D1583503

WITHDRAWN

712.03(44) DEL

Claude-Louis Châtelet (1753-1795). 'Frontispiece du Recueil . . . Trianon'.
Châtelet was commissioned to execute watercolours for the albums Marie-Antoinette gave to visiting royalty. This watercolour, representing various fabriques of the Queen's garden arranged in an arbitrary manner, is from the album in the Biblioteca Estense, Modena. Marie-Antoinette probably presented it to her brother, Archduke Ferdinand, Governor of Lombardy, who visited the Queen with his wife, Maria-Beatrice d'Este of Modena, in May 1786

Garden Pavilions

and the
18th Century French Court

Eleanor P. DeLorme
Preface by Jean Feray

WITHDRAWN

Antique Collectors' Club

To my mother and to Bonnie,
who planted the gardens of my childhood, and who knew the Gardener

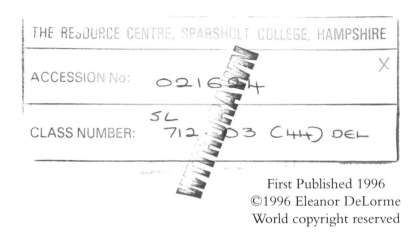

THE RESOURCE CENTRE, SPARSHOLT COLLEGE, HAMPSHIRE

ACCESSION No: 0216 24   X

CLASS NUMBER: SL
                  712. 03 (44) DEL

First Published 1996
©1996 Eleanor DeLorme
World copyright reserved

ISBN 1 85149 189 9

All rights reserved. No part of this publication may be reproduced, stored in a retrieval system, or transmitted in any form or by any means electronic, mechanical, photocopying, recording or otherwise, without the prior permission of the publisher

British Library Cataloguing-in-Publication Data
A catalogue record for this book is available from the British Library

The right of Eleanor DeLorme to be identified as author of this work has been asserted in accordance with the Copyright, Designs and Patents Act, 1988

Printed in England on Consort Royal Satin paper from Donside Paper Mills, Aberdeen by the Antique Collectors' Club Ltd., Woodbridge, Suffolk IP12 1DS

CONTENTS

Sparsholt College Library
Sparsholt, Winchester
Hants. SO21 2NF

WITHDRAWN

PHOTOGRAPHIC ACKNOWLEDGEMENTS

Arch. Snark/Edimedia © Musée du Château de Versailles, 66; Archives Departmentales de Loir-et-Cher, 153 (Fonds Ménars), 154, 156; Archives Nationales, Paris, 124, 133; Atelier, 31; Avery Library, Columbia University, New York, 208; Bibliothèque des Arts Décoratifs, Paris, 27, 38, 39, 148, 173, 196, 219, 231, 241 (top), 249; Bibliothèque Municipale de Besançon, Fond Paris/Courtesy Dr. Alain Gruber, 242; Bibliothèque Nationale, Paris, 18, 22, 23, 33-37, 40, 44, 46-50, 52-54, 56, 57, 60, 61, 64, 65, 69, 73-75, 77-79, 81, 90, 95, 97, 103, 105, 111, 112, 115, 116, 119, 122, 123, 129, 134 (bottom), 135, 137, 141, 142, 144, 145, 147, 151, 161, 165, 168, 172, 174, 175, 183, 186, 187, 193-195, 197, 200, 202, 204, 210, 214, 218, 225, 240, 241 (bottom), 248, 253, 257, 259, 261, 262, 266, 267 (bottom), 270 (top), 272, 273, 275, 277, 285, 293; Boston Athenaeum, 201; Boston Public Library, 303; Bowles Museum, Barnard Castle, Co. Durham, 89 (top); Cailleux & Cie., 181, 182; Caisse Nationale des Monuments Historiques et des Sites/SPADEM, 55, 67, 157, 169, 172; Cda/Ph. Guillmot/Edimedia, 32 (bottom © Musée du Château de Versailles), 227, 260, 268 (left); CdA/Guillot/Edimedia, 191; CdA/Ph. Hinous/Edimedia, 255; CdA/Ph. Orlandini/Edimedia, Frontispiece (© Musée du Château de Versailles), 243, 246 (top), 247 (top); Château de Versailles/Giraudon, 279; Olivier Choppin de Janvry, 209 (bottom), 212, 213, 216; © Frick Collection, New York, 162, 163; Calouste Gulbenkian Foundation, Lisbon, 281 (top); Editions Monelle Hayot, Yves Jannès, courtesy La Société historique et archéologique de Méréville, 294 (top and bottom left), 295 (top), 299 (left), 302 (bottom); by permission of the Houghton Library, Harvard University, 113; Claude Laroussinie, 217; Pascal Le Maître, 70, 125, 228, 229; Library of the Boston Athenaeum, 201; collection of the Library of Congress, Washington, D.C., 107; Francis Loeb Library, Harvard, 198, 234; Metropolitan Museum of Art, New York, 114 (Jack and Belle Linsky Collection, 1982), 143 (gift of Mr. and Mrs. Charles Wrightsman), 155 (Purchase 1966, Josephine Bay Paul and C. Michael Paul Foundation Inc., and Charles Ulrick and Josephine Bay Foundation Inc. gifts, and Rogers Fund), 268 (right, gift of J. Pierpoint Morgan), 269, 304 (William H. Huntington 1883); Musée d'Art et d'Histoire de la Ville de Meudon, 134 (top); Musée Carnavalet, Paris, 24, 25, 96, 176, 177, 185 (bottom), 203 (Giraudon); Musée Conde, Chantilly/Giraudon, 108, 109, 220, 221, 223; courtesy of Musée d'Ile de France, Château de Sceaux/P. Lemaire, 298; Musée d'Ile-de-France, Sceaux/Giraudon, 71, 128, 136; Musée du Château de Versailles/Réunion des Musées Nationaux, Paris, 17, 32 (top); Musée du Louvre, 84 (Réunion des Musées Nationaux); 91 (Giraudon), 301 (Réunion des Musées Nationeaux); Musée Marmottan, Paris/Giraudon, 206; courtesy Museum of Fine Arts, Boston, 82 (Marie Antoinette Fund), 309 (deposited by the City of Boston), 310; National Museum of Sweden, 295 (bottom); Newhouse Galleries, New York, 276; Photothèque des Musées de la Ville de Paris/SPADEM, 185 (top), 189; Preservation Society of Newport County, R.I., 243; Private collection, 233; Royal Collection © Her Majesty the Queen, 14-15; courtesy M. Dufresne de Saint-Léon, 294 (bottom right), 299 (right), 302 (top); Sotheby's London, 292; Eric Turquin, Paris, 100; courtesy Vaux-le-Vicomte/Photo Gérard Halary, 28; reproduced by Permission of the Trustees of the Wallace Collection, London, 93; Yale University Art Gallery, Trumbull Collection, 307.

Sparsholt College Library
Sparsholt, Winchester
Hants, SO21 2NF

ACKNOWLEDGEMENTS

This book grew out of a course of lectures presented in 1981 at the Fogg Museum, Harvard University. The response to the subject of garden pavilions (in the midst of a Boston winter) was so enthusiastic that my mentor, the late Howard C. Rice, encouraged me to turn the lectures into a book. Another friend and teacher, Jean Seznec, was also a real inspiration for the project, as were the Thierry de Ville d'Avray family. There are many people to be thanked for their help, among them: Jean Feray, Alain Gruber, Adolfo S. Cavallo, Olivier Choppin de Janvry, Louis de St.-Léon of Jeurre, Diane Baude, Doris May, Brigitte DeLorme, Marianne Roland Michel, Guy Stair Sainty, Deanna Cross at the Metropolitan Museum of Art, New York, Deborah Charlton at the Frick Collection, and at the Wellesley College of Art Library, Richard McElroy and Jeanne Hablanian. Especially I wish to thank my husband, Thomas L. DeLorme, and our sons who travelled many miles throughout France to take photographs. I also think with gratitude of my two publishers, Diana Steel and Monelle Hayot.

PREFACE

'L'art au service du prestige ne dure que le temps des honneurs qui le consacre' – Bruno Bentz.

The theme of this study brings to mind many of the challenges that confronted the Service des Monuments Historiques in our projects to salvage some of the finest garden buildings of the realm over the past thirty-five years.

A case in point is the extant Grand Trianon in the Versailles gardens. The Sun King's earlier Trianon de Porcelaine was purposely destroyed, for the faïence revetments could not withstand the onslaught of winter weather. In its place, and on the same site, was erected the Grand Trianon (Trianon de Marbre). It was set directly upon the ground, without cellars, and with weak foundations, so that it has always suffered from the problem of humidity. As a result, Louis-Philippe had to replace all the floors, for the *parquets d'assemblage* were rotted, but the new floors were of cheap parquet in herring-bone pattern.

After World War I, the roof of the Grand Trianon began to leak alarmingly, but thanks to the generosity of Mr. Rockefeller, it was completely renewed, and thus the building was saved. After World War II the *boiseries* were rotted from the floor up to the dado, along with the parquet floors, all due to the absence of heat for five years. The appalling state of the Trianon interiors was brought to the attention of General de Gaulle who decided to have it completely restored for the purpose of using it for state occasions.

Cellars were excavated under the building, electricity, heating and modern sanitation were installed, and the floors were covered with new *parquets d'assemblage* and marble. Since the only surviving original furniture was Napoleonic, this was reassembled, restored and covered with Lyons silks that were rewoven according to the original designs, with the same material used *en suite* for the hangings.

The paintings that had hung in the Grand Trianon in Louis XIV's day were brought out of storage from provincial museums and are again *in situ*. Today, visiting heads of state find the Grand Trianon a convenient and luxurious residence when they come to France for official business, and it is large enough to house both visitor and host.

Louis XIV's Marly was destroyed, but – in order to give an idea of the sites of the King's large, central pavilion and some of the smaller ones – the foundations have been restored to a certain height. Happily, some of the enamelled tiles that once lined the ornamental basins have been recovered in such quantity that a book has been written on the subject – *Les Bassins de Faïence du Château de Marly,* by Bruno Bentz.

At Chantilly, the Prince de Condé's Hameau has survived, well documented by the illustrations in the album of watercolours given as a souvenir by the Prince to the 'Comte et Comtesse du Nord', pseudonyms for the Grand Duke Paul and Maria Fyodorovna, the future Tsar and Tsarina of Russia, who were lavishly entertained there. As for the Ménagerie and the Laiterie at Chantilly, they are known to us only through plans.

Louis XV was especially fond of the hunt, and he ordered his *premier architecte,*

Jacques-Ange Gabriel, to build him several small hunting lodges, or *pavillons de chasse*. They were all in the hunting grounds adjoining the grand park of Versailles, and among those existing are Le Butard, Saclay (near the lake), La Muette (in the forest of Saint-Germain), Marcoussis, and Les Ulis. No longer extant are Les Metz, Le Pavillon des Bois de Verrières, Le Pavillon des Bois de Fosses Reposes, and the Pavillon du Pont Colbert.

As for Louis XV's Pavillon Frais at Trianon, it had disappeared, but thirty years ago there appeared on the market a Savonnerie carpet designed as a *parterre de broderie* in *trompe-l'oeil* – in green and yellow. Recently published documents reveal that this carpet was the one ordered for the Pavillon Frais. This charming, light pavilion has now been re-erected, with its original surviving *boiseries* for the walls. The panelling had been re-used in the Petit Trianon, but has now been returned to its proper place.

Marie-Antoinette's theatre at Trianon has been restored, and in it are to be seen the first life-size sculptures made of papier mâché, the work of Deschamps. In the Queen's Hameau the artificial rivulet has been leaking, because the clay lining was pierced by the roots of Louisiana cypress. The roofs of the cottages of the Hameau were originally not of thatch but of rushes, and it is difficult today to find workers in that particular craft.

At Ménars on the Loire, only the nymphaeum/grotto has survived, although others are known through documents recently given to Archives Departmentales du Loir et Cher. Among them are the Chinese pavilion by Charles de Wailly, which the architect of the Marquis de Marigny, Soufflot, refused.

The Pavillon de l'Aurore at Sceaux has also suffered from humidity, for the chariot of the Dawn Goddess was falling off the ceiling. With the help of a skilled craftsman, however, Aurora's horses are again pulling her chariot across the heavens through swirls of pink clouds.

★ ★ ★ ★ ★ ★ ★ ★ ★ ★ ★

Why pavilions? What is the purpose of these park buildings, large or small, solid or ephemeral, put up in France in the seventeenth and eighteenth centuries?

The reasons for these 'follies' are multifarious. They were a little more than just pretty garden ornaments. They were the pretext for a walk in the grounds, for enjoying the view, or to provide a pleasant shelter from the sun, wind or rain. Or just a resting-place after a stroll in the garden, and maybe for the privacy of a tête-à-tête. Or a comfortable place to kick off one's boots and dine with select company after the hunt.

They were a change of setting and a respite from the stuffy court, to escape the plague of etiquette, and a retreat for the sovereign among the happy few whom he invited. 'Marly, sire?' – the courtiers of Louis XIV would inquire, and it became a topic of conversation for those blasé courtiers who had not been invited.

In the case of that devoted pavilion-builder, Louis XV, the hunting boxes that he commissioned from his architect, Jacques-Ange Gabriel, served a highly practical purpose. His hereditary passion for hunting was not only a princely privilege, but also an ecological necessity. The large numbers of stags, deer and boar had to be brought under control, and even wolves still appeared in winter.

The hunting pavilions of solid materials were erected to meet the requirements of a noble gentleman hunting: to change horses, adjust the saddles, water the dogs. For the King and the few choice companions whom he entertained for supper after the *débotté* (shedding of boots), the royal architect designed a series of hunting pavilions – from Le Butard to Fausse Repose – like a musician practising his scales, and he relied only on line and proportion.

But a pavilion may also be the location for a larger surprise court entertainment: music, dance, supper, *medianoche* . . . Or, on the other hand, it may just fulfil the pleasure of building, become an eye-catcher in the layout of the vista, and an essay into a novel architectural style, be it rustic, Chinese, Turkish or Gothic. Or perhaps a grotto or fake ruin would be the romantic stage setting for a dream come true. All these reasons must be taken into account, and must not be seen as merely an attack of the building bug.

And what is the nature of these pavilions? Are they to be considered as ephemeral or lasting buildings? Follies for a season's delight, just a whim like a life-size toy, more ornamental than useful? Or a real house, an annex to the main residence for a retreat with a small, chosen company, *pauci sed electi*? If they are made of perishable materials, why do we try to maintain these fragile *fabriques*? For what purpose, if not to use? If made of solid stone to last, why are they so different from the main residence?

Eleanor DeLorme's achievement addresses these questions, in meticulously assembling the surviving or vanished examples of seventeenth- and eighteenth-century pavilions that mirror a certain civilisation. Her profound knowledge of the subject, carefully documented, allows her to present it in a scholarly yet entertaining way to the Anglo-Saxon public interested in French culture. It is a fine, historical, beautifully illustrated work on a subject which has rarely been treated in recent English texts.

It is hoped that the present work will be the point of departure for future research into this original architectural form, for these novel *fabriques* greatly influenced more conventional buildings. And for this reason, if for no other, these delightful structures deserve to be taken seriously, and preserved for the enlightenment and enjoyment of future generations.

Jean Feray
Inspecteur Principal Honoraire des Monuments Historiques, France

FOREWORD

The great Louvre curator and writer, Germain Bazin, maintained that one cannot isolate an artistic creation from its milieu, and this is eminently true for the pavilions that formed an essential part of French seventeenth- and eighteenth-century gardens. The present work makes no attempt to add anything new to the history of the French garden, nor are the pavilions discussed entirely unknown. The objective is to present them against the canvas of the age, within their social and physical contexts, and to identify these diminutive gems of architecture created for a privileged, discerning society as a valid and typically French art form. So I have approached the subject from the standpoint of social rather than art history. For the art historical perspective often isolates objects and treats them autonomously, which obscures the purpose for which they were created and ultimately robs them of their full significance.

Although most of the pavilions embellished gardens, some were erected on public squares for dancing and buffets to celebrate state occasions, and others along the river bank or on bridges, often serving as the *machine* from which the pyrotechnical displays were launched. The Pavilion of Hanover began its life in an urban setting, too, for it was attached to a house on the boulevards before its removal to the park of the château of Sceaux. These fugitive structures were often called *fabriques,* and the word was broadly interpreted, for it included not only pavilions, but such ornamental features as columns, obelisks, tents, tombs, decorative bridges, pagodas, belvederes, temples, pyramids, classical monuments, and probably the subterranean winter garden at Monceau.

They were invariably commissioned by the royal family and people closely associated with the court and its complex structure, for this princely group inherited a tradition of royal patronage, and possessed the taste, means and incentive to carry it on. The King's cousins were known as Princes of the Blood, whose stock might eventually ascend the throne, and who were represented by three families: the Orléans, who supplied the Regent, and were descended from Louis XIV's brother, Monsieur; the Condés, who provided Louis XIV with his finest general, the Grand Condé; and the Contis who were Bourbons, like the Condés. All possessed magnificent *hôtels particuliers* (town houses) as well as vast estates in the country, which they embellished with *fabriques* of epicene grace, suave sophistication or delirious fantasy.

Marriages in this charmed circle were often arranged for the purposes of social expediency, and the principals were often shockingly young. The Comtesse de Coislin announced to the Duc d'Harcourt: 'My niece . . . is to wed the only son of the Prince of Nassau. The disparity in their ages is . . . even greater than that of their fortunes. He is eleven, she is seventeen.' Louis XIV's minister, the Marquis d'Argenson, was even married without his consent, and the marriage eventually ended in divorce. Consequently, there were many unhappy marriages, which helps to explain – while it does not excuse – liaisons with *les belles impures,* the eighteenth century's euphemism for ladies of doubtful reputation. For some of the finest *morceaux d'architecture* both in Paris and in the country were associated with royal mistresses such as the Marquise de Pompadour and the Comtesse Du Barry, and women of the theatre – Sophie Arnould, Mademoiselles Dervieux and Guimard.

It is an arresting fact that as much care (and often money) was expended on these small garden caprices as upon a town house or château – 'le Bon Dieu est dans les détails.' For it was a society that was in earnest about its pleasures, and has often been reproached for 'doing frivolous things seriously, and serious things gaily' (Ducros). The Duc de Richelieu was preoccupied with the shape of a cornice in his salon, and took exquisite pains with the proper presentation of a dish prepared by his excellent chef Clouet. But at the battle of Fontenoy he rode gaily off into the face of enemy fire, waving his comrades to follow. And on the eve of his execution, the Duc de Lauzun dined upon oysters and wine, offering some to the executioner: 'C'est fini. Je pars pour le grand voyage.'

One aspect of life under the *ancien régime* that was never treated with sententious brevity were the fêtes – the spirit of a reign made visible. The royal fêtes figure prominently in this study because the provisional structures demanded for these occasions offered architects an excuse for flirting with new ideas for permanent buildings as they conjured up architectural fantasies that suited the theme of a particular occasion. Thus pavilions could be both economical and extravagant at the same time.

The closest affinity existed between festival structures designed by the architects of the Menus-Plaisirs and more enduring garden buildings. Both types were essential for the ultimate effect of the airy splendour of garden *divertissements,* and to court life as the Bourbon dynasty defined it. To the essays in architecture that were indispensable for these occasions were joined the contiguous arts of sculpture, painting, gardening, literature, dance, music, costume, cuisine, the manufacture of silver and porcelain, and especially engraving. Many of the Bourbon fêtes and garden buildings – from the time of Louis XIV to Louis XVI – were splendidly engraved, and Marie-Antoinette's were recorded in delicate watercolours by Châtelet, and bound into the luxurious albums she presented to visiting royalty. Others were evoked in drawings, like Saint-Aubin's haunting sketch of the pagoda of Chanteloup. The art historian Jean Seznac called them 'the fragile epitome of a civilazation, the signature of a century', which might apply to its pavilions as well.

The French officers and diplomats who came to America during the Revolution represented an extension of the court – by definition members of the nobility and gentlemen from old families. So they transplanted the royal French festival tradition to the New World. At West Point they fêted the Dauphin's birth in a ballroom of cut branches improvised by the military engineers, and at Philadelphia, the Chevalier de la Luzerne summoned a French engineer in American service, Pierre l'Enfant, to design a provisional ballroom for the same purpose.

★ ★ ★ ★ ★ ★ ★ ★ ★ ★

Since it has not always been possible to find acceptable English equivalents for some French terms, the French has been retained in such cases and when it lends a unique flavour that English words could not convey.

Eleanor DeLorme
February 1996

INTRODUCTION

What is a pavilion? In its simplest form a pavilion is nothing more than a tent which meets a ceremonial, social or military need. In the painting of the famous encounter near Calais in June 1520 between two monarchs, François I of France and Henry VIII of England, pavilions are depicted that served all three purposes (overleaf). The ceremonial dinner with ritual display of silver was held in the banqueting pavilion at right, with a fountain of wine before it; the social aspect was depicted by the monarchs embracing in the tent in the background; military tents with heraldic emblems were used for the participants in the tournaments, that 'soft and silken war'. Of such conspicious grandeur were the cloth-of-gold coverings (*drap d'or*) provided for the sovereigns and their entourages, that the meeting-place has traditionally been known as 'The Field of the Cloth of Gold'.

Such tents were always associated with members of the privileged class and often with hunting, which was a royal ritual and patrician sport. Two and a half centuries after François and Henry's celebrated gathering at Calais, the Prince de Conti, a Prince of the Blood, entertained the Hereditary Prince of Brunswick-Luneburg in a striped silk pavilion put up for the hunt supper after the chase in the forest of Conti's château at l'Ile Adam in 1776 (p.17).

Depending on which translation, the Old Testament uses the term pavilion to suggest a temporary shelter or tabernacle, and implicit therein are several concepts. The pavilion is a place of refuge: 'For in time of trouble He shall hide me in his pavilion' (Ps. 27:5). Or pleasure: 'How amiable are Thy tabernacles, O Lord of Hosts!' (Ps. 84:1). Or a covering for the earth: 'He stretcheth out the heavens as a curtain, and spreadeth them out as a tent to dwell in' (Ps. 40:22), so that the hymn writer speaks of the Lord as being 'pavilioned in splendour'. Or – in the most exalted imagery – as a covering for the sun: 'In [the heavens] He has placed a pavilion for the sun' (Ps. 19:4).

Similarly in the New Testament, the transitory nature of human existence (the earthly tabernacle) is contrasted with the permanence of the Christian's life after death (the eternal building) and this is expressed in different ways: 'For we know that if our earthly house of this tabernacle were dissolved, we have a building of God, a house not made with hands, eternal in the heavens' (2 Cor. 5:1). And the awe-inspiring words of the evangelist John, embodying one of the most profound concepts of Holy Writ, appear in one translation of the New Testament as: 'And the Word became flesh and tabernacled among us' (John 1:14).

Art, too, pays tribute to this association of pavilions with Divine Majesty, for in illuminated manuscripts a piece of drapery suggesting a tent is spread out above the head of the Deity, a saint or a king, setting him apart. This is why thrones are draped, why the state beds of French sovereigns were surmounted by a baldaquin with panaches of white feathers, for the king was divinely ordained for his office. It was not a matter of decoration, but of homage. One of the most moving visualisations of this concept is Leonardo's 'Virgin of the Rocks', in which the artist places the only true royalty, the Christ child, under the canopy of His mother's hand.

The pavilions that shall principally concern us here are the ornamental garden structures created for the French monarchy and royal circles. Most of them date from the

Attributed to Hans Holbein (1497-1543), 'The Field of the Cloth of Gold'.
In June 1520 François I of France played host to Henry VIII of England at an opulent occasion in northern France. So extravagant were the furnishings, so elaborate the display of gold, jewellery, and costumes that the meeting has since become known as 'The Field of the Cloth of Gold'. Tents of striped silk, embroidered stuffs, or gold cloth (painted by François' court artist) were set up to receive the distinguished participants who included Cardinal Wolsey, Erasmus, Thomas More, the Duke of Buckingham, Marguerite d'Angoulême, and Anne Boleyn. The sham castle on the right received Henry and his cavalcade, with wine flowing from the courtyard fountain. In the background the two kings embrace in a cloth-of-gold pavilion, and dine in the embroidered one on the right, with a brilliant silver display set out for the occasion.
    The meeting was so costly that, according to the French ambassador Du Bellay, more fortunes were destroyed here than in battle: 'The great outlay that was made cannot be over-estimated; but many carried their mills, forests, and meadows on their backs'

reign of Marie-Antoinette and Louis XVI, when the picturesque or *anglo-chinois* garden became fashionable, and pavilions proliferated. This type of 'natural' garden often looked like the setting for a comic opera, and the picturesque little *fabriques* contributed to the sentiments it provoked. A perfect example is seen in a watercolour by the architect of the Menus-Plaisirs under Louis XVI, P.-A. Paris, entitled 'Le Jardin de Cythère'. The English garden conceived by P.-A. Paris, with grotto, fountains and statuary placed at random, is adorned with a pavilion in the form of a neo-classsical temple half-hidden by the trees, its columns entwined with flowers and foliage.

The English counterparts of the French *pavillons* were called follies, referring to their ruinous cost, for they were built upon large estates by people with means and leisure. Decorative in nature and not generally intended for habitation, English follies lent particular emphasis to landscape features and punctuated a view. With another connotation, the word may derive from the French word *feuilles,* evoking thoughts of a small house lost in greenery. During the Regency the term *folie* was in fact used to designate these garden retreats. Finally, Michel Gallet has noted that *folie* was considered to be a pun, for lunatics were then confined in the Hôpital des Petites Maisons.

The Relationship of Pavilions to Gardens

Pavilions and gardens are inseparable, for these focal points in the landscape acknowledged man's essential place in nature. The garden provided the *mise-en-scène* for these capricious little gems of architecture, and as the French formal garden gave way to the picturesque garden in the second half of the eighteenth century, the character of the garden buildings reflected the new spirit soon to invade the art of French gardening. Without its pavilions, a garden could not be considered complete for, according to the Chinese, 'once a place has a *t'ing* (pavilion), we call it a garden,' writes Maggie Keswick.

Although French pavilions also complemented and embellished the garden, they were most often intended to be lived in. Built by the leading architects, they were of extraordinary stylistic diversity, commensurate with the purpose for which they were designed. The marmoreal grandeur of the Sun King's Grand Trianon proclaimed the nature of the absolute monarchy, serving a political as well as an aesthetic purpose. The Pavillon Français of his great-grandson Louis XV provided a centrepiece for his botanical garden, and in his Salon Frais made of *treillage,* outdoor meals were served. Marie-Antoinette's Belvédère, its interior painted in delicate Pompeiian arabesques, was given over to concerts and conversation. On Nicolas Beaujon's estate, a pavilion in windmill form with Gothic and Renaissance motifs, distributed water to the gardens.

The park of Monceau, created by the artist Carmontelle for the Duc de Chartres, boasted a collection of architecture 'from all times and places.' The principal pavilion became the scene of bizarre initiation rites into freemasonry; the Turkish tent housed a billiard room; the Théâtre de Verdure was really a Salle de Spectacles for theatricals; the Temple of Marble contained marble benches for 'reading, gazing, and weeping' (Wiebenson) which were considered proper pursuits in an age of *sensibilité*; and a small Gothic pavilion with pointed turret concealed the chemistry laboratory indispensable to a man of the Duke's class.

In the days of the Sun King, the younger set fled the punctilious court ceremonial and found refuge in the *treillage* pavilions of the gardens. In one, the Duc and Duchesse de Bourgogne are served liqueurs by her lady-in-waiting, the Duchesse du Lude (overleaf). Another offers a retreat for the younger princesses – one is doubtless the sister of the Princesse de Conti – who escaped there to indulge in pipe-smoking (overleaf). Others were places of assignations, which demanded an exquisite and clandestine setting, for pavilions could be associated with *la vie galante* (flirtations).

Not that pavilions were built for illicit purposes. They began as architectural components of the great French Baroque ensemble: the château with its furnishings,

Michel-Barthélémy Ollivier (c.1712-1784), 'Feast Given by the Prince de Conti', 1776.
Louis XV's cousin, the Prince de Conti (1717-1776), delighted in exquisite food, and fitted up for Louis a kitchen with silver utensils at the small château of La Muette. The dishes that emerged from it are said to have contributed significantly to the grande cuisine of France. Conti was famous for his English teas and receptions at the Temple, where Mademoiselle Fel sang and the young Mozart played.
Like all Princes of the Blood, Conti was fond of hunting, especially at his château of l'Ile Adam, designed by his architect, J.-B. André, who went to England to study the jardin pittoresque. In Ollivier's painting, which was intended to decorate the château, Conti entertains the Prince of Brunswick-Luneburg at a hunt supper under a tent put up in the woods near l'Ile Adam. Conti is seated, wearing a yellow coat. He offers a dish to a lady, at whose right sits the Prince of Brunswick in a black coat

Left: Anon, 'Monseigneur et Madame de Bourgogne Refreshing Themselves with Liqueurs', 1701.
The young parents of the future Louis XV have slipped out into the gardens for liqueurs and galettes in a treillage pavilion. The Duchesse de Bourgogne was the light of Louis XIV's latter years, brought new life to the court, and for her the old King decorated the pavilion of the Ménagerie. Her lady-in-waiting, the Duchesse du Lude, brings the glasses and carafes on a silver salver, her hair done up in the towering Fontanges coiffure popularised by an early mistress of the Sun King. Both the Duc and Duchesse de Bourgogne, still in their twenties, died of measles in 1712, as did their elder son. His two-year-old brother survived to become Louis XV

Right: Anon, 'The Charming Pipe-Smoker', c. 1710.
In her journals of 1704, the Sun King's sister-in-law, Liselotte, bemoans the lack of dignity manifested by the younger set at Versailles. She reported that people of highest quality got exceedingly drunk and used tobacco. Here, three princesses have retired to a pavilion, appropriately covered with grape vines, for wine, card games and pipe-smoking. They wear the ubiquitous pearls, Fontanges coiffures, and overskirts edged with lambrequins typical of the period

works of art, and gardens – these last an extension of the château into space and arranged on axis to the main dwelling. The ensemble reached its full development by 1661 at Nicolas Fouquet's château, Vaux-le-Vicomte near Melun, where Louis Le Vau and Charles Lebrun were reponsible for the château and its decoration, André Le Nôtre for the gardens.

Louis XIV, as we know, confiscated this remarkable team of artists to transform his father's hunting lodge at Versailles into the château that became the seat of government and home of the Bourbon family. Here Le Nôtre further extended his concept of the *jardin français*, the French formal vista garden. Even before its completion, the Sun King had built his first pavilion, the Grotte de Thétis, no doubt inspired by those grottoes in the garden of his Italian grandmother, Marie de' Medicis, at Saint-Germain-en-Laye, where Louis was born.

The ultimate source for the *jardin français* and its pavilions was to be found in Italian Renaissance gardens with their *casine,* grottoes, pools, fountains, cascades, statuary, and groves of trees *(boschetti)*. For in sixteenth-century Italy, the garden had ceased to be a mere afterthought, and architects began to conceive of it as an integral part of the principal dwelling. It was then that gardening truly became an art form in the western world.

Inspiration for Italian garden builders came not so much from the centuries just preceding, but from the spacious days of Rome's first and second centuries, the majesty they knew from the vestiges of the past that were daily before their eyes. For Renaissance gardens often enclosed actual ruins: the Orsini garden was placed on top of Augustus' mausoleum (1575). Ruins were so closely associated with Renaissance gardens that false ruins were to be constructed in French eighteenth-century gardens, looking back to antiquity and its Renaissance rebirth. Certain *amateurs* actually lived in them, such as François-Nicolas-Racine de Monville, who inhabited a truncated fluted column at the Désert de Retz. The remains of Hadrian's Villa at Tivoli became a model for later colonnades and *isolotti* in both Italian and French gardens. The famous Temple at Tivoli, drawn by both Hubert Robert and Fragonard, reappeared in countless eighteenth-century gardens in France, including that of Monsieur de Girardin at Ermenonville.

A Roman source for garden buildings – known through literature – was Varro's Aviary, a combination aviary/fish pond/outdoor dining pavilion in circular form. It became a prototype for the aviaries of later gardens such as the Villa Lante at Bagnaia (1556-89) and the château of Gaillon (just after 1501) of the Cardinal of Amboise. The Bourbons, too, were fond of aviaries. The engraving of a fête given at Versailles during the early years of Louis XIV's reign show the Cour de Marbre illuminated for a buffet, and aviaries of gilt *fer forgé* (wrought iron) in the corners of the elevated courtyard. When Louis' great-grandson, Louis XV, was living as a child at the Tuileries, the gardeners put up for him a tiny pavilion in the garden with a *volière* (aviary) entirely of white birds, an idea he would perpetuate later in his roof-top gardens at Versailles.

The most significant garden achievements of the Renaissance belonged to the great period preceding Vignola's death in 1573. In the 1550s Tribolo created for the Grand Duke of Tuscany at Castello near Florence, a garden with fountains, statuary, and even parterres. In Rome there was Raphael's never-completed Villa Madama (c.1516) as well as Vignola's gardens for the Farnese family: Villa Caprarola at Conciglione (c.1547), Villa Giulia outside the city (1550-5), and the Villa Lante at Bagnaia. After 1550 Ligorio's somewhat excessive conceits were to be seen in the gardens of the Villa d'Este at Tivoli. Then, there were the glorious Boboli Gardens in Florence (1550) with cypress-bordered paths and a celebrated grotto painted and stuccoed *à l'antique* (overleaf).

So the idea of a garden as complement to the dwelling is due to sixteenth-century Italian architects, and the underlying concepts of these Italian gardens were applied, in turn, to Renaissance gardens across France. They would ultimately be transformed and codified by that *architecte de plein air,* André Le Nôtre, into the distinctly French vista garden realised first at Vaux, the dress rehearsal for Versailles.

The predominant idea was an axial arrangement of garden paths *(allées)* with the villa itself as termination of the main axis, and the *casine* (pavilions) subservient to the principal building. There were groves of trees *(bosquets)* which, although they might be on a hillside outside the garden proper – as at the Villa Lante – were oriented to and visible from the garden. Flowers and clipped evergreens were confined to specific areas of the garden. Although flowers struggled to survive in hot Roman summers, they flourished under the Ile-de-France's temperate skies. Water was exploited in glittering

Left: Paths in the Boboli Gardens, Florence.
Charles VIII of France returned from his invasion of Italy just before 1500, bringing Italian garden designers with him. So the viotolloni *(straight paths) of Italian Renaissance gardens became features of the Italian-style gardens at Blois and Amboise, and in the seventeenth century a source of the wide allées of French formal gardens. At Versailles, a central, broad avenue – the* tapis vert *(green carpet) – led from the centre of the château to the Grand Canal, linking the King's residence to the horizon. Lined with statuary set against meticulously clipped trees to suggest an outdoor sculpture gallery, it provided a majestic passage to the Apollo Basin that enunciated the theme of Versailles*

Right: Grotto in the Boboli Gardens, Florence.
When Louis XIV's grandmother, Marie de' Medicis, arrived in France to become the Queen of Henri IV, she brought with her memories of the glorious Boboli Gardens with its renowned grotto by Bernardo Buontalenti with Bernardino Poccetti's dramatic fresco of impending disaster. The royal couple's terraced gardens at Saint-Germain-en-Laye were enhanced with grottoes built by Italian workmen and hydraulics executed by the Florentine specialist Thomas Francini, who made engravings of the grottoes in 1599. Francini's hydraulic system energised the curious automates *that charmed the Dauphin, Louis XIII, whose own son (future Louis XIV) was born in 1638 at Saint-Germain. Although the animated figures and animals – like 'Orpheus Playing to the Beasts' – were in disrepair by this time, the grottoes perhaps inspired Louis' Grotte de Thétis at Versailles, and possibly the Labyrinthe, where painted lead statues enlivened with fountains depicted the* Fables of Aesop

fountains, quiet fishponds, crashing cascades, and acquired an architectonic quality in the hands of the *fontaniers*, who treated it as a sculptor models clay. It also provided the power for hydraulic works that produced organ music, trumpet blasts and bird calls. Garden paths sometimes terminated in a nymphaeum based upon antique examples, and grottoes lined with moss and shells housed intricate waterworks apt to dowse the visitor unwarned of jets camouflaged in the floor. Sculpture, softening the transition from leaf to stone, made the gardens outdoor museums, and as in the Belvedere Court in the Vatican, much of it was ancient. A common garden feature was the vine-covered pergola in tunnel form seen at the Villa d'Este. It reappeared in French Renaissance gardens, and later in seventeenth- and eighteenth-century gardens as a *berceau de treillage* (tunnel of trelliswork) or a *berceau de verdure* (greenery clipped in the form of a barrel vault).

With Charles VIII's Italian invasions just before 1500, Italian gardening concepts began to be transplanted on to French soil, for the King set Italian gardeners to work upon the royal domains of Amboise and Blois in the Loire valley. In the gardens at Blois, each separate unit was self-contained, for there was not as yet any notion of relating the garden to the château or of treating it as a single entity. Anne de Bretagne's pavilion was little more than a covered garden seat with vines clambering up the sides to the roof,

Left: Grotto of La Bastide d'Urfé, France.
A rare extant example of the grottoes or nymphaea frequently seen in sixteenth-century gardens is the one built by humanist-diplomat Claude d'Urfé about 1551 at his château of La Bastide d'Urfé in central France. Like the later Grotte de Thétis, the interior is glimpsed through grilles of gilt ironwork, the walls ornamented with grey-blue, white, and rust-red mythological characters and geometrical ornament. The figures and animals stand forth in such astonishing relief that it is difficult to imagine how the artists could have modelled them of small stones.

A triumph of the Italian taste, the grotto of La Bastide was considered the most beautiful in the realm, especially when the water jets in the floor – worked in arabesques of tiny stones – were turned on to bathe with sprays of liquid silver the statues and reliefs set into the wall

Right: The round pavilion at La Bastide d'Urfé.
Erected by Claude d'Urfé to embellish his gardens, the restored pavilion is in French Renaissance style

where a gilded statue reflected the sun. At Gaillon an allée of trees, reminiscent of the *viotolloni* in the Boboli Gardens, led to an octagonal pavilion with a marble fountain at the centre and topped by a *lanterne.* There was a grotto as well, and parterres executed in box with coloured pebbles between the plants as foil for the green *broderies.* Box was the ideal plant material for parterres because of its slow growth, the small, intensely green leaves, and the density it acquired with pruning. Despite the presence of Italian gardeners, Blois showed itself an essentially French garden, with open galleries for *promeneurs* to admire from a higher vantage point the parterres of bright flowers bordered by box, like carpets spread out upon the ground.

The major influx of Italian artists, however, came under François I, who brought them to the Loire valley and to Fontainebleau in about 1520. The Fontainebleau gardens were expanded with flower beds, hedges, and statuary that included the young Michelangelo's 'Hercules'. Most significantly for our purposes, grottoes such as the Grotte des Pins were created, and of course, pavilions. One of the most precious documents of Renaissance France was the Pavillon de Pomone (overleaf), its walls painted in the 1530s by Il Rosso and Primaticcio with appropriate subjects: the story of Vertumnus and Pomona and the gardens of Priapus. It was the French who had given literary form to the modern notion of love – courtly love – in the twelfth-century allegory *Roman de la Rose.* Dealing with courtship in a garden, the idea remained forever fertile in the French imagination, from the time of the Renaissance Pavillon de Pomone to Josephine's Temple of Love in the Malmaison gardens.

Advanced though the gardens of François I at Fontainebleau may have been, it was one of his ambassadors, Claude d'Urfé, who created one of France's most elaborate grottoes in the Italian manner at his château, La Bastide d'Urfé, in central France.

Attributed to Israel Silvestre, 'The Grotte des Pins et Pavillon de Pomone, Fontainebleau'.
Erected by François I around 1543, the Grotto is pierced by three arcades that assume the form of rustic Atlantes. Its interior, with a central fountain, was stuccoed with figures of animals and birds, the walls painted in foliage. At the end of the allée stood the Pavillon de Pomone, and it was at this time that the word pavillon came to be generally employed in France as an architectural term. The original Latin word pavilio *meant a tent, underlining its temporary nature. The Pavillon de Pomone was apparently finished by 1540, one of the most curious manifestations of Mannerism in France. Small as it was, the King considered it significant enough to have it decorated with two large wallpaintings by the Italian artists whom he called to work at the château, Il Rosso and Primaticcio. This was among their first enterprises in France, and they depicted the history of Vertumnus, the Roman god of vegetation, and Pomona goddess of the fruit of trees*

Sent by the King to the Council of Trent in 1546, d'Urfé remained in Italy until 1551. On his return, he began to transform the old family château, adding a long gallery of two storeys as a covered promenade from to which to view the gardens below, the only extant example of its kind in France. To embellish the gardens he put up a round pavilion in the French Renaissance tradition, and before his death in 1558, he commissioned from his artisans a sophisticated grotto/nymphaeum in the Italian manner (previous page). Coloured stones were set into the wall as mosaics, and compartments separated by terms in relief. In the niches were placed antique statues brought from Italy, and water jets were concealed in floor and ceiling. It was precisely the type of décor that Louis XIV would employ in his Grotte de Thétis at Versailles.

At the château of Anet, built by Henri II and his mistress, Diane de Poitiers (1546), there appeared for the first time in France a specialist in garden design, Etienne Dupérac. When Dupérac returned from Italy in 1582, the subsequent owner of Anet, Diane's son-in-law the Duc d'Aumale, appointed him architect of the parterres. Dupérac is credited with the first *compartiment de broderie* as well as with treating the whole parterre as a unit, a revolutionary idea in garden design. Etienne Dupérac formed the theorist Claude Mollet who, in turn, opened the way for André Le Nôtre's formal gardens of the seventeenth century.

In 1589 France emerged from medieval feudalism to become an absolute monarchy, embodied in the person of the first Bourbon king, Henri IV. The concentration of power into the hands of the king was of utmost importance for the development of the French garden. In 1615 the King's Italian wife, Marie de' Medicis, began construction of the Luxembourg Palace, with a grotto and fountain at right angles to

St. Germain-en-Laye.
The château of Saint-Germain-en-Laye had been constructed in 1539 during the reign of François I. His son, Henri II, enamoured of Diane de Poitiers and much given to divertissements *in the garden, put up a pavilion for the purpose just below the old château. In 1597 Henri IV engaged the Italian engineer Thomas Francini to establish the water systems of his gardens, and in 1599 the King summoned Etienne Dupérac to Saint-Germain. Dupérac had created the revolutionary garden at Diane de Poitiers' château of Anet, and Henri IV asked him to develop a new château and garden at Saint-Germain. It was laid out in six levels of terraces leading down to the river, linked by stairs, each one ornamented with fountains, grottoes,* pièces d'eau, *and geometrical parterres separated by* allées

the principal façade (pp. 24 and 25). The Queen would have remembered the Boboli Gardens from her native Florence when she created at Saint-Germain-en-Laye a garden in the Italian mode — in fact, the full Roman architectural manner, terraced, and sloping down to the river.

Saint-Germain became the favourite residence of their son, Louis XIII, who as a child explored the grottoes with automata such as the Lady with the Organ, Perseus and Andromeda, and Orpheus moving about and playing to the beasts. In 1738 there was born at the château a grandson of Henri IV and Marie de' Medicis, the future Louis XIV, who was especially attached to the place. Although the hydraulics were in disrepair

The Luxembourg Palace today.
After the tragic assassination of Henri IV, Marie de' Medicis engaged the architect Salomon de Brosse in 1615 to build a luxurious palace for her, the central block flanked by end pavilions, providing a complete suite of rooms on each floor. A new unity appeared between the residence and the gardens, with dignified, embroidered parterres by Jacques Boyceau centred with fountains. It was here that Antoine Watteau came to draw the trees of the park which had reached abundant maturity, and to study the allegorical cycle that Rubens had painted in the Queen's gallery. Today the Luxembourg gardens, with the allées of clipped lime trees, flowered parterres, and reflecting pools are still a favourite retreat for Parisians

and the musical automata had ceased to perform as they had during his father's lifetime, the Sun King honoured their memory in his first garden pavilion at Versailles.

By this time France had absorbed the ideals of the Italian Renaissance, transplanting, adapting, transforming, making them her own, and western Europe completely surrendered to French taste as cultural and political leadership passed into her hands. Curiously, the Church had made scant use of the art of gardening to promote its aims, but André Le Nôtre was quick to perceive that the hierarchical principles of Italian and French Renaissance gardens could be applied to a landscape which would extend and amplify the powerful monarchial propaganda represented by the entire Versailles concept. Synthesising the components of the gardens at Blois, Anet, Saint-Germain, Le Nôtre boldly refashioned an entire countryside into a vista garden with infinity for the horizon, defining once and for all what a royal garden should be. This was a singularly French event. Finally, the Versailles gardens were laid out with their parterres, the *tapis vert*, *pièces d'eau*, bosquets, canals, fountains, cascades, and elaborate sculptural programme, all subservient to a central theme.

Jean-François Janinet (1752-1814), 'Vue du Chateau du Luxembourg du Côté du Jardin'

Although transformations and changes were always in progress, the stage was nevertheless set for the pavilions conceived by the Bourbon monarchs, from the Sun King's regal but tentative Grotte de Thétis to Marie-Antoinette's wistful and romantic

Grotto of the Luxembourg Gardens today.
Like the gardens of Saint-Germain, those of the Luxembourg featured grottoes with fountains. Today the fountain/grotto of Marie de' Medicis, with its congelations and bossages, still graces the gardens, but the sculptural programme in the niche by Ottin, 'Polyphemus ready to Crush Acis and Galatea', dates from 1863

Hameau. Since the rulers were not only 'makers of manners' but also pace-setters for society, it naturally followed that members of court circles and other fashionable people followed the example of their rulers, and that *fabriques* sprang up in their gardens.

The period from 1715 to the Revolution was characterised by almost unprecedented architectural vitality, and saw the transformation of the capital into the city that still entices us today. A primary concern of every cultivated person was building; the royal family, *grands seigneurs,* financiers, playwrights, artists, actresses and their 'protectors' ruined themselves with building projects.

Jean-François Janinet, 'Vue de la Grotte du Jardin du Luxembourg'

25

During the time when Marie-Antoinette was Dauphine and Queen, superb *hôtels particuliers* (town houses) with extensive gardens were going up along the boulevards, near the Place Louis XV, along the river, and near the Bois de Boulogne. In this time of architectural revolution and experimentation, what better place to give free rein to the imagination, to try out new solutions and fresh ideas than in the garden buildings of one's private Eden, the rediscovered world of nature represented by the new picturesque garden? There was no need for a vast country estate, for within sight of Paris one could create a landscape in microcosm.

The eighteenth-century pavilions that enlivened the gardens of these *belles demeures* achieved an encyclopaedic diversity. The interior of the Palladian villa adorning the Duc d'Orléans' Paris garden was painted to simulate a leafy forest glade, and was intended for theatrical performances. The neo-classical retreat designed by the architect A.-T. Brongniart and decorated by F.-J. Bélanger for the actress Mademoiselle Dervieux, was cooly Pompeiian, with medallioned mahogany doors and a bath painted with the 'Aldobrandini Nuptials'.

Some were in the Chinese taste, like the pavilion with lattice balustrades anchored in the middle of a lake, to which a convivial group of card-players is being conveyed in a small craft with dragon prow (opposite). The gardens of the Ruggieri brothers, firework manufacturers, were like a carnival, with a pavilion in kiosk form as the point of departure for little boats that ran the Niagara rapids. In his antique *folie* with elaborate *treillage* and Apollo reliefs by the sculptor Adam le Jeune, Monsieur la Bouëxière served exquisite dishes and chilled chablis. 'Supper is one of the four ends of man', wrote Madame du Deffand, whose favourite guest was Horace Walpole.

In Paris and in the country, the leaders of French society engaged the finest architects of the realm, the most accomplished cabinetmakers, bronzeworkers, painters, and sculptors to create 'the prettiest trinkets in the world', as the Baronne d'Oberkirch described the garden buildings put up for the Prince de Condé. Travelling with the Archduchess Maria of Russia in 1782, the Baronne attended the gala of the century, when Louis-Joseph, Prince de Condé, fêted the royal party in the pavilions of his dream park at the measureless Condé domain of Chantilly.

Jean-Demosthène Dugourc (1749-1825), 'Sallon de Jeu au milieu d'un Lac'.
The sheer fantasy of the garden with oriental pagoda, tropical trees, kiosk at the water's edge, and Chinese pavilion resting on stilts in the lake is echoed by the eccentric barque with banners and streamers in which avid card-players sit. Dugourc, one of the finest ornemanistes of the Louis XVI period, was married to the sister of François Bélanger, the Comte d'Artois' architect at Bagatelle. Working under Bélanger's direction, Dugourc invented for Bagatelle's grand salon — which opened upon the garden — eight great panels of arabesques and grotesques that are among the outstanding décors of the period

Vaux-le-Vicomte, aerial view.
The architect of Vaux-le-Vicomte, Louis Le Vau (1612-1670), came to the site fresh from triumphs in Paris such as the still-extant Hôtel Lambert and Hôtel Lauzun. Vaux was raised upon a moat for entirely pictorial purposes, for it was no longer needed for defence, and the domed salon on the garden side was among the first in France. The theme of three openings is used throughout, and the composition is 'stitched together with terms' — as the Comte de Vogüé has put it — at the entrance gates, in the Oval Salon, and in the gardens. After Vaux, Le Vau carried out the first enlargement of Versailles for Louis XIV. Ernest de Ganay regarded the gardens of Vaux-le-Vicomte, in their original form, as André Le Nôtre's masterpiece

CHAPTER 1

THE FRENCH FORMAL GARDEN

There were essential differences between Italian gardens and their *cassine* and French gardens and their *pavillons*. First, there was the climate. Affluent Milanese, Florentines and Romans left the city heat for their cool suburban villas which they occupied only in summer, but the French monarchs lived in their châteaux year round. This is why Versailles became a veritable city – the 'city of the rich' as Bossuet called it – for it housed the court and was home of the royal family. This is not to say that the court was not itinerant, for it was, travelling from one royal château to another throughout the *ancien régime*, but once the Sun King moved into Versailles in 1682, it remained the principal home of the Bourbons until the outbreak of the Revolution.

The climatic differences also meant that plant material which could survive Italian winters would not necessarily adapt itself to the colder, wetter French winters. Thus the *orangerie* – counterpart of the Italian *limonaia* – became an important French garden building.

The Bourbons were inordinately fond of orange trees which, in Louis XIV's day, were aligned along the wall of the Galerie des Glaces in silver tubs, and put into the garden each spring during the first half of May (the Florence season is 15 April to 15 November). In July an orange flower was gathered for Marie-Antoinette to send around to members of her household. Then in the autumn, between 1 October and 15 October, the gardeners summoned the sailors who manned the small ships in the Grand Canal to move all the tubs indoors. In short, if one had hundreds of orange trees in heavy tubs to be moved twice a year, it required a navy.

There were topographical differences, too, between Italy and France, for Italian villas were often built on hill sites so that water might cascade over rocks and flow swiftly through channels. But the flat plains of central and northern France offered a real challenge to the ingenuity of French garden designers, for it demanded the total transformation of an entire countryside to create an impressive garden on the virtually featureless terrain of Versailles.

The fine Italian gardens had been relatively few, but in the seventeenth century, Frenchmen such as Cardinal Richelieu at Rueil began to adapt, alter and expand the earlier Italian examples. So it is to the French aristocracy (and Louis XIV was the principal aristocrat in Europe) that credit must be given for having elevated the art of large-scale gardening to a more nationwide development.

Vaux-le-Vicomte

With the death of Cardinal Mazarin in 1661, Louis XIV's personal reign began, and France was approaching the period of her political and cultural zenith, as well as that of her greatest wealth. A particularly influential figure at the sunrise of this brilliant age was Louis' finance minister, Nicolas Fouquet. Fouquet was a man of taste as well as of wealth, and attracted to himself the illustrious names of a supremely creative age: the writers Corneille, Molière, La Fontaine, and the celebrated composer, Lully.

For the realisation of his newest château and its gardens there was the prodigious genius Charles Lebrun as designer, decorator and painter; the architect Louis Le Vau, fresh from his Paris triumphs such as the Hôtel Lambert; and that scion of a family of royal gardeners, André Le Nôtre, who was here given his first big commission. It was a formidable team, reminiscent of that which created the château of Anet – Philibert Delorme, Jean Goujon, and Benvenuto Cellini. In order to make space for his gardens, Fouquet bought three villages and swept them away.

At Careggi in Tuscany, the garden had been a quiet spot where an erudite owner might read Plato with his friends; at Bomarzo, the garden provided surprise, even horror; at the Villa d'Este the visitor was entertained, amused, and sometimes soaked; in the Borghese gardens, Cardinal Scipio – via an inscription over the gate – hospitably invited everyone in. But at Fouquet's Vaux-le-Vicomte the gardens were calculated not to entice, but to stun. They were designed to complete and set off the château and to provide a munificent setting for the garden fêtes. Saint-Beuve called Vaux 'ce Versailles anticipé', for at Vaux all of the arts conspired in a typically Baroque fashion to produce the hierarchical ensemble of château, furnishings, works of art, and gardens as the proper setting for a *grand seigneur*. And Vaux led directly to the ordered splendour of Versailles.

The stupendous garden built by Le Nôtre on Fouquet's behalf was already the vista garden that he would soon create for the King, and it contained all of the elements, similarly conjoined, that we shall find in the royal domain. It was intended to be taken in at a single glance from the *perron* (flight of steps) that extended from the oval salon down to the garden level, and the *broderies* and parterres suggested an enormous carpet spread out from the château to the remote distance, the vanishing point marked by a giant copy of the Farnese Hercules on the hill beyond. The garden architect left groves of trees on either side of the central avenue. The trees also provided a restful backdrop to the fountains, pools, and statuary, and a screen for the architectural surprises at the ends of the horizontal axes. Nature in its primitive state was annihilated, its forms wilfully regimented into architecture, with yews and box masquerading as green stone pyramids and cones, densely packed evergreen forming vaults, arches and walls.

The garden's purpose was not to show off particularly fine specimens of plants or flowers, but to provide a proper setting for the exalted *dramatis personae* who would inhabit it. Flowers, shrubs and trees were used as massed greenery or geometrical shapes of colour as foil for the stone château, and – later at Versailles – for the pavilions which would become focal points in the gardens.

With the help of the *hydraulicien* Claude Robillard, Le Nôtre used water in a dramatic way. Walking down the median axis, one passed grilles of water like shimmering walls, through which the parterres were perceived. Every step was accompanied by the sound of water, which reached a crescendo when the visitor arrived at the Grand Cascade beside the canal. A rectangular pool in front of the steps that ascended at either side of the nymphaeum reflected the château, and Madame de Sévigné stopped at Vaux 'to bathe in the ornamental waters' (Adams).

Louis XIV had already seen the work in progress on Fouquet's newest château, and although it was not yet complete, the Finance Minister invited Louis and the court to

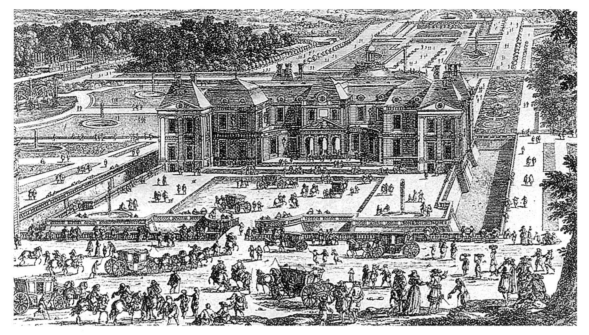

Vaux-le-Vicomte as it looked in the Sun King's day.
Guests' carriages will turn round in the courtyard which is traditionally kept free of greenery for this reason. The sombre utilitarian aspect of the entrance court was intended to contrast with the view that presented itself when the visitors reached the Oval Salon, where they looked down on the dramatic spectacle of Le Nôtre's gardens stretching out before them, punctuated with fountains, statuary, reflecting pools and a nymphaeum, and terminated by the statue of Hercules

Vaux for a *divertissement* on 17 August, 1661. The Queen was pregnant and could not go, but Louis was accompanied by a young blonde daughter of the provincial nobility whom he noticed in his sister-in-law's entourage, whose name was Louise de la Vallière.

The story of that warm August evening is too well known to be recounted in detail, but we know that Louis and his party were conducted around the château by Charles Lebrun, who explained the allegories in the *boiseries* and tapestries woven in Fouquet's atelier nearby, pointed out the glorious ceiling paintings, some of them his own work. Finally, they reached the Oval Salon, with Girardon's wonderful sculpted terms pullulating around the ceiling, the doors opened upon the vista of the spectacular gardens, all to the counterpoint of the King's mounting irritation. All the waters were playing, the parterres were aglow with four hundred lights in fleur-de-lis pattern.

There followed a supper prepared by the Condés' famous chef, Vatel, served upon silver-gilt plates in the gardens, a performance of Molière's *Fâcheux* before a glittering grille of water, music composed by Lully for the occasion. Then, an illuminated whale proceeded down the length of the canal, accompanied by fireworks and bouquets of light on the dome of the salon. Little gifts of diamond tiaras were made to the ladies and richly caparisoned horses to the men. Finally, Louis could bear it no longer, and was heard to exclaim: 'Luxe insolent et audacieux!' One can almost see that fine nose, delight of his sculptors, quivering with rage.

Fouquet was arrested shortly afterwards and, following a sensational trial, he was sentenced to Pignerol. Part of the loot that Louis took from Vaux (some of it paid for) included Fouquet's tapestry works, the orange trees, and Poussin's garden terms. Above all, there was the incomparable artistic triumvirate of Le Vau, Lebrun, and Le Nôtre – men who were in tune with the diapason of their own time – whom Louis appropriated for his own purpose, the enlargement of his father's hunting lodge at Versailles.

Patel, Versailles. 1668.
The royal family can be seen at right, coming over from Saint-Germain-en-Laye in 1668 to see the progress that is being made in transforming the château. The red/gilt coach bears the Queen, Marie-Thérèse, followed by the King's.

Already visible are the parterres that Le Nôtre was creating on the north side to be seen from the King's apartments in the north wing after the extensions by J.-H. Mansart. On the south side were the parterres below the Queen's suite.

The small rectangular structure with water on the roof on the north side is the Grotto of Thetis, which would be demolished when the north wing was later added. Louis XIII's old château has been retained as centrepiece for the enlarged Versailles that is emerging

Cotelle, Labyrinthe de Versailles.
The painting shows the lead animals and figures from Aesop's Fables. *André Félibien, preceptor to the Dauphin's son, the Duc de Bourgogne, described the Labyrinth as a metaphor for love, where one loses one's way. This delightful bosquet was destroyed in 1775*

Versailles

Louis XIII's 'little playing-cards chateau' (Saint-Simon) that Louis XIV decided to transform into the residence for the French court was hardly more than a pavilion. The Sun King's father had also been an ardent hunter, and his small *ermitage* at Versailles offered shelter when he followed the chase in forests teeming with the game that attracted him to the place. The hunt was more a ritual than a sport for the Bourbon kings, and the sites of the royal châteaux were chosen on the basis of abundant woodlands. This must have weighed heavily in the Sun King's decision to enlarge Versailles, for he was a mighty hunter. It was a taste inherited by each of his descendants – the Dauphin, Louis XV, and Louis XVI. It would be that inveterate builder, Louis XV, who would commission Jacques-Ange Gabriel and others to adorn his favourite hunting grounds with delightful *pavillons de chasse*.

Louis XIV's choice of Versailles as a home for the court was certainly not due to the natural beauty of the spot, for the swampy terrain had nothing to recommend it and threatened the health of the workers. The most formidable disadvantage, though, was the lack of water, which was needed in endless quantities for fountains, *pièces d'eau,* forests of trees transplanted for the bosquets, the emerald *tapis vert,* flowers and shrubbery. Charles Perrault lamented the paucity of water and expressed the views of most of the Court: 'On etait en branle de quitter Versailles pour aller bâtir dans un terrain plus heureux'.

The struggle to bring water to the site taxed the ingenuity – and the patience – of Louis' engineers almost to breaking point, but finally the Machine de Marly (1681-4) was devised to lift water from the river to reservoirs 162 metres above it. In 1685 the waters of the Seine came rushing in to fill reservoirs, reflecting pools, canals, basins with water-jets and cascades. Fountains like fantastic egret plumes punctuated the garden vistas, like Le Bassin de la Sirène, where the Siren, with a Triton who had emerged from the pool, blows sprays of water skywards from a large conch shell.

The Francinis (experts in hydrodynamics who had worked in the gardens of Saint-Germain-en-Laye) achieved astonishing water effects, collaborating with sculptors of the Versailles school. Although it was Le Nôtre's all-encompassing plan that brought order and harmony to the vast acreage, he achieved such rich complexity through the concerted efforts of hydraulics' wizards, engineers, sculptors, stone masons, and legions of workers whose prodigious task it was to excavate and level, arrange paths, flower beds, and parterres, and lay the foundations for the complex sophistication of the various bosquets.

Meanwhile, the château itself was gradually assuming the arrogant dimensions appropriate to the supreme monarchy of Europe. Its east front would soon be preceded by the great *place* (square) before it, the *avant-cour* (forecourt) flanked by the commons, wings projecting forward at either side to enclose the Cour de Marbre. The forecourts were intended for carriages or sedan chairs, and the bustle of arrivals

P. le Pautre, Le Bassin de la Sirène.
The animating idea of the fountain was to herald the arrival of Apollo: the Siren lifts her arm to greet him, and blows the conch shell to announce his arrival. Berger noted that the same Sirens and Tritons appear on the Grotto façade, with the putti on dolphins in the roundels, so that the Siren Basin becomes a prelude to the Grotto. The sculptural group was executed by the eminent sculptors, Gaspard and Balthazar Marsy.

On the ledges of the rectangular basin stand bronze vases holding shrubs and plants that have been allowed to grow naturally, but those bordering the gravel path are coaxed into spheres and pyramids

Apollo Basin and Grand Canal, Versailles.
The highly original Apollo Basin, with sculpture by Jean-Baptiste Tuby (1635-1700), depicts Apollo being pulled by his horses from the sea to begin his daily round of the heavens. It complements the iconography of the Grotto of Thetis, to which Apollo descends at the end of day.

The Apollo Basin precedes the Grand Canal, the lateral arm of which terminated in the Ménagerie to the south, recalling the glories of Solomon. The north arm was completed by the fragile folie covered in faïence, the Trianon of Porcelain, later replaced by the Grand Trianon

and departures, so greenery was inappropriate for these spaces and was reserved for the garden façade. Even today, Frenchmen wonder at the impropriety – in their view – of hyacinths and tulips planted in front of American or English houses, for they belonged in the garden parterres.

At Versailles, when one stepped out upon the western terrace that created a pedestal for the château, the gardens were seen as a vertical picture. At either side were the twin Water Parterres underlining and reflecting the dwelling, around which were disposed bronze figures representing the Rivers of France (1685-94). As one walked down the main axis, one encountered the Latona Basin with Apollo as a child, the *tapis vert* decorated at each side with statues and vases, edged by high clipped hornbeam, the Apollo Basin with Apollo as the adult Sun God, and the Grand Canal beyond, finally completed in 1672.

Under the windows of the King's apartments in the north wing, and the Queen's in the south, Le Nôtre created parterres, a concept that came from the ancient maze or labyrinth, carrying the scale of the house into the gardens to make the architectural transition. The relationship of dwelling to gardens was further enhanced by the manicured *broderies* – low, clipped greenery in arabesque forms against a background of coloured stones favoured by Le Nôtre. The Queen's Parterre du Midi was of flowers, for Louis liked flowers, the more fragrant the better. They heightened the 'visual temperature' of the scene, picking up the polychrome patterns of the Savonnerie carpets indoors.

If water gave scale and animation to the garden, statues and vases effected a liaison between the château and the greenery of shrubs, grass, and trees. Providing focal points

Vue des Cascades de Versailles.
The Neptune Basin in its first form is seen here, but the sculptural decoration could not be carried out under the Sun King because of the War of the League of Augsburg. Under Louis XV, the basin was entirely redone between 1739 and 1740 under the direction of Louis XV's architect Jacques-Ange Gabriel, with waterworks by the Francinis.

The gilt lead sculpture – by Bouchardon, J.-B. Lemoine and Lambert Sigisbert Adam – was of such distinction that Pierre de Nolhac called it 'the most grandiose lead decoration in the world.' Small boats could be accommodated on the Neptune Basin, but only the Grand Canal and Swiss Guards' Basin were large enough for the King's flotilla

were vases with sculpted relief, loaded with symbolic meaning and retelling Greek tragedies, for seventeenth-century imagery turned to allegory. Under Lebrun's direction, a team of sculptors interpreted Lebrun's drawings, peopling the park with statues and groups inspired by antiquity. Among them was the series of twenty-four colossal statues in white marble – the so-called 'Great Commission' – that elaborated the heliocentric theme of Versailles set forth by the statues standing on the western façade of the château.

Le Nôtre studied painting in the atelier of Louis XIII's First Painter, Simon Vouet, and it was here that his solid friendship with Charles Lebrun began. Vouet had travelled widely, bringing back sketches of gardens, including those for the Byzantine emperors by Greek gardeners. Applying the lessons he had learned from Louis XIII's painter and the science of perspective he had no doubt assimilated from his close association with the family of the architect *par excellence,* François Mansart, Le Nôtre proved himself to be a superb *ornemaniste* on a grand scale.

His design for the Cascades de Versailles in their original form is an example, the apotheosis of water manipulation at Versailles. The contruction of Le Nôtre's first design was directed by the architect J.-H. Mansart, beginning in 1679, and it represents the harmonious equilibrium that the garden architect achieved between the elements of his composition. Here he disposed the basin in the form of a vast hemicycle, 'a sort of antique theatre, of which the seats were turf, and the parterre (or stage, in this case) a sheet of water' (Ganay 1962). To create the effect of liquid fireworks was a prodigious ramp of forty-four water jets, half of them emerging from

Bosquet of the Labyrinth at Versailles.
The idea for the Labyrinth (1666-74) apparently came from Charles Perrault, and it is unusual in that the iconography is devoid of any political allusions. There were thirty-nine fountains, each one illustrating a fable by Aesop, and at the entrance stood metal statues of Aesop and Cupid who, according to Perrault, is himself a labyrinth

huge lead vases beautifully ornamented. Fan-shaped cascades tumbled into the enormous basin, from which spouted six tall sheaves of water. The perspective looking back towards the château was framed by tall trees. But the avenue was kept wide enough for the spectator to appreciate the Pyramid Fountain (designed by Lebrun), the centrepiece of the North Parterre, and suggested one of the fabulous pieces of *orfèvrerie* (silverware) from the King's illustrious collection.

Some of Le Nôtre's finest achievements were the bosquets hidden away in the recesses of the gardens. One was the Labyrinthe, inhabited by painted lead animals and figures from Aesop's *Fables*, and possibly intended for the instruction of the Dauphin (above and p. 32). Another was the Marais where, in the centre of a marsh, a metal tree spouted water. Its most extraordinary feature were the buffets at the side, another of the Francinis' miracles. For on the shelves of the buffet stood 'crystal' vases and pitchers, actually formed by water in jewel colours – again, a subtle tribute to the King's collection of hardstone vessels mounted in ormolu.

With 5,000 people in the palace, 15,000 more in the *maisons de ville,* 2,500 horses in the stables, and its incomparable gardens, Versailles was the world's greatest stage, and an edifice dedicated to the cult of royalty. The aura surrounding 'Apollo' and his attendants was maintained by physical distance, an extension in three-dimensional space of the ideological gulf that remains immutably fixed between gods and mere mortals.

Louis XIV particularly enjoyed the pleasures of outdoor life, and apparently no other aspect of Versailles delighted him more than the gardens, for which he wrote a guidebook. They provided a noble retreat for King and court, and their theatrical possibilities were exploited to the full as a stage for the garden fêtes that became an integral part of the Versailles routine – the 'government by spectacle', as Professor Treasure put it. The flaming bouquets of splintered radiance that lighted the sky during the firework displays were reflected in the shimmering waters of the Canal, and threw into stark relief the sculpted forms of box and yew, the dense, mysterious forms of the bosquets.

To celebrate the treaty of Aix-la-Chapelle and the bringing of water to the gardens, Louis staged a huge party on 18 July, 1668, known as the *Grand Divertissement*. The château itself appeared to be a real Palace of the Sun, for all the windows were filled with antique statues illuminated with various colours, the balustrades and terraces were edged with vases blazing with light, and in the garden parterres were luminous colossal figures. The royal party in coaches watched from the summit of the Allée Royale carpeted with the *tapis vert* at that time edged with terms.

Le Pautre, the Fête of 18 July, 1668, engraving, 1679.
The King's famous engineer, Vigarani, was responsible for all the 'machines' that governed the firework displays, illuminations, and stage machinery.
Here the King is seen in his carriage pulled by six horses, accompanied by the princes and princesses, being driven across the gardens by his able coachman, Millet, to see the féerique *illuminations of the parterres and château outlined in lights. The Latona Basin is in its original form*

Bosquet of the Etoile, Versailles.
The buffets for the fête of 1668 were presented in various garden bosquets, and the five buffets set up in the Etoile were all different, ranging from cold meats to almond cake palaces and sugared pastry. Vases stood between the buffets containing shrubs bearing preserved fruit. Trees with fresh fruit were placed along the five paths, and from them the courtiers could pick pears, gooseberries, apricots, peaches, oranges, cherries, and Portuguese oranges. When the court left the bosquet, the King customarily allowed the people following him to pillage the food

The bosquet of the Etoile became an open-air dining room, with five buffets centred upon a towering jet of water. One buffet supported a mountain whose caves were filled with cold meats. In the foreground were two others, the one on the left in the illustration above (with a top representing the parterres of a French formal garden) held a palace made of almond cake, the one on the right, silver vessels for drinks. A backdrop of living foliage was sculpted into buffets with volutes festooned with fresh flowers and precious vases containing large bouquets. As the courtiers wandered down the five paths that radiated from the Etoile, they discovered shrubs at either side bearing fresh fruit, and at the end of each path, a flowered niche with the King's gilt cipher lighted with hundreds of candles.

After the court left the Molière play, given before almost 3,000 spectators in a pavilion of foliage, they were conducted to another which sheltered the after-theatre buffet. At its centre stood a large rock formation representing Parnassus surmounted by the winged horse Pegasus, and studded with silver figures of Apollo and the Muses. The *feuillée* was elaborated with an enriched cornice with porcelain vases filled with fresh flowers and flower garlands suspended by silver gauze scarves; deep green piers of living greenery held basins from which water flowed and candlesticks blazed with torches; a niche behind the buffet displayed twenty-five enormous basins of chased silver and vases of precious metals. Flowing cascades bubbled from the summit of Parnassus, forming four little rivulets that flowed out upon the lawns. It was a way

Le Pautre, foliage pavilion for the Grand Divertissement of 1668.
This remarkable foliage pavilion is octagonal, with a round table supporting a great centrepiece of the Muses and Pegasus. Fruits and cakes were usually presented in the form of pyramids, like the pyramidal yews in Le Nôtre's gardens. Fresh flower festoons hung from the tops of the doors, with lighted chandeliers at the centre of each opening. Another chandelier illuminated the silver display at the back, and blazing torches flank dolphin fountains on the piers. A complex collective effort and many diverse talents were required to fabricate the intricate treillage, shear the greenery into flat walls, realise the sculpture and waterworks, and artistically arrange the sumptuous silver and oriental porcelain

of celebrating the bringing of water to the great preserve, for now effects could be achieved which had formerly been impossible.

The history of the bosquets is confused, for many were changed. One of the most highly refined was the Salle des Antiques, an outdoor sculpture gallery that was a favourite haunt of the court. The basins were surrounded by black and white marble walkways used as a promenade for the courtiers to study the twenty-four antique statues displayed on marble pedestals. They stood in shallow water, with jets interspersed, while at the centre and ends were fountains spilling over basins in the form of giant shells. To set off this exquisite composition were walls of sheared greenery, backed by bosquets of natural trees.

The classical spirit in which Le Nôtre's *jardin français* was conceived determined the form of the more permanent pleasure houses that Louis was to build. For even he became fatigued by the burden of exacting etiquette that governed every waking moment of court life. So he began to seek refuge from the huge château in a series of retreats which became satellites in the gardens – the pavilions that complemented and completed Le Nôtre's magisterial plan.

Jean Nocret, Louise de la Baume Le Blanc, Duchesse de la Vallière (1644-1710).
It has been said that Louis XIV fell in love with Louise de la Vallière and Versailles at the same time.
Louise was shy, did not like the glare of court life, and was no match for the authoritative personality of
the King. By the time of the Grand Divertissement of 1668, it was clear that her days as mistress were
numbered. In 1674 when still only thirty, threatened by the ascendancy of Athénaïs de Montespan,
Louise asked to leave court for good, to take Orders as a Carmelite. She gave Louis four children — two
sons who died very early, another who lived to sixteen, and a daughter, who grew up to become Mlle. de
Blois, who married Philippe d'Orléans, son of Liselotte and the King's only brother, Philippe. Louise
had other galants beside the King. One was Loménie de Brienne, who wanted her to pose for a repentant
Madeleine that he wanted to have painted for his collection

CHAPTER 2

PAVILIONS IN THE AGE OF
LOUIS XIV: 1661-1715

In August 1661, when Louis and the court were invited to the unfortunate party at Vaux-le-Vicomte, the Queen – who was pregnant – did not accompany him. It was at this time that a daughter of the provincial nobility caught Louis' eye – blonde, shy Louise de la Vallière. So it was she who went along with the royal party to Fouquet's château on that warm August evening.

His love affair with Louise became a factor in Louis' awakening interest in his father's hunting box at Versailles. For in this bachelor's retreat, the young couple could escape the prying eyes of the court – especially the two Queens (Louis' wife and mother). The gardens of the diminutive château extended along an axis from the parterres to a quatrefoil basin that would be the setting in 1664 for a famous garden fête to honour Louise before the court. Like Diane de Poitiers, the sixteen-year-old Louise de la Vallière was an expert rider, and in the forests that surrounded Le Petit Château she and Louis hunted and explored the countryside that was shortly to be transformed.

Despite the marshy soil and unpromising site, Louis gradually became attached to the small château of red brick with white quoins and a blue slate roof that was 'the colour of playing cards'. The following year he began to assert his own authority there, staking out portions of the terrain with garden buildings designed by Louis Le Vau, the architect he had taken from the fallen Fouquet.

The Ménagerie
The first of these was a zoo, the Ménagerie (1662-4), which the architect of Vaux-le-Vicomte conceived as a domed pavilion in octagonal form, preceded by two forecourts, and flanked by dependencies. It was surrounded by enclosures for Louis' collection of rare birds and animals, and he was so pleased with it that he ordered the artist Nicolas Robert to paint its exotic inhabitants, so the royal ostriches and peacocks were immortalised in Robert's famous vellums.

Louis was always especially fond of the Ménagerie. When Marie-Adelaide de Savoie (Duchesse de Bourgogne and future mother of Louis XV) arrived in November 1696, Louis was so smitten with her that he presented her the Ménagerie, and ordered the architect J.-H. Mansart, who succeeded Le Vau, to redecorate it for her. It was to Mansart that the King's often-cited directive was sent: 'Il faut de l'enfance répandre partout'. For a light-hearted, youthful manner was appropriate for the lively, dark-haired girl who was the joy of Louis' latter days.

The Ménagerie remained a favourite haunt of the courtiers as long as the Bourbons lived at Versailles. In Marie-Antoinette's day, the people of Paris made frequent excursions out to the grand château, where they followed the wide allées down to the

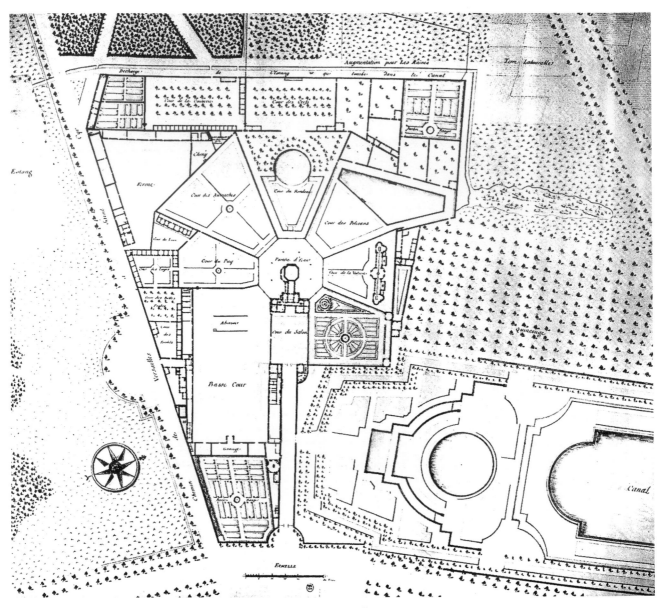

Le Rouge, Plan of the Ménagerie, Versailles.
The Ménagerie, which terminated the south arm of the Grand Canal, was an octagonal pavilion with domed roof. From the upper storey could be seen the courtyards where the unusual birds and animals were kept, an idea that reflects the collections of King Solomon. The Laiterie for the Duchess of Burgundy was added to it

Ménagerie. Here they could watch bears, tropical birds and zebras, or wander through the bosquets, hoping to catch a glimpse of the Queen, who liked to stroll in the gardens with her children.

To accompany the Ménagerie, in 1663 the King ordered another pavilion – the Grande Laiterie (Dairy) situated to the south of the allée that led to the Ménagerie itself. Ostensibly for practical purposes, the Dairy's chief *raison d'être* was to amuse the King and his mistress. The Versailles Dairy is usually considered to be the first *laiterie parée* (decorated pleasure dairy) in France, a type that would proliferate during the reign of Louis XVI. But in François I's day, there had been a dairy at Fontainebleau which was decorated for the King by Primaticcio himself.

Nothing remains of Louis XIV's Dairy except the plan, but it consisted of two rooms, the larger in octagonal form, and the smaller rectangular. The octagonal room, repeating the shape of the Ménagerie, was lighted by two windows, with a stone or marble console table that ran around the walls (a constant feature of later dairies), interrupted by a basin in the corner, and an octagonal table at the centre. The other room contained two basins and a well.

A true Bourbon, Louis was concerned with every phase of its construction, taking particular interest in the progress of this amusing little *folie*. The day that water was brought to the Dairy, thanks largely to the efforts of the *fontainiers* Francini, the King rushed over to open and close the faucets, getting quite wet. It was this *gamin* spirit that prompted him to incorporate into his next pavilion, the Grotte de Thétis, hidden jets in the floor that were activated when a visitor stepped on a button. His father, Louis XIII, had delighted in being soaked by the water jets hidden in the Saint-Germain-en-Laye grottoes, but these 'wetting sports', as the English call them, have never greatly appealed to the French spirit.

Plaisirs de l'Ile Enchantée

Even before Le Vau began to enlarge the château, André Le Nôtre was set to work on the gardens that were to be its majestic setting. An equally compelling reason for their ordered magnitude was the need for vast spaces, broad alleys, large reflecting pools, glittering fountains and hidden bosquets as an outdoor stage for the *divertissements* that were a traditional feature of court life. Ceremonies and celebrations that exploited drama, art and music had proclaimed French royal power since the Gothic age, and would continue to do so throughout the Bourbon reign. As Louis' power increased, the *mystique* that was a natural accompaniment of power had also to grow (Wolf). He understood that this could most effectively be accomplished through the sheer glamour and *panache* of a series of theatricals in the gardens.

One of the more spectacular early extravaganzas was the one staged in May 1664, the *Plaisirs de l'Ile Enchantée*. The Queen and Queen Mother (Anne of Austria) were both there, but everyone was fully aware there was a dual purpose behind the affair: to present Louise as official mistress (she had just given birth to a child in December 1663), and to efface forever the memory of the humiliating fête at Vaux-le-Vicomte that had been a model of the genre. Louise and many members of his court had been there, so the King got his conservative minister, Colbert, to loosen the royal purse strings to provide a three-day party for six hundred guests that would upstage Fouquet's party which had lasted only a single evening.

This memorable event of May 1664 set a precedent for all of Louis' future *divertissements*. It required the participation of architects, gardeners, mechanics, composers, playwrights, chefs, painters, sculptors, musicians, actors, singers, engravers, silversmiths and artisans of every kind. Carlo Vigarani conceived the constantly changing décors. Louis' great designer, Jean Berain, created the costumes of sumptuous materials especially woven for the occasion, heavily embroidered with gold and silver thread, and studded with real jewels.

The event also marked a collaboration between two men of genius who have become legend in the annals of the theatre, and who were indispensable to the court of Louis XIV. One was the composer Jean-Baptiste Lully who achieved a prodigious success in opera and a sort of monopoly on musical production in France. The other

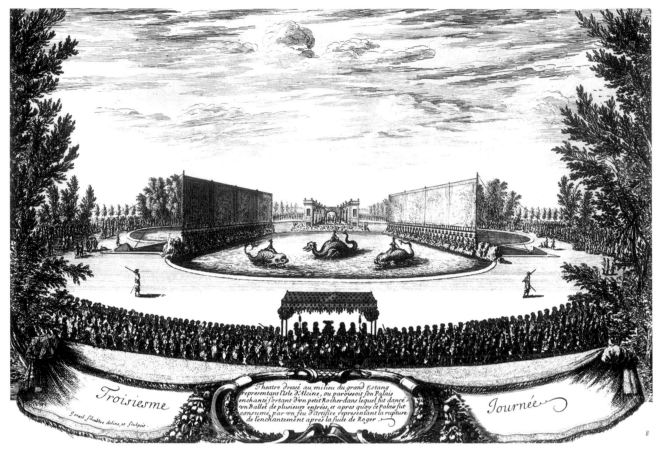

Troisiesme

Journée

Israel Sylvestre delin. et sculpsit.

Theatre dressé au milieu du grand Estang
representant l'Isle d'Alcine, ou paroissoit son Palais
enchanté sortant d'un petit Rocher dans lequel fut dancé
un Ballet de plusieurs entrées, et apres quoy ce Palais fut
consumé, par un feu d'Artifice representant la rupture
de l'enchantement apres la fuite de Roger

8

Israel Silvestre, 'Troisième Journée de l'Ile Enchantée'.
The three-day affair of the Plaisirs de l'Ile Enchantée in the burgeoning Versailles gardens really inaugurated the ambitious building programme. For the finale on the third evening, Louis is seated in his feathered hat under a portable pavilion of rich stuffs embellished with fleurs-de-lis, flanked by ladies of the royal family. The musicians are precariously perched upon rocks at either side of the basin, against a backdrop of the crown tapestries, and in the background, the enchanted palace of the magician Alcine rests upon an island. As the musicians began to play Lully's music, three enormous whales emerged from the water, Alcine riding on the back of one, her companions on the others. As they approach the shore they address complaints to the court, then retire to the palace, which opens to receive them. Six knights, prisoners of Alcine, try to escape, but are vanquished by her guardian monsters. When Alcine invokes the aid of the demons who serve her, a terrifying assault ensues, but the hero Roger quickly rubs his magic ring. A deafening roar of thunder splits the sky, followed by loud explosions, then a shower of fireworks which consume the palace, as the spell of Alcine is broken

was the immortal Molière who assumed the triple role of author/actor/producer for the King. The result of the Lully-Molière partnership was the *comédie-ballet*, for musical and literary history was being created for the entertainment of the Sun King's six hundred guests.

On the first evening, the stage in the garden was defined by towering clipped hedges joined by tall doors of living greenery bearing the King's cipher, and lighted by numerous white wax candles in immense chandeliers hoisted into the trees by complicated machinery. A herald in flame-coloured costume with silver embroideries announced the programme.

Versailles was to become an island over which the great magician, Alcine, was to cast a spell that would hold the court captive for three days, an idea taken from Ariosto's *Orlando Furioso*. The herald was followed by trumpeters, drummers, and finally the King himself on a dashing mount, wearing a costume lavishly worked with jewels and a casque trailing flame-coloured plumes.

Then came the noble members of his troupe, magnificently dressed, riding richly caparisoned horses, followed by four Centuries, twelve Hours and signs of the Zodiac. One munificent tableau followed another, as the actors spoke Molière's lines interspersed with Lully's music, and Vigarani busily rearranged the scenery with his able team of carpenters, mechanics and stage hands.

For the Seasons' tableau, the King's musicians took the front of the stage, and to the sounds of violins and oboes, four animals representing the Seasons lumbered out, no doubt reluctantly, upon the stage: bear, camel and elephant from the Ménagerie, and a horse. Tables in crescent form were set up in the exedra for the cold collation, and the gifts in heavy silver dishes were presented on the heads of 'shepherds' who were lined up behind the *tableau vivant*.

For the second night's performance, Molière had not even finished writing the play, but the *Princesse d'Elide* (interpreted by Molière's wife) was staged anyway for the august company. Molière's own performance as the buffoon/valet Lyciscas was, in fact, the hit of the evening.

The finale of the three-day event centred on the Lake of Alcine, with the stage set up on the Swan Basin (site of the future Latona Parterre and Apollo Basin). The engraver Israel Silvestre has depicted the moment before Alcine's spell was broken and the entire scene was destroyed in a dazzling fireworks display. An enchanted palace rises on the Island of Alcine in the background. The Crown's most gorgeous tapestries are hung at the sides to delimit the liquid stage in the foreground, below which the musicians perch precariously upon rock formations.

After the fête had officially ended, the King conducted the court over to the Ménagerie, where they fed the compliant animals that had taken part in the play and admired the fantastic fowl. One of the guests, Locatelli, recorded in his journal that the shining copper aviary must have contained every kind of known bird, for he counted more than forty different species in a few minutes.

In the evening, the salon of the Ménagerie was transformed into a stage for the presentation of Molière's *Les Facheux*. Those who had attended Fouquet's party perhaps made a mental comparision with the beautiful theatre at Vaux decorated by Charles Lebrun that stood at the end of an allée under a grille of water. If the improvised stage of the Ménagerie was not quite as appealing, the play certainly captured the attention of the audience, for it began with the appearance of a large shell surrounded by jets of water falling into a basin. When the shell opened, there stepped forth a nymph, the actress Madeleine Béjart (Molière's sister-in-law), who recited a prologue to the glory of the King.

The Ménagerie served as a salon for luncheon in the days that followed. For the night buffets, an eight-sided table was put up, with a centrepiece in the form of a pavilion with columns, floral festoons and papier mâché figures. The vestible of the château was converted into a stage for the renowned premiere of Molière's *Tartuffe,* a technical masterpiece and perfect model of the comedy of characters.

It has been observed that Versailles, before it became the theatre of the King's grandeur, was first of all the theatre of his pleasures. The next pavilion that he added to the gardens was a direct response to Louis' insatiable taste for theatricals, for it was used as the actual stage setting for performances, and its interior exploited the dramatic possibilities of space, lighting and water.

Façade of the Grotte de Thétis.
The façade bas-reliefs by Van Opstal repeat the imagery of the Siren Fountain. Pierre de Nolhac claimed the grilles were painted green, but paintings show them gilded. Inside the grotto were tiny invisible jets that suddenly turned on when one stepped on them, a great embarrassment to the ladies.
The complicated hydraulics that produced the water streaming over the walls, the bird songs, and water spouts were the work of Pierre and François Francini

Grotte de Thétis

By July 1665, if not before, work had started on the north side of the château for the new Grotte de Thétis, Louis' first major artistic enterprise in the gardens. It could properly be called a pavilion, for it was a free-standing cubical structure whose interior was treated as a grotto. The strange and bizarre Mannerist elements that had characterised the earlier caverns in the gardens of Saint-Germain-en-Laye, however, were suppressed in this new grotto/pavilion where the constraining principles of classical architecture prevailed.

To set forth the concept of the absolute (and divine) monarchy, Louis chose Apollo the Sun God as his emblem. In 1653 he had danced the role of Apollo in a court ballet, wearing a costume studded with shining suns and a beplumed hat sprouting golden rays. Sunbursts would become ubiquitous decorative motifs at Versailles, and the radiant theme was announced on the triumphal-arch façade of the Grotte de Thétis.

A complex iconography was worked out by Claude and Charles Perrault, referring to Apollo's descent into the sea to rest in the grotto of the nereid Thetis after his day's round of the heavens. A grotto was the proper setting for this event, for grottoes were consecrated to gods long before temples, as Naomi Miller has shown. As she points out, they were regarded as sacred places, associated with water as a source of poetic inspiration and rites of cleansing. The low-relief sculpture in the entablature and rondels on the façade carry out the theme of the Thetis Grotto, and the wrought-iron door grilles arranged as gilded rays suggest that the Sun himself inhabits the interior.

Left: Jean-Baptiste Tuby, Acis.
Acis was the Sicilian shepherd who was loved by Galatea, goddess of water. The sculptor Tuby had been in Rome and was a living link between Italian and French seventeenth-century artists, but it was due to the School of Fontainebleau that France had become a centre of classical influence. Mythology inspired most of the statues at Versailles, and the Thetis Grotto exploited the talents of the great team under François Girardon that comprised the Versailles School of sculpture

Right: Jean-Baptiste Tuby, Galatea.
Galatea was the adorable goddess of water with whom Acis fell in love. She also attracted the attention of the giant Polyphemus. When she and Acis were surprised by the giant, he crushed his rival with a rock. Since Galatea's abode was properly the sea, she is associated with the nymphs who are assisting Apollo in the central salon of the Grotto (p. 50). Tuby, an ingenious sculptor, was more interested in plastic effects than in the Apollo tradition

Just inside the door one encountered niches at each side holding white marble statues by the sculptor Baptiste Tuby of Acis and the nymph Galatea, her foot resting upon a dolphin. Under the direction of the *rocailleur* Delaunay, the walls were sculpted in low relief with shells and moss, and pillars were decorated with elaborate *rocailles*, marine deities with scaly bodies in high relief, and Neptune masques from which water plunged into shell-shaped basins surmounted by the King's cipher.

The grotto represented the synthesis of the Versailles style from its beginning, for a major feature of the gardens was announced here: water used in conjunction with sculpture. Water, a common symbol of Apollo and Thetis, played a central role in both the décor and iconography of the grotto.

By means of the hydraulics system installed behind the rear wall by the *hydrauliciens*, Pierre and François Francini, water was made to flow into basins and to activate music played by the hydraulic organ

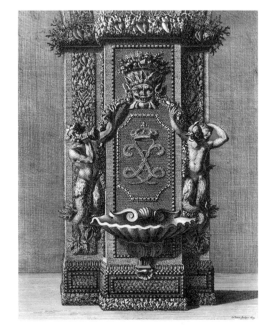

Le Pautre, decorated pillar in the Grotte de Thétis.
The architectural elements of the grotto received revetments of shells, mother-of-pearl and polished rocks. The pillar supports a shell-shaped basin into which water is spewed from the mask of Neptune, God of the Sea. The King's crowned, interlaced initials are flanked by marine deities like mermen with scaly bodies.
The intricacies of the rocailles lent a mysterious plasticity to the grotto, over whose walls poured thin streams of water, and which was totally dark – except for the chandeliers – until the doors were thrown open

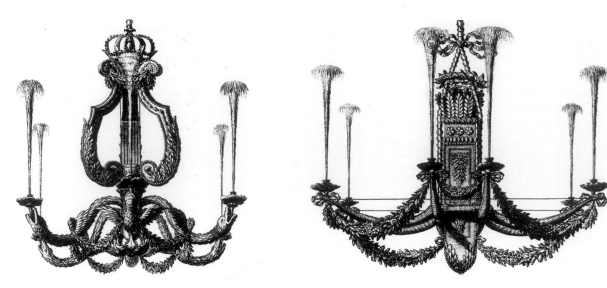

Chauveau, chandeliers of the Grotte de Thétis.
The lyre was Apollo's instrument. The chandelier on the left is surmounted by a crown, and the arms supporting the bobêches for the water spouts (liquid candles) are clothed in laurel leaves that form the scaly bodies of the serpents. The chandelier on the right features festoons of shells, a quiver crowned with a classical laurel wreath, suspended by a bow

that imitated the songs of birds. Thin streams trickled over the irregular wall surfaces, which were enhanced with mirrors, coral and shellwork, creating the effect of constant movement. Lighted sprays of water issued from chandeliers of classical lyres, crowns and swags, and from wall lights in the form of shellwork masks inspired by the Mannerist tradition (opposite).

Total harmony was achieved through subtle, complex, sophisticated relationships between the iconography of exterior and interior, the focal point of which was the far wall where the theme set forth on the façade acquired three-dimensional form (p.50). Three domed niches shelter sculptural masterpieces of the Grand Siècle: in the central niche stood 'Apollo Ministered to by the Nymphs of Thetis', a manifesto of the Versailles school by François Girardon, leader of the King's team of sculptors. In the flanking niches stood two groups by Gilles Guérin and Gaspard Marsy, 'The Sun King's Horses Tended by Grooms'. In Louis' garden pavilions and the immense atelier of Versailles, this distinguished group of sculptors would find a field in every way worthy of their talents, and they would influence European taste for almost a century (Souchal).

There was as yet no theatre at Versailles, so the grotto offered an opulent backdrop for concerts and plays. The façade embellished with rondels presented a noble proscenium, and when the grilled doors were swung open (or removed), the three splendid marble groups of Apollo and his horses were seen through the triple opening at the back of the stage.

The fête of 19 July, 1674 featured a cold collation in the Ménagerie, and a *promenade* upon the Grand Canal in the King's gondolas accompanied by his musicians. The evening ended with a performance of Molière's *Le Malade Imaginaire* before the Grotto of Thetis. The façade itself was seen at the back of the stage, with a painted backdrop representing the architecture and bas-reliefs of the grotto as a proscenium, a nice Baroque conceit.

By the beginning of 1667, before he left for the siege of Lille, Louis' interest in the faded Louise de la Vallière had already begun to wane, and during the campaign, a fresher court beauty attracted his attention. She was the witty, finely educated Athénaïs de Mortemart, Marquise de Montespan. It soon became apparent that she would replace Louise as the official mistress, for the King was as infatuated with her scintillating conversation as her physical charm.

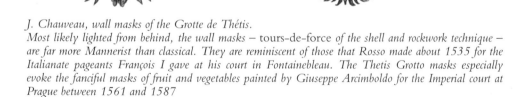

J. Chauveau, wall masks of the Grotte de Thétis.
*Most likely lighted from behind, the wall masks – tours-de-force of the shell and rockwork technique –
are far more Mannerist than classical. They are reminiscent of those that Rosso made about 1535 for the
Italianate pageants François I gave at his court in Fontainebleau. The Thetis Grotto masks especially
evoke the fanciful masks of fruit and vegetables painted by Giuseppe Arcimboldo for the Imperial court at
Prague between 1561 and 1587*

The eight-year-old Dauphin was smitten, too, and Athénais remained an important
figure in his life. When he was later decorating his apartments that became a major
attraction at Versailles, he received from Athénaïs some glorious embroideries to
complement his distinguished porcelain collection. The Marquise proved to be Louis'
most prolific mistress (she bore him nine children), three of them named Louis. The
youngest, Louis-Alexandre, Comte de Toulouse (1678-1737) interests us, for he
became the father of the good Duc de Penthièvre, whom we shall meet at the
pavilions of Rambouillet.

If the *Plaisirs de l'Ile Enchantée* had been the vehicle for presenting Louise as official
mistress, the *Grand Divertissement* of July 1668 (see Chapter 1) ushered in Athénaïs de
Montespan. She was given her own apartments at court, but Louis again found it
awkward to conduct an illicit affair under the eyes of the family. So he began to
consider – apparently during the winter of 1670 – a small house in the gardens to
which he could repair with the glamorous Athénaïs.

Le Pautre, the three principal sculptural groups in the Grotte de Thétis.
Félibien thought the art of Versailles succeeded best in the triumphal arch of niches sheltering the three superb groups of sculpture that set forth its theme. The central niche contains the group of Apollo after his descent from the heavens, and the nymphs of Thétis who prepare his toilette. His horses are in the niches at each side, attended by merfolk. Those on the right are by Gaspard Marsy (1667), showing the influence of Bernini, while the group on the left is by Gilles Guérin. The central tableau is by François Girardon and his assistants

François Girardon et al., 'Apollo Ministered to by the Nymphs of Thetis'.
It was an audacious act on the part of Girardon to undertake seven figures in one group, and to bring them together in a harmonious ensemble. Perrault advised him to study the antique in Italy, so Girardon's head of Apollo is inspired by the Apollo Belvedere. The nymphs exhibit the classical and balanced grace that characterises the sculptures of the Great Commission in the park of Versailles. In their attitudes and treatment of the drapery they recall the marvellous Muse in Poussin's 'Inspiration of the Lyric Poet'.

Kitchen wall in the Amalienburg pavilion.
Although the Amalienburg is one of the delights of eighteeenth-century German Rococo, its kitchen walls faced in tile give us perhaps the best idea of what the interiors of the Trianon de Porcelaine looked like. The tiles of the Trianon were either imported from Holland or by the new Compagnie des Indes founded by Colbert in 1664. They were a part of the symphony in blue and white established for the interiors, for the furniture and the taffeta covers were also the same colours. If the wall and floor tiles were not Dutch, they could have been faïence made in Paris, Saint-Cloud, Lisieux or Rouen, imitating the famous blue-and-white of Holland

The Trianon de Porcelaine

The new pavilion that Louis began to dream of, apparently during the winter of 1670, was to become a real innovation, for – as Erdberg remarks – it was the first Chinese garden building to appear in Europe. Where did Louis get the idea?

One remembers that he had been surrounded by beautiful objects since his youth, thanks to his mother, Anne of Austria, a woman of exquisite taste. Louis' own taste was also formed by that born collector, Cardinal Mazarin, his artistic mentor and virtual stepfather after Louis XIII's early death. Mazarin's extensive collections included rare Chinese ceramics, and he has been credited with having introduced the oriental taste into France.

In 1665 a French Jesuit travelling in China wrote of the marvellous Porcelain Tower of Nanking, and described it as 'enamelled and glazed in green, red, and yellow [giving it the appearance of] emerald, rubies, and gold . . . little metal bells lifted the depressed spirit . . . and its summit was topped by a solid gold pineapple'.[1] The tower was not really of porcelain, and whether the crowning pineapple was solid gold is a matter for conjecture, but engravings of the fabled pagoda were circulated in Europe and might well have come to Louis' attention.

So the Trianon de Porcelaine was begun during the winter of 1670, and by spring it was finished. Although it had been inspired by the Orient, no Asiatic forms appeared in the design, for it was indebted to French classicism. Placed at a point where three alleés converged and preceded by an oval courtyard, its frontispiece was marked by a triangular pediment supported by Doric pilasters, its corners by quoins, and a balustrade ran around the flat roof.

There were four dependencies, two small pavilions flanking the entrance gates (not shown in the engraving), and two more at either side of the courtyard; they were all intended to facilitate the serving of meals: one was for *confitures*, another for *entremets*, a third for the *potages*, and the last for the *buffet*. The Trianon could be used only

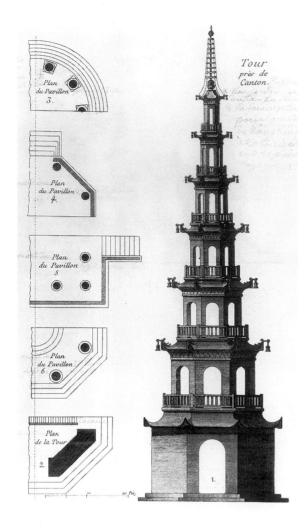

Tour
près de
Canton.

Plan
du Pavillon
3.

Plan
du Pavillon
4.

Plan
du Pavillon
5

Plan
du Pavillon
6.

Plan
de la Tour
2.

1.

*'Tour près de Canton'.
This type of engraving gave
impetus to the Chinese taste
that manifested itself in the
Trianon de Porcelaine,
although the wall revetments
were not of porcelain, but of
tiles. The tower shown never
seems to have appeared in any
gardens of the Sun King's
day, but in the eighteenth
century the British architect
William Chambers took up
this motif, and it would be a
feature of the Duc de
Choiseul's garden at
Chanteloup*

during the warm months, for it had no chimneys.

Its garden was a miniature version of the *jardin français* on two levels. Near the dwelling were ten smaller *parterres de broderies* with two fountains, from which one descended via the central alley to the lower garden where there was an adjustment of scale. This was divided into two large square parterres centred with fountains, and at either side tunnels of trelliswork that descend from Renaissance gardens. Blooming in the parterres were pinks, hyacinths, citron, myrtle and jasmine, but to hold the ubiquitous orange trees that were virtually symbols of the Bourbon dynasty, Monsieur apparently sent over huge blue and white ceramics tubs from his Saint Cloud porcelain factory.

The Trianon de Porcelaine derived its name from the blue and white tiles that clothed the exterior walls. The roof was paved with plaques of coloured faïence, there were lead birds painted in natural colours and faïence vases on the balustrade, so hailstorms could not be permitted.

The interior walls and floors were covered with faïence plaques, and must have looked something like the kitchen walls of the eighteenth-century pavilion of the Amalienburg near Munich (previous page). The furniture was 'Chinese', upholstered with white taffeta sprinkled with Chinese flowers, and a drawing exists of the elaborately festooned bed hung in the same precious material.

Louis was inordinately fond of this delicate, colourful little tea house, and it figured prominently in six days of fêtes – the last grand fêtes of the reign. They occurred in July 1674 and their purpose was to announce the completion of the gardens.[2] The garden of the Trianon was celebrated in the party that took place there on 11 July, for which the designers put up a *feuillée* – pavilion of living greenery – in the form of an octagonal salon with a large oculus open to the sky. Depicted in the engraving opposite are the loges for the musicians and chorus at the sides, Louis and his immediate entourage at the centre facing the exedra for the stage, the ceiling adorned with the King's interlaced L-cipher, underlined by bouquets of fresh flowers in vases on the cornice. After the theatricals, the court moved into the gardens for a supper in the brilliantly lighted, new bosquet known as the Salle des Festins (Room of Festivities).

Although the Trianon de Porcelaine had to be razed in 1687 because of its fragility, it started a fashion, for the *Mercure Galant* of 1674 reported: 'Le Trianon de Versailles avoit fait naistre à tous les Particuliers le désir d'en avoir; que presque tous les grands Seigneurs qui avoient des Maisons de Campagne en avoient fait bâstir dans leurs Parcs . . .' ('The Trianon of Versailles gave rise to a desire in all private individuals to have one; almost all the great gentlemen with country houses have had one built in their parks').

Furthermore, Louis XIV's first Trianon became the ancestor of numerous pavilions in the oriental taste that would adorn the *jardins anglo-chinois* in the following century. But none of its successors were ever built of real faïence, or quite attained the air of royal *insouciance* that marked the original. For Ernest de Ganay, the Trianon de Porcelaine was 'the freshest, most beautiful rose pinned to Versailles' gown of brocade and gold.'

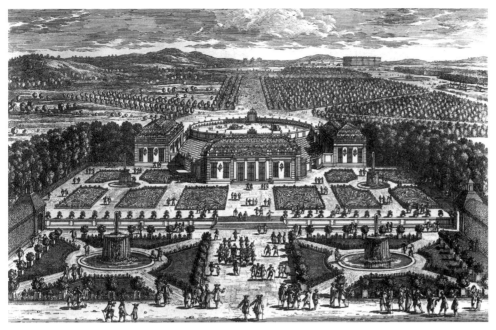

The Trianon de Porcelaine.
This first Trianon appeared at the end of the winter of 1670, 'as if it had sprung from the earth with the flowers', wrote a contemporary of Louis XIV. Its builder was François d'Orbay. A complex of five pavilions covered with faïence tiles said to be Delft blue and white, there were animals of painted lead intended to look like porcelain, as were the grilles and window frames. The gardener Le Bouteux filled the beds with such strongly-scented flowers – like tuberoses and Spanish jasmine – that the courtiers were compelled sometimes to avoid the gardens at night. The Trianon de Porcelaine was admired by everyone, and the court delighted in taking cold collations there during the warm months. It was such a fragile structure that it began to deteriorate after some fifteen years, was razed, and replaced by the Grand Trianon in 1687

François Chauveau, 'Pavilion in the Gardens of Trianon'.
This elaborate fugitive structure of living greenery was put up at the Trianon de Porcelaine in July 1674. The King's composer, Lully, directs his Eglogue de Versailles, *with words by the poet, Philippe Quinault who, from 1672 onwards, composed libretti for Lully's operas. Athénaïs de Montespan would be in the King's party, but as Trianon began to crumble, so did his infatuation with her*

Pierre-Denis Martin (1663-1742), ' Château de Marly', engraving by Devilliers.
Marly-le-Roi was the kingdom of water, as the Grand Trianon was the kingdom of Flora. The King's house at the centre is on an axis with the pièces d'eau, *beginning with the great cascade behind the pavilion, the rectangular reflecting pool in front of it, followed by the great basin, at either side of which the six pairs of pavilions for the court are situated. Next, water flows over shallow steps to fill the wide basin flanked by Coysevox's statues of 'Fame' and 'Mercury'. On a lower level is the* abreuvoir *(watering place), into which the courtiers have ridden to cool their horses.*

Guests eagerly sought invitations, inquiring, 'Sire, Marly?' as the King passed along the Gallery of Mirrors. Marly has disappeared, but Martin's painting from which this engraving was made, makes us understand why Frederick II believed that 'civilised Europe could only be French'

Marly

For his next pavilion, or rather pavilion complex of Marly, Louis chose a site in 1678 that was further away from the court. Saint-Simon reported that the King was 'convinced that he needed a small place and privacy on some occasions . . . [so] he searched around Versailles for something to satisfy this new fancy . . . [and] found . . . a narrow, deep valley with steep sides, inaccessible on account of the boggy ground, without any view, closed in by hills on all sides.'[3] In this wilderness Louis XIII used to hunt deer, and at Marly was installed the *machine de la rivière Seine* that supplied the gardens of Versailles.

The King's early pavilions had been the scenes of his youthful dalliance with Louise de la Vallière; the Trianon came into being as a love nest for his affair with Athénaïs de Montespan; Marly and Louis' last pavilion (the Grand Trianon) were associated with a woman whose character was above reproach – Françoise d'Aubigné, Marquise

Ferdinand Elle, 'Madame de Maintenon and her Niece'.

Françoise d'Aubigné, Marquise de Maintenon (1635-1719), was born a Protestant, married the famous Paris poet, Paul Scarron, and figured prominently in the salons. She was splendidly educated, wrote fascinating letters, and was misunderstood by the French. The King called her 'Votre Solidité' – a perfect description of a woman whose character was marked by an impressive specific gravity. After the Queen's death in 1783, she became Louis' second wife. Her close friend was the Abbé Fénelon, tutor to the Dauphin's son, the Duc de Bourgogne

The Octagonal Salon, Marly.
This great two-storeyed salon that dominated the King's pavilion was the scene of Louis' fêtes and buffets to which the courtiers were summoned from their own lodgings. It was furnished with consoles and tabourets along the walls to leave the centre free for the festivities.

The lighting conformed to the rule for all proper French salons, that is, at three levels: the lustres that hung from the ceiling, the wall lights that hung close to the mirrors for reflection, and the candelabra on consoles and other tables.

The décor of the Marly pavilions was much less subdued than that of Versailles, for here Louis indulged his love for polychromatic effects in coloured marbles and superb Savonnerie bench covers with bright yellow grounds, plumed helmets, and flowers. Although he acted the role of King at Versailles, at Marly he thought of himself as the rich proprietor of a country estate

de Maintenon. Following the Queen's death, a morganatic marriage between Louis XIV and Madame de Maintenon was arranged, and this circumspect lady reigned at Versailles from 1684 until the King's death.

Athénaïs de Montespan had made the serious mistake of committing the King's bastards to Madame de Maintenon's care, an arrangement that brought the governess into constant contact with the King, who began to spend long hours with her, discussing his children's upbringing. By the time that Louis was considering Marly as a retreat for himself and selected guests, Athénaïs had already fallen from favour, and the vacuum left by the favourite's departure had been quickly filled by the virtuous Madame de Maintenon, in whose apartments on the first floor the most significant aspects of court life now took place.

One is tempted to see the influence of Madame de Maintenon in the form that this new pleasure house assumed. In the atmosphere that now prevailed at Versailles, there was no longer a question of sequestered places in the gardens for clandestine meetings. Marly constituted a public announcement in artistic terms, that the King – whose own pavilion was on prominent view at the centre – would be in residence, surrounded by those members of the court who had been invited to accompany him. Of course, the imagery was lost on no one, for it proclaimed Apollo surrounded by the Signs of the Zodiac, for Marly, with its six pairs of pavilions for courtiers, was an entire complex arranged in the usual hierarchical order.

Given the uneven nature of the terrain and the marshes, it was not a simple matter to convert it into the most extraordinary of all Louis' accomplishments in this genre. Prodigious feats of levelling and filling were required: whole forests of trees had to be transplanted, a river was redirected to bring water for countless fountains, huge reflecting pools, faïence-lined fish ponds upon the terrace, and the thundering cascade behind the King's house.

The young J.-H. Mansart was the architect, but Louis himself closely surveyed the work, presenting his own ideas as decorator, gardener and architect, as one of his friends put it. The King's house that dominated the composition was based upon Palladio's Villa Rotunda, its huge central Octagonal Salon articulated by heroic pilasters with composite orders, and four vestibules in the principal axes. The royal house contained four apartments, distinguished by the colour of their damask hangings: the King's was crimson, of course – the royal colour; Madame de Maintenon's was a quiet, discreet blue; Liselotte's was a warm *aurore* (peach); and for her husband, Monsieur (Louis' only brother), a vibrant green to set off his jewel collection.

In a capricious spirit, the exteriors of the twelve courtiers' houses (six on each side of the reflecting pool) were painted with *trompe-l'oeil* pilasters of *rouge du Languedoc* marble with bases of *vert antique,* carried out under the direction of the King's First Painter, Charles Lebrun. From a distance the impression was of incomparable luxury, for the window frames and balustrades surmounted with figures and vases were all gilded, and the bas-reliefs of the pediments and window panels were picked out in gold against a royal blue ground. It was revealed as *trompe-l'oeil* only when one drew closer – a flamboyant theatrical gesture for this most unusual of all the King's pavilions.

ELEVATION DU PREMIER PAVILLON A DROITE.

Echelle de cinq Toifes.

COUPE DU PREMIER PAVILLON A DROITE.

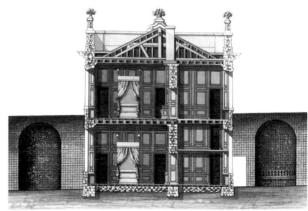

ELEVATION DU PREMIER PAVILLON A DROITE.

'Cross Section and Elevation of the First Pavilion at the Right', Marly.
The exterior of the pavilion was realised in trompe-l'oeil, *under the direction of Charles Lebrun. Quoins mark the corners, an oval mythological medallion is inserted between the windows of the* premier étage, *with vases at either side of the windows. On the* rez-de-chaussée *(ground floor), terms support the entablature while in the centre a pair of terms occupy a shallow niche. The interior consists of two bedrooms and two cabinets where clothes could be stored and which accommodated the* chaises percées *(commodes). There was a separate bathing pavilion*

Above and opposite: Antoine Coysevox (1640-1720), 'Fame' and 'Mercury', Marly.
It could be claimed that the entire eighteenth-century school of French sculpture proceeded from François Girardon and Antoine Coysevox, who created the magnificent 'Fame' and 'Mercury' for Marly, now in the Louvre. The pair may be seen in their original positions at either side of the abreuvoir *(watering pool) in the engraving after the painting by P.-D. Martin on page 54.*

Coysevox was the uncle and teacher of the sculptors Nicolas and Guillaume Coustou, who were the great link between the seventeenth- and eighteenth-century schools (see pp. 62 and 63)

Aveline's engraving overleaf portrays the King's arrival at Marly in the oval courtyard preceding the royal dwelling, with the guards standing at attention and flags flying. A spacious courtyard was needed for the purpose, for even at Marly Louis was attended by a large entourage, and the prescribed rituals for arrivals and departures were scrupulously observed.

An accompanying engraving by the same artist reveals the lavish use of *treillage*, which forms an enclosing wall, joins the courtiers' individual pavilions, and separates the living quarters from the countryside beyond.

The central theme of Marly was water, the 'principal ornament . . . and soul of the garden'.[4] Each pavilion was oriented towards the large reflecting pool, and that of the King appeared to float upon water, since it was placed upon the main axis running

Aveline, The King's Arrival at his Pavilion of Marly.
Whether Louis was returning to Versailles or arriving at Marly, it was always a stirring sight. Trumpeters went before him and the Swiss Guards accompanied him. Primi Visconti said that there were so many courtiers, valets and bodyguards all running about that it reminded him of the Queen Bee when she left the hive with her escort. This view is of one side of the King's pavilion, the cascade at far left, and formal parterres on either side

Aveline, the King's Pavilion at Marly seen from the rear.
The view down the principal axis terminating in the watering place. Intricate tunnels of treillage mark off the forecourt and connect the courtiers' individual pavilions. In the distance is the old chateau of Saint-Germain-en-Laye where Louis was born in 1638 and which served the court until it moved permanently into Versailles

Cascade at Marly.
The cascade was behind the King's house, and he loved the thunder of its waters. The caption of the engraving explains that, on the highest level, three gilt Tritons supported the basin into which a large jet fell. It overflowed to the lower levels that were interspersed with other fountains, from which the water shot with such force that it created a startlingly white foam. This contrasted with the trees and deep green living palisades marking off the bosquet. The cascade was bordered with a white marble retaining wall, upon which stood six white marble statues of water nymphs interspersed with gilt metal vases, a beautiful marriage of stone and water

through the *abreuvoir* (watering place), the rectangular basin, smaller pools, and the dramatic cascade with *girandoles* that provided a shimmering backdrop for the King's house.

Louis loved marble, precious materials, crimson – which became almost a neutral in his hands – and especially gilding. One can visualise the *éclat* of the white, foaming cascade as it played against the gleaming white marble and the dense, dark foliage of the trees – an effect that no engraving can capture.

The river motif was further perpetuated at Marly in sculpted personifications of rivers placed throughout the park. Beside the *abreuvoir* stood two of the finest sculptural achievements of the century: the 'Fame' and 'Mercury' of Antoine Coysevox (pp.58 and 59), later to be replaced by the famous Horses of Marly by Guillaume Coustou (overleaf and p.63).

The two groups provide a stark contrast between the exalted spirit of the Grand Siècle as exemplified by the Coysevox pair, and the humanistic tone of the eighteenth-century that Coustou's work represents. Coysevox's mythological figure of 'Fame' trumpets the King's renown, and the god 'Mercury', buttressed by trophies, carries the message to the four corners of the earth. In Coustou's groups, technically competent though they may be, mere grooms hold the reins of the King's horses, which now have nothing to do with Pegasus.

At Marly the gardeners carried out intricate tunnels of greenery, with ball finials to mark the springing of the arches, straight walls and columns of clipped shrubbery as backdrop for sculpture (pp.64 and 65). If one wandered beyond the formal parterres,

Above and opposite: Guillaume Coustou (1677-1746), 'Chevaux de Marly'.
The groups by Coysevox (pp.58 and 59) and these by his nephew, Guillaume Coustou, were brought
from Marly back to Paris where they graced the Place Louis XV (Concorde), before they were removed to
the Louvre to protect them from the effects of pollution. After Louis XIV's death, those in charge of
embellishing the royal gardens thought that the Coysevox pieces were not of sufficient volume to fill the
space they occupied at Marly. So Guillaume Coustou was set to work on the 'Chevaux de Marly' to
replace them. Models were completed about 1740, and the finished groups were carried from his Paris
atelier to Marly by water in July 1745, where they were received with unbounded enthusiasm. They were
so admired that Lalive de Jully had terracotta reductions made of them for his salon

Berceaux et Galeries de Verdure à Marly.

Portique et Cabinet de Verdure, executé.

Above and opposite: Clipped greenery at Marly.
Marly was renowned for the art of topiary. Here the topiary specialists created sheared walls of greenery as a foil for white marble statuary (opposite right), arcades that framed vistas (above), colonnades topped with vase-shaped finials (opposite left), and walkways sheltered by small trees trained to form berceaux (top). Madame de Maintenon complained that these intricate affairs and the tall avenues of sheared shrubbery gave no relief from the sun. She wrote that there was — mercifully — one part of the Marly gardens to which she often repaired to rest in the shade, for here the trees were allowed to grow as they wished

it was possible to discover a delightful *cabinet de verdure* that featured a small pavilion in temple form designed by Belin de Fontenay. Its dome was painted in *trompe l'oeil* trelliswork entwined with leaves and flowers in which birds perched, after the manner of Italian *cassine*.

Invitations to Marly were highly coveted, for it offered refreshing diversion from the stifling atmosphere of the pompous château. Guests were provided with all they needed in their individual lodgings. The women were allowed to wear *robes de chambre*, happy to be liberated from the uncomfortable *grand habit* of Versailles, and they took charming lace caps with embroidery, purchased from Alexandre's fashionable shop on the Pont Neuf in Paris.

Marly provided all sorts of amusements, such as La Roulette, a chair on rails to descend the hill, a scenic railway called La Glissoire, a menagerie of rare birds and colourful military reviews. Even Louis was given to a little horseplay, flipping bread pellets during a meal. When he grew old, he would appear at fancy-dress balls at Marly with a gauze robe over his clothing, to show that he wanted to enter into the spirit of revelry although his dancing days were over.

Louis was so proud of Marly that he wanted to show it off to the English court which was lodged at Saint-Germain. James II had given up his throne in 1688. He arrived in France in 1689 with Mary of Modena, and Louis took care of him for the rest of his life. So in August 1704 Louis arranged a party to take place in the usual pavilion of greenery called a *salle verte*. Liselotte reported that the *faux marbre* table was in horseshoe shape, and the centrepiece consisted of a superb marble Galatea on an island in the middle of a lake in which multi-coloured fish swam in golden nets.

Marly became Louis' preferred retreat, for as Pierre Verlet put it: 'With age, the influence of Madame de Maintenon, and great sadness (the deaths of three Dauphins and the Duchesse de Bourgogne), there was the attraction of Marly, where the King took refuge more and more often during the last years of his reign. Still maintaining his world and his great château with a firm hand, he revealed for another château [Marly] an attachment that was only too visible. In this way he gave an unhappy example to his successors, and contributed to the loss of prestige suffered by the château of Versailles itself . . .'[5]

Madame Campan, who knew Marly before its destruction by the Revolution, considered it the most palpable example of the King's taste. 'The centuries all have their own colour', she observed, 'and Marly still gives a more authentic idea of Louis XIV than Versailles itself. Everything there seems to have been constructed by a magic power, the wand of a fairy. The palaces and gardens of that pleasure house could be compared to the theatrical decorations of the fifth act of an opera.'[6] But Marly was not the final act, for there was yet one more pavilion to come, and this one would be designed by the the Sun King himself.

Pierre-Denis Martin (1663-1742), 'Vue perspective du Grand Trianon prise de l'avenue en 1723'.
The Grand Trianon is a one-storey pavilion with the roof hidden by the balustrade in the Italian manner.
The faces are articulated with Ionic pilasters in rose Languedoc marble, and the door and window
openings are enriched with crisply sculpted flowers mingling with musical instruments, a décor that is
repeated in the interior decoration. In Martin's painting, the skyline sculpture may still be seen.
  In the foreground, Louis XV as an adolescent is returning from a ride. Louis XV did not appreciate the
appeal of the Grand Trianon until about 1750, when he began to add his own little garden buildings to
the majesterial composition

The Grand Trianon

If Marly was the kingdom of water, Louis XIV's last pavilion was the kingdom of
flowers, the Palais de Flore as it was known at court. The fragile Trianon de
Porcelaine gradually became so dilapidated that it had to be razed in 1687, and almost
immediately there arose on its site at the northern arm of the Grand Canal the most
brilliant satellite of Versailles – the Grand Trianon.

Peristyle of the Grand Trianon.
This was a favourite place for Louis XIV to dine with courtiers, since they could look down upon the gardens (which one always must with a formal French garden). It was constantly used for cold collations; a cool spot with breezes, it was often lighted for special effects, and Louis became increasingly fond of it.

The peristyle underlined the prevailing taste for a garden building entre cour et jardin. *The brother-in-law of J.-H. Mansart, Robert de Cotte, is credited with the peristyle that joined the two wings which were conceived as two small châteaux. But the King himself apparently instigated the design.*

After the Sun King's death, the Grand Trianon was used only infrequently during the next two reigns. Yet shortly before the storming of Versailles, the Duc de Croÿ reported that it had been greatly renovated, and that the marbles were just as they were when they came from the hands of Louis XIV

A sovereign gesture, this long one-storey building *entre cour et jardin* was designed by the King himself.[7] The painted *trompe l'oeil* effects of Marly now yielded to real *rose Languedoc* marble with sculpted stone surrounds for windows, pilasters with Ionic capitals, and coupled columns in the open peristyle (opposite). Except for the stone ornaments that adorned the balustrade – *pots à feu* (vases with flaming torches), baskets of flowers, groups of children – the Grand Trianon remains much the same today as when it was built.

A range of columns in-the-round tie the building together, physically and visually, for the coupled pilasters articulating the full-length doors become coupled columns in the elevated peristyle. The peristyle serves the same purpose as the Cent Marches descending on either side of the Orangery at Versailles – to provide a view of the garden below. Trianon's garden was a model of profuse but elegant refinement, and here Louis collected flowers as works of art.

In his day the first terrace below the peristyle was embellished with green embroidery patterns centred by statues of children in gilt metal. This restful greenery prepared the eye for the stunning impact of the lower parterre where flowers were massed in floral designs – violets, pinks, hyacinths, tulips, feverfew, bellflowers carnations, valerian, white lilies, jonquils, tuberoses, anemones, double snapdragons, Constantinople narcissus, heliotrope and jasmine. Saint-Simon tells us that the flowers in all the *parterres* were changed every day. This daily rotation was possible because thousands of pots were always kept ready in the greenhouses – during six months in 1687, the gardens required 125,352 pots. The parterres of Grand Trianon might be filled with mauve hyacinths and pink tulips in the morning, but they could be quickly transformed into islands of white narcissus and crimson anemones in the afternoon.

Water animated the perfumed gardens in various ways: the flower compartments were set off by sparkling fountains; water buffets featured rushing cascades; from the Grand Canal courtiers mounted majestic staircases that flanked a horseshoe basin into which tumbled towering crystal jets.

The most intriguing, though, was the Bosquet des Sources, a shady part of the garden where fifty springs created rustling brooks, with tiny irregular islands of grass large enough to accommodate a table and two chairs. Perelle's plan (opposite) shows the King's formal garden of embroideries (19), contrasted with the Bosquet des Sources (20). The meandering brooks in the latter were interspersed with islands shaded by dense, natural foliage, anticipating the new gardening style that would appear soon after the Sun King's death.

Grand Trianon was a retreat where especially designated courtiers came by water for card games, a stroll in the garden, an opera, supper, or *médianoche* (a supper served at midnight after a fast day). Ample provisions were made for culinary needs, for the plans show rooms for 'les viandes . . . le rost . . . les entremets . . . pain . . . vin . . . dessert . . . confitures . . . chocolat et le café.'[8] Coffee was just being introduced, and chocolate was a favourite of the Queen, who as a Spaniard, drank it black, without sugar.

When we remember the conditions under which Louis dined at Versailles, we can understand how appealing supper in a pavilion might have been for him, for when he dined at the ceremonial *grand couvert*, the courtiers all stood about paying close attention. Louis' sister-in-law, Liselotte, said that she ate as quickly as possible because twenty valets watched every bite she put into her mouth and counted every swallow. Even when dinner was served to Louis in the antechamber off his bedroom, an endless train of attendants presented the meal in a strictly prescribed order. So delighted was Louis with the Grand Trianon that he could hardly wait to use it for a supper in the gardens.

The excuse he found was the marriage in 1685 of his legitimised daughter, Mademoiselle de Nantes (fruit of his union with Athénaïs de Montespan), to the Duc de Bourbon. The Marquis de Sourches reported on 23 July that the dinner was served upon four tables in the four *cabinets* (small rooms) at the end of the covered walkways, all of which were brightly lighted by a large number of crystal chandeliers. The Marquis de Dangeau recorded in his diary on 11 June 1691 that Louis supped with seventy-five ladies under the peristyle above the flowered parterres and the fountains.

Louis XIV's great château dominated the 'spatial and sequential phenomena' of Le Nôtre's incomparable gardens. Although constantly changing in its details, the master plan of Le Nôtre remained the same – an aesthetic, intellectual, horticultural triumph of the highest order, unprecedented in garden history.

The Sun King's pavilions were fitting additions to this majestic enterprise, and each was intimately associated with the garden that completed it. They reflected, too, the dramatic change in Louis' character, from the young man in his late twenties who led the smart set in Paris, frolicking with Louise de la Vallière at the Grotte de Thétis, to the dignified sovereign who ordered the Grand Trianon in his late forties. By this time Louis had acqured 'le gravité d'un roi de Théâtre', in Primi Visconti's words, and the Grand Trianon clearly reflected the civilised nobility of the court style. Yet, in its relaxed atmosphere, its floral décor, the frivolous Bosquet des Sources, the intimate association of the dwelling with its garden, the Grand Trianon presaged the delicious garden pavilions that would be realised for Louis' great-grandson, Louis XV, the Bien-Aimé.

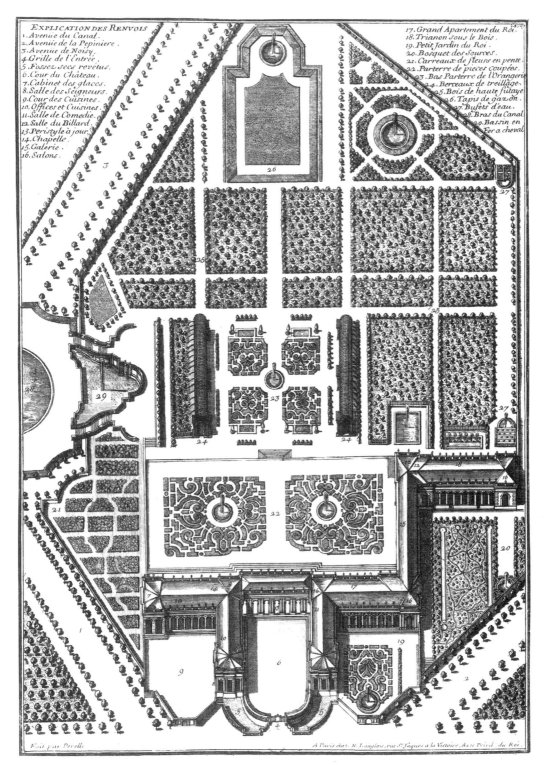

EXPLICATION DES RENVOIS
1. Avenue du Canal.
2. Avenue de la Pepiniere.
3. Avenue de Noisy.
4. Grille de l'Entrée.
5. Fossez secs revêtus.
6. Cour du Château.
7. Cabinet des glaces.
8. Salle des Seigneurs.
9. Cour des Cuisines.
10. Offices et Cuisines.
11. Salle de Comedie.
12. Salle du Billard.
13. Peristyle à jour.
14. Chapelle.
15. Galerie.
16. Salons.
17. Grand Apartement du Roi.
18. Trianon sous le Bois.
19. Petit Jardin du Roi.
20. Bosquet des Sources.
21. Carreaux de fleurs en pente.
22. Parterre de pieces coupées.
23. Bas Parterre de l'Orangeri
24. Berceaux de treillage.
25. Bois de haute futaye
26. Tapis de gazon.
27. Bufets d'eau.
28. Bras du Canal.
29. Bassin en Fer a cheval

Fait par Perelle

A Paris chez N. Langlois, rue St. Jaques a la Victoire, Avec Privil. du Roi.

Perelle, plan of the Grand Trianon gardens.
When courtiers came over by boat to the Grand Trianon, they arrived via the horseshoe-shaped fountain at left (29). Then they walked up the stairs seen at either side, and up another short flight to find themselves on the level of the lower parterres that were framed by berceaux de treillage (24). Having glanced down the axis beyond to the tapis vert (26) with a fountain beyond, they turned to mount the short central staircase that led to the upper parterres (22). These were planted with the most exquisite flowers at Versailles, for they were visible from the portico where dinners were often given. The wing on the right was called the Trianon sous Bois because the garden in front of it – the Bosquet des Sources (20) – was overshadowed by trees, under which little tables were placed on tiny islands between the flowing rivulets. Liselotte wrote that her rooms at the Grand Trianon looked out upon this enchanting water garden

Above: The Pavillon de l'Aurore, Sceaux.
The lovely Pavilion of Aurora has been restored, but when it had fallen into a state of romantic abandon, it inspired the novelist Alain Fournier as a setting for his haunting novel Le Grand Meaulnes, *and was the subject of a famous photograph of 1910 by Eugène Atget. The château of Sceaux was razed, and the present château, which houses the Musée de l'Ile de France, is a replacement, reflecting the style of the seventeenth century. But Perrault's Pavillon de l'Aurore still stands in the garden, evoking memories of glorious fêtes by Colbert, the Marquis de Seignelay, and the recklessly extravagant Duchesse du Maine*

Opposite: 'The Poet Philippe Quinault Inspired by the Nymph of Sceaux'.
It was usual for writers, composers, and a small orchestra to be attached to a great house like Colbert's at Sceaux. Philippe Quinault worked closely with Jean Berain and Jean-Baptiste Lully in devising numerous 'rejoicings' at court. They were almost invariably celebrated with an opera, for which Quinault wrote the libretto, Lully the music, and Jean Berain designed the costumes that illuminated the peculiarities of each character and which were works of art in themselves

Sparsholt College Library
Sparsholt, Winchester
Hants. SO21 2NF

CHAPTER 3

PAVILIONS BUILT BY MEMBERS OF LOUIS XIV's COURT CIRCLE

While Louis XIV was planning the Trianon de Porcelaine in 1670, his indefatigable and devoted Superintendant of Buildings, Jean-Baptiste Colbert, acquired the domaine of Sceaux, some eighteen miles south of Versailles. The energetic superintendent, whom Madame de Sévigné called 'Le Vent du Nord', was not a man to waste time, so he set about converting the existing manor house into a château commensurate with his position. Colbert's architect at Sceaux was his principal assistant in the Royal Buildings Office, the writer Charles Perrault. André Le Nôtre was on hand to redesign the garden with trelliswork pavilions, a canal and cascades, and parterres of elegant green *broderies.* From the Versailles atelier, Colbert summoned two of its finest sculptors, François Girardon and Nicolas Coysevox, to decorate the entrance pavilions with a dog and unicorn (symbols of fidelity and integrity) and to embellish the cascades designed by Charles Lebrun.

Le Pavillon de l'Aurore at Sceaux
Also symbolic was the important garden pavilion for which Colbert's favourite architect apparently provided the design, although there are no documents to prove Perrault's authorship. The Pavillon de l'Aurore was situated beyond the parterres and at the centre of the *potager.* It symbolised Colbert himself, for this intrepid minister – like the dawn – prepared the way for the Sun King's ascension.

The design is a perfect example of academic classicism, which – as André Gide remarked – says less in order to express more, and it demonstrates the intellectual equilibrium and harmonious elegance representative of the Grand Siècle. Elevated upon a terrace with flowing steps at either side and a marble fountain as centrepiece, the pavilion was conceived as a circular salon lighted by six windows, flanked by two *cabinets*. Over the salon bays, six small paintings after Lebrun designs portray putti performing seasonal gardening tasks, reinforcing the pavilion's affinity with the gardens. Here Colbert set up his office in the summer months and, according to tradition, to flee the abrasive personality of Madame Colbert.

The interior walls are articulated with six Ionic pilasters supporting a frieze displaying Colbert's emblem (the grass snake), above which the gilded cornice enframes a (recently restored) ravishing cupola painting of 'Aurore' by Charles Lebrun – a delicate compliment to the Sun King. We remember that the Oval Salon at Vaux was covered by a cupola, and Lebrun was to have painted the interior with an allegorical composition, but Fouquet's fall came before the artist could begin. At Sceaux, Fouquet's victorious rival, Jean-Baptiste Colbert, ordered *two* cupola paintings from Lebrun. One was intended for the now-destroyed chapel, where Perrault certainly worked, and the other decorated the Pavillon de l'Aurore.[1]

In this dignified garden house, the superintendent received the King in July 1677, and the following October the French Academy, of which Sceaux's owner was a member. Lully's associate, Philippe Quinault, composed a poem praising the beauties of Sceaux, and a drawing at Chantilly portrays the poet, inspired by the nymph of Sceaux, standing before the Pavillon de l'Aurore, with its dome and triple-pedimented exterior (p.71).

One supposes that Colbert's garden fêtes were properly circumspect. He was always urging economy, arguing for the Louvre as royal residence rather than Versailles. Furthermore, after Fouquet's disgrace (in which Colbert was largely instrumental), Louis' ministers realised that it was imprudent to call attention to the ambience of one's own residence. Or to attempt, even in honouring the King, to rival the court spectacles that were at once an art form and psychological weapon.

When Colbert died in 1683, however, the domaine of Sceaux passed to his son, the Marquis de Seignelay, Secretary of the Marine – a far less prudent man than his father had been. For Seignelay lived in unabashed splendour, surrounded by the finest tapestries with marine triumphs designed by Jean Berain (1697), silver and gold appointments, and an enviable art collection. Almost immediately upon his succession, Seignelay began to stage extravagant fêtes in the marvellous gardens that lent themselves so well to these occasions that were *de rigueur* for a man who figured so prominently in the Sun King's train.

Seignelay's *divertissements* were of such unbridled magnificence that they provoked angry comments from Louis' Minister of War, Louvois. (Louvois had hated Colbert, and was jealous of the attention Seignelay had drawn to himself in the merciless naval bombardment of Genoa in May 1684.) In that year, the Marquis de Louvois – who was himself involved in the cruel devastation of the Palatinate – wrote to a colleague that the King was highly displeased by Seignelay's conspicuous display. It was a peculiar comment from the man who had just spent over 100,000 livres for a single evening's entertainment at his château of Meudon.

Not to be outdone by Louvois' spectacles at Meudon, the new owner of Sceaux planned a garden party for the King and Dauphin in the summer of 1685. While keeping an eye on expenses (no one could forget Fouquet), Seignelay had to invent an evening of unusual interest to flatter his master and the heir to the throne, for both

Jean Berain, 'Fête donnée au Roi par le Marquis de Seignelay à Sceaux, Juillet 1685'.
The improvisations of Jean Berain were legend. In his design for this fête he has used only two sides of the basin to accommodate the guests, leaving the others free for the disposition of the great silver buffets which are reflected in the water. Set against the tunnel of trelliswork at the rear is the traditional buffet featuring large silver and silver-gilt ewers and basins from the Colbert collection. The lights that top the pavilions and fill the girandoles on the tables are echoed in chandeliers suspended in the apertures of the trelliswork berceaux. Berain conceived these as a sort of vestibule through which the royal party entered the outdoor room.

Louis and the Grand Dauphin were notable connoisseurs. The Dauphin, in fact, lived perpetually *en fête,* rushing about from masquerades to operas with his sister and inseparable companion, the Princesse de Conti (daughter of Louis and Louise de la Vallière), and his wardrobe boasted a vast collection of ingenious costumes designed for him by Jean Berain.[2] Clearly, a fête of subtle artistry that would impress this professional *bon vivant* and the King required all the talent that Seignelay could muster.

So Seignelay summoned – who else? – Jean Berain. After Charles Lebrun's departure, Berain dominated the artistic life at court (and in Paris, too, for that matter). 'Nothing was made of any sort whatever without its being in his [Berain's] style, or his having given the designs,' declared the famous collector Pierre Jean Mariette. This enormously versatile artist was already working on the interior decoration of Seignelay's château, and another of Berain's specialities was his remarkably original designs for garden parties.

For that summer evening at Sceaux in 1685, Berain adapted his plans to the possibilities and the resources of the topography. Choosing a part of the garden where tunnels of trelliswork surrounded a *boulingrin* (bowling green), he treated the central basin as a 'canal' which would mirror the ingenious lighting devices he invented for the occasion. Evoking the solar myth, Berain produced *machines de lumière* – a type of candelabra that held up to twenty-five white wax candles in the form of lyres (Apollo's instrument), fleurs-de-lis, and crowns.

His *pièces de la resistance* were two pavilions made of greenery that he had put up at either end of the 'canal' – Berain called them 'arcades de la feuillée'. The one at right housed the King's party, with the Duc de Bourbon and other court personalities. The one on the left was for the Dauphin, accompanied by the Princesse de Conti and others of the younger generation. So the ruler and the heir apparent faced each other across the ornamental basin.

From the centre of the basin a water jet ascended like a tumult of liquid light, reflecting the numerous candles in the *machines de lumière* that surmounted the pavilions and that stood on the buffets laden with the magnificent Colbert silver and

Louis-Auguste de Bourbon, Duc du Maine (1670-1736).
One of the Duc du Maine's legs was shorter than the other,
so the artist has ingeniously posed him with crossed legs.
Madame de Maintenon, who was like a mother to him,
refers to Maine as 'the man to whom my heart is tenderest'.
Her letters reveal that the Duke loved his wife, the Duchesse
du Maine, so much that he preferred to spoil her rather than
try to curb her wanton excesses

colourful, pyramidal arrangements of fruit. The extraordinary refinement of Berain's design was commented upon for days, and it was considered by a court already surfeited with luxury to be 'la plus belle [fête] jamais donnée au Roi'.

Three years later Berain surpassed himself, this time for a princely *divertissement* that we shall see in the gardens of the Condé family at Chantilly. In 1690 the Marquis de Seignelay died, and the domain of Sceaux passed to a legitimised son of Louis XIV, the Duc du Maine, whose Duchess was a daughter of the house of Condé. With the advent of the new châtelaine, an even more festive chapter in the history of the Pavillon de l'Aurore and its gardens opened.

By the 1690s the King's children by Athénaïs de Montespan had reached marriageable age. In 1692 their haughty youngest daughter, Madamoiselle de Blois, became the bride of her first cousin, Philippe d'Orléans, the future Regent. In March of the same year, Athénaïs' oldest son, Louis-Auguste de Bourbon, Duc du Maine, married one of his Condé cousins, Anne-Louise Bénédicte de Bourbon-Condé.[3]

Maine had been reared by Madame de Maintenon, for Athénaïs had given to this circumspect lady the care of some of her children ('this equivocal race', as Sainte-Beuve called the legitimised royal bastards). One was the charming little Duc du Maine, who quickly gained a place in Madame de Maintenon's affections. Although a childhood disease had left him crippled, when Maine reached his teens he followed his illustrious father on campaign. His younger brother, the Comte de Toulouse (reared by Madame de Louvois), was far more popular, and at only thirteen he exhibited remarkable *sang-froid* at the Battle of Mons, later becoming a fine admiral and father of the Duc de Penthièvre. Despite Toulouse's accomplishments, it was the Duc du Maine who always remained the apple of Louis XIV's eye.

When it came to choosing a wife for him, the King naturally turned to his Condé cousins, despite certain peculiarities of personality that were said to have been inherited from the wife of the Grand Condé, Louis' most famous marshal. The present prince, Henri-Jules (eldest son of the Grand Condé), was no exception. He was an outstanding student, a connoisseur of art, and in his country house at Chantilly he presided over a particularly brilliant salon of the leading writers. But sometimes he imagined he was a dog, and prowled about the gardens baying at the moon. These spells sometimes came upon him when the King was present, but 'he could sufficiently control his madness to withdraw into a window, from where his barkings, muffled by the end of the curtains which he would stuff in his mouth, would be faintly audible to the company.'[4]

Despite these unsettling qualities, Jules-Henri was still First Prince of the Blood, so in an unprecedented gesture, Louis XIV himself called at the Condé establishment on 16 February 1692 to announce to Jules-Henri that he required the hand of one of his daughters for Maine. Love matches were not considered to be in the best taste for a person of Maine's standing, but he was at least allowed to look over the three tiny

Condé daughters, and his eye fell upon the petite Anne-Louise.

A few days later the engagement was announced in the King's private apartments at Versailles, followed by an evening party at the pavilion of Trianon with a concert and supper for eighty guests. In March they were married in the Versailles chapel, with the affair reported fully in the *Mercure Galant,* and eight years later, the King bestowed upon the Duc and Duchesse du Maine Colbert's magnificent estate at Sceaux.

The tiny Duchess was known at court as a 'Doll of the Blood' because of her diminutive size, but she was an independent little creature who found the constraints of court life not at all to her liking. When the King gave them the domain of Sceaux, Anne-Louise set about to convert it into her own private kingdom. The gardens were among the finest in the Ile-de-France, and there was the lovely Aurora pavilion, now planted with a garden of flowering *plates-bandes* to replace the old seventeenth century kitchen garden. Liselotte bustled out to Sceaux to see the Maines in the autumn of 1704 and recorded her impressions in her journal:

Anne-Louise Bénédicte de Bourbon, Duchesse du Maine (1676-1753).
The self-centered little Duchess of Maine holds a fan and mask, perhaps her theatrical accessories, although women also carried masks to protect their skin from the sun. She stands beside a console table decorated with the insignia of her own order of chivalry, the Order of the Honey Bee. The motto was taken from Tasso: 'The bee, though very small, can do great things'

> In front of the house is a big parterre with a bower . . . at the side of an alley is a fine mall, then another alley which runs to the grand canal, much longer than that at Fontainebleau, and which is the source of a large and pretty cascade. In all the parterres are fine fountains, and what I find even prettier, there is near the house a little wood, decorated with springs and fountains. One is in the form of Aeolus chaining a wind, with four other winds at the corners . . . Then there is Scylla, surrounded by dogs, barking and spitting water. There are two fountains of bronze, beautiful workmanship. Next come two fountains of white marble, representing children spitting into the water . . . All the paths . . . are decorated with antique marble busts.[5]

The Scylla Fountain was designed by Charles Lebrun, who had collaborated with Le Nôtre when Colbert was laying out the park, and it was one of Lebrun's happiest ideas. Dezallier, who saw it late in the eighteenth century, described it as a huge basin through which ran an allée. On one side was the Fountain of Aeolus, with allegorical figures of the winds at the corners spouting tall jets of water; on the other was the Scylla Fountain, with dogs spitting water at the central figure of Scylla. All the figures were of soft gilt, malleable lead that partook of the life of the waters.

Seemingly oblivious to the outside world, the Duchess regarded Sceaux as her own private playground, where she lived the life of a fairy queen who needed neither food nor sleep. Hilarious example of the escapist mentality, Anne-Louise was fond of theatricals staged in the Aurora Pavilion, the Orangery, or on improvised stages set up in a broad allée. She always assumed the leading role herself, and the entrepreneur of these events was the peculiar Nicolas de Malézieux, a mathematician, poet and fabricator of operas. His work must have shown some merit, however, for the prelate/author Fénelon was his friend, and the audience that filled the seats for the performances at Sceaux included the President of Parlement J.-F. Hénault, the writer Fontenelle and Saint-Aulaire, a member of the French Academy.

Among the Arcadian pleasures of her country seat were the Duchess' famous Nuits Blanches de Sceaux. For these occasions, the park would be transformed into a fairyland with hundreds of lanterns sparkling in the trees, the islands in the lake illuminated, barges decorated with coloured torches for the musicians, and the supper laid out in the bosquets on U-shaped tables lit with hundreds of white wax candles reflected in the enormous silver wine coolers. There were cards, the inevitable play starring the Duchess, and a musical or recitation in the Pavillon de l'Aurore, from which the guests would be conducted through the gardens with lighted flares to their coaches, inevitably to the counterpoint of a finale of fireworks.

It was the inexhaustible Malézieux who converted the Duchess' park into a realm populated by nymphs and shepherdesses; deputations from Greenland who had come to take her away as their Queen; troupes of musicians emerging from the bosquets to perform ballets upon a stage above the cascades; and knights in scarlet velvet robes bespangled with golden bees – her Order of the Honey Bee – who knelt in homage at the foot of her throne. But the Duchesse du Maine was not so prejudiced as to neglect the finest talents of the age, and sometimes works by Molière, Racine, and Lully were performed in her theatre at Sceaux.

Once Voltaire hid away in the château when he had to flee Paris. Later he wrote from Berlin that he longed to be there again 'At the feet of Madame la Duchesse . . . hers is an elect soul; she will love comedy to her last moment, and when she falls ill, I advise you to administer some fine play to her instead of extreme unction. People die as they live.'[6] As an 'ancient child of seventy', she was still playing the role of virgin shepherdess in the stately Pavillon de l'Aurore in her enchanted fairyland of Sceaux.

The Pavilions of Chantilly

Grand as the château of Sceaux may have been, it could hardly have impressed the Duchesse du Maine, who was grown up in the Condé enclave at Chantilly, a château that represented six centuries of civilisation. Everyone who could wangle an invitation went up to Chantilly north-east of Paris, and even the Kings of France wanted to own it. When the famous author of the *Princesse de Clèves,* Madame de Lafayette, was a guest there in June 1673, she dashed off a letter to her friend, the impeccable letter-writer, Madame de Sévigné: 'De tous les lieux que le soleil éclaire, il n'y en a point un pareil à celui-ci'. The prestige of Chantilly had rivalled even that of the royal châteaux ever since the Renaissance, when the old feudal, moated castle was transformed into a dwelling in the exuberant, new Renaissance style by Anne de Montmorency (1493-1567), François I's chief military officer. This unusually cultivated King, a passionate, erudite collector, came yearly to visit Anne de Montmorency, who was himself the major patron of his day after the King. In the château was a remarkable art collection (as there is today), splendid gardens with parterres in the Renaissance style, and an unusually fine hunting preserve where François and his captain of the military hunted stag and wild boar.

Later, that most Parisian of Kings, Henri IV, always welcomed invitations to Chantilly and coveted this enchanted preserve. So did his son Louis XIII, who was enraptured by its setting, and treated it as his own until his death in 1643.

When Louis XIV came to the throne, he and the Dauphin, with the entire court, would stay for a week at a time at this glorious château which was like a private art

BOURBON-CONDÉ
(Louis II, LE GRAND)
1621–1686

*Louis II de Bourbon-Condé,
Le Grand Condé.
After Marshal Turenne, the
Grand Condé was the foremost
soldier of his day, known at
court as 'Monsieur le Prince',
among the people as 'Monsieur
le Héros'. A remarkably
cultivated man who patronised
all the arts, Condé's
knowledge was encyclopaedic.
He read all the best new
books, had been a leading light
of Madame de Rambouillet's
famous salon in his youth,
then conducted his own
brilliant literary salon of
leading writers. Passionately
fond of theatre, Condé
maintained a troupe of
comedians, including the
celebrated harlequin
Dominique Biancolelli.
Condé's players divided their
time between Chantilly and
the Hôtel Condé in Paris*

museum. These court peregrinations involved hundreds of people, who were lodged, fed and entertained at the expense of the Duchess' grandfather, the Grand Condé.[7] The great marshal was an outstanding art patron, collector, a major protector of Molière, and an intimate of Boileau, Racine, Bossuet, Mesdames de Sévigné and Lafayette, La Bruyère, and La Fontaine. So his salon at Chantilly included the major composers and literary lights of the day, with whom he could hold his own on any subject. Passionately fond of theatre, the Grand Condé called the Italian Comedy to his country seat, and in 1677 the commander's own troupe made its début, when his guests were entertained in the garden structures.

After his retirement from military life in 1675, the renowned marshal devoted his energies and resources to a continuous embellishment of the family seat which André Le Nôtre had endowed (beginning in 1663) with a vast formal garden, the basic lines of which may still be seen. The Grand Canal at Chantilly was the finest in France because it was fed by living water from abundant springs and the river Nonette. Towards the west the thunderous Grand Cascade was a marvel of hydraulics, divided

Grand Cascade of Chantilly.
Le Nôtre was called to Chantilly about 1663, with his nephew Claude Desgots, and the great vegetable
gardener, Jean de La Quintinie. A central feature of the gardens were the waters which, as Bossuet remarked
in his famous funeral oration for the Grand Condé, 'were silent neither day nor night'. The Grand Cascade
is a particularly satisfactory invention, playing upon a series of curves. In the tall clipped palisades at either
side in the rear are niches with segmental heads; the stairs descend beside the cascades in a gentle Baroque
curve, and the central cascade below falls from a curving basin from which springs a tiered fountain

into two parts, and set off by a pair of winding Baroque staircases. There were water jets of varying heights, tall liquid chandeliers, masques spouting water, foaming buffets, marble statues, and an immense water bouquet at the highest point, for which tall, living palisades with niches provided a dark green backdrop.

Chantilly was one of Le Nôtre's greatest challenges, for he could not lay out the gardens on an axis with the irregular feudal château, which had been rebuilt during the Renaissance.[8] But the garden architect was so pleased with his accomplishments there that he wrote to the Earl of Portland in 1698: 'Remember all you have seen of French gardens, Versailles, Fontainebleau, Vaux and *especially* Chantilly'.[9] The reader must bear in mind the opulence of these gardens as they were left by Le Nôtre, for they will be the setting for Condé garden parties during the next two Bourbon reigns.

Another charming but minute garden within the grand design of Chantilly was the one Le Nôtre designed for the Maison de Sylvie. This little pavilion had been built in 1604, and became famous as a refuge for the poet Théophile de Viau. His protectress was the châtelaine of Chantilly, Marie-Félice des Ursins, Duchesse de Montmorency, whom Viau addressed as 'Sylvie'. Henri IV admired this garden house so much that he wanted it for himself, and when it had fallen into disrepair the Grand Condé had it rebuilt in 1670.

Le Nôtre's tiny garden for the Maison de Sylvie was composed of three triangles, one of green embroideries, the other two of grass, with a round parterre like the dot

La Maison de Sylvie, Chantilly.
Le Nôtre was especially gratified by the work he performed for the Condés at Chantilly, and wrote to the Prince de Condé in 1682: 'I am continually thinking about the embellishment of your parterres, fountains, and cascades of your great garden.' He created a tiny jardin français *for the Maison de Sylvie, joining it to trelliswork tunnels of greenery with the fleur-de-lis over the doorways – an intimate association of house and garden. The pavilion was enlarged, but it is still at Chantilly, and used for private dinner parties*

of an exclamation mark. It was all enclosed with trelliswork berceaux topped with finials in the form of fleur-de-lis, a device to which the Condé family were entitled. Most of the trelliswork was put up by specialists in this garden art whom the Grand Condé brought from Holland, and they executed numerous *cabinets de treillage* for the bosquets in the park and the Island of Love.

In 1668 Condé had conquered Franche-Comté, so the victorious marshal invited Louis XIV and the court to Chantilly in April 1671 for a three-day fête which became one of the most widely discussed parties of the century. The *Gazette* reported the details of the elaborate collations that were served in *salles de verdure* erected in the gardens and the royal family's visit to the recently refurbished Maison de Sylvie. It was on this occasion that the famous Condé chef, Vatel, committed suicide. Madame de Sévigné's letter describes how the unfortunate man, overwrought by the demands of Condé hospitality, found it impossible to meet the culinary demands of a large and sophisticated entourage.

Royal hunting parties regularly took place in the forests of Chantilly, with the Duc du Maine's equipage often lent for the stag hunt. They enjoyed the patrician, vanishing sport of falconry, and the Grand Condé and Louis XIV were probably among the last falconers in France. The hunts inevitably concluded with a *divertissement* at the pavilion of Sylvie, which now featured a menagerie nearby with birds from all parts of the world, comparable to the King's at Versailles.

After the death of the Grand Condé in 1686, his son, Henri-Jules de Bourbon-Condé (father of our Duchesse du Maine), carried on the family tradition. 'Greedy even by Condé standards', as Lewis put it, this peculiar man staged even more lavish parties than his father. Despite his eccentricities, Henri-Jules' innovative fêtes were always in exquisite taste, for he had a genius for entertaining, for building and for decoration.

In August 1688, when the future Duchesse du Maine was only twelve, her father offered the Grand Dauphin a series of festivities. It will be remembered that only three years before, Colbert's son, Seignelay, had engaged Jean Berain to design the party for the King and Dauphin that took place at Sceaux around the lighted basin, with pavilions of greenery for the two principal guests. A Prince of the Blood like Condé could certainly upstage a family descended from wool merchants, so *he* called in the King's designer to provide the décors for *his* parties.

For one of them, Berain ordered a huge foliage pavilion to be erected, its sides pierced by twelve openings that revealed twelve allées through the forest, bringing the woodlands themselves into the composition. It was an appropriate and fascinating invention, appreciated by the Grand Dauphin, an ardent hunter.

In the same series of *divertissements*, Berain ordained a collation in the middle of a labyrinth (opposite). Since the weather was unusually warm, he chose a cool bosquet backed by a woodland, and presented the cold collation in a manner that vividly evoked features of the fabled Chantilly gardens.

The guests were summoned to an open-air salon with walls of living greenery, an exedra at each side, and the ubiquitous silver buffet centred at the back. In the corners of the roofless pavilion, he set up tiered buffets, the shelves of which were covered with refreshing green lawn in which grew tiny field flowers, as a display for the Condé silver and porcelain, also garnished with flowers. Berain's favourite accessories – cartouches with the royal arms – form a prominent part of the decoration.

The table in the foreground, with an orange tree in a mammoth silver vase as *surtout*, was festooned with fresh flowers and also covered with green lawn, upon which were placed shallow silver compartments shaped like the parterres in the Chantilly gardens. In them were arranged fruits in miniature scale to resemble the flowered parterres, so the whole elaborate display became an edible formal garden, a subtle tribute by the King's designer to the King's garden architect.

The Dauphin's suite had been conducted to the spot by oboes, and after the meal, the King's composer Lully, dressed as Pan, accompanied by dancers and musicians clothed as other sylvan divinities, emerged from the woods, executing a ballet and singing the music Lully had written especially for the occasion.

Although the park already abounded in garden structures and trelliswork bosquets for the incessant fêtes, there was another type of pavilion that was gaining favour among people of Henri-Jules' class, and that was the *laiterie d'agrément* (pleasure dairy). So the avant-garde Prince de Condé called J.-H. Mansart (who had succeeded Le Vau as the King's architect) to direct the construction of one of the earliest laiteries in France (1689-94). Built by Daniel and Pierre Gitard, the Chantilly Laiterie was attached to a menagerie in horseshoe form, and consisted of a suite of four rooms arranged *en enfilade*. The salon was vaulted in fine white stone, and on a buffet of violet marble was displayed a table service of faïence emblazoned with the Prince's coat-of-arms. Water issued from sculpted rams' heads and flowed into a marble trough to refresh the visitors, who were served dairy products on faïence plates.

Scenes of pastoral life were represented by the paintings hung throughout the Laiterie, as well as by *Fables* of Fontaine executed by R.-A. Houasse, one of the King's painters at Versailles. On the other side of the courtyard stood another pavilion ornamented with paintings inspired by the cult of Isis, the Egyptian goddess of marriage and the family. In the Chantilly paintings she was symbolised appropriately by a cow, and the dramatic

Jean Berain, 'Dessein de la Colation qui fut donné à Monseigneur par Mons. Le Prince dans le Milieu du Labirinte à Chantilly, le 29 aout 1688'.
Berain's design for the collation given by the Prince de Condé for the Dauphin took place in an outdoor room with walls of sheared greenery as backdrop for the incredible table in the foreground, the centrepiece a huge orange tree. Silver containers in the form of rectangular or oval garden parterres are filled with fruit, imitating the floral parterres of Chantilly's formal garden. At either side are buffets displaying silver and porcelain, the shelves covered with fine grasses, with the incomparable Condé silver displayed on Baroque consoles at centre back. Ranged around the room are boxes painted to resemble blue and white porcelain, holding orange trees. The next Condé generations, avid collectors of oriental porcelain, produced at the château one of the finest soft-paste porcelains, the famous Chantilly with milky-white glaze that became the rage of Europe

poet Racine provided a detailed critique of the Isis decoration.[10]

Although destroyed in 1799, the Laiterie of Chantilly was the most sumptuous and best known of all the ornamental dairies of France, vaunted by poets and imitated by architects.[11] When Grand Duke Paul of Russia came to Chantilly in 1782, he was so impressed by it that he asked for its plans.

When considering the laiteries of the next century, the reader should bear in mind that the form was given impetus by the innovative Condés in the great park of Chantilly, and at the Ménagerie of Versailles. For dairies will proliferate in the most fashionable gardens of the new century: at the Orléans château of Le Raincy, the Prince de Ligne's estate of Beloeil, the Duc de Chartres' Monceau, J.-J. de Laborde's English garden at Méréville, and Marie-Antoinette's Laiterie at Rambouillet – the most complete and sophisticated manifestation of the type, a veritable dialogue of the arts.

Antoine Watteau (1684-1721), 'La Perspective', the château of Montmorency.
Watteau's inspiration came not only from the theatre, but also from the spirit of the times in which a longing for the simple life was reflected in less formal and less rigid attitudes. Here his painting shows Lebrun's gardens as they appeared after the château of Montmorency was acquired by the artist's patron, Pierre Crozat, during the first quarter of the eighteenth century. Watteau portrays Crozat's guests strolling in the gardens, the casino that closes the perspective glimpsed through trees that have been allowed to grow naturally. The view is in stark contrast to that of Israel Silvestre's view of the casino on page 84

CHAPTER 4

THE BEGINNING OF
THE PICTURESQUE GARDEN

Friedrich Nietzsche was right when he described the seventeenth century as the age of will power. For it had required a prodigious will – and of course the means – to consummate in a grand manner the determined objectives of such men as Louis XIV, Colbert, Lebrun, and Le Nôtre. Colbert put it another way, and just as succinctly: 'Ours is not a century of *petites choses'*.

Yet, as the Grand Siècle drew to its close, winds of change were blowing through the lofty corridors of Versailles. The fast young set were beginning to rebel against the unyielding formality of court life, setting off fireworks under the palace windows, and slipping off to the further reaches of the gardens for a bit of drinking and smoking in the arbours. The licence of the younger generation was beginning to undermine respect for authority, and even before Louis' death there were symptoms of 'that underground movement' (Lewis) that would erupt in 1716 as Regency France.

When Louis XIV died in September 1715, rule passed to Liselotte's son, Philippe d'Orléans, the Regent. Pierre Verlet called him 'un roué presque parfait', and he did prove to be the most accomplished rake of the century. Someone said that Philippe regarded the day as a desert he had to cross to get to the oasis of night.

Although one cannot credit (or blame) Philippe with the revolution that was taking place in manners, domestic life, and gardens, it is fair to say that the brief period of the Regency gave impulse to the breakdown of old constraints. Rigid protocol and correct deportment yielded to a desire for pleasure, comfort and diversion. It was reflected in the curving lines of interiors, chairs with deep cushions that, for the first time, took into account the shape of the human body, dresses that fell into loose, sibilant taffeta folds *à la Watteau,* and gardens that were more often than not allowed to revert to a more primitive state.

But this change had already been noticed with the arrival of the young Duchess who had so entranced Louis XIV, Marie-Adelaide de Savoië, Duchesse de Bourgogne (future mother of Louis XV). A granddaughter of Henrietta of England, this spontaneous little creature showed the same capability for enjoyment as her great-uncle, Charles II. It was for Marie-Adelaide that Louis refurbished the pavilion of the Ménagerie and introduced a new bosquet in her honour into the formal symmetry of Marly.

It was called the Bois de la Princesse, and it announced a new gardening style. The straight allées of the older garden were retained, but in and out of the allées wandered winding paths that led capriciously into green *cabinets.* In one of these outdoor rooms was placed a small temple with a dome supported by marble pillars. Its interior was painted with trelliswork sprinkled with birds and flowers against a blue sky, and there were two semicircular benches. It must have been a gem, for the painter was Bellin de Fontenay, who executed some of the beautiful overdoors with bouquets of flowers for the Grand Trianon.[1]

'A daintier, less assertive age had succeeded. Watteau was its painter, not Le Brun; the lute replaced the drum.'[2] And in this more delicate age, the measured, stately cadences of the heroic landscape imposed by Le Nôtre gradually yielded to the lighter fancies and idyllic scenery of a pastoral – the incipient *jardin pittoresque* of the Regency.

The difference between the old and new attitudes become abundantly clear when we look at a garden pavilion that belonged to Charles Lebrun as seen through the

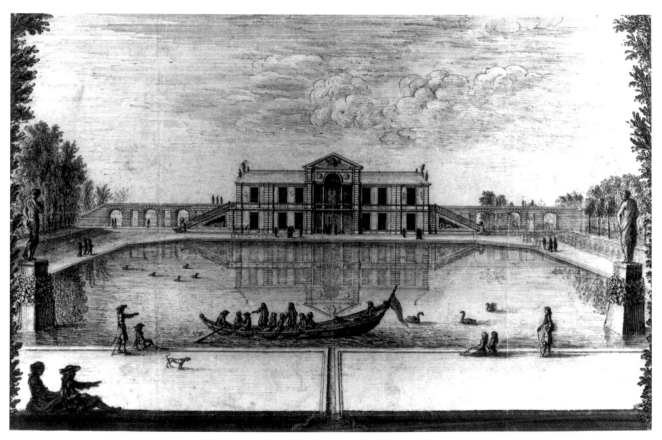

Israel Silvestre, Montmorency, c.1670.
The artist emphasises the perfect symmetry of Lebrun's garden at Montmorency. The pedimented frontispiece of the Château d'Eau is exactly centred upon the rectangular pool, with two tiers of three windows at each side, and a staircase descending from each wing, backed by an aqueduct with segmental openings. There is no doubt that Lebrun intended this Italianate casino to serve the dual purpose of functional garden building for visitors or supper parties, and as a theatrical device to close the perspective of the gardens. Lebrun had visited Italy, and the triumphal arch recalls the architecture of Andrea Palladio

eyes of a contemporary about 1670 (opposite), and then at the same building as depicted by Antoine Watteau during the early part of the eighteenth century (p.82).

In the early1660s Charles Lebrun had acquired an estate north-west of Paris by the name of Montmorency. When he could snatch a moment from the onerous burdens of his official position, he indulged in his favourite pastime – laying out formal gardens with fountains, pools, cascades and grottoes. For entertaining, Lebrun put up a pavilion in the form of an Italian casino with a two-storeyed open colonnade linking rusticated wings – the Château d'Eau. It is seen in the drawing opposite centred on a rectangular reflecting pool flanked by classical statues, on an axis with a tunnel of clipped greenery from which the viewer has just emerged. In the triangular niches formed by the twin staircases sit river gods like those in the nymphaeum at Vaux-le-Vicomte, where Lebrun was labouring at this time in the interests of Nicolas Fouquet.

Lebrun died in 1690, and around 1708 Montmorency acquired a new owner – Pierre Crozat, probably the most formidable collector of the century, and agent for Philippe d'Orléans, the Regent. Crozat engaged his architect, Jean Cartaud, to build a new château at Montmorency with an oval salon giving upon the garden, inspired by the one at Vaux-le-Vicomte. Crozat retained the essential lines of the gardens as Lebrun planned them, but in concession to the new Regency taste, he allowed the trees to reach maturity and the grass to grow naturally. To these more informal gardens Crozat added pavilions in the form of a kiosk, a belvedere and a mill, for which he engaged the sculptor Robert Le Lorrain to execute bas-reliefs of sea gods. He retained Lebrun's old casino, which was probably used as an orangery.

When the inimitable Watteau painted the guests in Crozat's garden (p.82), he disposed them about the long grass with languorous delicacy. And Lebrun's pleasure house was treated as a picturesque element, for it is glimpsed through the feathery trees and closes the perspective.

Hence the name of the painting – 'La Perspective' – for the pavilion looks (and functions) like one of those painted backdrops in seventeenth-century gardens that both defined the space and extended the view into the distance. Richelieu's garden at Rueil (c.1638) had featured a triumphal arch painted on a wall in *trompe-l'oeil,* and the same motif appeared at both Marly and Saint Cloud, where the flat backdrop viewed at the end of an allée was executed by Bon Boulogne. The painted perspective at Saint Cloud was described as a circular temple of Flora in three dimensions, surrounded by nymphs holding baskets of flowers. An intriguing subtlety of Watteau's painting is that the perspective *is* architecture, part of a real *folie* that evoked the classical past, but which has been made to serve the same purpose as the painted ones.

Regency gardens were subtly seductive, and the temptress was Nature herself. She loosed her stays, and what had formerly been confined within rigid, inflexible lines now burgeoned forth into the flowing Rococo curves of Regency and Louis XV gardens. Now Nature's gestures were rounded too, and the trees that once grew in straight, wind-swept allées, providing no shade during the heat of the day, were permitted an artless asymmetry. These are the trees of Watteau's gardens that Horace

Walpole saw as 'tufts of plumes and fans . . . that nod to one another like the scenes of an opera. Fantastic people! who range and fashion their trees, and teach them to hold up their heads, as a dancing master would if he expected Orpheus should return to play a minuet to them.'

Watteau's inspiration from the theatre is always apparent – its spatial ambiguities and dramatic lighting – and it was the Regent who called the Italian comedy back to France. But above all, Watteau evokes a spirit of nostalgia, a longing for the simple life associated with pre-Louis XIV France, the uncomplicated existence – or so the theorists thought – of an 'impossible pastorale' (Walpole). Regency gardens opened themselves up to the countryside, and this new orientation was reflected in the revival of interest in pastoral romances like Honoré d'Urfe's *Astrée*, published c.1608.

It is almost invariably the artists who announce new concepts. François Boucher is most often remembered for his scented canvases of boudoir subjects, but he was one of the most versatile and accomplished artists of the century. The perfect professional, and a true disciple of Watteau (whose drawings he collected), Boucher left no field of art untouched.

As early as 1743, he presented a preview of the informal, irregular garden in his 'Landscape with Watermill' (p.89). An eminence at left is crowned by the ubiquitous Temple of the Sibyl at Tivoli which inspired so many French garden buildings, and artists like Joseph Vernet and Hubert Robert. But along with the classical reference, Boucher introduces into the scene a rustic cottage with romanticised inhabitants, much like the *maison bourgeoise* that he designed for Monsieur Watelet's model landscape garden at Moulin-Joli after 1754.

A picturesque negligence typifies Nature – fallen branches and a meandering stream that replaces the straight canal of the formal garden. References to the ancient world (the temple and broken column upon which the lady rests) mingle with the pastoral (the water wheel and peasant's cottage). The tree shapes recall those of Watteau's *fêtes galantes,* and a part of the painting's subject is the personality of the dominant *repoussoir* tree. Clearly this is Nature ordered to a new vision, the consequences of which will be far reaching. Its attitude is no less aristocratic, although in a different way, than Le Nôtre's had been, and its artistic objective is not so much decorative as expressive.

The *jardin pittoresque* or *jardin anglo-chinois* fully manifested itself in France by the middle of the eighteenth century. As opposed to the *jardin français* – which achieved terminal drama through distance and whose main lines could be perceived at a glance – the aim of the new garden is surprise, novelty, variety and strong contrasts. The seventeenth century wanted a vista, but the eighteenth century demanded a view.

Although we cannot be concerned here with the primacy of France or England in this momentum towards the picturesque garden, it must be noted that the Englishman William Kent was among the first to see that 'all nature is a garden', as Horace Walpole remarked. During Kent's Grand Tour of Italy about 1719, he was struck by the *natural* beauty of the landscape, as well as by Claude's canvases and the wildly romantic landscapes of Salvator Rosa.

When Kent returned to England, a strange thing happened. Whereas painting had previously tried to record what it saw in nature, now nature began to copy what it perceived on canvas. English gardens, such as Henry Hoare's landscape garden at Stourhead, strove to look like a Claude painting with *repoussoir* trees, temples that imparted an air of antiquity, and bridges whose arches were completed in the reflections of lakes. Nature was *again* transformed, as artfully contrived as at Versailles, although the hand of man is carefully concealed.

Once it had been discovered that all of nature was a garden, then it became only a matter of 'fencing in' Nature herself, with appropriate garden buildings and monuments to complete the vision. 'Fencing in' is a figurative expression, however, for barriers have in fact now disappeared. At Versailles there had been grilles of *fer forgé* through which one could look out to the countryside, but these were gradually replaced by the *fossé* or ha-ha, as the English called it – a concealed ditch which prevented any visual interruption between garden and surrounding countryside.[3]

The new approach to gardening that began to infiltrate Europe was based ultimately upon eastern practices, and in 1749 there appeared in Paris the first complete description of Chinese gardens, a treatise on the royal gardens in Peking by the Jesuit Père Attiret, a painter to the court of Ch'ien-lung. Every valley in this fantastic garden was embellished with a pavilion with the curving, upturned roof that lent such charm to the type. Each one contained a collection of books, precious objects, and antiquities, and one was linked to the next with zig-zag bridges over rushing brooks.[4]

Maggie Keswick remarks that it was these small buildings – whether large enough for habitation or merely shelters from the rain – that effected 'one of the most fundamental transformations in the gardens', and evoked multiple associations. A character in a Ming dynasty novel comes upon a group of reed-thatched cottages and exclaims: 'Ah! now here is a place with a purpose. It may have been made by human artifice, but the sight is none the less moving. In me it awakens the desire to get back to the land, to a life of rural simplicity. Let us go in and rest awhile!'[5]

The spirit of this Chinese Jean-Jacques Rousseau invaded French gardens, and we find Louis XV creating a space adjacent to his botanical garden that featured winding paths suggestive of a primitive retreat, although the royal garden architecture followed traditional lines. In a peculiar reversal, the Jesuits tried to impose *French* taste upon China, for there were Jesuit pavilions at the court of China in the 1760s.[6] The walls were hung with mirrors and Gobelins tapestries sent out by the French court in 1767, and many of the details – including the furniture – were copied from French engravings. The architect Gordon Morrill suggests that this taste might be called 'françoiseries'.

If Louis XV did not actually indulge in oriental forms for his own garden buildings, his Directeur des Bâtiments, the Marquis de Marigny, toyed with the idea of a Chinese belvedere for his gardens at Ménars. Architectural *chinoiseries* were the perfect complement to the endlessly movemented forms of the Rococo, that delightful aberration in French art that took its inspiration from nature, in which there are almost no straight lines.

Marigny, as an arbiter of public taste, thought it more prudent to adhere to the classical manner, but many oriental *fabriques* did appear in French gardens. One is the Chinese pavilion at Cassan, at one time part of an ambitious waterscape near l'Ile

Adam built by Bergeret de Grancourt after a year's trip to Italy from 1773 to 1774. He was accompanied by Jean-Honoré Fragonard, while Bergeret's guide was Pierre-Adrien Paris, whose taste was formed in the French Academy in Rome and who worked for thirteen years at the Menus-Plaisirs, designing most of Marie-Antoinette's festival architecture, much of it inspired by Fragonard.

The eclecticism of Cassan is interesting in its marriage of the classical nymphaeum of antiquity with oriental caprice. The substructure is a sort of subterranean salon, supported by eight massive Doric columns, containing a circular pool fed by the waters of the lake. Above is the Chinese pavilion in red, ochre and green, with whimsical finial and bells tinkling in the wind.

The oriental influence persisted throughout the Revolution and beyond, and was carried to the most theatrical extremes in gardens of the last Bourbon reign. These eastern fantasies were perfectly at home in the French landscape garden, with its rock formations hollowed out in the Chinese manner, cascades and rivers coursing through artificial meadows crossed by oriental lattice bridges. In the environment of the natural garden, pavilions really came into their own, and it is a curious fact that even those immaculate incarnations of the antique spirit – the Belvédère and Temple of Love designed for Marie-Antoinette – found places in a garden setting that was denied every formal element.

It would be wrong to suggest that the traditional *jardin français* was totally eclipsed by the new landscape gardens. For the Le Nôtre garden that had provided the Sun King an 'illusion of absolute and timeless sovereignty' never really disappeared.[7] The compelling reason for its longevity was the perfection with which it set off classical French architecture, which has usually been the norm for France.[8] The age of Louis XV is regarded as the heyday of the Rococo, but his new botanical garden would be laid out in straight, converging lines, and the garden of Madame de Pompadour's Hermitage at Fontainebleau was arranged in geometrical parterres with boxwood *broderies*.

So for those who could afford to maintain them, conventional parterres, sheared trees, reflecting pools and ruler-straight allées enframed châteaux of prestige. And the newer, irregular plantings appeared beyond the immediate reaches of the dwelling, as the picturesque garden gained momentum.

François Boucher (1703-1770), 'Landscape with Watermill'.
Boucher won the Prix de Rome when he was twenty-one, and three years later he went to Italy. Enormously successful on his return to Paris, he became Louis XV's premier peintre and a favourite of the powerful Marquise de Pompadour. In this striking landscape, the brilliant blue sky provides foil for the billowing tree and white temple, while the human figures are treated as merely units in a decorative design, for the real interest resides in the landscape. Each element is pleasing in scale as it relates to the others, and the mingling of the classical with the pastoral would be characteristic of the new landscape garden

The Chinese pavilion at Cassan.
Pierre-Jacques Bergeret de Grancourt (1742-1805) went to Italy in October 1773 and returned in September 1774, enamoured of Italian gardens like Hadrian's Villa and the Villa d'Este that exploited the magic of water. The extensive water garden that he created at Cassan was obliterated in an air raid in 1945, but most of the Chinese pavilion with its stone substructure escaped. It has since been restored.

petit houssar du Roy

Madame de Ventadou

Madame de Ventadour and Louis XV as a boy.
Charlotte de La Mothe-Houdancourt, the Duchesse de Ventadour (1661-1744), is credited with saving
Louis from the doctors in the fatal epidemic that wiped out his family. Here she holds Louis XV on a
leash as he reviews his troops, the Gardes Françaises and the Swiss Guards, at the old royal château of
Vincennes, while his small companion, the petit houssar, *teaches his dog tricks*

Louis XV, 1748, Maurice Quentin de La Tour (1704-1788).
It has been claimed that Louis XV discovered the unique talent of the fine pastellist Quentin de La Tour. La Tour was an emotionally disturbed man, but an unusually shrewd observer of character. His excellent likeness of the King conveys a nobility, tempered with reserve. It was painted in 1748, three years after the Battle of Fontenoy, when Louis' popularity was at its height, and in the hearts of his people he became Louis le Bien-Aimé

CHAPTER 5

LOUIS XV, PATRON OF ARCHITECTURE:
1723-1774

The orphaned Louis XV was only five when the Sun King died, so he was placed under the tutelage of a governess, Madame de Ventadour, the only real parent he had, for he had barely known his own mother, the Duchesse de Bourgogne. At age seven, weeping copiously, Louis was taken away from Madame de Ventadour, and put into the hands of men, according to royal tradition.

At the beginning, the responsible Duc du Maine was superintendent of the young King's education, but in 1718 he was replaced by one of the Condés, Louis-Henri de Bourbon-Condé, known as Monsieur le Duc (1692-1740). It was Louis-Henri's grandfather whom we have already met lavishly entertaining the Grand Dauphin in

Louis XV and his petit
houssar.
*The young Louis XV stands
in what appears to be a garden
pavilion, a basin with water
jets behind him. He is wearing
court dress (habit de cour)
with the Order of Sainte
Esprit, and he watches his little
hussar playing with two small
dogs, one of which stands on a
tabouret*

the bosquet at Chantilly, and Monsieur le Duc surpassed even
Condé standards of hospitality when he received Louis XV at
the family château just after the King's coronation.

Although Monsieur le Duc was a fixture (for a while) in the
King's entourage, it was Cardinal Fleury who took charge of
the King's education – a modern education in every respect,
with teachers who were active in the Academies, at the
centres of research, and authorities in every field. To be
instructed in the great and noble profession of kingship, Louis
had to learn geography, history, diplomacy, classics,
mathematics (under François Chevallier), and military
strategy. Louis XV was one of the most beautifully educated
monarchs in Europe.

There was a deeply serious side to his nature. Even as a
child, he was surrounded by books, and all his life he
diligently and patiently carried out his official duties. The
Council Chamber – where he spent so many hours –
adjoined his bedroom, and when it was very cold he slept there, with a large white
angora cat curled up on a crimson damask cushion. The King's duties were far more
onerous than we might imagine, for the divisions between the executive, the
legislative, and the judiciary that exist today were unknown, and at that time they
were *all* concentrated in the person of the King. As Antoine remarked, this is why the
Coronation was so significant . . . and it was no doubt why Louis XVI wept when the
oil of Clovis was sprinkled upon his brow.

In spite of the Regent Philippe d'Orléans' disastrous moral example, he did try to
keep his official and private lives separate. He was intelligent, eloquent, generous and
conscientiously fulfilled his duties to the King, who seems to have been genuinely
fond of him. And in dramatic contrast to the two tumultuous regencies that had
preceded it, the Regency was a peaceful era, as Louis XV's own reign would be, with
the exception of the Seven Years' War. Jean Feray remarks that war is an art that
destroys all others, so in Louis XV's stable, prosperous age, the King was able to
indulge in one of his favourite arts – the princely art of building.

The court had abandoned Versailles at the time of Louis XIV's death and moved to
Paris, so the life of the capital took over the cultural functions that had been
performed under the Sun King at Versailles. When Liselotte lamented that there was
no longer a court in France, in a real sense she was right, for the solemn majesty of
the old King's court was never regained, even after Louis XV re-established it in the
grand château on 15 June 1722.

*François Boucher (1703-1770), 'La Marquise de Pompadour devant le Groupe de Pigalle, l'Amour et
l'Amitié, dans les Jardins de Bellevue, 1759'.
Jeanne-Antoinette Poisson le Normant d'Etiolles became Louis XV's official mistress in 1745 and
assumed the title of Marquise de Pompadour. She has usually been considered* arbiter elegantiarum *of
her age, and although her taste was unquestionably superb, it was Louis who took the lead. She did,
however, know how to encourage and consult with him, as the Queen never did. After she ceased to be
Louis' mistress about 1752, she became his friend. So the group by the sculptor Pigalle depicts both stages
of their relationship: the figure is shown in the state of undress authorised by mythology as Friendship,
and the putto who reaches up to her is Love*

Philippe reclaimed the splendid town house of the Orléans, the Palais Royal, and made it one of the show-places of Europe, a point of convergence for the new aesthetic. The *rocailles* that Gilles Oppenordt insinuated into the elegant new panelling, and that Charles Cressent executed in superbly chased ormolu for the Regent's splendid commodes, were among the first appearances of that motif that would characterise the age of the Rococo over which Louis XV would preside.

The pleasures of a fashionable life, the lively art trade, the intellectual vitality of the capital made Paris an emporium of the arts. It certainly affected the young King, who lived at its very centre. For just as the Sun King's taste had been formed by the foremost collector in Paris, Cardinal Mazarin, so must Louis XV have absorbed – by association – principles of connoisseurship from the Regent. A cultural excitement surrounded the Regent's establishment, and Paris throbbed with pleasure. New town houses were being fitted out for the Duc d'Antin, the Princesse de Conti, and Louis XV's uncle, the Comte de Toulouse, *grand veneur de France* (master of the hunt). He shared Louis' love for the chase, and from the spring of 1724 onwards, Louis was making regular excursions to his uncle's château of Rambouillet for the hunt.

The young King did not live at the Palais Royal, but in the old Tuileries Palace that Philibert Delorme had begun for Catherine de Médicis in 1563. The immense formal gardens planted by Marie de' Médicis about 1628 became a favourite haunt of Parisians, and one of the terraces was converted into a tiny kingdom for Louis XV. Here he played with his *petit houssar*, a small boy of simple background who wore a hussar's uniform, and his other companions.

On the terrace was installed a small menagerie, and for his amusement a jeu de bague (carousel) that was turned by men stationed in an area hollowed out below. In a nearby bosquet stood a light pavilion where he took his supper on warm summer evenings. It was Louis' first pavilion, and he was so pleased with it that he instituted an Order of the Pavilion, with heraldic emblems for his friends' coats, in imitation of his own Saint-Esprit. There were only two rooms, one used as a summer classroom, the other a billiard room, for all Bourbons were expected to excel in billiards.

In his own private garden surrounded by *treillage* the small boy cared for the parterres with a rake, shovel and watering-can, all made of silver. In Marie de' Médicis' day, the Tuileries gardens had contained aviaries that were concealed by branches to give the impression of a primitive forest, so – following this tradition – a *volière* of white birds was put up in Louis XV's garden. He was never again without an aviary, soon acquiring a scientific interest in ornithology, and it is certainly no accident that paintings by the King's artist, François Boucher, are often adorned with white birds. There was even a small yacht anchored on an adjoining reflecting pool, with a sailor to navigate it. It was intricately sculpted and gilded, and painted by the influential artist who taught Watteau, Claude III Audran (1658-1734), Keeper of the Luxembourg Palace.

So Louis le Bien-Aimé grew up in Paris under the admiring eyes of his subjects, a beautiful, spoiled, highly intelligent, sensitive chid. For his birthdays, the office of the Menus-Plaisirs planned elaborate fêtes, with fireworks displays in the Tuileries gardens. The structure for the fireworks that were set off to celebrate his ninth birthday evoked memories of his great-grandfather's first pavilion, the vanished Grotte de Thétis. The grotto from which the fireworks were launched was probably of canvas and papier mâché, and portrayed the sun shining from the interior of the cavern surmounted by cascades and flanked with river gods.

When he was only fifteen and a half, Louis was married (1725) to a princess six years his elder. She was Marie Leczinska, daughter of the former King of Poland, Stanislas Leczinski, who would become sovereign of the Duchy of Lorraine in 1738. Marie was a dignified girl, worthy of respect, and her father had given her a fine education, but she lacked the capacity to understand Louis XV's personality or be a real companion to him. By the time Louis was twenty-seven, Marie had borne ten children, but after she suffered a miscarriage, the doctors forbade any further intimacy between them, an arrangement that the Queen seems to have preferred. In any case, from that time onward, as Pierre Verlet remarked, the only one who crossed the gilt balustrade guarding her bed was the cat.

At twenty-eight, Louis was extraordinarily handsome and robust, and had inherited his great-grandfather's sensuality. In the dissolute society of the so-called Age of Enlightenment, a man in Louis' position was expected to find a mistress, but one who came from the right stratum of society.

La Grotte de Thétis. Although the grotto at Versailles was nothing but a memory by 1719, the designer of the support for the fireworks used the Thétis theme to celebrate Louis' ninth birthday. Water cascades down in three tiers and from the sea monster's mouth. Dragons – a popular motif in Regency interiors – spew water over the rocks. As the fireworks were ignited, they lit up the interior of the grotto. There is an affinity between fireworks and water, not only for water's reflecting properties, but also to ensure safety

This delicate matter was taken in hand by one of his favourite cronies, Armand de Vigneron du Plessis, Duc de Richelieu, a great-nephew of the famous Cardinal. Like his great-uncle, Richelieu was a true taste-maker, with magnificent residences filled with treasure, and one of the few people who knew Versailles under three reigns – from the time of the Sun King until Louis XVI's ascension. The lecherous Duke was the very incarnation of the eighteenth-century libertine and an unfortunate permanent fixture in Louis' suite, so he quickly provided a list of candidates for the King's mistress.

By the 1730s the four daughters of the Marquis de Nesle filled this role in sordid succession. In order to avoid having them at court, Louis would take his earliest mistresses – Mesdames de Mailly and de Ventimille – out to the château of Rambouillet that belonged to his cousin, the Duc de Penthièvre, after the death of Toulouse.[1] Rambouillet was one of Louis' favourite hunting preserves, and these clandestine affairs took place in a little rustic hunting pavilion ('une vilaine petite maison de chasse')[2] at Saint Leger that was part of the Penthièvre property. After the sudden death of Madame de Ventimille, Louis suffered a deep depression and spiritual crisis, sequestering himself in this *hermitage sylvestre* hidden in the woods. In the forest of Rambouillet are still to be seen stone tables where the mighty royal hunter and fine marksman stood for the ceremonial removal of his boots after the chase.

Finally one of the de Mailly sisters – Richelieu's special friend, the ambitious Madame de Chateauroux – gained ascendancy over her sisters, and became Louis' favourite. She and Richelieu were with the King when he fell seriously ill at Metz (Moselle), but at the end of 1744 Madame de Chateauroux died too, leaving the way open for a woman who has come to be regarded as the epitome of the royal mistress.

During the summers, it was the King's custom to hunt stags in the forest of Sénart near his hunting pavilion of Choisy. On the edge of the forest stood the château of

VUE DE LA PLACE DE LOUIS XV.

Grandeur de 9 pouces 9 lignes sur 7 pouces 9 lig

Jean-François Janinet (1752-1814), 'Vue de la Place Louis XV'.
The architect for Place Louis XV (today Place de la Concorde) was Jacques-Ange Gabriel. It was conceived to be the most beautiful square in Europe, but became – ironically – the setting for Revolutionary activities. On 11 August, 1792 the statue of Louis XV by Edmé Bouchardon was toppled from its pedestal, and on 21 January the following year Louis XVI was taken there for his execution. David's statue of the goddess Liberty was set up in the Place, and in the presence of the statue, the scaffold was erected for the execution of Marie-Antoinette on 16 October, 1793

Iᵉʳᵉ VUE DE L'HÔTEL DES MONNOIES DE PARIS,
DU CÔTÉ DE LA RIVIÈRE.

De la grandeur de 9 pouces 9 ligᵗ sur 7 pouces 9 ligᵗ

Jean-François Janinet, 'Première Vue de l'Hôtel des Monnoies de Paris, du Côté de la Rivière'.
Jacques-Denis Antoine (1733-1801) was one of the most prolific architects of Paris. His Hôtel des Monnaies (King's Mint) built on the site of the Prince de Conti's town house, is typical of the dignified architecture with which Louis XV endowed his capital. Antoine has emphasised the strength of the two top storeys which rest on the rusticated ground floor. The projecting frontispiece is articulated with heroic columns, and the attic embellished with horizontal panels enclosing bas-relief sculpture. The building still animates the riverscape of Paris

Charles-Nicolas Cochin, 'Décoration du Bal Masqué donné par le Roy'.
Versailles was brilliantly lighted for the Ball of the Clipped Yew Trees. It was one of the elaborate events at court and in the capital to celebrate the Dauphin's marriage to the Infanta Marie-Thérèse of Spain. Eight thousand white wax candles in chandeliers and massed girandoles illuminated the Hall of Mirrors. The guests sat in the window embrasures, looking out over a sea of marvellous costumes – Italian Comedy figures, Turks with immense turbans and grotesque masks, shepherdesses, and ladies in dominoes (hooded capes). One of the yew trees (to the right) is the King in disguise

Etiolles, and its châtelaine – Jeanne-Antoinette Poisson le Normant d'Etiolles – rode there as well. Madame d'Etiolles was a flower of the Paris bourgeoisie, well-known for her social graces. Her uncle, Le Normant de Tournehem, built a private theatre for her at Etiolles that was as large as that of the Opéra, and her performances there were admired by a circle of friends that included Voltaire, and the dukes de Duras, Nivernais, and Richelieu. It is uncertain when she first attracted the King's attention – possibly when she drove through the forest of Sénart in a blue phaeton, or during the celebrations in Paris and at Versailles the following Shrovetide to celebrate the Dauphin's first wedding.

As First Gentleman of the King's bedchamber, the Duc de Richelieu was in charge of all the arrangements for the series of fêtes following the Dauphin's marriage to the Infanta Marie-Thérèse of Spain on 23 February, 1745 in the chapel of the château. The first was a ballet, and since the château did not yet contain a theatre, he summoned the office of the Menus-Plaisirs, and within twenty-four hours they had converted the Versailles stables into a suitable structure. It was this office that put up the temporary pavilions for all the court fêtes, and for the occasion of the ballet, the Slodtz brothers designed an exuberant Rococo décor with great flourishes of palm branches along the walls, statues in niches, a false roof painted with cherubs floating among pink and blue clouds, and hundreds of lights garnished with fresh flowers.

The most elaborate event was the masked ball given by the King on 24 February in the Hall of Mirrors, again planned by the Duc de Richelieu. All the beauties of the court were there, and the Avenue de Paris was lined with carriages bringing the guests from Paris, among them Madame d'Etiolles. In the rules of *ce pays-ci*, the King was now fair game and Madame d'Etiolles was appropriately dressed as Diana. The King was disguised as a clipped yew tree with a vase on top inspired by the yew trees from Le Nôtre's garden.

In September 1745, Louis brought Jeanne-Antoinette to court, and she was to remain there for the rest of her life. Since she could not be presented officially without a title, she was given – by her own choice – the title of Marquise de Pompadour, and with her formal presentation on 14 September it was tacitly understood that she had become the King's official mistress.

Carlyle claimed that history is the essence of innumerable biographies, and with the advent of Jeanne-Antoinette, the history of French court life – and certainly the art of living – entered a new phase. In the strange mores of the 'City of the Rich', Madame de Pompadour came to occupy a prominent place, for she knew how to stage plays and ballets that amused the King, and arrange delightful *divertissements* for the court. She was a performer of professional calibre, and would appear as the only woman in a cast of excellent dancers and acrobats. Her radiant charm and graceful gestures were seen to best advantage on the stage, provoking the comment of Dufort de Cherverny: 'She was rounded in all her forms, as in all her gestures.'[3]

Towards the Queen, she showed both deference and tact, and Marie-Leczinska even came to like her. The Queen was especially grateful for Madame de Pompadour's efforts to amuse the moody King, and on one occasion she reproached Louis for not having been appreciative enough of a soirée that the Marquise arranged on 3 September, 1748. The Queen's constant confidant, the Duc de Luynes, reports in his *Mémoires*: 'The King was displeased. Madame de Pompadour rose from the table to sing the role of Night, the King put on his mask to dance in the ballet. The Queen . . . said that she did not approve the King not taking part in a fête that had been prepared with so much care and so great a desire to please him, that she was angry on behalf of Mme. de Pompadour, for she pitied her very much.'[4]

Even before Jean-Antoinette arrived at court, Louis had already created the *petits appartements* where he lived in a clandestine manner on the fringes of official life, attempting to carry on a private existence as discreetly as possible. He was delighted that she shared his love for architecture, painting, sculpture, interior decoration, natural history and gardens. Louis was so fond of horticulture that he ordered hanging gardens for the terrace along the Cour des Cerfs, with fountains, flowering plants and bird cages by the trelliswork master Langelin, and he filled them with white birds. To these aerial parterres he added two small pavilions joined by a gallery and surmounted by more birdcages, with the encouragement of the Marquise, who engaged J.-B. Oudry to paint some of her exotic specimens. The hanging gardens were one of Louis' favourite retreats at Versailles, for – without being seen from below – he could look out from the roof to the stables on the entrance side, and towards the formal gardens on the other.

Although architectural history and theory had been part of his education, it was apparently not until this time that Louis' practical interest in the subject was aroused. In April 1742 Jacques-Ange Gabriel – descendant of a long line of architects – had been made First Architect, and from this moment, there began a close, sympathetic, and fruitful collaboration between Gabriel and his master that lasted for thirty-two years, until Louis' death. A friend of Madame de Pompadour, Charles Pinot Duclos, claimed that Louis XV actually spent more on buildings than his great-grandfather Louis XIV, who has been so consistently reproached by historians for his unbridled extravagance.

The memorialists tell us that nothing pleased Louis XV more than to sketch plans for his friends, and we may imagine him working in his sunny corner room *(cabinet intérieur)* at Versailles overlooking the courtyard, the magisterial *bureau du roi* for state papers at the centre; or making architectural sketches, bending over the beautiful flat-topped desk of red lacquer and ormolu that Gilles Joubert made for him (today in New York).

Louis was so fond of building that the royal houses remained perpetual construction sites, and he shortly began to turn his attention to Paris. When he was living there as a child in the 1720s, there was still no Panthéon, Ecole Militaire, Place Louis XV (Concorde), Monnaie (Mint) or Madeleine, and the Louvre was about half the size it is today. So Louis began to commission a series of distinguished monuments for his capital.

In 1751, at the insistence of Madame de Pompadour, he endowed the Rive Gauche with the Ecole Militaire, an academy for five hundred boys whose families claimed noble descent, and its imposing silhouette still dominates the Champ de Mars. On the same side of the river towards Saint Germain, the church of Saint Sulpice was finished in 1755 by the Florentine architect Giovanni Servandoni, who had designed the spectacular firework displays in 1739 for the marriage of Louis' daughter, Louise-Elisabeth. The Place Saint Sulpice is a fine piece of theatre itself. On long summer evenings it looks like a monumental stage set with the light playing against the façade of the church, picking up reflections from the waters of the fountain over which Bossuet and Fénelon benevolently preside.

In 1763 the City of Paris ordered Edmé Bouchardon's equestrian statue of the Bien-Aimé as centrepiece for the last great square of Paris, the Place Louis XV. It was again Gabriel who imparted the grave and tranquil beauty to the twin-colonnaded buildings that still dominate it today (p.96). In 1764 Louis himself laid the first stone of the domed Sainte-Geneviève (Panthéon) by the confirmed neo-classicist, Soufflot, who would later design an austere pavilion for the Marquis de Marigny's Paris house and the garden architecture for his estate at Ménars. The same year, the dramatic Madeleine began to rise at the moment when the Rue Royale was being opened up, and five years later, in 1769, ground was broken for the celebrated Ecole de Chirurgerie by Jacques Gondoin – 'the classic monument of the eighteenth century', according to de Quincy. It was designed by the son of Gondoin, an especially favoured gardener of the King, who extended his favour to the son, Jacques, and enabled him to attend Blondel's school. By the time Gabriel's buildings on the Place Louis XV were being finished about 1770, the architecture of the capital was fully comitted to the new style. In 1771, J.-D. Antoine's dignified Monnaie (Mint) appeared on the river (p.96), and the following year, the Comédie-Française by M.-J. Peyre and Charles de Wailly, known since 1797 as the Odéon.

At Compiègne the King's architect completely transformed the handsome château to which Louis gravitated for the hunt, and Versailles finally received its court theatre when Gabriel's Opéra was inaugurated 16 May, 1770 to celebrate the Dauphin's marriage to the Archduchess Marie-Antoinette. The town of Versailles was embellished with up-to-date urban projects, and the cities of Orléans, Nantes, Rouen, Rennes, and Bordeaux acquired monumental ensembles. The celebration for the erection of the King's statue at the new Place Royale at Reims called for an illuminated arch leading to the dancing pavilion. Svend Ericksen has called Louis XV the greatest patron of French art of his time, and he was fortunate to be served by the foremost artists.

It must have been soon after Madame de Pompadour's arrival in 1745 that she and Louis began to discuss the possibility of a little house removed from the court. She understood his desire for a private life, his attachment to gardens and the country, his respect for *des biens de la terre*. So Louis began to take a special interest in the retreats of his close friends.

Etiènne-Michel Bouret (1710-1771).
Bouret was a prominent figure in French society, holding influential positions under Louis XV, admired by men of letters like Voltaire and Marmontel, and enjoying the dubious distinction of having his natural daughter, Adelaide de Flahaut, become the mistress of Talleyrand. After 1742, when Bouret built his château of Croix-Fontaine near Nancy, he commissioned his architect, Le Carpentier, to put up an unusually luxurious hunting pavilion for Louis XV, the Pavillon de la Croix-Fontaine, to which Bouret is gesturing in the portrait. This elegant pavilion with its gardens, was said to have cost Bouret twelve million francs

A regular guest at the dinners in the *petits appartements* was the Marshal Prince de Soubise. Together Louis and Madame de Pompadour went out to visit Soubise's small pleasure house at Saint-Ouen, where the Marquise would acquire a large château dominating the Seine. Soubise was an inveterate pavilion builder, but neither Louis nor Pompadour lived long enough to see the famous Paris *folie* that the architect Cellerier designed for Soubise in 1787, just before his death.

The King and Marquise went also to Les Porcherons and Gennevilliers to see pavilions designed for the gourmand Duc de Richelieu, and the notorious Marshal entertained them with supper in a *glacière*. Then there was the folly built at Neuilly by Louis' minister, the Marquis d'Argenson, his forthright secretary of state – sometimes called d'Argenson la Bête – with whom Madame de Pompadour never got on at all, and the Machaults' garden house at Arnouville. One of Louis XV's most luxurious hunting pavilions was the Pavillon de la Croix-Fontaine near Nancy which the Farmer-General Etiènne-Michel Bouret had Le Carpentier design for the King's use.

Louis was also invited out to the château of Dampierre by the Queen's closest friends, the Duc and Duchesse de Luynes – 'mes honnêtes gens', she called them. They always maintained apartments for Marie Leczinska at Dampierre, the Duke dutifully recording her frequent visits in his carefully kept journal. Louis would have seen the pavilion on the lake where the Duke and Duchess – with the dull, neglected Queen – nodded over endless games of *cavagnole*.

There were, of course, the extant royal pavilions which were always at the King's disposal, and we shall note in a moment his rediscovery of the Grand Trianon. But etiquette still had to be observed even there, and courtiers were allowed to accompany him to Marly or Trianon, where he would be assailed with requests for favours even by such close friends as the Duc de Croÿ. Besides, the new gardens at Trianon were open to the public, and de Croÿ wrote in 1757 that people came from everywhere to admire them. Just as the Sun King's gardens had suffered vandalism during his lifetime, and even afterwards, the curious visitors who investigated Louis XV's new plantings took away flowers, fruits, and even dug up the bulbs (Verlet).

Marly was a little further away from court, but Louis found it musty and humid. Besides, it held painful memories, for his father (the Duc de Bourgogne) had died here during the terrible winter of 1712 when he lost his mother and brother.

There was yet another small royal residence, though, and it was happily further removed from Versailles, hidden away in the Bois de Boulogne. This was the château of La Muette, which had been occupied by the Regent's scandalous daughter, the Duchesse de Berry, for whom Watteau himself decorated some of the rooms. Upon her death in 1719, the Regent – in one of his finer gestures – had given it to the nine-year-old Louis XV. Saint-Simon said that the Regent was offering him a *galanterie* quite suitable to his age, for the little boy could amuse himself as he chose, away from the constant attentions of the Parisians. Although Saint-Simon must not be accepted uncritically, we may believe him when he reports that Louis was ecstatic, for now he had something of his very own.

Louis went to La Muette for vacations away from the Tuileries, and he would spend two or three days in this small house in the forest with a walled courtyard before it. According to Liselotte (who lived until Louis was twelve), here he first demonstrated his love for animals. She noted that he established there another menagerie, with such democratic inhabitants as cows, goats, hens, sheep and pigeons – white ones no doubt. At either end of a long canal filled with carp, and with ducks nesting along its banks, stood two aviaries filled with birds.

One of the joys of the pavilion life was being able to cook for oneself. Under the tutelage of Louis' cousin, the Prince de Conti, and his celebrated chef Lazur, Louis learned how to prepare an exquisite cuisine. The kitchen of La Muette, furnished with silver cooking utensils, became a small centre of gastronomy, and later Louis indulged in this peculiarly French art in his private apartments adjoining the Cour des Cerfs just under the roof-top terraces at Versailles.

At La Muette a carousel with wooden horses was installed, similar to the one that Louis-Henri de Bourbon-Condé had put up for a fête he had organised at Saint-Maur for Louis' mother, the Duchesse de Bourgogne. Louis became adept at tilting-at-the-ring, for he was a precocious rider, one of the finest *cavaliers* of his age. His expertise contributed to his love for the hunt, and the chase was traditionally regarded in French royal circles as an heroic virtue.

This game of tilting-at-the-ring (*jeu de bague*) was not merely an idle pleasure, for equitation was a necessary skill for a King who was expected to go with his troops into battle, as Louis did at the battle of Fontenoy in May 1745, taking the Dauphin with him. Louis remained with his men until the outcome was assured, and Napoleon credited Louis XV personally with the victory because he refused to leave the field. As Louis and the Dauphin surveyed the terrible carnage after the battle (accompanied by d'Argenson who had to take smelling salts to manage it), the King remarked to his son: 'You see what a victory costs. The blood of our enemies is human blood. True glory consists in sparing it.'

Louis retained his affection for the hideaway in the Bois de Boulogne, and as the Duc de Luynes noted in 1746, he showed at La Muette a genuine proclivity for building. He engaged the Gabriels (father and son) to transform the diminutive château on both court and garden side, and in the spring of 1751 he and the Marquise inaugurated the project with a small dinner for twenty-four friends.

D'Argenson complained four years later that the treasury could not afford the enlargements to La Muette's gaden. One can understand the minister's anxiety, for it became almost a miniature Versailles, with *parterres de broderie,* a green carpet *(tapis vert),* allées of carefully clipped trees, an orangery, and kitchen garden, to which was added – inevitably – a house for pheasants.

Louis' favourite château of Compiègne acquired its complement of pavilions too. We do not know when the first ones were added, but the ambassador Mercy-Argenteau provides a glimpse of him there two years before his death. It was the King's custom, Mercy reports in a letter of 14, August 1772, to take his supper each Tuesday in a 'pavilion detached from the palace . . . which was known as the little château. The favourite [then Madame Du Barry] did the honours of the pavilion.' Mercy attributed the absence of the Dauphin (future Louis XVI) from the pavilion suppers that year to the fact that he was offended by Du Barry's presence.[5]

True to form, Louis XV ordered Gabriel to rebuild Compiègne, even though it kept the members of the court (who had to accompany him) sneezing and breathing the dust of a construction site for almost twenty years. Building and rebuilding would become a pattern throughout the reign, for this restless King was always enlarging the crown châteaux, and rearranging or updating the gardens with new parterres and pavilions.

Among his favourites were at least twelve hunting lodges scattered throughout the Ile-de-France, where he would stop for refreshment in bad weather, for supper, or to pass the night. Four of these were designed by Gabriel,[6] one of which is the extant pavilion of Le Butard constructed at La Celle Saint-Cloud between 1750 and 1751, executed by the *contrôleur* Mollet. The exterior is simplicity itself, with the entire surface rusticated, and the pediment sculpted with a wild boar attacked by hunting dogs. The interior contains a vestibule with marble chimney-piece, a round salon under an azure blue cupola underlined by a frieze of putti in rinceaux (scrolls of foliage), a warming room, and a closet for the *chaise-percée*. Sleeping quarters were provided in three rooms above.[7]

Perhaps the most interesting of all was the *pavillon de chasse* that stood on the margin of a pond near the village of Saint-Hubert, north of Rambouillet, whose specifications Gabriel drew up in 1755. In 1757, and again in 1764, Louis ordered extensive alterations to the original hunting lodge – additional storeys and wings, several courtyards, commons, and stables. So the relatively modest *rendezvous de chasse* turned into the splendid château of Saint Hubert!

Verberckt provided models for some of the interiors, and four of the finest sculptors who worked for the Crown – Pigalle, Falconet, Coustou and Slodtz – executed bas-reliefs, while the master Clerici provided the stucco work. In two niches stood busts by Slodtz of Diana, Goddess of the Hunt, and Louis XV, a logical combination. With its site and the finesse of its interiors, the former hunting lodge of Saint-Hubert became one of the most satisfying of the royal châteaux.

Like the Sun King before him, Louis XV followed each detail with a connoisseur's eye, and everything created for him was marked by a special tact and refinement. He was an expert judge of *boiseries,* porcelain, fabrics, bronzes, sculpture, painting and architecture, and everything created for him was marked by a special tact and refinement. Jean Feray claims that whereas in England taste is determined by the merchants, in France it was defined by the monarchy itself.

The old maxim, 'Bâtir, c'est imiter le Roi', remained as true as ever. The court, his cousins, the nobility, the aristocracy and bourgeoisie followed Louis' example. But it worked both ways, for even before the King had conceived of his garden buildings at Versailles, his Condé cousins were further domesticating the Chantilly park with architecture. At the château of Lunéville, Louis' father-in-law, Stanislas Leczinski, had already begun to create a garden of follies, and certain aspects of these amusing caprices will be reflected in the Bien-Aimé's own aesthetic choices.

Ce vend à Paris chez Jacob rue St Jacques chez Mr Armand attenant la rue du Plâtre.
avec Privilege du Roy.

CHAPTER 6

LOUIS-HENRI DE BOURBON-CONDE
AND CHANTILLY

The powerful Condé family – cousins of the ruler – were permanent fixtures at the French court, and Louis XV's entourage abounded in Condés.[1] Serving as his principal minister was the Duc de Bourbon, Seventh Prince of the house of Condé, known as Monsieur le Duc. He was an ugly man with a rounded body perched upon tall skinny legs, so that he looked like a heron. But his taste was as exquisite as his body was malformed. His son, Louis-Joseph, was Master of the King's Household when he was only eight, in which role he was required to solve burning questions of protocol at court. Then there was Monsieur le Duc's younger brother, the Comte de Clermont – only a year older than Louis XV – who had begun to appear regularly at court in the summer of 1722. Clermont invariably accompanied the King at the hunts of La Muette, where he showed himself to be a far better hunter than he was a soldier, since most of his military career was spent in retreat. He also appeared in plays with Madame de Pompadour, taking the role of the 'American' (actually, an inhabitant of the Antilles)

Louis-Henri de Bourbon-Condé, Monsieur le Duc (1692-1740).
The embellishment of the great château was the aim of Monsieur le Duc's existence; he added the superb stables by Jean Aubert, he initiated the manufacture of porcelain, and he called in the finest artists of the realm to decorate the interior. The gardens were a marvel under Monsieur le Duc, and the parterres, bosquets, canal, and cascades formed a living backdrop for the perpetual Condé fêtes

when the Marquise played the role of Alzire in Voltaire's play of that name in the theatre of the *petits appartements* on 28 February, 1750.

Finally, there was the Duke's younger sister, Marie-Anne de Bourbon-Condé – who was known as Mademoiselle de Clermont. We find her, with her sister, among the members of the King's party on 8 March, 1722, at a ball in the Tuileries theatre. She was appointed Superintendent of the Queen's household after the royal marriage at Fontainebleau on 5 September, 1725, a post she held until her untimely death at the age of thirty.

Naturally, the Condés were conspicuous in the ceremonies surrounding the King's Coronation at Reims at the end of October 1722, when Monsieur le Duc and his brother, the Comte de Clermont, rode in the royal carriage with the Regent, Philippe d'Orléans. It must have been a painful trip for all, for the Condés and Orléans branches of the Bourbon family detested each other. (The rivalry stemmed partially from the fact that if Louis XV died without issue, Monsieur le Duc would find himself the subject of the insignificant Duc d'Orléans, son of the Regent.)

After the Coronation mass on 2 November, Louis was taken to the Regent's estate at Villers-Cotterêts, for he was granted the honour of entertaining the King after the coronation mass before the Condés' turn came. So for two days Villers-Cotterêts was the scene of pastoral revels and sumptuous feasts, and in the evenings the château and entire village were lit up like a carnival.

Since the ancestral mansion was smaller than Chantilly (a plus for the Condés), Philippe d'Orléans could lodge only Louis XV and his immediate party there. A solution for putting up the rest of the court had to be found, for there were numerous officials, the Gardes Françaises and Swiss Guards who escorted the King, and one hundred actors, musicians and dancers who had been engaged for the fêtes. So the designers, carpenters, and painters got busy, and soon the lawns blossomed with wood and canvas pavilions that looked like small country houses, and a military encampment of colourful tents for the soldiers.

After Louis' arrival, a round of cannon fire heralded the beginning of the festivities, and invited the innkeepers of the village and nearby countryside to partake of Orléans hospitality during the King's stay. The Orléans were always solicitous of popular support, and the Third Estate was later to become a major factor in the Orléans' bid for power. The gazettes reported that the villagers consumed 29,045 pieces of meat, 3,071 *livres* of ham, 14,039 of fish, 36,464 eggs, 80,000 bottles of Burgundy and champagne, 800 of Rhine wine, and 65,000 oranges, without counting cakes and pastries.[2] A stag hunt – where Louis' famous commander, the Maréchal de Saxe, shone brilliantly – was followed by the customary illumination of the gardens, and banquets laid out in the bosquets.

The climax was reached on 3 November when the Regent summoned the thespian and theatrical resources of Paris, for he was especially adept at dramatic *divertissements*. It was Philippe d'Orléans who had recalled the Italian Comedians in 1716, and a company of comedians whom he had had recruited by the Duke of Parma performed at his town house, the Palais Royal. Philippe also inaugurated the first public ball at the Opéra, and when he led out the dance 'French civilisation followed'.[3]

For the fête of 3 November the park of Villers-Cotterêts was transformed into a fairground that exactly reproduced the Paris fairs of Saint-Germain and Saint-Laurent. In canvas pavilions painted in vivid carnival hues, the Italian Comedy performed, with

Palais Bourbon, Paris, engraved by J.B. Rigaud.
In 1722 Monsieur le Duc's mother, Louise-Françoise de Bourbon, engaged the Italian architect Girardini to plan a town house for her, the Palais Bourbon. The work was carried on by Lassurance, then finished in 1728 by Gabriel and Jean Aubert, who was decorating the Chantilly stables and château for her son. She formed a long liaison with her brother-in-law, the Marquis de Lassay, and in 1720 they acquired all the terrain between the Quai d'Orsay, Rue de Bourgogne, Rue de l'Université and Boulevard des Invalides. Here they put up two neighbouring hôtels, first the Palais Bourbon, then the Hôtel de Lassay, though both were simply folies. The engraving shows the Palais Bourbon as it was enlarged c.1765 by Louis-Joseph de Bourbon (1736-1818), for whom the new informal garden at Chantilly was built. One entered the grounds from the street, where the elaborate entry is framed by pairs of columns surmounted by the Condé arms. In 1756 Louis XV bought the Palais Bourbon so it would not be demolished, and for the decoration of the Place Louis XV, for the low pavilion seen across the river made a pleasing contribution to the elegance of this last great square of Paris

diverse entertainments by ballet dancers, marionettes and acrobats. Wooden boutiques decorated with flags, ribbons, flowers, and insigniac were manned by dancers from the Opéra who sold coffee, ices, chocolates, conserves, jewellery, faïence and porcelain (Saint-Cloud, most likely, since this was the Orléans' own factory).

On the next day came the Duc de Bourbon-Condé's turn to entertain the royal party. Affluent though the Regent was, Monsieur le Duc managed to outshine even his Orléans rival, for in addition to his Condé inheritance, his estate had been further enhanced in 1719 as a result of astute investments in the stock exchange.

One tangible manifestation of the Condé fortune appeared in Paris the year of Louis XV's coronation: the marvellous Palais Bourbon which the Duke's mother, Louise-Françoise de Bourbon (known at court as Mademoiselle de Nantes) commissioned from Girardini. The suggestion of an Italian architect may have come from her brother-in-law, the Marquis de Lassay, who had travelled in Italy, and who built his own town house beside the Palais Bourbon. Since they consisted of only a ground floor, they gave the appearance of low, classical pavilions rather than town houses, and an aerial plan by Turgot of 1734-9 shows the two colonnaded houses with a narrow band of parterres between them and the Seine.

When Girardini died, the eminent French architect, Lassurance, continued the work at the Palais Bourbon, making it one of the most innovative houses in the capital. It was the first French house with large panes of glass, and it soon became the talk of Paris, for it represented a milestone in the art of commodious living, according to the architect Pierre Patte. In its garden was an even smaller pavilion than the Palais itself. The windows of its salon were covered by mirrors that rose from the floor at the touch of a button, an invention that perhaps inspired the same feature in Marie-

The écuries at Chantilly.
The vast stone stables by the architect Jean Aubert (d.1741) were built between 1719 and 1735 and are typical of his uninhibited genius. The composition is centred with a pair of tall doors surmounted by a Baroque cartouche of fleur-de-lis, emblem of the Condés, who were direct descendants of Saint Louis. Behind the noble centrepiece stands a huge central domed salon, from which two wings depart, housing the horses in their stalls, the carriages, and accoutrements of equitation and the chase. There is a balcony for the musicians, and water buffets were embellished with statuary of subjects related to the hunt

Antoinette's boudoir at the Petit Trianon fifty years later.

When it came to Chantilly, Monsieur le Duc unblushingly declared that his one aim in life was to make the famous château even more impressive than it had been in the days of the Grand Condé. Louis XV had already spent some time there during the summer of 1715 (before he received La Muette). At the great Condé preserve, Monsieur le Duc taught the five-year-old King to love hunting, and presented him a special gun decorated with gold and mother-of-pearl.

For Louis XV, it was the beginning of a life-long, unabated love for the chase, and he could spend hours on end in the saddle without the slightest sign of fatigue. He and his uncle, the Comte de Toulouse, carried to perfection the art and science of *vénerie,* especially the stag hunt. Among Louis' favourite haunts were the woodlands of Chantilly, and Monsieur le Duc ordered a specially designed equipage to be kept in his stables for Louis' personal use.[4]

The fêtes that Condé offered to Louis XV in November 1722 came at a propitious moment, for the Duke was updating the château, which still held the fantastic collection

Detail of the cartouche over the doors of the Chantilly écuries

of furniture, paintings, and tapestries so admired by the Sun King. The Dairy that the Gitards had constructed under the direction of Mansart was being enlarged, suites with new white and gold Rococo panelling were installed in the château, and the chapel was redone.

All of this was fresh and new when Louis arrived with his suite, and his host arranged a superb apartment for the King that catered exactly to his tastes. The salon commanded a view of the aviary, and his *salle des gardes* was hung with paintings relating to the hunt by Wouvermans, Van der Meulen, and Desportes. A special favourite of Louis XV J.-B. Oudry, received a commission for portraits of the King's hunting dogs in 1725, and for the unusually fine series of tapestries, 'Les Chasses de Louis XV'.[5]

Wedding festivities in Parma for Prince don Fernando of Spain and Archduchess Maria-Amalia of Austria, 1769.
The French kings who invaded Italy at the end of the fifteenth century became enamoured of Italian art and the Italian influence persisted with France's two Medicis queens and beyond. The most promising French artists were sent to the French Academy in Rome, and Louis XV's daughter became Duchess of Parma. This cultural interchange was reflected in garden fêtes, and those of the Parmese court were almost indistinguishable from the parties that the Prince de Condé offered to Louis XV in 1722. Here the guests are descending the broad allées to the axis marked by classical statues

A special delight for the King were the new *écuries* (stables) housing 250 horses. Of cream-coloured stone, Monsieur le Duc commissioned them from the architect Jean Aubert, who also put the finishing touches to the Palais Bourbon. A triumph of Regency architecture, the *écuries* of Chantilly are the finest in France if not in Europe, the 'the work of a prince of architecture for a prince of the realm' (Gallet 1972).

Often the stables served as a vast pavilion for Condé *divertissements*. On one occasion the guests were led through the dark gardens by torchlight from the courtyard of the château to what appeared to be a temporary pavilion under a huge dome. The buffets with fountains were laden with the feast, and the openings at each side of the large room were covered with magnificent tapestries from the family's collection. At a given signal, the tapestries were dropped, and the guests suddenly realised they were dining in the *écuries* when they caught a glimpse of the horses in their stalls at either side, and the unrivalled Condé equipages.

On the evening of 4 November, 1722, as the King's carriage approached the château, it was greeted by three salvoes of artillery and the principal entry was lighted by a double range of *pots à feu*. The Renaissance façade and moat were outlined with lights, an illumination which was repeated each evening of the King's visit. Louis and the entire court were treated to five days filled with extravagant festivities that were typical of Condé prodigality. There were hunting expeditions in the Chantilly forests, where four generations of Condés had followed the chase. The vast woodlands were punctuated by *pavillons de chasse* where the hunting party – Louis and the numerous *privilégiés* entitled

Jean-Marc Nattier (1685-1766), 'Mademoiselle de Clermont'.
Marie-Anne de Bourbon, Mademoiselle de Clermont (1697-1724) was the daughter of Louis de Bourbon, Prince de Condé, and Louise-Françoise de Bourbon, Mademoiselle de Nantes. Here Nattier has portrayed her as a river goddess, with her pavilion in the background

to accompany him – stopped for refreshment or to take shelter from the rain.

Once again Le Nôtre's gardens became the setting for the fêtes. Still there were the majestic canal and sweeping cascades, the classic allées that denied growth or change, the marble statues of mythological figures obtained in Rome by the Paris merchant Louis Alvarez, the grand staircase with nymphaeum below.

All details were arranged by the Controleur-Général of the Condé house, Destin, who oversaw everything from the King's ceremonial dinner (the *grand couvert*) to the illumination of the gardens at the Maison de Sylvie. The hunts were followed in the evenings by comic operas in the garden kiosks, ballets in the Orangerie, performances by the three Paris theatres, and naval combats upon the Grand Canal. The décor of the pavilions, the entertainment, and the cuisine were of such prodigious artistry that the *Mercure de France* carried detailed accounts of them, and the events were later engraved.

The morning after his arrival, the King went straight to the Maison de Sylvie, where his grandfather (the Grand Dauphin) had been entertained almost fifty years before. The garden of this little house with its *tour de force* of trelliswork – porticoes, tunnels, domed pavilions all worked in lattice with the Condé arms – intrigued the King. Workers in *treillage* were employed a few years later on the terraces above Louis' own private apartments at Versailles, and decorative trellis later appeared in both his and Madame de Pompadour's gardens.

Then Louis went off to the Ménagerie to study the collection of rare birds, for he was already forming his own Ménagerie with aviary at La Muette, and another was later added to his Trianon garden. The Maison de Sylvie and Ménagerie provided the focal points for the brilliant festivities, where the host's strikingly beautiful sister, Marie-Anne (Mademoiselle de Clermont) was a centre of attraction. She and Louis XV were the same age, and on this occasion she rode in his carriage, dressed as an Amazon.

Variations of the post-coronation extravaganzas were repeated in 1724 when Louis spent the entire month of July at Chantilly. Marie-Anne usually presided at dinner, seated between the King and Monsieur le Duc, and afterwards accompanied their guests to a concert in a garden bosquet, a collation on the Ile de l'Amour, or an illumination of the Grand Canal.

Among the guests at Chantilly during the July fêtes was a young man of good lineage but not of royal blood, the Duc de Melun, and during the course of the King's visit, Louis de Melun and Marie-Anne fell in love. Both of them knew it would have been out of the question for either the King or Monsieur le Duc to give consent to their marriage, for Marie-Anne was a Condé princess destined to become the queen of a foreign sovereign, and Monsieur de Melun was only a member of the lesser nobility.

But, as Félicité de Genlis recounted the story, love triumphed over the demands of

Detail of the Nattier portrait of Mademoiselle de Clermont.
The rusticated pavilion built at the site of the spring of mineral water was often illuminated for the evening parties in the huge park of Chantilly. The light that was reflected in the pool and cascades setting off the pavilion contributed to the nocturnal drama of the spirited Condé fêtes

rank, and on a luminous summer night, the young couple slipped out of the great château to meet in the dark recesses of the park. Near the Laiterie they entered one of the *chaumières* that had been decorated by the milkmaid Claudine with flowers cut from the gardens. And there, in a milkmaid's thatched cottage, with two peasants as witnesses, the marriage of the exalted Princesse de Condé and Louis de Melun was celebrated by a priest before a marble table from the Laiterie that served as an altar.

The fêtes for the King went on as before, and about a week after the clandestine marriage (of which the court and Monsieur le Duc were still unaware), the bridegroom joined the royal stag hunt, followed by Mademoiselle de Clermont and her ladies in a carriage. At the very moment when the stag was brought to bay and trying to defend itself, the animal charged into the allée down which Louis de Melun was riding to join the hunt and, turning suddenly upon the horseman, mortally wounded him. A few days afterwards he died in the huge château, leaving Mademoiselle de Clermont prostrate with grief. The allée at Chantilly in which the tradgedy occurred still bears his name.

Although the matchless gardens of the Condé château had been the scene of her greatest happiness and her deepest sorrow, the bereaved princess sought consolation in their ever-changing beauty. In 1725 a spring of mineral water was discovered there, and to commemorate this additional source of natural water, Marie-Anne ordered a pavilion be erected close by the spring, with a formal garden of its own.

In the summer of 1729 the portraitist Jean-Marc Nattier was summoned to execute Marie-Anne's portrait. Louis XV must have liked it, for Nattier was to become one of the King's favourite portraitists, especially for likenesses of his adored daughters. In his 'Mademoiselle de Clermont', Nattier personifies the sitter as a river goddess, leaning upon an urn from which flows water from the spring, attended by an impish marine putto and nymph with pearls entwined in her dark hair. The graceful nymph pours the beneficial water from a magnificent rock crystal ewer with gold mounts, probably one from the comprehensive Condé collection that rivalled even the King's. Figuring prominently in the background is the pavilion of rusticated stone, with steps descending to the gardens.

Louis was at Chantilly again for two months in 1725, from 8 June to 8 August (during which time there were twenty-nine days of rain), and Monsieur le Duc extended his accustomed hospitality. To thank him, Louis ordered four large paintings by two eminent artists who specialised in scenes of the hunt – from Oudry a pair of hunts for fox and roe-deer, and from Desportes a pair of boar and deer hunts. In that same year, Monsieur le Duc hung them in the Salle des Gardes of the immense château. The two artists were also called in for interior decoration at Chantilly, and in about 1735 Christophe Huet was engaged to paint the most ravishing room of *singeries* and *chinoiseries* of the Louis XV period that is extant, with the possible exception of the salon in the Hôtel Soubise.

But the days of the Duc de Bourbon as minister were numbered, and on 11 June, 1726 his dismissal was finally decided. Although the unpopular Duke begged Louis to keep him, he was ordered – amidst general rejoicing – to Chantilly until new orders were given. None of this seems to have affected his personal relationship with the King, for Louis was back at Chantilly in December 1725, and again the following summer.

Monsieur le Duc's retirement from public life had the happiest results for the domain of Chantilly, and for the history of French porcelain in particular. He had already become enamoured of oriental art, and now he set up an atelier for making lacquers in the Chinese manner, adding a large chest of antique Japanese lacquer to the furnishings of the Maison de Sylvie. For his amusement, the ateliers produced painted *toiles* that perfectly imitated those from the East, and he gave them as gifts to Monseigneur, the young Dauphin.

Monsieur le Duc furnished his forced exile with a huge collection of oriental porcelain and began to experiment in the laboratory of his estate with the manufacture of porcelain. The Cirou family of professional ceramists was called in, a privilege was granted for the manufacture in 1735, and the legendary porcelain factory of Chantilly was born.

At first the wares imitated pieces from the Duke's oriental collection, which he mingled with his own to confound his dinner guests. Some were decorated with oriental herons, with silhouettes like the Duke himself, but as time went on they became more French, and were marked with the Condé arms. Some were painted with insects from the nearby forests, where Louis XV loved to follow the hunt, others with a French interpretation of quixotic oriental personages in beflowered robes. But among Chantilly's most delightful products were those inspired by the pleasure houses themselves: yellows and cornflower blues from the Maison de Sylvie gardens, where the Grand Condé walked when the battles were over. Or bears and great cats from the Ménagerie, which stood near the *chaumière* where Mademoiselle de Clermont and the Duc de Melun were secretly married on a bright moonlit night.

Chapter 7

King Stanislas Leczinski and the Chateau of Luneville

The Queen's father – jovial, and often tactless Stanislas Leczinski, the exiled King of Poland – was not one of Louis XV's favourite visitors. He would suddenly appear at Versailles to see his royal son-in-law, who made the best of his sojourns and lodged him in proper style. Not always in the château, but usually in the Grand Trianon at the nothern end of the Grand Canal.

Stanislas was living in the château of Lunéville, where he received eminent French

Stanislas Leczinski (1677-1766).
Stanislas was elected King of Poland at the age of twenty-seven, but was replaced in 1714. He, his wife and daughter Marie, wandered about until they found a home in France. Marie's marriage to Louis XV was an unbelievably good stroke of luck. Stanislas gave up his claims to the Polish crown and received the duchies of Lorraine and Bar for his lifetime. He cut a portly, picturesque figure as he was driven around his estate in a light carriage, smoking a long Turkish pipe. Kind and generous, he greatly promoted the prosperity of Lorraine

The Trefoil Pavilion at Lunéville, engraving by Jean-Charles François.
François made excellent engravings of the Recueil des châteaux, jardins, et dépendances que le Roy de
Pologne occupe en Lorraine *(1750) by Stanislas' architect, Emmanuel Héré de Corny (1705-63). The*
clover-leaf-shaped pavilion was the largest pavilion. It was built in 1737 opposite the petits appartements
at the end of the canal, and could accommodate overnight guests in its two bedrooms with alcoves. It was also
a favourite place for meals, which often ended with a dessert in the form of an extravagant centrepiece – a
gastronomic and visual delight concocted by Stanislas' highly-acclaimed chef, Joseph Gilliers

visitors like the philosophers Claude Helvétius and Montesquieu, or Madame du
Deffand's friend, J-.F. Hénault, the President of Parlement. Voltaire came for extended
periods, before he went off to Frederick II's establishment, Sans Souci, at Potsdam,
where hung perhaps the finest Watteau collection in Europe. The impertinent
philosopher occupied a three-room suite on the west side of the Lusthaus, which
Frederick was decorating after 1753.

That Voltaire was welcome at Stanislas' château is a measure of the crassness the
former Polish king displayed towards his own daughter, for the philosopher was
sponsored at the French court by Madame de Pompadour. Voltaire's cynical presence
and his gauche rhymes complimenting the Marquise's relationship with Louis was yet
another cross that Marie Leczinska had to bear. When it became too much for even
the self-effacing Queen, Voltaire was sent packing . . . into the open arms of her own
father, Stanislas Leczinski, in the duchy of Lorraine. The philosopher was sometimes
even accompanied by Madame de Châtelet.

In 1744, after Louis' serious illness at Metz (Moselle), he found it convenient to
stop off to visit Stanislas in his château of Lunéville. The French party – which
included the Queen's loyal friend, the Duc de Luynes – arrived on 29 September.
The Duke recorded that they were received with fêtes, cannon salutes from the
terrace, and a magnificent illumination of the entire town.

Louis knew that Stanislas was turning his château into a showplace inside and out,

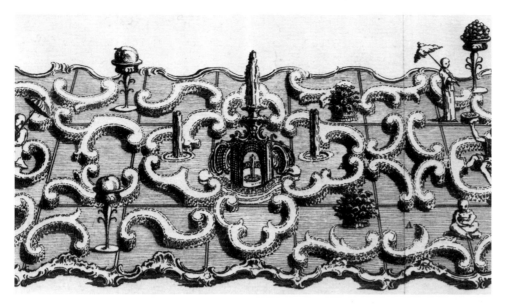

Detail of table decoration from Gilliers' Le cannemeliste français *(Nancy, 1751).*
Designers of table tops followed the examples of landscape architects, building miniature gardens of wax, biscuit dough, sugar pastes and coloured sugar along the centre of the table. By the mid-eighteenth century the centrepiece and terrines would be of porcelain or silver, but Gilliers' surtouts, brought in at the end of the meal, were of chestnuts, glazed fruits and meringues

and one thing they had in common was their fascination with architecture; in fact, there were seventeen architects in Stanislas' employ, along with marble workers and painters. In the eighteenth century, a knowledge of architecture – and often a draughtsman's abilities – were universally understood to be part of a royal education, and this held true for the *gens de qualité*. Stanislas showed a proclivity for drawing architectural designs himself, as did Frederick the Great (whose sketches are still in the Sans Souci library), and we know that it was also one of Louis XV's favourite pastimes.

Louis took a special interest in what his pleasure-seeking host was doing with his gardens, for within the year the King was to begin planning his own at Versailles. The grounds of Lunéville were laid out in the traditional French formal manner, copying Le Nôtre, and Stanislas was ornamenting them with an unusual ensemble of garden buildings destined for dining *en plein air*. There is no doubt that they gave Louis ideas for his own later commissions, although these would not take the same form.

One of Stanislas' pavilions was the two-storey Kiosk, where an elaborate dinner party was offered to Louis XV during his visit, and subsequently Stanislas built others along the same lines. The Trefoil Pavilion (the *Trèfle*) with its double flaring roof was used as an outdoor gaming salon. Its centre was circular, there were two alcoved bedrooms, and a third room containing the staircase and bath. The affinity of the Rococo with oriental forms was reflected in the *chinoiserie* wallpaper with pagoda motifs and swaying trees. The *Trèfle* became an important source for other European garden buildings, like Frederick the Great's Chinese Pavilion at Sans Souci between 1754 and 1756 by Johann Büring. For Lunéville was on the direct route to Germany.

The designs for Stanislas' pavilions mingled exotica from many sources, and one of them was described by Voltaire as 'half Turkish and half Chinese'. In August 1761, two of Louis' daughters, Mesdames Adelaide and Victoire, went to see their grandfather in Lunéville, and were entertained in the Kiosk. For this occasion the appointments were particularly lavish and the tables were crowned with *surtouts*, or centrepieces, created by Stanislas' famous chef, Joseph Gilliers, author of *Le cannemeliste français* (1751), with engravings by J.-C. François.

Sometimes Gilliers' spun-sugar *surtouts* looked like playful Rococo garden buildings, for the confectioner drew upon the vocabulary of the landscape designer, the garden architect, and the delectable art of porcelain. For Mesdames' party, Gilliers

Frankenthal porcelain centerpiece, c. 1770, model by Karl Gottlieb Lück (working 1760-75).

As chinoiseries took eighteenth-century Europe by storm, gardens and tables sprouted kiosks and Chinese pavilions. Typical of this taste is this porcelain centrepiece of brilliant natural colours in the form of a Chinese pavilion from the Frankenthal factory. Although the swirling base and curving stair are typically Rococo, the lattice of the balustrade, repeated in the openwork basket, is an oriental motif, but also reflects the treillage *that was a feature of most European gardens. The finial with dragon is not original to this piece*

chose a nautical theme for the centrepiece, with decorated confections arranged on silver shells. Its appearance – and taste – can only be imagined, for Gilliers specialised in elaborately moulded desserts, and his edible *surtouts* were cataracts of liqueur-flavoured meringue, and spun sugar laced with brandy, chestnuts and glazed fruits.

Standing behind the Kiosk was another summer dining room in the form of an open arcade, adorned with two gilt Rococo buffets carved with sea shells, dolphins and coral. A novel feature was the mechanical table that could be lowered to the kitchen below, obviating the need for servants in the room. It was exactly the type that Loriot would later devise for Louis XV's château of Choisy, where he liked to dine in an atmosphere of suave flirtation.

Stanislas' architect was Emmanuel Héré de Corny, who had returned to Nancy c.1740 from Paris, where he had been trained under the outstanding French architect working in the Rococo manner, Gabriel Boffrand. Boffrand had just finished his spectacular addition to the Paris hôtel of the Prince de Soubise, which the King took Madame de Pompadour to see. This was the beautiful Salon Oval with Natoire's scenes from the legend of Psyche enframed in curving white and gold *boiseries* and enlivened with gesticulating putti on the cornice. Boffrand's pupil must also have seen his master's veritable gem of pavilion architecture at the château of Saint Ouen – a tiny three-room pavilion of such ingenious simplicity that it served as a model of the genre for years to come.

For the friends who came to visit, the ruler of Lunéville had Héré design an entire village of pavilions (called *chartreuses*) along the Grand Canal, in which they stayed

The Perspective at the end of the Grand Canal, Lunéville.
Like the Italianate casino that closed the perspective of the Montmorency gardens (pp.82, 84 and 85), this backdrop for the cascades at the end of Lunéville's Grand Canal appears to be an impressive Italian palace, although the pillars, trophies and statues were executed in grisaille. It looked like a real building, but was only a clever example of trompe-l'oeil, *although the staircases that led up to it were real, as were the jets of water at either side. Behind the cascades was a pavilion used as a music room, with the walls of Lunéville faïence painted in pink roses with green bands, a colour scheme favoured for Sèvres porcelain of the Louis XV period*

during the summer months while Stanislas occupied the château. It was an arrangement reminiscent of Marly, where Louis XIV's dwelling had dominated those of the courtiers, whose pavilions bordering a reflecting pool were painted in *trompe-l'oeil*. But the tenor of Rococo society was more informal, and at Lunéville each *chartreuse* was equipped with dining room, cabinet, kitchen, and garden. As benevolent seigneur, Stanlislas invited himself to dine with his guests in their *chartreuses*, and fruits and vegetables from the gardens were expected to appear on the table.

The two tiers of cascades at the far end of the Grand Canal were surmounted with a perspective that looked like a Palladian villa, and – like Marly – its architectural features were executed in *trompe-l'oeil*. On the occasion of Louis XV's visit in 1744, a firework display was staged in front of the cascade. Behind it was a pavilion used for a music room, with wall revetments of pink and green Lunéville faïence, recalling the Sun King's vanished Trianon de Porcelaine.

Lunéville's most spectacular garden feature was Le Rocher, the automated village over 250 feet long resting upon a rock formation. Eighty-two figures, motivated by water power, gesticulated and made sounds appropriate to their activities – men singing as they worked at a forge, peasants hammering or carving wood, shepherds

'Vue et Perspective du Rocher,
Lunéville'.
The engraving shows members
of Stanislas' court on a covered
terrace (right), from which they
watch the figures at their work
on Le Rocher. It was intended
to represent a mountain village,
animated by water power, some
of its wooden figures portraits of
people who lived in Lunéville.
Possibly one was Stanislas'
dwarf, Nicolas Ferry, known
as Bébé, who was at his court
from 1741 until 1764

playing pipes. This ambitious group of automata was created by Stanislas' gifted clockmaker, François Richard.

The idea of animated figures was not new, for there had been *automates* in Renaissance gardens, and at Marly, Père Truchet had invented a *tableau changeant* for the Sun King's amusement. But the animating idea of Stanislas' Rocher has nothing to do with exacerbated Mannerist conceits or a novelty to entertain a great king. Its spirit is entirely *dix-huitième*, for it probably was meant to represent an ideal society, the impossible dream of the philosophers, with Stanislas cast in the role of protective and benevolent seigneur.

The make-believe world of the Rocher was as unreal as the collection of follies and mirrored grottoes later seen in the Duc de Chartres' fairyland of the Parc Monceau, with its encyclopaedic collection of architecture 'from all times and places'; or as Marie-Antoinette's somewhat childish *jeu de bague,* a royal merry-go-round for the amusement of her guests at the Petit Trianon.

There is an important link between Lunéville and Versailles, for Emmanuel Héré's assistant at Lunéville was Richard Mique, whom Stanislas Leczinski ennobled in 1761. In 1766 Mique returned to Paris, with memories of the gardens of Lunéville, and he succeeded the great Jacques-Ange Gabriel as architect to Louis XVI. It was Mique who would participate in the design of Marie-Antoinette's gardens, drawing up plans for her theatre and her *fabriques* like the Belvédère and the Temple of Love. Less fortunate than his friend, Hubert Robert, Mique became too closely identified with the unhappy Queen, whom he followed to the guillotine on 8 July, 1794, less than a year after her own execution.

Stanislas lived to the age of eighty-nine, and he proved himself to be truly the *grand seigneur* of Lorraine, building bridges and roads, endowing hospitals and schools, and founding chairs at the university. After his death the château reverted to the French Crown, and has today become a museum. Nothing remains of the fanciful pavilions and animated village that once enlivened the gardens, but the lovely town square at Lunéville does remain. With its sense of urban scale and subtle elegance, the Place Stanislas is the outstanding example of Rococo urbanism in Europe. The square that Emmanuel Héré designed for his generous patron, Stanislas Leczinski, represents one of the unusual gems of town-planning of all time.

CHAPTER 8

LOUIS XV'S PAVILIONS AT VERSAILLES

While he was still living at the Tuileries in 1722, Louis XV ordered his page, Calvière, to go over to the Pont Nôtre-Dame, which was then lined with merchants' boutiques, to find the engravings of all of the bosquets of Versailles. Louis was only twelve, but he wanted to become better acquainted with the great château of which he was soon to become the master, and he was especially curious about the gardens. The engravings revealed the grand abstractions of Le Nôtre's seemingly limitless formal garden, vistas framed with groves of trees, shrubbery regimented into pyramids and cones, and floral *broderies* which were maintained as a frame for the dwelling even after the vogue for the *jardin anglais* had been launched.

When the court moved back to Versailles, Louis carried out repairs to both the interior and exterior, and made it apparent that the gardens belonged to the people. On one occasion, he gave a *fête villageoise* for the populace, with food and drink for all, and ballets with the dancers dressed as shepherds and shepherdesses, evoking pastoral pleasures years before Marie-Antoinette came to France.

The Sun King had been unable to finish the huge Neptune Basin, so Louis XV completed it with scrupulous care, ordering three great symbolic sculptures by Lambert-Sigisbert Adam, Jean-Baptiste Lemoyne, and Edmé Bouchardon, who would execute the King's equestrian statue for the Place Louis XV in the last years of the reign. On 14 August, 1741, Louis drove out in his *calèche* to admire the basin, perpetuating the Sun King's tradition of showing himself in the park. In 1743 the dutiful Duc de Luynes reported that the monarch visited almost all the bosquets and ordered the waters to play.

The public face of Versailles, the state apartments, and Hall of Mirrors remained essentially the same, although new Gobelins tapestries and fresh Lyons silks were put up, and the beautiful Salon of Hercules was finished. But the fine Ambassadors' Staircase, in disrepair and used infrequently, was demolished in 1752, and for a while the space was used for Madame de Pompadour's theatre.

Louis began to relax the exacting etiquette of his ancestor, and from 1738 he ceased to use Louis XIV's state chamber except for the ceremonies of the *lever* and *coucher*. For his own bedchamber he ordered a second fireplace. 'As soon as I wake up, before any of the servants come, I light my own fire', he said, 'and I do not need to call anyone . . . I must let those poor people sleep. I bother them often enough as it is.'[1]

So he gradually shaped the private apartments to his own needs – small, delectable rooms with multiple staircases, filled with exuberant light-saturated paintings, exquisite furniture, and the rarest ormolu-mounted porcelains. He could not abide dark colours or even the sombre bronzes of the royal collection. Louis' rooms resounded with the idea of pleasure – sunny, cheerful, warm hues for light-reflecting materials and panelling. The walls of one *cabinet* were lemon yellow lacquer picked out with silver, with Lyons silk to match for the hangings and furniture.

Art no longer served the state but the individual, and under the aegis of Louis XV the arts attained a moment of perfection, a majesterial depth, colour and grace. There were rich, flowered Lyons silks, Savonnerie carpets with yellow fields, white marble sculptures by Lemoyne or Bouchardon, superbly chased bronzes by Caffieri, porcelains with pulsating green grounds and Boucher cupids surrounded by a network of polished gold from the King's manufacture at Sèvres, extravagant pieces of silver by Thomas Germain, and furniture masterpieces by the great *ébénistes* Cressent, Oeben and Joubert.

To complement the private apartments were Louis' roof-top gardens, and after Madame de Pompadour's arrival he turned his attention to the immense formal park. Here he began to think of secret *enclos* that he might embellish with delicious hideaways, fountains and trelliswork in *rocaille* curves. Sculpture was of a more intimate and personal nature than the Sun King's, chosen for visual pleasure rather than profound meditation.

At the end of 1744, with the sudden death of his mistress, Madame de Châteauroux, Louis XV fled to the Grand Trianon to hide his grief. The impact of his mother's presence was still felt at the marble Trianon, although the Duchesse de Bourgogne had died when Louis was only two. The older courtiers remembered how the animated young duchess had brought gaiety to the last sombre days of the great King, and the elaborate round of festivities in 1697 to celebrate the Bourgognes' marriage. They culminated on 17 December, as Saint-Simon records, when the court went over to Trianon to hear André Destouche's pastoral opera *Issé* performed at the Salle de Comédie. At another time the Sun King arranged a dance at Trianon for Marie-Adelaide, and the Marquis de Dangeau reports that she and her party embarked upon the Grand Canal for the Ménagerie after the ball was over.

The Grand Trianon also held fond childhood memories for Louis XV, for he liked to ride in its broad allées, although he had not been attracted to it in his teens. Even though the Sun King's pavilion needed repairs and was *triste* in winter, Louis XV now became attached to it, and ordered Gabriel to have it refurbished.

The following year, Madame de Pompadour came to court, and she encouraged the King's interest in Trianon and its gardens. Apartments were fitted up for them there, and they would spend two or three days at a time. The lawyer/diarist, Edmond-Jean-François Barbier (another inveterate Versailles-watcher) reported that 'Trianon has become [the King's] *maison de campagne*' (Verlet).

In this country house of Trianon the spirits of two kings met: Louis XIV who had been its architect, with a 'compass in his eye' for proportion and symmetry (Saint-Simon), and his great-grandson Louis XV who was to make its nearby park a model of horticulture. Although much less formal in spirit than his ancestor's, Louis XV's gardens and their architectural components would not be randomly placed, but situated on the axes already established for the Grand Trianon. The eighteenth century was a time when buildings, like people, showed a courtesy in relationship to each other, and the pavilions of the Bien-Aimé would co-exist easily with the Grand Trianon, and with the impressive Cartesian gardens which complemented the arrogant château. But unlike those of his predecessor, they would be utterly devoid of any political allusions.

So the Grand Trianon gradually came to life again under Louis XV. By 1746 the ha-has were rebuilt, and by the end of 1749, most of the furniture, mirrors and appointments were in place. In March of that year the Department of Buildings

Charles-Nicolas Cochin (1715-1790), 'Sa Majesté Louis XV Estant Acompagné de Monsieur le duc d'Antin à la Cascade de Trianon'.
Even before his return to Versailles in 1722, Louis XV was fascinated by his great-grandfather's gardens. After he moved the court back to the great château, he regularly took certain courtiers with him to make the rounds of Marly, La Muette and Trianon. Strolling with him in the gardens of the Trianon is the Duc d'Antin (c.1665-1736), the son of Athénaïs de Montespan and her husband, who owned a fine house in Paris. Louis especially liked the Trianon gardens, where the Sun King's parterres were carefully maintained. The water buffet before which he stands is surmounted by a river god and goddess. Water pours from the volutes and spews from the mouths of the hunting dogs at either side

provided the plans that Louis had requested for a new flower garden – a *jardin fleuriste*.

The presence of the King in this part of the garden called for a small house, so he began to work almost continuously with Gabriel on the building and garden projects, as the Duc de Luynes reported: 'M. Gabriel . . . travaille presque continuellement avec le Roi pour tout ce qui s'appelle bâtiments et jardins'. And the minister d'Argenson confirmed the close personal association between Louis XV and his architect: 'His Majesty did not breathe except with plans and designs upon his table'. Tables were, in fact, among his favourite pieces of furniture, for in addition to the two famous bureaux in the study, he ordered a *table de campagne* (folding table) from Antoine Gaudreaux in 1740, with beautifully crafted mathematical instruments furnished by the trellis artist Langlois – compasses, crayons, inkwells and rulers used by professional architects. The result of this collaboration between Louis XV and Gabriel was a transformation of the gardens south-east of the Grand Trianon as a setting for what would eventually become a new Trianon.

Gabriel's Pavillon Français of 1749-50.
This is one of Louis XV's most attractive pavilions, with its tall French windows and insistent horizontals of cornice and balustrade, reflected in the gilt frieze of the circular central room. Emil Kaufmann regarded it as a key document in breaking Baroque rules, for the departure of the four short wings is stopped short, cutting it off from its environment

The Ménagerie

The Sun King's Ménagerie still stood at the southern arm of the Grand Canal, and before the spring of 1749 Louis XV had asked Gabriel to design a new menagerie near the Grand Trianon, with the enthusiastic support of Madame de Pompadour. Her own gardens were laid out by one of the Le Nôtre family, Jean-Charles Garnier d'Isle, and her hermitages were equipped with hen houses and small barns for Dutch cows. The King's mistress was so fond of animals that she ordered porcelain figures for her residences, and judging by her purchases from the Paris *marchand-mercier* Lazare Duvaux in 1751, she must have owned an entire farmyard of them.

By July 1749, the Ménagerie was in progress, and it was conceived in a more informal spirit than the Sun King's Ménagerie or the Condés' at Chantilly, for Louis XV's Ménagerie was that of a gentleman farmer. There was a Laiterie, all sorts of fowl, including poultry, and the King and Marquise collected the eggs themselves. No matter how bucolic it all appeared, the interior was as refined as the *petits appartements,* with supple panelling sculpted by the eminent wood-carver, Jacques Verberckt, and napkins of *petite Venize superfine.*[2]

The parterres were finished in the fall of 1750, the gardener Belleville put down bulbs, extraordinary ensembles of *treillage* were added, and in 1751 the Ménagerie domain was extended to the south with an enclosed garden of orange trees, an indispensable accessory to the Bourbon dynasty, for as we have seen, orange trees in silver tubs had lined the Hall of Mirrors when Louis XIV created it. And one of the

Detail of the roof balustrade of the Pavillon Français

horticultural sights of Versailles was the so-called 'Grand Condé', an orange tree that had been planted in 1421, was taken to Chantilly in the 1590s, and moved to Versailles during Louis XIV's reign (it finally expired in 1895).

Ladies who wanted to stroll in the gardens of the Ménagerie were furnished with parasols of crimson *gros de Tours* with gold borders, a nice foil for the greenery, and twenty-four folding chairs, ancestors of those still to be seen in the Tuileries gardens, were also provided for their convenience.

The Pavillon Français (1749-50)

Louis XV's predilection for building and his life-long zeal for science was directly linked to his new Ménagerie, and his increasing interest in the botanical sciences would shortly find expression in his celebrated botanical garden. If he were to enjoy fully this fascinating realm developing around the Grand Trianon, however, there needed to be a pavilion for cards, music and conversation, and as shelter when he came to admire the rare birds in the Menagerie beyond.

So the trio of King, Madame de Pompadour, and Gabriel began to plan the Pavillon Français in the form of a Saint Andrew's cross, situated at the intersection of two allées. To capitalise upon the view of the gardens, there were full-length doors and windows, an octagonal salon with Corinthian columns flanked by four small cabinets, and *boiseries* again executed by the master, Jacques Verberckt. The superb gilt frieze of waterfowl, hens and geese in gilded cages links it thematically to the Ménagerie. It is of considerable importance to the incipient neo-classical movement, for Tadgell regarded it as a landmark in the progression from the Rococo to the Louis XVI style.[3] To perpetuate the playful note struck in the interior, the roof balustrade was surmounted by stone statues of children and pots of flowers.

All of the elegance of the century seems to be summed up in this delicious pavilion which so delighted Louis XV. He regarded it as an example of 'the taste in which one should build', according to the often-cited note of the Duc de Croÿ:

> The King loved plans and building very much. He took me into his pretty pavilion [the Pavillon Français] in the gardens of Trianon, and remarked that it was in this taste that one should build. He ordered Gabriel to give me two plans that they had made together. He sketched his ideas himself for a long time, and with Gabriel, returning this proposition . . .[4]

How profoundly the architect was influenced by the King's own ideas we do not know, but it is certain that Louis XV's taste was noble, refined, and sure. In spite of the Goncourts (and others) who speak of 'France Pompadour', Louis XV's

The Pavillon Français.
The engraving shows Marie-Antoinette walking in the Trianon gardens in 1788, holding the hand of her son. The Pavillon Français, with urns holding flowers along the balustrade, faces the Petit Trianon in the distance at left. The berceaux de verdure from the old formal gardens under which the Queen walks have been retained, and the orange trees have been set out in the traditional orange boxes for summer

connoisseurship was superior to and quite independent of the Marquise's; it was he who directed the arts of the nation, and his taste was fully manifested in his elegant pavilions at Versailles.

The Botanical Garden

Louis XV would have agreed with Baltrusaitis that 'the laying out of a garden is an act of architecture'. Perhaps the finest piece of architecture executed for Louis XV in floral form was the new *jardin botanique* created by Claude Richard, whom Linnaeus called 'the ablest gardener in Europe'.

Louis' interest in the study of botany was stimulated by his conversations with the Duc d'Ayen, one of his favourite cronies and a good friend of the Marquise. Another was the ubiquitous Duc de Croÿ, who was always stopping by to see what was going on in this corner of the gardens, and to admire the exotic fowl that he liked so much, for he was about to embark upon writing his *Histoire naturelle.* It was de Croÿ who claimed that the Marquise had given the King 'tous ces petits gouts',[5] meaning Louis' taste for the bucolic.

In 1750 Claude Richard was officially appointed *jardinier-fleuriste* to the Crown, and the King immediately set him to planting his new botanial garden. It was of such comprehensive excellence that it became renowned throughout Europe, for it contained 4,000 types of plants, including coffee plants, strawberries and Reine Marguerite pears, carefully classified by the excellent botanist Bernard de Jussieu. In 1733 two cuttings *(oeilletons)* of pineapples had been brought from Central America to Louis XV. Le Normand, the head gardner who succeeded La Quintinie, nursed them in the hot houses, and by 1745 he was able to offer the King the two first home-grown pineapples. They were painted by François Desportes, and the canvas is now at

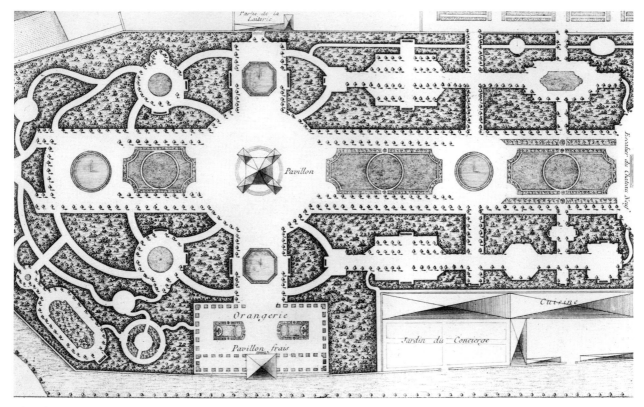

Plan of Louis XV's garden, 1754.
The steps to the Petit Trianon are seen on the extreme right of the plan ('Escalier du Château Neuf'), and beyond them are the Petit Trianon and then the botanical gardens laid out in regular rows. The Pavillon Français (marked 'Pavillon') stands at the rond-point and is the centrepiece of the garden. Below it on the plan is the small trelliswork Salon Frais (the summer dining room, marked 'Pavillon frais') with its own parterres, while the Laiterie terminates the upper arm of the axis. Curving paths wander throughout the bosquets that form the backdrop to the formal layout of the Pavillon Français gardens

Versailles as an overdoor in the Queen's *petits appartements*. The pineapples were so successful that two more hot houses were provided for them, and in 1754 Louis ordered espaliered peaches for the walls. Another fascinating addition was what the French called 'evergreens', using the English term, and de Croÿ often mentions galleries filled with these non-deciduous trees that the King found so amusing.

Although the botanical garden was laid out in rectangular form, there were also bosquets laced with meandering paths, looking forward to Marie-Antoinette's picturesque garden at Trianon twenty-five years later, and backward to the old Bosquet des Sources of Louis XIV's days, or to the Marly gardens, where Madame de Maintenon had fled the grand avenues cut straight as a wall and swept by the elements to find sanctuary in the apartments of greenery, sitting on a bench to watch the royal carps swim in their faïence-lined pools.

The Salon Frais (1751-3)

As Louis became ever more committed to botany, he decided to extend the landscape composition with trelliswork, and yet another pavilion, the Pavillon Frais, which was built on axis with the Pavillon Français and the Laiterie. It has long since disappeared, but its foundation was of small stones, and the exterior walls were entirely of *treillage*. This intricate work was carried out by the expert Langelin, who had already provided the trellis pavilions for the terraces of the King's private apartments, as well as the complex Bosquet du Baldaquin for Madame de Pompadour at Bellevue (pp.133 and 134)).

The tiny Pavillon Frais was a summer dining room, its floor covered with a large

The Salon Frais.
This echoed the stone Pavillon
Français in the medium of
treillage: the doorways take the
form of segmental arches, while
the rectangular windows are
adorned with cartouches at the
top, and the balustrades are
crowned with urns holding
flowers to provide the transition
between the pavilion and the
sky. The floral garlands that
depend at either side of the
windows link the façade to the
interior, where Verberckt's
boiseries echo the same theme

carpet in *camailleux vert,* executed to Chevillon's design by the royal Savonnerie factory, and recently rediscovered. The interior panelling was sculpted with baskets and garlands of flowers by Verberckt in 1753, its design extending the exterior into the interior, for the same motifs appeared on the façades and porticoes. Mirrors were installed during the spring of 1753, and in July the *treillageurs* were at work on the delicate baskets that topped balustrades. The trelliswork for the arcades and the outside walls of the Salon Frais seems to have been made of iron since it was easier to manipulate than wood.

But two elements that were inevitably associated with eighteenth-century pavilions were still missing: orange trees in their traditional square boxes with round finials, and garden sculpture. So from La Muette, Roule, Versailles, and even faraway Compiègne, orange trees were brought for the Pavillon Frais. In 1756 the Salle des Antiques of the Louvre provided the sculpture – two statues, selected with the help of the engraver Charles-Nicolas Cochin, to be placed at either end of the berceau of greenery.

The Petit Trianon (1762-4)

Louis' preoccupation with his new garden complex, where he liked to spend pleasant hours with his friends and Madame de Pompadour, became a royal pastime. As he surveyed the layout of the Ménagerie and Laiterie, the botanical garden and greenhouses, the Pavillon Français with its formal garden at one side, the 'evergreen' on the other, he decided that a larger, more important pavilion was needed to complete and dominate the entire composition. So the trio that had planned the Pavillon Français set their minds upon the culminating project for the gardens, the Petit Trianon.

The Petit Trianon has been the subject of exhaustive studies,[6] so it is inappropriate to discuss it here. However, the true *raison d'être* of this famous pavilion must be pointed out: Louis XV apparently wanted a distinguished dwelling that not only commanded and crowned the Trianon complex, but which afforded an interesting view from every side – the entrance court, the botanical garden, the *jardin fleuriste,* or the Pavillon Français with its own small garden ensemble and trelliswork dining room.

Construction on the new project was delayed by the Seven Years' War (1756-63), and Gabriel's first proposal of 1761 was disappointing. He then simplified the original plan, and the new drawings so delighted the King that he approved them in May 1762. Work began soon afterwards, and Pierre Verlet pointed out that the new building celebrated the end of a war, in the tradition of the Sun King. In this case, it was the Treaty of Paris, marking the end of the Seven Years' War in 1763.

Christian Baulez has remarked that the first plan would not have been notable, but that the final one was a masterpiece. Pierre Verlet calls the Petit Trianon 'le chef-

d'oeuvre du siècle', and the devoted nineteenth-century curator of Versailles, Pierre de Nolhac, wrote: 'Never had one achieved a purer line. In this fine dwelling of French stone, which occupies the privileged site of the domain of our kings, seems to be reborn some image of Hellenic perfection.'[7] Even in an age of exemplary French architecture, the acknowledged masterpiece was not a monumental public building, like the Ecole Militaire or even Soufflot's dramatic Panthéon, but a pavilion of modest size, imbued with an undeniable charm, set within the context of a royal garden.

The art historian Fiske Kimball believed that there was an influence from English Palladianism, but Fleming and his colleagues rightly discern that 'this perfectly proportioned cubical composition is wholly French and achieves a serenity and distinction different in kind and quality from any other contemporary building'.[8]

The four different façades show Gabriel's habitual modulations according to the levels of each. He established a rhythm of five openings for each one, varying the ornament according to its orientation. Two are adorned with pilasters, while the façade giving upon the botanical garden is without ornament, and that oriented towards the Pavillon Français is embellished with columns. The terrace before it opens at each end with steps, and again at the centre with a short flight, establishing the relationship to the axis of the Pavillon Français, and inviting the visitor to explore the garden.

As his predecessor had done at the Grand Trianon, Louis XV constantly surveyed the work, approving or correcting details as they were presented, no doubt ratified by the Marquise, who had rallied in her last years to the antique mode. The exquisite *boiseries*, which were still being installed in November 1773, six months before the King's death, were executed by Honoré Guibert, brother-in-law of one of Louis XV's favourite painters, Joseph Vernet. Guibert's name must always be associated with Gabriel's in the success of the Petit Trianon, for the sculptors from his atelier were responsible for the Corinthian capitals of the façades and modillions of the entablature. Especially well adapted is the lovely interior staircase with its fine iron balustrade showing the monogram of Louis XV and fleur-de-lis. It was achieved by Louis Gamain, the artist in wrought iron who also worked in this medium for Louis XVI.

This enchanting retreat seems to have grown directly out of the gardens, and it became again the Realm of Flora, for the garden theme was carried throughout. The overdoor paintings were adorned with a profusion of flowers, and the panelling of the salon is of an exquisite and restrained beauty. Here lilies are encircled with a wreath of

Façade of the Petit Trianon giving on to the Pavillon Français.
Although built for Louis XV and Madame de Pompadour, she died in 1764, the year it was finished, although the King briefly enjoyed it with Madame Du Barry. The Petit Trianon is regarded as the first manifestation of the new type of building that conformed to the ideal of the 1750s – a classical temple or pavilion set in an open landscape. This would be fully realised when it was acquired by Marie-Antoinette upon her accession, and Richard Mique built a landscape garden for her in 1778

Boiseries of the Petit Trianon.
Louis XV intended that the interiors of the Petit Trianon reflect his interest in botany and its garden setting. This panel shows the royal fleur-de-lis surrounded by laurel leaves, surmounted by a crown of roses. The carving is exceptionally fine, much of it executed by Honoré Guibert, who carved the frames for paintings by his brother-in-law Joseph Vernet

laurel leaves, and crowned by a garland of roses in full relief.

The dining room paintings represented allegories of Fishing, Hunting, the Grain Harvest and the Grape Harvest.[9] Four overdoor paintings in the salon, by Lepicié and Jollain, depicted Adonis and Anemone, Narcissus, Clytie as a sunflower, and Hyacinth changed into the flower that bears his name. On the ground floor was installed the King's valuable botanical library.

The Petit Trianon already represents the neo-classicism that would be a hallmark of Louis XVI's reign, and greatly extended its influence. Even before the principles of the new style were so liberally and rigorously applied by Claude-Nicolas Ledoux and Etiènne Boullée, Jacques-Ange Gabriel simplified a volume by reducing it to its barest essentials. But in spite of its compact composure, solid equilibrium, grandeur and monumental simplicity, the Petit Trianon retains a lightness and grace that is purely *dix-huitième*. It became famous throughout Europe, so that the word *trianon* became synonymous with a garden building of special distinction. As such, it became the foundation document for almost all the pavilions that graced princely gardens throughout Europe, including Ludwig II's Bavarian interpretation of it at Linderhof in 1878.

Madame de Pompadour died in April 1764, so she never enjoyed the marvellous garden house she had helped to plan. In April 1774, while he was relaxing at Trianon with his last favourite, the Comtesse Du Barry, Louis fell fatally ill with smallpox. His doctor, who considered it unseemly that a King of France expire in a pavilion, insisted that he leave for Versailles, so he was hustled into a carriage, shivering with fever, and carried back to the great château. Madame Du Barry was sent away, the King sincerely repented, asked the forgiveness of God and of his people, and on 10 May, 1774 Louis le Bien-Aimé was gathered to his fathers.

After Louis' death, the Petit Trianon was presented by his grandson, Louis XVI, to Marie-Antoinette upon their accension to the throne. The young Queen would extend and modify its gardens even more extensively, and commission other ravishing pavilions in the style that Gabriel had initiated in his work for the Bien-Aimé. For it is with the name of Marie-Antoinette, and the final, halcyon days of the *ancien régime,* that the name of the Petit Trianon is inextricably and forever associated.

CHAPTER 9

THE PAVILIONS OF
THE MARQUISE DE POMPADOUR

Of all the wealthy French women of her time, Madame de Pompadour owned the largest number of properties, about thirty in all. Her country houses, invariably surrounded with woodlands, extended the hunting grounds of the peripatetic King, and allowed him to escape the invariable routine of Versailles, Fontainebleau, and Compiègne. Some of her residences were sizeable châteaux like Crécy and the glorious Bellevue, but others were no more than large pavilions in the form then known as *hermitages* – to which she added dependencies like theatres, dairies, and conservatories. It was these that seemed to give her the greatest pleasure, for she was inordinately fond of gardens, having assisted in the restoration of the Trianon gardens, and she is credited with winning the King over 'to her taste for flowers, fresh fruits, and exotic produce'.[1]

A more compelling reason for her delight in the country was a desire to flee the 'terrible life' that she lead at court (she died at forty-two), where she acted as the King's indispensable hostess. The demands made upon her were relentless – presiding over all the entertainments, rehearsals and performances twice a week, as well as the constant travelling with the traditional progressions of the court. Even though she was granted spacious, beautifully decorated apartments at Versailles and Fontainebleau, and could have all the room she needed when Gabriel began to remodel Compiègne in 1751, she deliberately chose to receive the King in her own little houses where tiresome court etiquette was not allowed to penetrate.

All her *hermitages* featured Dutch cows, aviaries and hen houses, and this artfully edited version of the country life appealed to the King's retiring nature. The Prince de Croÿ observed them together early in 1751 at the château of Choisy: 'Le roi en paraissait plus charmé que jamais, et elle se conduisait auprès de lui avec beaucoup d'art, d'attention, et de respect'.[2]

With Louis XV's stamp of approval, the taste for such retreats (*pavillons de repos*) became firmly established, and from this time onward the concept of a rustic house or cottage gained currency among the culturally enlightened who would incorporate them into their *fermes parées*. A pavilion of this type, large enough to be lived in, but not as big as a château, evoked rural delights and participated in the ineffable joys of a garden.

Choisy

When the King bought the château of Choisy in September 1739, there was a small pavilion at the corner of the garden near the river, which he liked to use as a hunting lodge. The garden was enlarged in 1743, and in 1745 he asked Gabriel to add a

Papillon de la Ferté, the 'petit château' of Choisy.
This view of Madame de Pompadour's pavilion is by de la Ferté, the cultivated Director of the Menus-Plaisirs, whose own garden was well known. The Italianate pavilion put up by Gabriel for the Marquise de Pompadour between 1754 and 1756 was removed from the château itself, but linked by the narrow Gallery of the Baths. Choisy was one of Louis XV's favourite châteaux, and in the autumn of 1750 he had a new road built from Versailles to Choisy for easier access. The following January the Marquise came with the King to the château of Choisy, surrounded by all the royal family, whose confidence she had gained during her five years at court

Ménagerie. Jean-Antoinette commissioned the royal architect to put up a small house for herself close by in 1754-6 which was nothing more than a one-storey pavilion in the form of an Italian villa opened upon the garden. Its projecting frontispiece, supported by coupled columns, is surmounted by a triangular pediment, with a balustrade along the skyline.

The engraving made by Papillon de La Ferté, Director of the Menus-Plaisirs, shows the traditional Le Nôtre garden with *broderies* traced at either side, while in the narrow bands flowers are allowed to grow naturally. The interior perpetuated themes of flora and fauna, for the bays were appropriately sculpted by Guillaume II Coustou with garlands of fruits and flowers. There were animal paintings by Oudry and Desportes, groups of birds by Bachelier, and a superb Savonnerie firescreen with parakeets on a mauve ground, owls and monkeys on pale blue. Even the marquetry of the tables was enhanced with flowers and birds.

For the dining room of the Marquise's pavilion at Choisy, a mechanical table was devised by Guérin, similar to the one Louis had seen at his father-in-law's château of Lunéville in 1744. At the sound of a bell, the *table volante* rose from the kitchen, accompanied by four smaller ones, with the meal already laid out.

Versailles

Madame de Pompadour's one-storey hermitage at Versailles situated in the park seems to have been finished by 1749, and consisted of only five rooms, three on the courtyard, two on the garden; its hangings were of cotton, its furniture of painted wood: 'I spend the better half of my life in my hermitage', she wrote to her friend Madame de Lutzelbourg.[3] Here the King came to visit her after the hunt, and to admire the lilacs, oleanders, myrtle, olives and roses that chimed perfectly with the bucolic character of the place. In spite of its rusticity, the King's gardener, Richard, planted a *jardin français,* the centrepiece of which was the octagonal antique bath of Ronce marble from Louis XIV's magnificent Appartement des Bains at Versailles (now in the Orangerie).

Fontainebleau

Lassurance seems to have had a hand in the first design of the extant Fontainebleau Hermitage de Madame de Pompadour, as it is usually called. In 1749 the King accepted Gabriel's proposal for an absolutely square pavilion, surmounted on each façade with curvilinear pediments evoking the Four Seasons, vases of flowers on the balustrade to soften the transition between leaves and stone, and with nothing rustic about it.

The Hermitage was deliberately placed outside the grounds of the royal château, and was not intended for long stays, although bedrooms were provided on the first floor. As often happened with the King's commissions, an addition was ordered, and six years later Gabriel extended it at either side. At the left of the entry is a low building covered with *treillage* intended for a dining room (p.131), balanced on the other side with an identical one in the form of an open-air salon (*salon de verdure*).

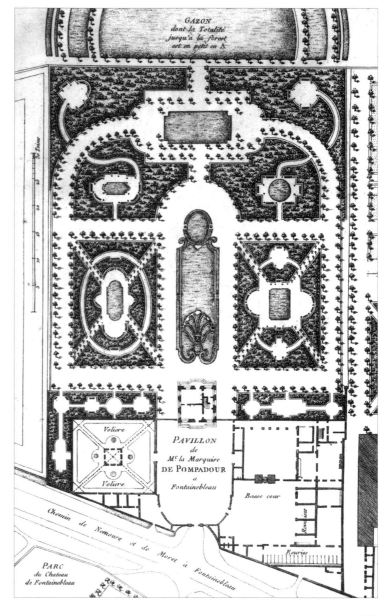

Plan of Hermitage and garden at Fontainebleau.
The first project for the Hermitage was given by Lassurance, and this is his idea for a rectangular pavilion entre cour et jardin. *The principal axis runs through the entrance court, pavilion, formal parterres, rectangular sheet of water and semi-circle of lawn with forests beyond. The central parterre of broderies was designed by Garnier d'Isle, with a basin of water at each extremity and at each side bosquets featuring straight paths radiating from central basins. The aviary for the Marquise's beloved birds is on the left of the entrance courtyard*

The Hermitage of Fontainebleau (above and opposite).
Since her teens, Madame de Pompadour had been initiated into the arts of architecture and gardening.
Louis gave her the Hermitage in January 1754, but in December 1754 Gabriel began to enlarge it with
the dining wing to the left of the entrance court (opposite), balanced by an addition, on the right of the
entrance court, both covered with treillage *to emphasise the bucolic character of the place. The Marquise*
kept the pavilion all her life

In 1749 Gabriel installed a Laiterie at the Fontainebleau Hermitage in the Cour des Belles Poules, and another at the Marquise's château of Crécy in 1752 at one of the extremities of the park. It was either circular or octagonal, and decorated with four stone statues designed by François Boucher of young women engaged in rustic occupations, and executed by the sculptors Coustou, Allegrain, Falconet and Vassé. Although the original statues have disappeared, they were copied for small table statuettes at Sèvres, a type that would be especially favoured by Louis XVI.

Except for the *porte-cochère*, the masonry of the Hermitage was finished by 15 May, 1750, although the King did not give it to the Marquise until January 1754.[4] With its *boiseries* sculpted by the renowned Verberckt, its paintings and appointments chosen by Pompadour's discriminating eye, it was one of the most delightful retreats of its time, as it is still is today. A synthesis of formality and intimacy, 'freighted with class', the Fontainebleau Hermitage, which precedes the Petit Trianon, already announces the antique style that will shortly prevail.

Compiègne

Although Gabriel planned a large apartment for her use when he began reconstructing Compiègne in 1751, the King's favourite engaged the architect in 1754 to build a hermitage for her there which was almost identical to the one at Fontainebleau. Its size was between the Fontainebleau Hermitage and the Pavillon Français at Trianon, although it contained only a *rez-de-chaussée*.

A significant feature of the Compiègne Hermitage was an important pavilion which

was not treated as a dependency at all, but as an autonomous architectural entity. This was the Dairy (*Laiterie parée*) with its own entrance courtyard and garden. It contained a *salon frais* with stone floor (no doubt with water running through it, hence the name), and the ceiling was probably vaulted. Like those at Fontainebleau and Crécy, it had nothing whatever to do with the utilitarian structure we think of a dairy, but was purely for amusement.

These immaculate dairies were 'for the diversion of the aristocracy', as the century's finest teacher of architecture, J.-F. Blondel, tells us:

> One may now count on there being among the dependences of our beautiful pleasure houses . . . dairies . . . where women come to take milk, beat butter, make cheese, abandoning themselves to all sorts of country distractions.[5]

These dairies, which became so popular from the middle of the eighteenth century onwards we have already seen as features of princely châteaux from Versailles to Chantilly during the days of the Sun King.

Bellevue

None of Madame de Pompadour's properties so completely epitomised her delightful personality and refined taste as her favourite château of Bellevue, which Nancy Mitford called the 'finest flower, inside and out, of eighteenth-century domestic architecture'.[6] In 1750 the Marquise turned to her own architect, Lassurance, for the designs of this legendary country house that dominated a large terrain above the Seine between Sèvres and Meudon, and was approached, unusually, through a garden.

The large vestibule was presided over by Falconet's statue of 'Music' and Lambert-Sigisbert Adam's 'Poetry', a fitting tribute to the Marquise's promotion of the arts. In the gallery, Boucher's paintings were linked with garlands carved by Verberckt. Lampas, especially woven for the rooms at Bellevue, was used for hangings and to cover the furniture. It perfectly complemented the exquisite ormolu furnishing, bronzes, the Sèvres porcelain services for the dining table and *garnitures* for consoles and mantelpieces.

In the gardens were numerous statues, among them Pigalle's 'Louis XV' and Guillaume II Coustou's 'Apollo.' It was at Bellevue that Madame de Pompadour indulged in the ultimate extravagance, according to the Duc de Richelieu's well-known anecdote. On a cold, dreary winter day she invited the King to the château, where he discovered that the parterres were filled with scented flowers of Vincennes porcelain. The pastilles lighted in the perfume-burners wafted the fragrance of carnations and roses through the air. 'To affect the quality of the day, that is the highest art', Thoreau observed.

At Bellevue, the Marquise gratified her passion for the theatre. In the gardens was installed an exotic pavilion in the Chinese taste, with lacquered wall panels by Charles-André Tremblin, a decorator of carriages and festival architecture. Numerous performances were given there of works by Quinault, Dancourt and Rousseau, and by an intricate mechanical system, the size could be reduced or augmented as needed.

Also at Bellevue, on a terrace overlooking the Seine at the base of the future domain of the Marquise's château, stood a simple but dignified Regency pavilion with mansard roof called Brimborion. Madame de Pompadour was especially fond of it and purchased it in 1750, adding it to the Bellevue estate, and naming it affectionately Babiole. It appears in the cartouche of a plan of Bellevue, at the centre of the terrace dominating the Seine. In the background may be seen the Bois de Boulogne and Montmartre across the river.

Brimborion played a role in one of the few unsuccessful fêtes that Madame de Pompadour ever gave – the inauguration of Bellevue in November 1745. As usual, she had gone to endless trouble over the details, even providing costumes for the guests who were to have them embroidered as they wished. But the weather was damp and raw, with a high wind which worsened as evening approached and caused the fires to smoke. So all of the carefully prepared food had to be transported to the pavilion of Brimborion. The firework display in the garden that Madame de Pompadour had planned as a climax to the evening's entertainment had to be abandoned when a courier from Paris brought news that an unfriendly crowd had assembled across the river on the plain of Grenelle.

But Brimborion was more than the setting for one of Pompadour's parties, for during the summer and fall of 1755 the small house under the terrace of Bellevue – from which Paris could be seen far away below – was the scene of secret diplomatic meetings that were of utmost consequence for the future of France. Not only would the next seven years of French history be affected by what went on there, but the talks would also seal the fate of a child who would be born on 2 November of that year to the Empress Maria Theresa of Austria. The Empress was urging her ambassador to France, the Prince of Stahrenberg, to try through Louis XV's powerful mistress to persuade the King to an alliance with Austria.

So Madame de Pompadour met day after day at Brimborion with Stahrenberg, and when she finally gave place to Cardinal de Bernis as the French representative, the negotiations were all but concluded. By the end of February 1756, it was clear that Frederick I of Prussia had determined upon war (the Seven Years' War), and Louis XV had no choice but to accept the plan of Maria Theresa, for he needed an Austrian ally. By 1 May the signatures were affixed to the document – when Marie-Antoinette was only six months old. It was implicitly understood that the alliance was to be cemented by the marriage of the Austrian archduchess to the heir to the French throne. The clandestine negotiations at Brimborion meant that Marie-Antoinette became the living pledge of the Austrian alliance, a pledge fulfilled in 1770, when she was brought to France as the new Dauphine.

The most extraordinary feature of the Bellevue gardens was the unusual bosquet composed of trelliswork pavilions with fountains and water jets. The Bosquet du Baldaquin represented a real *tour de force* of the art of *treillage* and was realised by the ingenious Langelin, who executed both the Salon Frais for the King's botanical garden at Versailles and the trellis pavilions for the Versailles terraces. Its name derived from the central canopy (or baldaquin) of gilt-lead supported by four palm trees, and with a

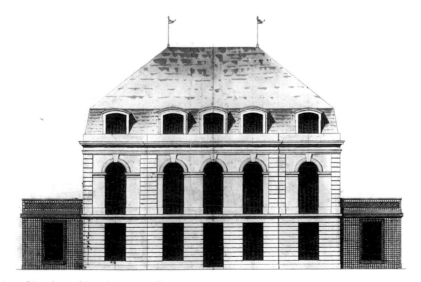

Elevation of Pavilion of Brimborion, Bellevue.
The château that best reflected the personality of Madame de Pompadour was Bellevue. It occupied a site chosen by the King on the summit of a hill in the Seine valley near Meudon, with a marvellous panorama of the river. In 1750 Lassurance and Garnier d'Isle completed the château with its two gardens, one dominating the château on the court side, the other extending from the façade to the Seine. The small Regency pavilion of Brimborion standing at the foot of the future garden on the Seine may well have influenced the conception of the château itself, for it had a mansard roof, the façade articulated with nine openings, conceivably a response to Brimborion's five apertures, rectangular below and segmental above

Treillage at Bellevue – the Bosquet du Baldaquin.
Among the wonders of Bellevue's gardens was this extraordinary bosquet of treillage, *the Bosquet du Baldaquin, referring to the central canopy of gilt-lead crowned with quivers of arrows, supported by palm columns. Beyond it is a berceau of* treillage *with a fountain in the niche flanked by two trelliswork pavilions used for summer meals. The concept of a Rococo trelliswork bosquet on several levels, with* treillage *worked in classical orders, enlivened by water jets that tumbled into pools on the lowest level, is typical of the sophisticated designs carried out for the Marquise de Pompadour at Bellevue*

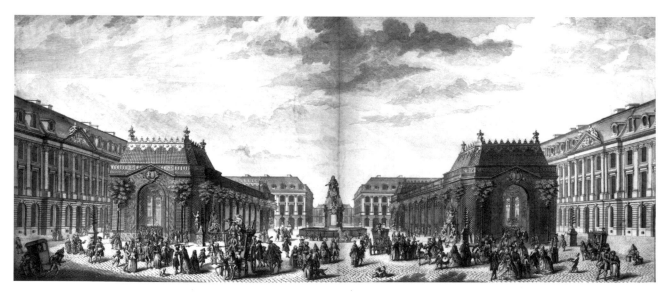

Perspective View of Place Louis le Grand.
The first marriage of Louis XV's son, the Dauphin, was celebrated with four days of fêtes in Paris, from 23 to 26 February, 1745. The great squares of the capital were decorated at enormous expense to accommodate the buffets, wine service and dance halls for the populace. The twin Rococo pavilions of treillage *with long colonnades on the Place Louis le Grand (today Place Vendôme) flanked the Sun King's statue. To further suggest a garden setting, trees were brought in and fountains with statuary were set against the piers*

Interior of the Bal de Bois.
Since the festivities for the Dauphin's marriage took place during the coldest days of winter, the trelliswork
walls of the ballroom were probably lined with heavy canvas. Numerous wall lights, each holding ten candles,
were suspended from ribbons, and the canvas ceiling was painted to simulate a blue sky with floating clouds.
The people of Paris ate and drank at the buffets, left and right, which are painted in faux bois

curving balustrade. This was flanked by *treillage* pavilions with broken pediments; on axis with the canopied feature at the centre was a curving gallery with a fountain in a niche.

The predilection for trellis pavilions continued throughout the eighteenth century, and became a speciality for designers who worked in the idiom of the Rococo, with sinuous curves, sweeping palm tree supports, and foliate volutes.

One of the memorable examples was the décor that had been created for the festivities in Paris during February 1745 to celebrate the marriage of the Dauphin. In the form of large halls with vestibules at each end, twin *treillage* pavilions were erected as ballrooms for the populace in the Place Louis le Grand (today Place Vendôme) by the Prévôt des Marchands and Echevins, and fortunately an anonymous engraver has left a record of their appearance (opposite). The vestibule of the Bal du Bois, as one of the halls was called, contained buffets painted in imitation marble, their shelves groaning with delicacies. Beyond was the ballroom with musicians in tiers at either side, a sky of painted canvas, real trees and living foliage growing from the 'ground', and clusters of lighted candles attached to the trellised walls. Although it was taken down after only two days, festival architecture was the eighteenth century's way of 'paying tribute to the divinity of the moment', to borrow Lady Dilke's phrase.

At Madame de Pompadour's death, her houses reverted to the King, although Ménars on the Loire went to her brother. Bellevue was wantonly destroyed, along with the historic pavilion of Brimborion, and her fine Hôtel d'Evreux became the Elysée Palace. None of the smaller pavilions on her country estates remain. The hermitage at Versailles is no longer recognisable, but the Fontainebleau Hermitage is still there behind the portal on the Avenue de Nemours, although the once-glorious formal gardens have long since disappeared.

J.-A. Chauvet, Richelieu's Pavillon de l'Aurore at Gennevilliers.
Richelieu acquired the property of Gennevilliers in 1749 and the pavilion probably dates from 1752 when he engaged the architect Servandoni to redesign both the château and the park. Chauvet (born 1826) recorded Richelieu's rotunda and ice house (glacière) in 1896 before it fell completely into ruin. The rotunda surmounting the ice house was used as a place for refreshment during the hunt, and during hot weather the Duke sometimes used the ice house (which probably included a decorated salon) for serving meals

CHAPTER 10

THE DUC DE RICHELIEU AND THE PAVILION OF HANOVER

Among the subversive influences at court, Armand-Jules II de Vignerot, Duc de Richelieu, was the most consistent and the most durable, living proof that the good do die young. He had been presented to the Sun King's court when he was only fifteen, and Saint-Simon recorded that he was so delightful that he became its idol, even adopted by the scrupulous Madame de Maintenon.

At the Court of Louis XV, Richelieu was positively scintillating, the nobility regarded him as a model, and he served the King at his *levers* and *couchers* for forty-four years. 'Charming, handsome, brave, wicked and corrupt, a traitor in his soul, one of those to whom all is permitted and all forgiven',[1] he was sent to the Bastille at least three times,

Armand-Jules II de Vigneron du Plessis, Duc de Richelieu (1696-1788).
Although Richelieu had been a star of Louis XIV's court, spoiled by everyone from the King and the Duchesse de Bourgogne downward, Liselotte – wife of Monsieur – detested him. When he was appointed ambassador to Austria, Richelieu's entry into Vienna on 7 November, 1725 – with running footmen, and silver shoes on his horses – was so sumptuous that he set a precedent the Duc de Choiseul followed later when he entered Rome. All his residences and garden pavilions exhibited his superb taste, but his influence on Louis XV was anything but salutary

but always turned up again in the King's entourage as if he had been away on holiday.

This Alcibiades of the age even flourished under Louis XVI (dying a year before the Revolution), and it was acknowledged that 'he survived every change of fashion'. Although thoroughly disreputable, Richelieu seems at least to have respected religion, which was more than could be said for Louis XV's minister, the Duc de Choiseul, or for either of Louis XVI's brothers, although d'Artois reformed later in life.

Richelieu is most often encountered in the archives busying himself in the matter of the King's mistresses, and is said to have been responsible for bringing to court from the Paris underworld that 'bacchante crowned with ivy and roses' – as George Greive, her avowed enemy, called Madame Du Barry. A combination of evil and erudition typical of the century, the Marshal-Duke's senile concupiscence was undiminished in his late eighties. One of his more ingenious devices was a hinged chimney-piece communicating from his Paris hotel to the adjoining house of a female acquaintance, and even Madame Geoffrin – who was not easily shocked – described him as 'l'épluchure des grands vices' (refuse of the great vices.)

Richelieu was a fixture in the most fashionable salons of Paris and cut a dazzling figure in the capital, but he was just as impressive on the battlefield. He was with Louis at the moment of the monarch's greatest popularity – the Battle of Fontenoy on 11 May, 1745. Richelieu was in fact one of the heroes of the day, for when the French had only four guns left and all seemed lost, Richelieu – with the Duc de Biron and the Marquis d'Estrées – boldly took the King's bodyguard into action. This courageous stroke succeeded brilliantly, for the Duke of Cumberland gave way and retreated from the field.

Invariably the Duc de Richelieu was included in Louis XV's intimate suppers in the private apartments at Versailles. We find him with the King and the Marquise at a small house party at Choisy, and he accompanied Louis to Madame de Pompadour's pavilion at La Celle Saint Cloud. He never failed to amuse the King, and was among the few who were with Louis when he died.

Great-nephew of the illustrious connoisseur Cardinal Richelieu, the Duke became a renowned collector himself. Besides numerous princely residences filled with some of the finest objects of the *ancien régime*, and the marvellous town house where his famous chef, Clouet, presided as *maître d'hôtel,* Richelieu inherited perhaps the largest French collection of paintings by Nicolas Poussin, rivalling that which had been formed by the master's friend in Rome, Cassiano dal Pozzo.

This incorrigible pacesetter for royal and fashionable society was naturally a connoisseur of architecture, and a notable builder of *folies* designed by the best architects. One of them was decorated with wallpaper from China – an expensive rarity at the time – with the adjoining bath tiled in Dutch faïence. His fondness for oriental motifs was reflected in a lacquered room for his Hôtel d'Antin, and in an unusual lacquered Chinese study (*cabinet de la Chine*), sections of which are conserved in the Musée Carnavalet in Paris. It was installed in the old family town house on the Place des Vosges which Richelieu inherited from his father, whose extraordinary Rubens collection is today in the Pinakothek, Munich.

Another of the Duke's pavilions contained Michelangelo's so-called 'Slaves', and four enormous vases made from porphyry columns brought from Italy. Still another

Pavilion of Hanover in the Park at Sceaux.
In 1933 the wing of Richelieu's Hôtel d'Antin, known as the Pavilion of Hanover, was moved to the grounds of the château of Sceaux. Having been wrenched from its architectural context of the Hôtel d'Antin and the Boulevard des Italiens, the pavilion is today a forlorn morceau d'architecture

of his garden houses was panelled with *boiseries* depicting 'The Mythology of Love'; the Marquis d'Argenson described an evening party there in 1740, when the host conducted the aged Duchesse de Brancas (a lady-in-waiting to the Dauphine) around by candlelight, explaining the allegories to her.

Along with his King and most of the French aristocracy, Richelieu discovered the joys of the country, but it was not so much Nature they sought as 'the *idea* of Nature, a fiction that would enable [them] to escape from everyday life.[2] So in 1749 the Marshal-Duke acquired a large property at Gennevilliers, where he enlarged the gardens and embellished them with a variety of architectural hideaways.

Among them was the theatrical Pavillon de l'Aurore, represented in the watercolour by Chauvet (p.136) as a round pavilion posed upon a *glacière* or ice house. Every important property of the *ancien régime* owned an ice house, and Madame de Pompadour's at Crécy is still intact. A *glacière* was an excavated subterranean room usually located in densely wooded areas so as to be sheltered from the sun. Here ice, cut into squares and insulated with earth and straw, was stored to be used for dining. The existence of these eighteenth-century refrigerators was reflected in the arts of the table, with the addition of wine coolers and ice cream cups to elegant Sèvres table services.

Richelieu's pavilion at Gennevilliers was constructed by that born stage designer, the architect G.-N. Servandoni.[3] It probably dated from 1752, when the Duke engaged the architect to redesign both the château and park. The pavilion was in circular form with a peristyle of twelve columns, surmounted by a statue of Mercury, although Eros would have been far more appropriate. Beneath it was a grotto containing the ice house, which must have included a decorated salon, for it was here that the Duke served lunch to the King and Madame de Pompadour on a hot summer day. The property later passed to the Duc de Choiseul, and in 1783 the first performance of the inflammatory *Mariage de Figaro* was presented there.

During the Seven Years' War, Richelieu greatly augmented the already considerable family fortune. It has usually been claimed that the proceeds of his treachery in the ruthless sack of Hanover enabled him to buy the beautiful Hôtel d'Antin in Paris in 1756. Around 1757-60 he engaged the architect Jean-Michel Chevotet (1698-1772), who had worked at the Hôtel de Croÿ and on various *folies*, to transform the Hôtel d'Antin, adding a wing that terminated in a pavilion with a view over the fields. Known as the Pavillon d'Hanovre, its style is *retardataire* for its date, retaining the rhythmical sequences of the Baroque with its undulating walls, a balcony embellished with wrought-iron supported by ornate consoles, and doors with segmental heads crowned by smiling faces that look back to the Regency.

The interiors were apparently painted by Gaetano Brunetti and his son, who had worked in *trompe-l'oeil* in England, and applied their talents to the residences of people who moved in the King's circle. They executed Madame de Pompadour's splendid staircase in the Italian manner at Bellevue, painting it with *trompe-l'oeil* mythological figures and architectural elements. In Paris, they were employed by Louis' close friend, the Prince de Soubise, at his superb hôtel in the Marais, and by the Queen's intimate companion, the Duc de Luynes, for his town house which – although destroyed – is perpetuated in the Brunetti murals from the Hôtel de Luynes in the Musée Carnavalet. For the Duc de Richelieu's Paris house in the Rue Neuve Saint-Augustin, the Brunettis painted an illusionistic staircase, with Corinthian columns and a ceiling with Fame holding a trumpet and distributing laurels.

The Pavilion of Hanover created a seductive setting for the amorous adventures of the Duc de Richelieu, who bore for the appointed time the appropriate title of First Gentleman of the King's Bedchamber. Soon the courts of Europe were talking about his garden house with its superb furnishings, in which the architect Chevotet collaborated with the owner.

Horace Walpole was as curious as everyone else to see the celebrated *folie* that Voltaire called 'the fairies' pavilion', and on his next trip to Paris he succeeded. 'I have seen it!' he wrote. 'There is a chamber surrounded with looking glasses and hung with white lutestring,[4] painted with roses. I wish you could see the antiquated Rinaldo who has built himself this romantic bower. Looking glass never reflected so many wrinkles.'

Its furnishings would have been as interesting as its architecture, although we have no

Jean-Michel Chevotet, Pavilion of Hanover.
Chevotet was a member of the Society of Arts and Sciences, a personal friend of the Duke, and a highly favoured architect in Richelieu's affluent circle. He was also known as a garden designer, working with such distinguished patrons as the Duc de Croÿ. According to the usual practice, Chevotet no doubt provided a folio of drawings, including the arrangement of the furniture. The Marshal-Duke was accused of pillaging Hanover to pay for his unrestrained building projects, hence the name of the pavilion

Debret, Boulevard des Italiens and the Pavilion of Hanover.
The essence of the Boulevard des Italiens, which grew up around the Pavilion of Hanover in the nineteenth century, is captured here with strollers and horse-drawn carriages in the shop-lined streets

inventory. But there must have been exotic items, for Richelieu patronised that purveyor of desirable objects, the *marchand mercier* Lazare Duvaux, who delivered to him 'a chest in old pagoda lacquer, ornamented in bronze gilded with ormolu, and an Italian griotte marble top.'[5] Richelieu's taste was renowned throughout Europe, for in 1765 a correspondent of Horace Walpole sent him news of the refurbishing of the Pitti Palace: 'They are now furnishing all that part . . . painted by Pietro da Cortona . . . Marshal Botta has got models of chairs from France, one of the Duke of Richelieu's, the frame of which cost 700 livres.'[6]

After the Duke's death, the Hôtel d'Antin was destroyed – that is, all but the wing still known as the Pavillon d'Hanovre, and we must think of it as it looked when it stood on the corner of the Boulevard des Italiens and the Rue Louis le Grand. For a while it served as the Café Velloni, and Artur Rubinstein remembered it as the seat of Gabriel Astruc's Société Musicale, an agency to promote the performing arts

The Duke would have been gratified to know that his graceful pavilion survived to participate in the bustling life of the boulevards, which were still focal points of Paris artistic and social life in the early 1900s. At that time it consisted of a large reception room, with three wide windows affording a wide panorama of the view that was often painted by Pissarro. In 1933 it was removed to the park of the Duc du Maine's old château of Sceaux,[7] where it stands today in isolated splendour (p.139).

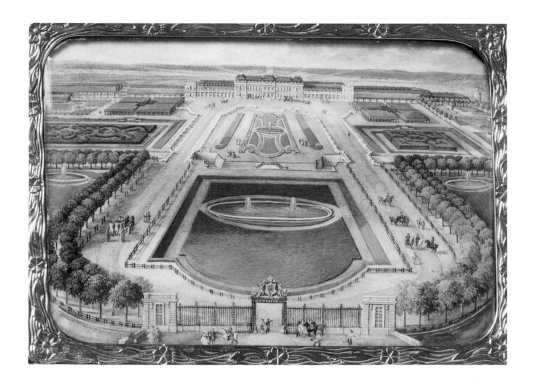

CHAPTER 11

THE DUC DE CHOISEUL AND CHANTELOUP

It has already been seen that many of Louis XV's closest friends figured prominently in the military, and the camaderie of the battlefield was perpetuated within the King's private circle. Among them were the ubiquitous Duc de Richelieu; the Maréchal de Saxe, whose many victories in the early spring of 1745 paved the way for the exhilarating success of French arms at the battle of Fontenoy; the Maréchal-Prince de Soubise, who bore one of the oldest and most honoured names in France, but was disgraced at the battle of Rosbach in 1757; and the Comte de Noaïlles, the governor of Versailles who became a marshal in 1766.

Another military figure and intimate of the King's circle (and rival of the Prince de Soubise) was Etienne-François de Choiseul, Comte de Stainville, Duc de Choiseul (1719-1785). He and the Duchess dined with Louis and Madame de Pomadour three times a week, and Louis felt at home with this aristocratic man. Choiseul and his father were both Chevaliers of the Golden Fleece, the only known instance of a father and son

Louis-Nicolas van Blarenberghe. One (of six) paintings in gouache of the château of Chanteloup on a gold box.
The Choiseul's château of Chanteloup was reputed to be one of the most complete and magnificent estates in Europe. Like an elegant town with a square before it, the grounds stretched out on all sides to the horizon. The château was ironically destroyed by the grandfather of the famous dandy of Proust's circle, Robert de Montesquiou. At the Prefecture of Tours is the beautiful entrance grille of fer forgé with the Choiseul coat-of-arms, through which guests passed

Etiènne-François, Duc de Choiseul.
Until his disgrace, the Duc de Choiseul was an immutable fixture of the King's inner circle, his most energetic and effective minister, and in Chatham's view the greatest minister since Richelieu. His advancement at court is attributed to Madame de Pompadour and, like her, he was one of the real taste-makers of the reign

receiving this coveted honour in the eighteenth century, except for the royal family.

Furthermore, Choiseul's wife was a member of the Crozat family, whom Louis had known from childhood. Although he had been a young boy at the time, Louis would have remembered that Pierre Crozat, as the Regent's agent, had bought most of his spectacular art collection for him. Pierre's brother, Antoine Crozat, was one of the richest men in Paris, lived in the first house constructed on the Place Louis le Grand (today the Place Vendôme), and founded Louisiana. Antoine Crozat's granddaughter,[1] Louise-Honorine, became the wife of the Duc de Choiseul in 1750 and remained devoted to him all her life, despite his many infidelities.

The Duke served Louis XV for twelve years with conspicuous distinction as his ablest minister. A key figure of the age of Louis XV, Choiseul operated at the centre of a web that stretched out to almost every significant figure in Europe. He was a man of such diversified talents that he was regarded as 'one of the most extraordinary phenomena of the century'.[2] Saltau went even further, describing Choiseul as 'one of the most interesting figures of the eighteenth century . . . and [embodying] most of the qualities and vices of the time . . . He was not only the man, but also the minister of the century.'[3]

Choiseul owed his advancement at court to Madame de Pompadour, but the King appreciated the military distinction Choiseul had achieved as a cavalry leader until the peace of Aix in 1748, and his subsequent service as marèchal-de-camp under the Prince de Soubise. His letters to the military from Vienna in 1757 show Choiseul to have been an expert in strategy and tactics as well as diplomacy, so the following year he succeeded Cardinal Bernis (whom Louis never liked) as Foreign Minister. It was a position that included the direction of the army and navy, and it presented the new minister with an opportunity to bring about sorely needed reforms.[4]

Some of them would have far-reaching consequences for future French military campaigns. For one thing, Choiseul understood that a new kind of warfare was being adopted in Europe, and he brought to France in 1765 the first artillerist of Europe, Vaquette de Gribeauval, whose lighter cannon were easily adaptable to the type of battle that would be fought during the Revolution and First Empire.

Besides his consummate knowledge of military affairs, Choiseul was among the most skilled diplomats of Europe. In 1754 he was appointed Ambassador to Rome, and sent back delightful objects to his friend, Madame de Pompadour. In April 1756 he made his famous entry into the Eternal City with the spectacular entourage recorded by Panini, for Choiseul was renowned for his prodigality in an age when luxury abounded.

Three years later Ambassador Choiseul was sent to Vienna, where he became an architect of the Austrian alliance in 1757, which signified that France was no longer at the mercy of Frederick the Great.[5] The French alliance with Maria-Theresa also meant that her daughter, Marie-Antoinette, would come to France as Dauphine. Although she and Choiseul were worlds apart in spiritual matters, Marie-Antoinette was alway grateful to Choiseul and remained his staunch supporter.

Another facet of this extraordinary man's personality was his expertise in the world of banking. He named as banker to the court his friend, Jean-Joseph de Laborde, making him the principal commercial functionary of the realm. The honourable Laborde, a partisan of the alliance with the Viennese court and member of the powerful *choiseuliste* party, was the owner of France's most extensive landscape garden at Méréville. Many of its pavilions were designed by the painter Hubert Robert, who accompanied Choiseul to Rome, and whose career was launched and enormously abetted by his generous patron.

There was yet another realm in which Choiseul shone, that of enlightened protector of the arts and true connoisseur. It was a role he was able to assume largely because of his wife's fortune and her own proclivities. In Rome, she and the Abbé Barthélémy would visit the museums, monuments, exhibitions, and attend courses on the ancient world taught by the Abbé Venutta. One of the Duchess' visitors wrote years later that 1756 was the happiest year of his life, for he was able to live at the very fountain-head of the *beaux-arts*, as he described the Choiseuls' Roman establishment.

The same was true of the Choiseul house in Paris, for Louise-Honorine had inherited from her great-uncle, Pierre Crozat, the famous town house that was a cultural centre of Paris under the Regent, along with a large part of Crozat's renowned collection. To this impressive assemblage of works of art, the enterprising Choiseul – encouraged (if not guided) by the Duchess – added so extensively that he amassed one of the finest art collections in European history.

The famous hôtel became the political, literary, artistic centre of Paris. When they were not at court, the Choiseuls held a perpetual open house where as many as eighty people might stay for dinner. Madame du Deffand, a special friend of the Duchesse de Choiseul, described these evenings – along with the inadequacies of eighteenth-century heating: 'They entertain in their gallery [which] is enormous and needs seventy . . . candles to light it; the fireplace is in the middle, there's always a huge fire and stoves at each end, but in spite of that, one's frozen or else one scorches if one stands near the fire or the stoves; everywhere in between is an ice-box. There's a vast crowd . . . all the beauties, all the young girls, great lords and little ones, a big table in the middle where every kind of game is played, which they call a *maçedoine* . . . there are four backgammon boards which split one's ear-drums . . . It's only being alone that I find worse than such a jam.'[6]

Suddenly and incredibly, the day before Christmas 1770, Choiseul's fortunes were completely reversed, for he was abruptly dismissed by the King.[7] It was said that Choiseul's political enemies used Madame Du Barry to influence the King, for the minister had never concealed his dislike for her, but Maugras discounts this, since Du Barry never wanted to play a political role.[8] In any case, two years later, in straitened circumstances (for a Choiseul), the Duke had to sell his spectacular collections, and the

Louise-Honorine, Duchesse de Choiseul.
In Rome she kept open house to the most illustrious families. On the Choiseuls' return to France, the Duke and Duchess were always included in the King's private dinner parties. Neglected by her husband, the Duchess became an outstanding patron of the arts

145

sale that took place from January to June in 1772 has been called 'one of the most singular phenomena in the history of the arts.' It almost broke Choiseul's heart, for he passionately loved his paintings and had bought with a rare discernment. The dispersal of his treasures ultimately enriched the major museums of Europe, and in 1772 four hundred paintings from the Crozat-Choiseul collection arrived at the Hermitage.

As a condition of his disgrace, the King ordered his former minister to go into exile – as it was euphemistically put – at his estate near Amboise in the Loire valley. Life there was bearable, however, for the Choiseul's château of Chanteloup was reputed to be the most complete and magnificent estate for a *grand seigneur* in all of Europe, a fact that is made abundantly clear in Louis-Nicolas van Blarenberghe's miniatures depicting Chanteloup and its environs on a gold box (p.143).

The château was like an intimate, elegant town with a square before it, a long, impressive entrance for carriages, and gardens stretching out on all sides to the horizon. The minister had purchased it in 1761, and greatly enlarged it so that it contained eighty-four suites of guest rooms, for his extravagant hospitality in Paris was matched by the luxurious quarters he provided for his guests in the country. One of them, who spent the summer at Chanteloup, complained that the château was so vast that it took him twenty minutes to get through the corridors from his own suite to reach the rooms of his friend, the Abbé Barthélémy.

With all of the artistic resources of France at their fingertips, the Choiseuls might have been expected to create one of the most fascinating garden ensembles in France, and they did. As usual, the gardens in the immediate environs of the dwelling were laid out in the Le Nôtre style – elaborated with parterres, waterworks, allées and bosquets. But beginning in 1774, the Duke and Duchess laid out an irregular English garden to the west of the château.

Hubert Robert – who owed so much to the Choiseuls and remained close to them – was often at Chanteloup, and it seems almost certain that he would have been consulted for the garden as well as the pavilions. It was at just this time that the painter was helping the new Queen, Marie-Antoinette, plan her English garden at Versailles which, like the Choiseuls' garden, had to take into account a pre-existing formal scheme. Robert became adept at meeting these problems, and even as late as the Revolution, he was designing a garden described as *mi-anglais, mi-français* for Madame Houdetot, mother-in-law of the statesman Mathieu Molé, another member of the Choiseul-Laborde circle.

For those who were firmly committed to the picturesque school, there had to be a complex elaboration of pavilions, and within the Chanteloup park was scattered an interesting collection – a rural cottage, a kiosk, grottoes that could be used for parties, a shell pavilion, hermitage, windmill, and an aristocratic ice house. Although Hubert Robert's ideas for the Queen's Hameau would come somewhat later, one wonders how much the artist contributed to designs for the Choiseuls' rural cottage, hermitage, and windmill, all part of the tradition of the Queen's Hameau.

We may be certain that the Duchesse de Choiseul was directing the work, for Maugras tells us that she had 'l'amour de la truelle' (a love for the trowel). As a

Engraving of plans of the Pagoda at Chanteloup

PAGODE
QUIOSQUE
de *Chanteloup*
a *M. le Duc*
DE CHOISEUIL

5 Pieds
Cinquieme

6 Pieds
Quatrieme

9 Pieds
Troisieme

12 Pieds
Second

18 Pieds

3   6 pie

D

A

D

C

B

Plan
du
Quiosque

A

24 Pieds

Premier

36 Pieds

Plan du
Rez de chaussée
de la Pagode

147

La pagode de Chanteloup, état en 1855.

Sargent and Francais, lithograph of the Pagoda at Chanteloup in 1855.
The abandoned Pagoda stands like a lonely sentinel in the open fields that had once been Chanteloup's gardens. The Pagoda and van Blarenberghe's paintings of the château and gardens are all that remain of the patrician establishment, although the Duke's paintings are found in collections throughout the world. Nineteenth-century artists found the pagoda a singularly romantic object

knowledgable and avid gardener, she oversaw the creation of the cascades, water jets, and quincunxes. Under her supervision colonnades were added to the château, and the elaborate stables that were renowned throughout Europe. She was an excellent rider and took the horses out daily, accompanied (when he was in residence) by her nephew, the Duc de Lauzun, one of the more impetuous young nobles from the Queen's circle who accompanied the French army to America.

During the summers of 1776 and 1777 both Choiseuls were preoccupied with a new construction that faced the southern side of the château at the centre of the garden: a seven-staged Chinese obelisk or pagoda to pay homage to friends who came to visit them in their exile. Distributed on the different floors were sofas, stools, armchairs in the Chinese taste, while eight large windows lighted the first salon. Between these windows were tablets of white marble on which were engraved in gilt letters the names of friends who came to Chanteloup.

The prominent position of the Pagoda may be ascertained in some of the van Blarenberghe paintings on the gold box. A splendid cascade descends on the principal axis of the dwelling on the south side, flowing over twelve levels to fill a semi-circular basin or lake. Beyond it, the Pagoda rises as the predominant visual emphasis and focal point for all the allées converging from the park and woods. It is the only garden building that remains, and 'a classic example of pavilion-making with that dash of aggression inseparable from the search for perfection.'[9]

Based upon the Pagoda at Kew by the architect William Chambers, the Chanteloup structure is not a true pagoda because the roof does not overhang the storeys below and it is composed of dressed stone. It has usually been attributed to an obscure architect, Louis-Denis Le Camus,[10] but Hubert Robert's biographer, Jean Cayeux, believes that it was most likely by Robert himself, noting that its first floor is similar to Bramante's Tempietto as Hubert Robert sketched it in Rome in 1762.

One of its purposes was to provide a panoramic view of the spectacular gardens, and anyone who climbed to the top of the 131-foot structure was rewarded with a view of Tours cathedral. Like Louis XIV's Trianon de Porcelaine (although in different form), it was intended to evoke the memory of the Pagoda of Nanking, and provided

The Pagoda, Chanteloup, today.
The Pagoda is all that remains of the once-fabulous gardens of Chanteloup to which the Duchesse de Choiseul gave her constant attention. The interior was once embellished with furniture for the illustrious guests who made the pilgrimage to visit the Choiseuls in their exile. Choiseul had their names engraved on white marble plaques that were set into the walls

just that element of playful surprise sought for a landscape garden. The Chanteloup Pagoda is a blend of exotic architectural chinoiserie and classical details, like the peristyle of sixteen columns that encircle its *rez-de-chaussée*.

Its other purpose, as we noted, was to honour those who came to visit the Choiseuls, for the former minister had left Paris in triumph, followed by numerous *dévotés* to his court on the Loire, maintained, of course, at Choiseul's expense. It was the era of the triumphant exiles, as Maugras put it, for the Orléans and Condé princes were in disgrace, too, for taking the part of the old Parlement against the Chancellor Maupeou, and Louis XV had them packed off to their respective estates of Villers-Cotterêts and Chantilly. (It was a time when people of their class were becoming so impregnated with a taste for country life that, exiled or not, they began to leave Paris in April to pass the summer on their country estates, leaving the city deserted until autumn.)

The Choiseuls spared no expense to make life pleasant for their guests in their magnificently decorated château, for there were billiards, theatricals, elaborate dinners and garden parties in the evenings, and music by the band from Choiseul's military company. For those who were *amateurs* of horticulture like their hosts, there were rare specimens of flowers and shrubs in the park, and for the gentleman-farmers, an enormous marble stable housing pedigree Swiss cattle and prize pigs.

Braving the King's displeasure, people bearing Europe's most illustrious names beat a retreat to Chanteloup, and at the château on the Loire there occurred a curious phenomenon. As the King went out of fashion, virtually isolated in the boudoir of his last mistress, Madame Du Barry, Louis' disgraced minister and his wife became objects of love and veneration. Horace Walpole said that glorious Chanteloup was turned into an obligatory pilgrimage for *le monde*, and there were many friends from their Roman days who rallied round the Choiseuls as well.

There was the Prince de Beauvau-Craon, and the Duc de Chartres of the Orléans family. Chartres was accompanied by his hedonist companion, the thirteen-year-old Comte d'Artois (younger brother of Louis XVI), whose mentor was Chartres and whose idol was Choiseul. From the military came the Maréchal and Maréchale de Ségur, and the wives of the prominent marshals de Mirepoix and de Luxembourg.

There were Italians like the flamboyant Casanova and the Florentine Doctor Gatti, the apostle of inoculation. Among the Choiseul protégés were the Abbé Barthélémy, who found the château near Amboise the perfect place to write. This erudite Frenchman composed his *Voyage du jeune Anacharsis en Grece* largely at Chanteloup, and it was destined to become an unqualified success among the avant-garde who had become enamoured of the Greek taste. Hubert Robert was often at Chanteloup, and was always grateful to the Choiseuls for underwriting his Italian studies and for the patronage that came his way from their affluent friends.

Louis XV's death in 1774 and Marie-Antoinette's petitions to Louis XVI marked the end of the Choiseuls' exile, and they were allowed to return to Paris. The Duke went directly to the Bois de Boulogne to thank the Queen, who was staying at Louis XV's beloved old château de la Muette. The ex-minister died just in time to be spared by the Revolution, but the Duchess' sister, Madame de Gramont, was condemned to the scaffold. So was the Duchess' nephew, the dashing young Duc de Lauzun, who had ridden with his aunt at Chanteloup as a boy. The Duchesse de Choiseul died in prison in a terrible state, and on the last day of her life she was writing to Napoleon Bonaparte, asking him to intervene on her behalf.

Although the château at Amboise and its pavilions have long since disappeared, the Pagoda still stands as a sentinel by the reeded lake. And the Choiseuls' delicious garden fêtes at Chanteloup, which lent such lustre to summer life, were remembered for many years by their guests. One was the Neopolitan Ambassador, the Marquis Caraccioli, who lived on the Place Vendôme, and had come to feel that France was his home. When he was appointed Viceroy of Sicily, Louis XVI congratulated him on going to live in one of the most delightful places in Europe, but Caraccioli sadly replied that the most delightful place in Europe was the one he was leaving.

Writing later of the soirées that the exiled Choiseuls offered their guests at Chanteloup, Caraccioli recalled how the Pagoda looked on a warm summer night when the party left the château after dinner to wander through the cool, fragrant gardens. They descended past the rushing cascades to the ornamental lake, where they embarked in gay little frigates hung with lanterns, serenaded by the Duke's musicians. The Pagoda reflected in the lake was a vision, hung from top to bottom with parti-coloured lights swinging in the breeze, as the pale moon rose over the water.

CHAPTER 12

THE MARQUIS DE MARIGNY AND MENARS

At the moment when the Duc de Choiseul was reconstructing his gardens at Chanteloup, another château on the Loire – Ménars – was being embellished with *fabriques* designed by some of France's leading architects. Driving south from Paris towards Blois, one is astonished at the sight of the long, low château of creamy stone looming up from the opposite river bank. Its magnificent terraces command a view of some thirty miles along the Loire, and the gardens ramble down to the edge of the river, which is unusually wide at this point.

Ménars had belonged to Madame de Pompadour, but it passed at her death in 1764 to her brother, Abel-François Poisson de Vandières, who had acquired the title Marquis de Marigny in 1754. When he was not yet nineteen, he had been introduced at court by his sister, who determined that he would inherit the important post of Director-General of Buildings, Gardens, Arts, Academies and Royal Manufactories. When Pompadour became official mistress, she saw that the directorship went to her husband's uncle, Le Normant de Tournehem, and she intended that her brother should succeed Tournehem, for the Director stood at the centre of power and influence, and gave cultural direction to the nation. At least it may be said that both Tournehem and Marigny, who replaced him in November 1751, displayed exemplary administrative ability, and for over twenty years Marigny presided over the artistic life of France, generously supporting the arts for which he entertained a genuine appreciation.

How Madame de Pompadour groomed her brother to assume this key position is

Abel-François Poisson de Vandières, Marquis de Marigny (1728-1781).
Only a year after her installation at Versailles, Pompadour introduced her younger brother at court, and in April 1747 he accompanied her to the King's loge at the Opéra. Thanks to his sister's position, in 1751 he was appointed Director-General and given the title Marquis de Marigny three years later. As Director he became a principal influence upon the arts of France, and served Louis well for twenty-two years

151

well known – she sent him off to Italy to study the arts of another cultural tradition, and to find himself in the vanguard of Europeans who were flocking to the exciting excavations that had begun at Herculaneum in 1738, and only the year before at Pompeii, recalling Goethe's famous remark: 'No catastrophe had ever yielded so much pleasure to the rest of humanity as that which buried Pompeii and Herculaneum'. The Marquis de Marigny and his party were no exception.

The sensational discoveries at the cities that had been buried in the eruption of Vesuvius in 79 A.D. triggered unbounded enthusiasm among the intellectuals, for until then the only known example of classical painting was the Roman mural, 'The Aldobrandini Nuptials', but now numerous paintings and art objects were coming to light. So titled Frenchmen, German aristocrats, and throngs of Englishmen descended upon the ancient ruins, and the Grand Tour came to be an essential part of a genteman's education.

So Madame de Pompadour dispatched her brother off to Italy in 1749 for three years' study. Her letters of advice awaited him at stops along the way, and she shipped off appropriate suits for his important social engagements. He went with an accomplished trio whom the engraver Nicolas Cochin called the young man's 'eyes'. There was Cochin himself, who assisted the Marquise with her endless fêtes and theatricals and engraved a number of them, as well as official court functions; the influential art critic Abbé Leblanc, who advised the Marquise in her art purchases, and wrote the erudite notes on the Salon of 1747 that established his reputation; and the architect Jacques Soufflot, who was already interested in buildings of the past, and whose election to the Royal Academy of Architecture the Marquise arranged.

This much-discussed journey is usually held to be a major contributing factor to the mid-century artistic crisis in France whereby the antique manner eclipsed the prevailing Rococo. Marigny stood with Leblanc in agreeing that the only proper arbiter for judging a painting or work of art was personal taste, but both Cochin and Soufflot returned to Paris as champions of Neo-classicism. Cochin, however, had been disappointed in the paintings that were unearthed, and considered them representative of the decline of Roman art.

In 1755 Soufflot received through Marigny the important commission for the marvellous Eglise Sainte-Geneviève (now the Panthéon), the design for which was a fruit of his stay in Italy. In 1768 the Director engaged the architect of the Panthéon to transform his Paris house, the Maison du Roule, then at the corner of the Rue de Courcelles and the Rue de Monceau. Here Soufflot created a wholly Palladian villa, introducing the Venetian manner in the form of an unembellished Doric order on the two main floors, and a large Venetian window.

The gardens of Marigny's Paris hôtel were a different matter. Although he and his architect had committed themselves to classical canons in the dwelling, the Director of Buildings, who never became a staunch Neo-classicist, indulged his preference for the lingering Rococo in some of the garden buildings. There were the ubiquitous statues and busts from the ancient world, and a fashionable tent furnished with a suite of furniture à la Grecque. The tent was probably of durable material, for the furniture by Antoine Godefroy consisted of twelve chairs, twelve armchairs, four begères and five canapés (sofas). Marigny also added a wooden kiosk in the oriental manner which must have looked something like the project he ordered for one of his sister's fêtes at Versailles.

Michel-Barthélémy Hazon, oriental pavilion.
In his official position as Director-General of Buildings, Marigny was expected to embrace the classical mode championed by the companions of his Italian trip, the architect Soufflot and engraver Cochin. But he toyed momentarily with the idea of Hazon's whimsical oriental fantasy with curving roof of fish-scale tiles, palm tree pilasters, and adjoining tents of striped canvas. The structure is perched upon a rock and a magot figure sits in the grotto beneath

When he inherited Ménars upon the Marquise's death, an enticing prospect opened up for the creation of new gardens, and Marigny brought in Soufflot to create ramps leading down to the river. Although he maintained the old manicured formal garden on the entrance side, he ordered landscape gardens for the river façade that exhibited the *savant désordre* prescribed by the garden theorists.

The English garden at Ménars was laid out around 1770, with meandering paths among the trees, winding brooks, a *boulingrin* (bowling green), and a desert, all probably designed by Jean-François Neufforge, a student of the century's greatest teacher of architecture, J.-F. Blondel. Neufforge was an architect whose great number of published drawings (1757-77) would have attracted Marigny's attention, and he expressed the stylistic aspirations of his age.

So the château, and the gardens wandering down to the river's margin, became a constellation that brightened the riverscape. It had been even more colourful in the Marquise's day, for the river bank was enlivened by a ferry dock, fishermen's huts, and no doubt laundresses washing clothes in the Loire, recalling Italian scenes painted by Hubert Robert, one of Marigny's favourite artists.

To enhance the gardens, architectural elements were sprinkled throughout. There were trelliswork houses, a *jeu de bague* (perquisite of an aristocratic élite), and an assortment of pavilions indicative of Marigny's eclectic taste, for their architecture ranged from outrageously Rococo to Neo-classical structures in 'the correct manner', as the classicists saw it.

As a *grand amateur* with a fine collection of oriental porcelain, Ménars' owner considered a Rococo fantasy in the form of a Chinese pavilion (1770) presented by the architect Michel-Barthélémy Hazon. It was a theatrical piece with curving roof supported by palm trees, topped by a mast, and a Chinese magot sitting in the grotto substructure. Marigny rejected it, however, in favour of a Chinese belvedere (1772)

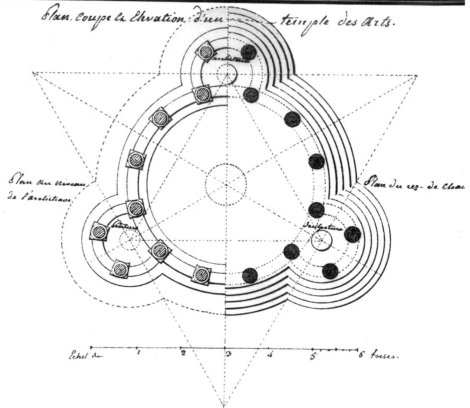

Charles de Wailly, Temple of the Arts.
The architect Charles de Wailly was greatly in demand for garden pavilions, giving a grandiose design for a pavilion with curving portico to Catherine of Russia, a Temple of Apollo for the park of Enghien, and a pagoda with tinkling bells and curving, exposed staircase for the park at Ménars which was executed, with certain modifications, in 1772

Pair of vases by Jean-Baptiste Pigalle (1714-1778), left, and Nicolas-Sébastien Adam (1705-1778), right.
The vases, with attributes of Autumn, were part of a set of four designed for Louis XV's château of Choisy by his architect, J.-A. Gabriel, but were never sent there. Louis XV gave this pair to Marigny, who placed them in the garden at Ménars, where they stayed until early in the twentieth century. They are now in the Metropolitan Museum of Art, New York. Of the other pair, decorated with attributes of Spring, one is in the Louvre and the other in the Empress Josephine's château of Malmaison

designed by his most important protégé besides Soufflot, Charles de Wailly (1730-98). Like Choiseul's Pagoda at Chanteloup, it was doubtless inspired by William Chambers' famous pagoda at Kew of 1758. Marigny owned all the important architectural books and he greatly admired Chambers' publication on the gardens at Kew (1763). William Chambers and de Wailly were both students of Blondel, and the English architect seems to have been influenced by de Wailly's work at Ménars. The effect of Blondel's teaching upon de Wailly's generation was immense. His celebrated *Cours d'Architecture* states that the garden should be planted even before the house was started, and he insisted that it be an integral part of the house's design. Blondel's best students, like Charles de Wailly, liberally applied these principles to their pavilion designs.

For the terrace overlooking the Loire, de Wailly submitted a highly innovative proposal in the Neo-classical vein – a domed round Temple of Venus with baseless Doric columns, a form still rare in France, but which would proliferate from about 1770. Another proposal was a prostylar edifice enclosing the Barberini Faun to symbolise repose. Neither scheme was carried out. His most original (and flattering) project was a visual metaphor for Marigny's position – a Temple of the Arts (1770), with central dome surrounded by three smaller ones (opposite) to commemorate architecture, painting, and sculpture, stating that his aim was to give perfect equality to the three arts.

The Marquis' special interest was painting, with Cochin as his chief adviser, and his collection was noteworthy. Marigny's numerous commissions went to such major artists as J.-B. Greuze, Joseph Vernet and Hubert Robert. For the vases and statuary in Ménars' gardens, the owner chose works by the master sculptors Guillaume II Coustou, Nicolas-Sébastien Adam and Jean-Baptiste Pigalle, all of whom worked for the King and Madame de Pompadour.

Although some of the garden pavilions were designed by de Wailly, Hazon, and

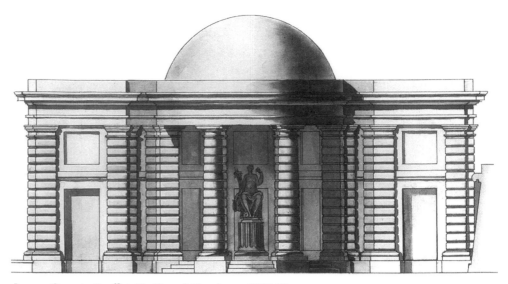

Jacques-Germain Soufflot, Pavilion of Abundance, 1768-70.
Soufflot's design for the Ménars garden structure is typical of the severe classicism associated with his name,
such as the projecting semi-circle supported by heavily rusticated Tuscan columns. Yet Soufflot also
provided a Chinese kiosk that Marigny added to the gardens in 1775

Nicolas-Marie Potain, it was to the companion of his Italian voyage that Marigny accorded the major role. Soufflot designed an orangery to serve as a *salon frais* where the host received numerous visitors, many of whom were on their way to Amboise to visit the Choiseuls. Still to be seen at Ménars on the river side is Soufflot's Pavilion of Abundance with rusticated walls, intended to connect the château to the orangery. Emil Kaufmann criticised it for being heavy and revivalist, but praised the modernity of the contrast between the smooth surface of the dome with the rusticated columns and pilasters. It once appropriately sheltered a statue of 'Abundance' with the features of Madame de Pompadour, and Coustou's life-size statue of the King whom Marigny served so well and so long.

Neither the architect nor his patron – for whom the Italian voyage had been the high point of his youth – had forgotten the Renaissance gardens they had seen near Rome. For the *viviers* (fish ponds) at Ménars were quintessentially Roman, fed by a spring that flowed from an antique nymphaeum/grotto which the Marquis christened 'piccola ma garbata' (small but enchanting).

Nothing in the spacious terrain surrounding Ménars, however, was so evocative of Italy as the towering obelisk that Soufflot designed for the roundpoint that terminated the grand allée. The obelisk as a piece of architecture evoked thoughts of Egypt, and was featured in other French gardens like the Parc Monceau (where it perched illogically upon a stone bridge), at the Comte d'Artois' Bagatelle, and in Monsieur de Bergeret's water garden at Cassan. But the distinction of Soufflot's obelisk lay in its purely *Roman* form, for it was – like the one at Bagatelle – properly supported by tortoises, and surmounted by a gilded sphere. It still stands at Ménars, soaring into the trees at the principal intersection of the great park, a fitting memorial to one of the most renowned and productive Grand Tours of the century.

Pavilion of Abundance, Ménars today.
The Pavilion of Abundance is almost the only extant pavilion in Ménars' garden

CHAPTER 13

MADAME DU BARRY AND LOUVECIENNES

The glories of Fontenoy, the progress of the kingdom, the significant reforms he instituted were dimmed by Louis XV's egregious violations of morality, and historians have been particularly severe in dealing with this aspect of his life. Although we cannot excuse what should be condemned, it must still be pointed out that Louis' well-bred depravity appears circumspect when his behaviour is compared to that of other monarchs of the time – the cynical Frederick II, the regicide and debauchee Catherine of all the Russias, or the insane Ferdinand VI.

The suffering of Marie-Leczinska came to an end when she died in 1768; Madame de Pompadour had died four years before, so a vacuum was left in that paradise of iniquity at Versailles. The more affluent members of the royal circle, therefore, were busily putting forward their own candidates for the position of official mistress. The 'cocher de l'Europe' as the still-powerful Choiseul was called, promoted his sister, Beatrixe, Duchesse de Gramont, for the position of new favourite.

Many of the courtiers, including the old Duc de Richelieu, First Gentleman of the Bedchamber in 1769,[1] had noticed a young, blue-eyed blonde with an abundance of golden hair who had been attracting a great deal of attention at the Opéra balls. Her name was Jeanne Bécu (1743-93), daughter of a seamstress and an unknown father. She was educated in a convent until she was fifteen, and then became the companion

Augustin Pajou (1730-1809), bust of Madame Du Barry.
The portraits of Madame Du Barry are generally unsatisfactory, but the bust by Pajou avenges her, and is one of the sculptor's masterpieces. The terracotta was done in 1770, shown at the Salon in August 1771, the same year it was executed in biscuit de Sèvres. *It is more restrained than Caffieri's showy interpretation of the same subject, where she appears to be an actress with a cascade of roses falling over her shoulders. Her vicious enemy, George Greive, who wrote inflammatory pamphlets against her and persistently hounded her to the scaffold, once described her as 'a bacchante crowned with ivy and roses'*

of a rich tax farmer's widow. By her late teens, Jeanne was apprenticed to the successful milliner Labille, father of the future painter Adelaide Labille-Guiard with whom Jeanne visited the artists' studios. At nineteen she was living under the 'protection' of Richelieu's friend, the collector/connoisseur Jean Du Barry, whose name and fortune opened doors into the world of letters to Jeanne Bécu, including the sophisticated literary salon of Mademoiselle Legrand.

Through the King's *premier valet de chambre,* Dominique-Guillaume Lebel, a surreptitious meeting was arranged between the enchantress and the King, who was impressed by the grace and irreproachable beauty of the former *modiste.* Since a title was requisite for an official mistress, a hasty marriage with Du Barry's brother was arranged for 1 September, 1768 – known as a *mariage à la détrempe* – and three months later, the new Comtesse Du Barry was installed at Versailles.

The propitious day for her presentation at court was set for 22 April, 1769, the usual preparations were made, and it was clear to her mentors that she would easily adapt herself to court manners. The leading dancer, Gaetan Vestris, rehearsed her in the mandatory *révérences;* the couturiers created a delicious confection for her presentation gown; the jewellers brought her diamonds from the crown repository.

Everything went off perfectly, for the Comtesse performed with admirable finesse the required *révérences,* even the last three, when she was required gracefully to kick her long train out of the way as she made her exit, still facing the King. Her appearance and *savoir-faire* even met with the approval of such arbiters of etiquette as Madame de Genlis, Talleyrand, and the Prince de Ligne. They naturally compared her with her predecessor Madame de Pompadour, and the prince declared that the Comtesse Du Barry projected 'un meilleur ton que l'autre'.

One wonders how a woman of Jeanne Bécu's background could have accommodated herself so easily to the grandest court in Europe, become an enlightened patroness of the arts, and a leader of the avant-garde. Although she received a good education at the convent, it need not have been more than rudimentary, if we are to believe the cynical Jean-Jacques Rousseau, who said that the education of women 'must be relative in regard to men, and achieve only the end of making them [women] pleasing to them'. But Jeanne had shown a refined taste and an interest in art when she was still a child of fifteen, and at least the time she spent in the Paris house of the collector Jean Du Barry was culturally profitable. For into his Paris hôtel came the *beaux esprits* in literature, philosophy, and poetry to converse with Jeanne, the artists Quentin de La Tour and Drouais to execute her portrait, and the sculptor Augustin Pajou, who would present at the Salon of 1778 the sensual bust that is said most faithfully to represent her (previous page). The year of her presentation at court, her two portraits by Drouais were the sensations of the Salon, although one cannot imagine why. They are insipid, and portray her with a coy expression that was denied by those who knew her. In fact, a considerable part of her charm was 'the engaging frankness of her wide blue eyes', as an officer of the King's light cavalry put it.

Du Barry's installation at court cleaved it into two factions, and the lines would be even more clearly drawn the following year. Although Choiseul had to endure Du Barry's presence, he achieved a major victory in 1770 when, as a result of the Alliance of which he was the principal architect, the young Austrian archduchess Marie-Antoinette arrived in May to become the new Dauphine. She inadvertently found herself a part of the Choiseul faction, among whom were many princes of the blood. Opposing them was the Du Barry cabal led by the favourite's sponsor, the Duc de Richelieu, and his nephew, the Duc d'Aiguillon, who would soon replace Choiseul as minister.

At the end of the year came Choiseul's disgrace, and much ink has been spilt over Madame Du Barry's possible role in the minister's fall and consequent exile to Chanteloup. We do know that Louis wrote to the Comte de Bröglie in 1772 that Choiseul's principles were against religion and royal authority,[2] but the loss of a minister of such calibre as Choiseul was nevertheless a severe blow to the King.

What made the matter even worse was the extreme popularity of the expelled Choiseul for, as we have seen, the high nobility began to make pilgrimages to Chanteloup, for which the King had to grant permission. Little by little, the Choiseuls were gradually alienated from court, and appeared there only to fulfil their duties. The Prince de Ligne summed it up bluntly: 'They run off to Chanteloup, insult Madame Du Barry, abandon for an entire season Compiègne and Fontainebleau . . . for Versailles had already fallen.' And from Madame Du Deffand, an old friend of the Choiseuls: 'Never was a disgrace accompanied by such glory'.

The Abbé Barthélémy's letter to Madame Du Deffand described the 'perpetual ebb and flow; I might imagine myself in the harbour of a port watching a crowd of vessels of all nations continually come and go'.[3] It was to counter this ebb and flow from Versailles to Chanteloup that the last sombre five years of the Bien-Aimé's life were set.

Louis still punctiliously attended to official business, waited patiently through tiresome ceremonies, and then hid himself away with the Countess at the Petit Trianon, in which he found increasing pleasure and which was being refurbished. The stern purity of its antique design was ratified in the décor that Madame Du Barry chose for the apartments granted her on the second floor of Versailles. Already accustomed to the superb appointments offered by the Paris furnishers of luxury goods, she purchased a garniture of splendid Sèvres vases with the King's medallion from the shop of Simon-Philippe Poirier, who also provided her bronzes, clocks and other *objets d'art*. Her furniture was supplied by the fine cabinet maker Louis Delanois, and the bathroom bronzes were by Gobert. There was a bed with four fluted columns, embellished with billing doves and wreaths of myrtle and roses carved by Lanoix and gilded by Jean-Baptiste Cagny, the steps covered with a carpet of figured Chinese silk. The billing doves motif also surmounted her famous dressing-table mirror created by the master goldsmith Roëttiers de la Tour. The execution of this suite of furniture – principally in the Louis XVI style – was without peer, and it included a mantel clock with the Three Graces supporting a vase, and a writing table covered with green Sèvres porcelain plaques.

The completed work at the Petit Trianon was inaugurated 3 September, 1770, and Louis XV was able to spend the night there on 9 September. Here were used for the first time the flying tables invented by Loriot: the large one upon which supper was laid in the kitchen below, accompanied by four small ones (*servantes*). They ascended from the kitchen, the King and his companion served themselves, and sent the table below when supper was over.

When the court made the customary autumn pilgrimage to Fontainebleau, the Countess asked the King's architect Jacques-Ange Gabriel to put up for her in the garden of Diana a small octagonal one-storey pavilion in the antique manner, covered with a terrace, and reached by a passage from the François I gallery. It was executed by the finest artists in their fields: the *boiseries* were by Jules-Antoine Rousseau, the important chimney-piece ornamented with children by the sculptor Louis-Simon Boizot, and the bronzes by Pierre Gouthière himself. Descriptions of the pavilion's salon

Entrance façade of the pavilion at Louveciennes.
The pavilion was acquired by the banker Lafitte in 1818 and throughout the nineteenth century had numerous owners. Almost all the decoration has disappeared, and one can understand why. When John Adams visited Louveciennes in August 1778 he recorded in his diary: '[it is] the most elegantly furnished of any place I have seen.' In 1929 its owner was Monsieur Coty, who began to excavate to install servants' quarters and a swimming pool, at which point the whole structure began to cave in. So it was reconstructed and enlarged for modern living, and is no longer a true document of the eighteenth century

and the vestiges that remain attest to its unusual refinement. The chimney-piece was remounted at Versailles in Louis XVI's beautiful library where it is today, and the sumptuous firedogs with hunting scenes and stags by Q.-C. Pitoin are in the Louvre. Sadly the pavilion was later destroyed by Mesdames (Louis XV's daughters), apparently with the approval of Marie-Antoinette, who always disapproved of the King's liaison with the woman whom the Duc de Croÿ scornfully labelled *la dame*.

The real triumph of the new style, however, was yet to come. On 24 July, 1769 Louis XV had given his mistress the old château of Louveciennes which Louis XIV had commissioned Arnold de Ville to build near the Machine de Marly. It belonged for a time to Mademoiselle de Clermont (sister of the Prince de Condé), then to Louis XV's aunt and confidante, the Comtesse de Toulouse, who gave it to her son, the Duc de Penthièvre. Louis acquired it from his cousin to present to Madame Du Barry, who had it completely redone. The following year she decided to add a pavilion for supper, music, and games, and in 1770 the white pleasure house of Saint-Leu stone began to rise on the terrace overlooking the Seine.

Her architect was among the most sought-after in Paris, Claude-Nicolas Ledoux, with the possible collaboration of Charles de Wailly. Ledoux, who greatly admired Gabriel, was highly favoured by the Richelieu-Du Barry coterie, which inevitably included the old Duchesse de Valentenois and the Princesse de Montmorency. Ledoux designed for the Montmorencys their exquisite Paris hôtel in the Chaussée d'Antin quarter, and it was in this fashionable district that he began in 1770 the ravishing town house that pleased all the critics, the hôtel for Mademoiselle Guimard.

Ledoux had proclaimed, 'If you want to be an architect, begin by being a painter.' What he 'painted' between December 1770 and December 1771 for Madame Du Barry at Louveciennes was directly inspired by Gabriel's Petit Trianon (as was the

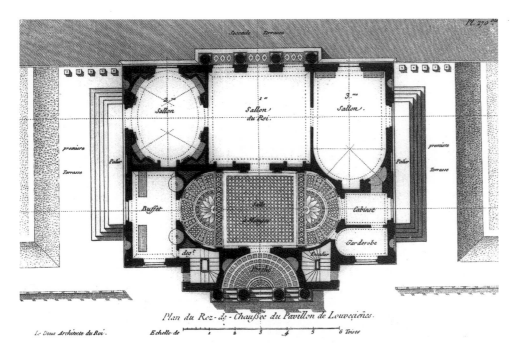

Pl. 270

Plan du Rez-de-Chaussée du Pavillon de Louveciennes.

Le Doux Architecte du Roi.　　Echelle de　1　2　3　4　5　6 Toises

Plan of Louveciennes.
Ledoux had already achieved some of the finest town houses in Paris when he was called to Louveciennes. His plan shows that it was intended as a pleasure house for dining and fêtes, for there are no bedrooms. One enters directly from the portico into the oval dining room with the rectangular salon beyond that overlooking the river

Hôtel Guimard). The Louveciennes pavilion was a square structure twenty-five feet high of Saint-Leu stone, with five windows on the river side. The entrance was articulated by four columns supporting a portico, niches with statues, and a bas-relief by Félix Lecomte of a Bacchanalian scene, with the unframed windows at each side which were almost a Ledoux trademark (p.164).

The artists whom Du Barry employed for the interior were among the foremost of their time: the sculptors Jean-Jacques Caffieri, S.-L. Boizot, Augustin Pajou; the leading *bronzeur-ciseleur* Pierre Gouthière; the *ébéniste* Jean-François Leleu, who worked chiefly for the disciminating Prince de Condé; the silversmith Jacques Roëttiers, whose commissions for Catherine of Russia at the same time marked the beginning of a new era in the history of French silver; the painters Jean-Honoré Fragonard, F.-H. Drouais, Joseph-Marie Vien, and the Queen's portraitist Elizabeth Vigée-Lebrun.

Here Madame Du Barry also gave impetus to the fashion for furniture decorated with Sèvres porcelain plaques, having already introduced pieces of this type into her Versailles apartments. So profound was her impact upon the taste of her time that a contemporary wrote: 'Elle faisait la mode à Paris et dans toute l'Europe'.[4]

Visiting monarchs paid court to Madame Du Barry, and in February 1771 she was visited by the future Gustavus III of Sweden, who left a diamond collar for her white greyhound, Mirza. To the great discomfiture of the Queen, her brother Joseph II called upon the former mistress in May 1777, and Vigée-Lebrun recorded in her memoirs that Monsieur de Monville – who lived at the nearby Désert de Retz – was frequently seen at Louveciennes. Even the most popular composers paid homage to the Countess, for in the same year as Gustavus' visit, Grétry dedicated his comedy-ballet, *Zémire et Azor*, to her.

The Louveciennes plan shows it to be a true *maison de plaisance*, for there are no bedrooms. Beyond the portico one entered the oval dining room (square with two hemicycles) with walls of grey marble, Corinthian pilasters with capitals and frieze of putti in ormolu (p.165). Between the pilasters were niches containing marble goddesses

Jean-Honoré Fragonard, 'The Lover Crowned', 1771-2.
One of Fragonard's series of paintings for Louveciennes, the airy, light-hearted 'The Lover Crowned' is one of the masterpieces of eighteenth-century French painting. The paintings had hardly been placed in Louveciennes before Madame Du Barry decided to replace them by a quartet of cold, classical paintings by J.-M. Vien. The girl's gesture is repeated in the billowing tree that bends towards the left. Flowers and foliage tumble about them in rich profusion, and the lush, untamed orange trees are blown by the wind

Jean-Honoré Fragonard, 'Love Letters', 1771-2.
Another in Fragonard's series 'Progress of Love' at Louveciennes. It is linked to 'The Lover Crowned' both formally and through the greenery of the landscape garden that must once have been a formal park. Trees part to reveal a blue sky behind the lovers, and light filters through the gay pink parasol at the base of a classical statue, perhaps Venus with Cupid at her side. Fragonard's marvellous workmanship is everywhere apparent

Elevation du Pavillon de Louveciennes du coté des Jardins.

Claude-Nicholas Ledoux, elevation of pavilion of Louveciennes, entrance façade.
Ledoux distinguished the entrance façade of Louveciennes with four free-standing Ionic columns, classical statuary, and a low-relief Bacchanalian frieze by the sculptor Félix Lecomte. Typical of the neo-classical movement is the recession of the steps within the portico, setting the dwelling off from its surroundings

holding cornucopias by the sculptors Augustin, Martin-Claude Monot and Félix Lecomte.[5] The vestibule/dining room led to the grand salon overlooking the river, for which three tapestries were ordered from the Gobelins after paintings by Jean-Baptiste Pierre, François Boucher and Carle van Loo, although they were never finished. It was apparently here that the celebrated bust of the Countess by Pajou stood on a classical altar of marble embellished with ormolu by the master bronze worker Pierre Gouthière.

In the salon on the right was a chimney-piece with ormolu and chased silver decorations by Gouthière, and for it Fragonard painted one of the most exquisite ensembles of the *ancien régime,* the superb 'Progress of Love' series, now in the Frick Collection (pp.162 and 163). Strangely, the Countess rejected these masterpieces in favour of cold, Neo-classical subjects by Vien – a choice symptomatic of the change of taste, whereby the Rococo was abolished in favour of the antique.[6]

The oval salon was mirrored, with a painted ceiling of rural pastimes by Gabriel Briard, firedogs by one of Marie-Antoinette's favourite bronze workers, Claude-Jean Pitoin, and surprisingly, two seventeenth-century canvases, no doubt admitted because of their classical subjects. One was thought to have been Simon Vouet's 'Toilette de Venus', now in Pittsburgh. The other was possibly the Boston 'Bacchus et Ariadne', now attributed to Lesueur.

By the summer of 1771 the pavilion was well enough along for the favourite to entertain the King's new minister, the Duc d'Aiguillon. On 2 September, 1771 it was inaugurated with a fireworks display and supper for the King who was accompanied by the indispensable Duc de Richelieu, again d'Aiguillon, the caustic Chancellor Maupeou, and the delightful Marquis de Chauvelin, the ideal diplomat. Moreau le Jeune gives us a glimpse of this 'small bright world' of Louis XV's last years (opposite).

The guests are seated in the oval dining room, musicians playing in the tribunes, the table decorated with a monopteral temple, its dome engarlanded with flowers, the columns entwined with greenery. The table appointments include Madame Du Barry's new 322-piece soft-paste Sèvres dinner service designed by Saint Aubin, one of the royal factory's most important commissions. In attendance are the Swiss guards and Louis-Benoist Zamore, the Countess' spoiled little Indian page upon whose costumes alone she wasted a fortune, and who betrayed her in the end.

The Louveciennes pavilion represents Neo-classicism *pur sang*, 'the first consistently

Jean-Michel Moreau (Moreau le Jeune, 1741-1814), fête given at Louveciennes in September 1771. Louveciennes was officially inaugurated on 2 September, 1771 by the dinner Du Barry gave there for the King in the oval dining room. The chairs by Louis Delanois, with straight legs and medallion backs, are already in the Louis XVI style. In niches at the back holding gilt bronze candelabra stand nymphs by Du Barry's sculptor Pajou; half-lustres hang against the mirrors. Although the illusionistic ceiling painting looks back to the previous century, the rest of the room is entirely in the Neo-classical taste: shallow pilasters framing plaques in low relief, the apses with coffered ceilings, the pedestal in the left foreground with a classical nymph supporting another candelabrum. The entire table top has been turned into a French garden with monopteral temples, the same type of décor that would be used in January 1782 for the Paris fête given for Marie-Antoinette on the occasion of the Dauphin's birth

conceived decorative ensemble' in a thoroughly Neo-classical style.[7] From every point of view — architecture, furnishing, appointments and works of art — it was a remarkable achievement for a woman with Jeanne Becu's antecedents. And it was not for nothing that the armorial bearings of the King's last favourite were surmounted with a banner that brandished the words: 'Boutez en avant' (Forge ahead).

Above and detail opposite: The Baths of Apollo, Versailles.
When the Sun King's Grotte de Thétis was destroyed to make room for the addition of the north wing to Versailles, the three groups of statues adorning the niches of the grotto (p.50) were moved to bosquets in the gardens. When Louis XVI's replantation of the Versailles gardens began, he engaged his garden designer, the painter Hubert Robert, to arrange a permanent setting for them. Typically, Robert planned the Baths of Apollo as a rustic grotto with cascades and vines trailing over the rocks. This was a constant feature of the picturesque garden, but totally inappropriate to the dignified Baroque classicism of the Versailles school. The centre group by Girardon is Apollo ministered to by the Nymphs of Thetis; those on the left and right by Guérin and Marsy respectively show Apollo's horses

CHAPTER 14

THE APOGEE OF THE PICTURESQUE GARDEN

When Louis XVI succeeded his grandfather, he was barely out of his teens. Even given his extreme youth, he apparently never wanted to rule, and Cobban noted that he often appeared to be a disinterested spectator of his own reign. An intelligent man with a lively intellectual curiosity, as Girault de Coursac has shown, Louis XVI – like the grandfather he so esteemed – was always surrounded with books. Also like Louis XV, he loved nature, and ordered the replanting of the park of Versailles.

Louis introduced a note of *bonhomie* at court which had been unknown in the measured gestures of Louis XIV or the refined distinction of Louis XV. He ordered simple wool suits for himself, and would sit in the gardens like any ordinary stroller and chat with his sisters-in-law. Sometimes he lacked the sense of occasion that was expected of a monarch. The Comte d'Hézècques recalled an incident in the Oeil de Boeuf where some remodelling was being done, and the King jokingly lifted a pail with a heavy page boy in it (hardly kingly, but not as outrageous as the English King, 'Silly Billy', with his head shaped like a pineapple, who spat from the state coach). Louis XVI's bearing was not impressive and his posture was poor, which counted against him, for it contrasted sharply with the Queen's dignified beauty and unusually graceful carriage.

Yet morally, Louis XVI stood head and shoulders above that cesspool of a court, and he hoped to save Christian France for the people: 'The King served God at a time when the Devil was in fashion'.[1] But Louis lacked the resolution necessary to lead the nation, and got no help from either the nobility or the church, and least of all from his own family. His brother, the Comte de Provence, called up Satan. His younger

Anonymous, German school, Marie-Antoinette, 1768.
This portrait of Marie-Antoinette aged thirteen was painted almost two years before she left her mother's court at Vienna. Maria-Theresa's was 'the chief bourgeois family in Europe', as someone remarked. Even at this age, Marie-Antoinette displays the dignified grace and charm that captivated Louis XV when he went to meet her in 1770. The Viennese chair and table are in the full Rococo manner, but her own interiors and furnishings would be in the fully developed Neo-classical style synonymous with her brief reign

brother, the Comte d'Artois, even mocked the processions of the Saint Esprit, participating with his dangerous cousin, Chartres, in rites of the occult. Of the three brothers, only the King was a model of fidelity. Ironically, it was he who lost his life in the Revolution, while Provence survived to become Louis XVIII, and d'Artois mounted the throne as Charles X.

Marie-Antoinette, on the other hand, always found the *mot juste* for everyone, and her contemporaries universally commented upon her charm. As the spontaneous, spirited Dauphine, she enchanted Louis XV, who went to meet her at Compiègne when she arrived from Austria, and presented her with the pearls of Louis XIV's mother, Anne of Austria. Not yet fifteen when she was married and nineteen when she ascended the throne, the vivacious new Queen was made of too lively mettle to endure the tedious ceremonial, scandalising older members of the court by a failure to venerate the established etiquette that had undergirded its dignity since the days of the Sun King.

Claude-Louis Châtelet (1753-1795), fête in the Trianon Gardens.
Marie-Antoinette created an English garden at Trianon because it was in fashion in the 1770s, but another compelling reason was the fact that it offered the ever-changing mise-en-scène, *according to season, that she desired for the official entertainment she was expected to offer to royal guests and foreign ambassadors. Her imaginative fêtes called upon all the resources of the Menus-Plaisirs, for there were concerts, country fairs, plays, illuminations and fireworks, followed by supper in the gardens presented with consummate French artistry. Here the Temple of Love is illuminated*

Her great love was fêtes, but in 1778, due to her first pregnancy, she was unable to participate in a masked ball. To console her, the King brought to her apartment an odd assemblage of characters in masks and costumes, all in their seventies. Naturally the Duc de Richelieu was commandeered – in the costume of a Titan – for he was still only seventy-four. With him were the Comte de Maurepas (back at court after thirty years' exile) disguised as Cupid and his wife as Venus. The ancient Maréchale de Mirepoix appeared as Aurora, and the Princesse d'Hénin as a Fairy. After bowing deeply to the Queen, Richelieu performed a minuet with the Maréchale de Mirepoix, gallantly kissing her hand at the end, and declaring that the younger courtiers could not have done it as well.

The Queen's taste for music and dancing brought to court people who were appreciated for their talent, so there was gradually a mingling of classes that had never been seen there before. Informal in her manner and unwise in her choice of courtiers, Marie-Antoinette was warned by her brother, Joseph II, in 1787 of the *soi-disant* society which was taking advantage of her, but to no avail.

Jean Pillement, chinoiseries, 1770.
The eighteenth century fell in love with chinoiseries, and in 1767 Louis XV had sent furnishings especially made in France for the garden pavilions of the Chinese court. The oriental kiosks at Bagatelle and Rambouillet featured upturned roofs like that in the Pillement engraving

Despite her poor judgement, her acting out in ignorance a disastrous political role, her final defence was so eloquent, intelligent, and courageous that even her enemies were moved. She remained, as the Comte de Tilly wrote, every inch a Queen: 'Whereas one would offer a *chair* to the other ladies, to Marie-Antoinette one could offer nothing less than a *throne*.'

The Queen became the cynosure of all Europe, a prominent figure in the aesthetic revolution already taking place in gardens and *folies*, and her own experiments in this realm would be carried out as châtelaine of the Petit Trianon. This is not to claim that she was among the first to build a natural garden in France, for a landscape garden already adorned the country houses of people in her own class such as the Prince de Ligne, the Comte de Caraman, and members of the Orléans family.

Long before Louis XV's death, political theorists were laying the groundwork for an entirely new way of looking at the world which would undermine the concept of a sovereign monarch, Versailles as the seat of government, and even the French formal garden, whose geometrical abstractions symbolised that concept.

The *philosophes*, in particular, enunciated 'enlightened' ideas. Not that they actually advocated revolution, for they were even conservative in practical matters,[2] but by condemning the existing order in church, state, and society, they opened the road to secular humanism. One of their most damaging instruments – a copy of which was to be found in Louis XV's library – was the *Encyclopédie*, in which man (mankind) was defined as 'seeming to stand above the other animals'. So with one blow, man's status as a contingent being created in the image of God was thoroughly undermined.

Another factor that opened wide the door in France to the prevailing current of opinion was the American Alliance of 1778, whereby the French nobility went off to war. The pacesetters within Marie-Antoinette's circle, represented by such privileged families as the de Lauzuns, the de Ségurs, the de Noaïlles, sailed to America with the Comte de Rochambeau to fight for American independence, leaving behind their French mistresses, and the pavilions and gardens of their ancestral châteaux. Their experiences in the New World 'gave a whole new dimension to ideas of liberty and equality made familiar by the Enlightenment'.[3]

When they returned to France, they brought with them a new mistress by the name of Liberty. Transplanted to modern France, Liberty-turned-Licence committed adultery with the so-called 'natural man'. Its product was the monster Anarchy, which was shortly to destroy the *ancien régime* and much more besides. For it has been observed that a society that could no longer tolerate a sovereign God could not tolerate a sovereign King, and rationalism led to revolution.

In this climate of purely secular ideals, the hierarchical concept of the garden as an ordered complement to the house fell before the liberating principles of the *jardin pittoresque,* and the so-called freedom possessed by Rousseau's natural man was now granted to gardens. His *Nouvelle Héloise* militates against *treillage,* parterres with coloured sands, porcelain flowers and vases. His heroine, Julie, sat in an Arcadian garden free of man-made structures, midst flowering meadows and shadowy glades

Jean Pillement, chinoiseries, 1770.
Chinese fabriques added an exotic touch to the landscape, and Pillement's designs could be adapted to fabrics and wallpapers. Oriental motifs were in such demand that François Boucher designed Beauvais tapestries depicting the Emperor of China seated in his garden, with a full complement of canopies similar to those in Pillement's design

through which natural streams meandered.

We are often reminded that the architect William Kent, in crossing over the fence, discovered that 'all nature is a garden'. But a rationalistic age, in which man comes to think so highly of himself, demands that 'improvements' be made even upon nature itself. So garden builders of the Queen's generation began to criticise Versailles and its park: 'Versailles est triste' complained the Prince de Ligne, and 'Le Nôtre a massacré La nature' chimed in the Vicomte d'Ermonville.

Henceforward, innovative garden-builders began to reject the old formal *jardin français* in favour of the new English landscape garden which looked as if it had just naturally grown there.[4] One of these was the Prince de Ligne, whom we saw nodding approvingly at Du Barry's presentation. In 1769 he had already asked the architect, F.-J. Bélanger, to build a new garden for him at his Belgian estate of Beloeil.[5] So authoratative had de Ligne become on the subject of gardens, that he immediately became counsellor to Marie-Antoinette upon his arrival in France, as well as to the Duc de Chartres in the Parc Monceau, and Monsieur de Monville at the Désert de Retz. The articulate Prince summed up the difference between the formal and the natural garden: the former were *jardins de l'intelligence*, while the latter were *jardins du coeur*.

So the stately cadences, the mathematical precision, the intellectuality of André Le Nôtre's manicured *jardin français*, with its splendid disregard for the ways of nature, gradually gave way to the playful caprices and *sensibilité* of the natural landscape garden which was allowed to go its own way. Or so it appeared. But – as Baltrusaitis pointed out – once nature had been rediscovered, it had to be transfigured – into a domain that was at once visionary and symbolic. The transformation of nature required by the new garden style dramatically affected the components with which one constructed a garden.

Trees, which once had been clipped and regimented into straight platoons, were now free to lounge beside a river bank, to billow and furl with rhythmic animation, acquiring an anthropomorphic character, as in Ermenonville's *ormes heureux*. In paintings of landscape gardens by Hubert Robert and C.-J. Vernet, weeping willows dip their branches into rivers, stiff poplars repeat the shapes of columns, and sometimes decaying, almost leafless trees cut diagonally across the canvas, suggesting evanescence.

New varieties of trees were introduced, too, and evergreens were planted along with lilacs and rhododendrons. The garden designers followed the advice of the Abbé Delille – 'Be a painter' – and disposed trees in a 'natural' but painterly manner to evoke the forfeited garden of Paradise.

Flowers, formerly confined to geometrical parterres, now sprang up beside serpentine streams, like an afterthought of nature. Tall flowers swayed in the breeze, intermingling with grass that was now allowed to grow long to suggest a meadow. The study of botany became a passion, and illustrations by Moreau le Jeune for Jean-Jacques Rousseau's *Emile* sentamentalise the virtues of gardening.

Rousseau even composed a manual of botany for beginners. A famous engraving represents his charitable presence, seated under a cedar in Girardin's landscape garden

Cascade at Ermenonville.
Ermenonville was one of the triumphs of the landscape garden. It was particularly pleasing for the contrast between still waters and rushing cascades, smooth white marble temples and rough-hewn grottoes. Looking past the cascade, the visitor could catch a glimpse of the ruins of a circular classical temple on the hillside, and at the centre of the lake, the Isle of Poplars with the tomb of the philosopher Jean-Jacques Rousseau

of Ermenonville, an antique temple in the background. Rousseau is benevolently explaining the classification of plants to his patron's son.[6]

Water, that indispensable element that had been coerced into cascades, fountains, canals and ornamental sheets to add sheen to the landscape, now threw itself imperiously over rocks. At other times it became a slumbrous stream wandering through quiet fields as at Ermenonville, where the scene was to be regarded as a picture seen from the dwelling. This effect satisfied the demands of the influential theorist Abbé Laugier who, like the Abbé Delille, declared: 'Il faut qu'un jardinier soit un excellent peintre'.

Rivers, with sinuous, winding courses, cascades tumbling over rocks, were regarded as great assets to the new gardens. They reflected the trees, afforded an excuse for picturesque bridges, and were indispensable for linking the parts of the composition. Water lent an inimitable charm, and the mill at Charles-Henri Watelet's picturesque garden of Moulin-Joli was made to span the river, so the scene looked like a painting by Hubert Robert, who had been Watelet's guide in Rome when he returned to the Eternal City in 1763.

Since gardens were intended to be composed with a painter's eye, French artists actively participated in this living art form. François Boucher designed the *maison à l'air champêtre* for the owner of Moulin-Joli. Fragonard's portfolio of drawings from his Italian expedition with the elder Bergeret in 1773 was consulted by Bergeret's son, Pierre-Jacques, for their park at Cassan, with its Chinese pavilion (pp.88 and 89). Hubert Robert transformed the gardens of Louis XVI's sister, Madame Elisabeth, at Montreuil, painted the replantation of the Versailles gardens for the King, and orchestrated the Baths of Apollo grotto (pp.166 and 167), and was consulted for the pavilion complex that Louis XVI built at Rambouillet for the Queen.

As for the famous gardens of Ermenonville and Méréville, Hubert Robert's canvases 'both recorded and inspired the creation of those sylvan domains composed of . . . romantic views'.[7] What is more, the artist actually worked for several years with

Temple of Love at Petit Trianon.
The Temple of Love was usually illuminated for the Queen's garden parties, for at night it seemed to float upon the waters, an ethereal classical object with the Bouchardon statue 'Love Making a Bow from the Club of Hercules' within. Sometimes bridges decked with flowers were built across the pond so that courtiers could pass over to the temple and look back to the lighted gardens where musicians played and tables were set up for the cold collations

Girardin on the gardens at Ermenonville – where water formed a great part of the composition – and after Bélanger's departure, Hubert Robert was totally responsible for the vast park, one of the most ambitious of the century. For a princely and aristocratic clientele (and the bourgeoisie as well), Robert designed numerous *fabriques*. One of his favourite motifs was the Temple of the Sibyl at Tivoli which appears – with a tumbling cascade – in his paintings, and in the form of a pavilion the Temple came to inhabit the garden that Robert conceived for one aristocratic owner – Jean-Joseph de Laborde at Méréville.

Statues, which had formerly been ranged as sentinels along the royal promenades, now crouched within the cavern of a gloomy grotto, lay half-hidden in the haunted shadows of an antique temple, or became incidental ornament in a never-never land of obelisks, windmills, Gothic ruins, and Chinese bridges. Temples of Love, like Marie-Antoinette's on the island at Trianon, sheltered statuary by the most celebrated sculptors.

Grottoes, once architectural focal points within the symmetry of the formal garden, began to assume a picturesque irrationality. In the Folie Saint-James at Neuilly and the Laiterie de la Reine at Rambouillet, the grotto blended the rustic with the Neoclassical. Marie-Antoinette's grotto near the Belvédère in the Trianon gardens was an eerie cavern whose floor and benches were covered with spongy moss. The romantic grotto that Hubert Robert designed for the Baths of Apollo in the Versailles gardens provided an inappropriate sanctuary for Girardon's great sculptural group from the Grotte de Thétis (pp.46-50 and 166). The garden that Louis XVI bought for his sister, Madame Elisabeth, at Montreuil was designed almost entirely around grottoes, a little river, and a *niagara*. It impressed even the Prince de Ligne, who praised the architect, J.-J. Huvé, for having achieved the greatest effect within a limited space.

Closely related to grottoes was another feature of Chinese gardens that appealed to French garden builders – the unusual rock formations that orientals prized as natural works of art. Le Rouge's publication *Cahiers de jardins anglo-chinois* contained plates

ÉLEVATION DU TEMPLI
ET DU ROCHER

VUE DU ROCHER, TEMPLE ET CASCADE DE S.ᵀ LEU *Prise du point E.*

View of the Rocher at Saint Leu.
The garden at Saint Leu is typical of the landscape gardens in France that were supposed to look like nature itself: trees scattered at random, 'natural' rock formations, winding canals with rustic bridges – an invitation to set out in pirogues or take sketchbook in hand. The source of the cascade that feeds the canal is, however, highly contrived: an artificial rocher *crowned by a Doric temple whose entablature, supported by vermiculated bands, is graced by a flower box! Dora Wiebenson pointed out that the picturesque garden in France was intended as a retreat into nature in a period of political and economic crisis*

with suggestions for constructing rocky outcrops for the new irregular garden. Rock formations ('bones of the earth') were especially valued by Hubert Robert, as seen in the huge grotto for the the Baths of Apollo as noted above, and the dramatic *rochers* for Jean-Joseph de Laborde at Méréville. Robert even engaged sculptors from the Academy to shape the boulders according to his meticulous instructions.

The picturesque *rocher* at Saint Leu was surmounted by a square temple with Doric columns banded with vermiculations and enlivened by cascades that flowed over the rocks to feed the river below, and this incongruous blending of the classical tradition with the natural was quite acceptable for the new gardens. In the Comte d'Artois' gardens at Bagatelle, a colourful Chinese tent perched upon a similar rock composition was the setting for aerial picnics.

A vista had been the object of the Sun King's garden, which achieved terminal drama through distance, but the garden of Marie-Antoinette's day sought a view. Vistas could be apprehended at a glance, but views were the reward of a landscape garden's leisurely elaboration of turning paths, enticing the visitor to further exploration, opening up to ever-changing scenes 'comme le décor de l'opéra', as Carmontelle put it in the preface to his book, *Le Jardin de Monceau*.

One moved as through a Chinese scroll, with one scene flowing into another. Always there was an object of interest in the décor – lattice-work benches, an island floating in a stream, hidden bosquets with singing birds, a white temple on a hill to close a perspective, and funerary monuments. A notable feature of the Marquis de Girardin's garden was the tomb of Jean-Jacques Rousseau, who conveniently died at Ermenonville.

The theorists insisted that all the elements be assembled as if they had grown there by chance, or as one of them put it: 'Art should not be allowed to set foot in the province of nature.' And from Voltaire, the shrubs of whose garden at Ferney were nevertheless clipped into geometrical forms as rigid as Le Nôtre's:

Jardins, il faut qu je vous fuie,
    Trop d'art me révolte et m'ennuie.

174

Tomb of Jean-Jacques Rousseau, Ermenonville.
One of the favourite pilgrimages for country outings was a visit to the Marquis de Girardin's Ermenonville, twenty-five miles from Paris. Here he introduced as a melancholy note into the 'canvas' of the park the Isle of Poplars which held the grave of Jean-Jacques Rousseau, who was buried there 4 July, 1778. Among the distinguished visitors were the Queen herself, Gustave III of Sweden, Benjamin Franklin, and Marie-Antoinette's brother, Joseph II of Austria. The tomb, surrounded by trees, looks like an antique monument, a pictorial element in the overall design in which Hubert Robert had a hand. In his itinerary for visiting Ermenonville (1791), Girardin wrote: 'The art of gardening . . . consists uniquely in executing Pictures upon the terrain, following the same rules as upon a canvas. These two Arts of imitation have the same aim'

For art was as rigorously applied to the new gardens as it had been to the formal ones, and was employed on every hand to 'improve' nature, accent her best points, interject colour, and introduce a spirit of play. Nature was appealing as long as it was ordered to suit one's philosophy in this era when rural life was endlessly discussed. But as Carmontelle put it in his Parc Monceau preface: 'The description of rural life was loved more than the practice. To depict the country as it *was* would destroy for the French the taste they *thought* they had for it'.

Nowhere was art, or rather artifice, more surprisingly employed than when bizarre elements were introduced – searing deserts, wastelands with gallows blowing in the wind, or haunted swamps. Sometimes the bizarre joined hands with the exotic, as in a garden that boasted a fantastic piece of zoomorphic architecture – a stable in the form of a cow, its interior lighted by a bull's eye opening in the 'Etruscan' vase on its back. At Bonnelles, huge rocks were arranged in the shape of an enormous animal carrying a painted Chinese teahouse on its back. The motivating concept was surprise, novelty, variety, and dramatic contrasts.

The chinoiseries that had already appeared in Rococo interiors and gardens reflected France's fascination with the Orient. It was a taste to which impetus had been given by Jesuit missionaries' descriptions of the Emperor of China's garden with its four hundred pavilions, all of different design. So from the 1760s onward, garden designers found that capricious oriental garden structures were the perfect points of accent in their new landscape gardens.

Nor were they confined to the countryside. In Paris, in the garden of the Hôtel de Montmorency by C.-N. Ledoux (1771), a dimunitive painted Chinese pavilion projected over the public path, lending a note of exotic gaiety to the Boulevard Montmartre below, and all but erasing the line between private and public space (p185). And as late as 1792, Nicolas Lenoir built the Chinese Baths directly upon the

Nicolas Lenoir, the Chinese Baths, Paris.
The watercolour shows the baths with treillage pagodas on the roof, and huge rochers – so prized in China – at either side of the entrance. The Chinese Baths were destroyed in 1856, and occupied the place where 29 Boulevard des Italiens now stands

boulevards, complete with rock formations, gilt lattice, and pagoda roofs.

Although critics did not always agree on the propriety of such whimsicalities, they were defended by the authority of the Prince de Ligne, that infallible judge of gardens:

> I love my dear Chinese isle, where in the shelter of the parasol that my big Mandarin holds, I visit in the midst of my water folk; I am excused on the ground of the beautiful vermilion of my balustrades, of my little bridge, of the three posts surmounted with gold apples . . . One does not wish to give the appearance of truth to that which he recognises with pleasure to be illusion.[8]

Illusion . . . As the storm clouds began to gather around 1787, for Marie-Antoinette and her coterie make-believe became more a necessity than a luxury. The keynote of Versailles' gardens and pavilions in the sunset years of the monarchy was fantasy, and of all the *pays d'illusion* created for an élite society none was more escapist in its aspirations than the Queen's private world at the Petit Trianon.

Luxury had become a bore, and in this realm of extravagant simplicity removed from the great château, the studied rusticity of cracked plaster, rough-hewn beams, and roofs made of rushes at the Queen's Hameau suggested unkempt peasants' huts. Cauliflower and beans grew in the little garden, and supper was served in a thatched-roof cottage, followed by country dances accompanied by mandolin and tambourine. It was like a scene from the comic opera, or from a fairy tale in the Queen's library at Trianon. It was an age when *les grands* were devouring fairy tales, and in the parks of great seigneurs, magic tricks were performed. What appeared to be a simple cottage from the world of Cinderella turned out to be, when one opened the door, an enchanted palace with white marble fireplaces, gleaming gilt-bronze appointments, pink silk embroidered hangings, and delicate Sèvres porcelain.

At Stanislas' château in Lunéville, his court had watched with detached fascination the carved wooden peasants working in the animated toy village. But in Trianon's life-size village – with its waterwheel and cabbage patches – the inhabitants *were* the court. Fairy tales abound in stories of peasant maids and Cinderellas who are suddenly transformed into princesses or queens. But was it ever the other way round?

CHAPTER 15

PAVILIONS IN THE AGE OF LOUIS XVI AND MARIE-ANTOINETTE: 1774-1793

By the time of Marie-Antoinette's ascension in 1774, the taste for country life was one symptom of the Anglomania that was sweeping over France. English novels were being read and discussed, Shakespeare was becoming the rage of Paris, younger members of the oldest French families – like Charles de Noailles – were affecting English accents, and from the Palais Royal, Parc Monceau, Villers-Cotterêts, and Le Raincy the Orléans family were disseminating Anglo-Saxon taste. The Duc d'Orléans sported English tweeds and *redingotes,* his gardens were filled with *l'evergreene* and his kennels with hunting dogs.

In 1766 the Comte de Lauraguais, a protector of the actress Sophie Arnould, had organised the first race-track in France, following English examples, and Louis XVI's brother, the Comte d'Artois, was one of the most avid spectators at the races on the Plaine des Sablons. Here the English system of betting gained popularity, especially with such *bon vivants* as the seductive Duc de Lauzun of the Queen's circle. This nephew of the Duchesse de Choiseul, with whom he rode at Chanteloup, also maintained his own stables near Paris.

D'Artois lost his shirt, but his penchant for gambling at least provoked one of his few humorous remarks. When he appealed to the King to bail him out of a gambling debt, Louis XVI refused, and the exasperated Prince exclaimed: 'My brother should not be called Roi de France et Navarre, but Roi de France et avare [miser].' Even Madame de Genlis joined the general criticism of the race-tracks, and eventually the Queen stayed away. But not before she had been noticed there in 1777 by the Countess Spencer, who admired her costume: a dress with closely fitted bodice, slashed skirt of flesh-coloured *gros de Tours* embroidered with garlands, a white mantle and hat. It is no wonder that the Comte d'Hézècques maintained that Marie-

Jean-François Janinet, Hôtel de Lassay.
The Hôtel de Lassay began its life as an eighteenth-century pavilion, along with its neighbour, the Palais Bourbon. Even though the Hôtel de Lassay was smaller, it was equally distinguished. These two low, classical pavilions embellished the eighteenth-century riverscape until they were swallowed up by immense government edifices. Today the Hôtel de Lassay is the Présidence de l'Assemblée Nationale

Antoinette was one of the people who was 'most attractive of her time.'[1]

The Peace of 1763 opened the door for the English to flock back to Paris (as they had done during every peace since the days of Charles V), and the Duc de Croÿ claimed that it was after the Peace that the English garden began to be imitated in France.[2] It was certainly helped along by that confirmed Anglophile, the Comte de Lauraguais, who seems to have been the first (1776) to seek the services of the dour Scottish gardener, Thomas Blaikie, who became an important figure in planning the royal and princely gardens.

The Count introduced Blaikie to several members of the Queen's group – the Baron de Besenval, the Duc de Chartres, and the Comte d'Artois. By the fall of 1777 Blaikie was in London acquiring seeds and trees for d'Artois' château of Maisons, and at the end of 1778 the Count asked his advice on the English garden for the pavilion of Bagatelle. Its architect, F.-J. Bélanger, studied garden structures in England, and the sketchbook of his trip became an important document in the cultural exchange between the two countries.

The fervour of garden- and pavilion-building that occurred during the decades of the 1770s and 1780s contributed to an undermining of the court's authority, a phenomenon for which the royal family itself was largely responsible. The uncertain King shut himself up with his locksmith Gamain to fabricate intricate locks, when he was not charging through the forests with his hunting companions. The Queen frequently explored the pleasures of Paris during the early years of the reign, and then retreated to the Petit Trianon, with increasingly fewer companions as time went on, devoting herself to her family.

Monsieur, Comte de Provence, fled as often as possible to his *maisons de plaisance* at Brunoy, or slipped out of the palace to the charming pavilion that his architect Chalgrin built in 1786 for the Comtesse de Balbi behind the King's Potager at Versailles.[3] Madame (Provence's wife), who loved music and patronised Gluck like the Queen, consoled herself in a lovely pavilion designed in 1784 by Provence's architect, Chalgrin, at Montreuil near Versailles. Although the property has been truncated, the Pavillon de Musique de Madame is extant, its vestibule like a garden, for the *trompe-l'oeil* decoration suggests a loggia with flowers massed in the foreground, and seen through the pillars of the tholos is a landscape garden with tiered fountains and flowing trees *à la Fragonard*.

The brazen Comte d'Artois divided his time between the races, orgies with the Duc de Lauzun and Chartres at the Palais Royal, and hunting at Saint-Germain or Maisons. By 1777 he was preoccupied with the pavilion of Bagatelle, a Neo-classical gem with a formal garden behind it, a courtyard before, and a landscape garden filled with follies. But it became a den of iniquity presided over by the actress/singer Mademoiselle Duthé (known as 'le passage des princes') and the captain of d'Artois' guards, the notorious Prince d'Hénin.

Next to the Queen and her brothers-in-law, the pacesetters of society were the princes of the blood. In 1764 the King's cousin Louis-Joseph, Prince de Condé, inherited from his grandmother the Palais Bourbon, and the next year he summoned his architect, Claude Billard de Bélisard, to transform it. The previous generation had indulged in a décor that made a fetish of mirrors, and these could now be made in large sheets and were highly prized for they reflected the glories of the garden.

Bélisard's décor underscored the garden setting, 'opening up' the ceiling of the billiard salon with trelliswork from which descended garlands of flowers to support

Perspective of the entrance to the house of Madame Thélusson. The triumphal arch before the Hôtel Thélusson visually links it to the boulevard, serving as a framework for the grand portico of Corinthian columns seen through the opening. The exterior of the arch is rusticated, and the interior is coffered like the Pantheon in Rome

the chandeliers with wax candles, evoking the spirit of Louis-Joseph's Hameau at Chantilly a decade later, where the dining room was painted to suggest a forest grove.

In the salon of the Palais Bourbon, the ceiling cupola swung back to reveal a circular gallery for Condé's musicians. It was probably Bélisard's tribute to antiquity, for in Nero's Golden House the ceiling enclosed movable panels that presented one appearance after another, as perfume was sprinkled upon the guests.

Some of the painted décor at the Palais Bourbon was the work of J.-F. Callet, an artist patronised by the Comte d'Artois, who called him in to execute six paintings interspersed with mirrors for a boudoir at Bagatelle. Another boudoir at Bagatelle was entirely mirrored, and the doors of the Palais Bourbon salon were glazed too, repeating the ever-changing spectacle of the gardens.

Bélisard mastered the vocabulary of the garden, for it was he who erected the delightful trelliswork pavilion at the nearby Pavillon de Lassay to house J.-B. Pigalle's sculpture of 'Love and Friendship'.[4] This 'Parisian Trianon' (Gallet 1972), with its segmental openings separated by rusticated pilasters, partook of the life of the river, for its stairway led down to the edge of the Seine.

This was typical of a tendency to link the dwelling with the river or the boulevards. Madame Thélusson's pavilion by Ledoux was preceded by a huge triumphal arch half-buried in the ground, inviting strollers to glance in at the garden. Although Ledoux thought of it as 'buried architecture', the actress Sophie Arnould grudgingly remarked that it looked 'like a great mouth that opened without saying anything.' The Prince de Condé acquired so much surrounding property that the Palais Bourbon became an estate in the Faubourg Saint Germain which he shared with the Princesse de Monaco, who lived for a while in its dependence, the Hôtel de Lassay (p.177). In 1774 she engaged the Orléans' architect, A.-T. Brongniart, to build the Hôtel de Monaco for her, with a circular vestibule and arcades of clipped greenery in the garden to shelter classical statuary.

Not to be outdone by their Condé rivals, the Orléans also assumed the mantle of patronage, and to them we owe some of the most innovative garden architecture of the day. They were even given credit for having built the first landscape garden, for Alexandre de Laborde stated that it was the Orléans who first 'broke with the melancholy regularity of classic gardens'[5] at their château of Le Raincy (1769-83).

There was naturally an English village, and engravings depict Orléans strolling by the lake with his page Narcisse at his side, followed by an English hunting dog (p.206). The houses for the locksmith, fountains' expert and gardeners were of wood and plaster painted to look like brick, similar to those of the Le Raincy Hameau, which included a dairy attached to the orangerie.

By 1773 the Duc de Chartres (who became the Duc d'Orléans in 1785) had engaged the artist Carmontelle to design the Parc Monceau. This ambitious undertaking purported to give a lesson in architecture 'from all times and all places.' The mechanical devices beloved of architects in the Louis XVI age were exploited, too, such as the door that swung open at the touch of a button concealed in the engraved mirrors of the Chinese kiosk. The open door revealed a little staircase that led to a subterranean salon, whose lighted chandeliers were infinitely multiplied in the mirrored walls.

The Prince de Conti (1717-76) also preferred his Paris residence to Versailles. At the Temple, this Prince of the Blood was preoccupied with his remarkable art collection,[6] entertaining his friends at English tea, where the young Mozart's performance was recorded by Conti's artist, Ollivier. For hunting, there was Conti's château of l'Ile-Adam, and Ollivier's painting depicts the fashionable striped tents Conti put up for suppers following the chase (see p.17).

The advent of the *jardin anglo-chinois* into France was accompanied by such a proliferation of garden structures that the decades just preceding the Revolution marked the summit of this feverish activity, in the countryside as well as Paris. What struck Thomas Blaikie about the French interpretation of the new garden style was the sheer number of buildings crowded together within the space of a single domain, such as Monceau. Nor did he care for the mingling within the same garden of the antique, the oriental, the Gothic, the rustic, the Egyptian, for he thought this artless *mélange* quite destroyed the effect. His criticism of French prolixity was often justified, for gardens like Méréville or the Désert de Retz were like pages from the *Encyclopédie* come to life.

Before discussing in more detail some of these new gardens that were renewing the countryside, we must look briefly at the salient types of architecture that appealed to this epicurean, pampered society.

The Rustic

The most surprising and apparently the earliest was the taste for the rural — hermitages, windmills, *chaumières* (cottages with thatched or rush roofs), dairies, and farms. This impulse was apparently initiated in large measure by Charles-Henri Watelet (1718-86), and it has been pointed out that as early as the 1740s 'such Frenchmen as Boucher, Watelet and Hubert Robert [were] observing, collecting, and illustrating . . . rural scenes with rustic buildings.'[7]

Watelet made his first Italian tour to study the gardens, with the intention of creating a picturesque garden on a property he had not yet acquired. On his return, he found near Bezons in 1754 exactly the diversified terrain that he needed, and on it stood an abandoned windmill named Moulin-Joli — precisely the *morceau d'architecture* required to evoke the desired associations.

The names of two artists whom Watelet engaged to help him carry out his project are inextricably associated with our subject. The first is François Boucher (adept at painting dovecots, hermitages, and watermills), who designed for the owner of Moulin-Joli a simple bourgeois house. The other is Hubert Robert,[8] to whom Watelet turned for the dairy and watermills, and who was later indispensable to Louis XVI and the Queen in their garden projects.

Moulin-Joli became so renowned that Marie-Antoinette visited it, as did her garden adviser the Prince de Ligne, Fragonard, Robert's patron the Abbé de Saint-Non, Horace Walpole and Benjamin Franklin. Its influence would be far-reaching, and *moulins* also graced irregular gardens in Paris. There were Dutch windmills at Monceau,

Claude-Louis Châtelet, 'Bellevue – Mesdames' Garden at Meudon', 1784.
The château of Bellevue was Madame de Pompadour's finest decorative achievement, but after her death it belonged to the aunts of Louis XVI (Louis XV's remaining daughters) known as Mesdames. In 1780-3 they commissioned an English garden, complete with artificial lake and a Hameau similar to Marie-Antoinette's, most likely designed by the Queen's architect, Richard Mique. The Marlborough Tower in neo-Gothic taste on the rock formation appears to be almost a replica of the Queen's at Trianon. It was a drain on the treasury to maintain Mesdames, and it has been said that Marie-Antoinette cost the state much less than the King's brothers or Mesdames, who were escorted to take the Vichy waters by 250 people and 160 horses

and the functioning windmill of the Folie Beaujon which distributed water to the gardens. It was of composite style, the rotunda base embellished with pointed arches in the Gothic manner, and at the top, a curious structure suggesting a minaret (p.185).

Hermitages were found in the Duc de Penthièvre's Rambouillet garden and at Bagatelle, where it was made of branches that reached out to offer a seat to the stroller. Almost invariably their roofs were of thatch or rushes, like the *chaumières* seen in the most up-to-date gardens, such as the Chaumière des Coquillage built by the Duc de Penthièvre for his daughter-in-law, the Princesse de Lamballe. In Paris the Duc de Chartres' sister, Bathilde d'Orléans,[9] received clairvoyants in her garden with a *chaumière* and *potager* to give an illusion of the country on the Champs Elysées. At Chaillot the façade of the *chaumière* built by Francois-Henri, Duc d'Harcourt, expressed extreme poverty, but the interior was smartly fitted up as a striped military tent with trophies.

The vogue for this type of pavilion with impoverished exterior and luxurious interior had been launched by the Hameau of Condé at Chantilly and Marie-Antoinette's Hameau at Versailles. These hamlets and farms invariably included a dairy, which acquired a sophisticated anti-Rococo sobriety in the Rambouillet Laiterie de la Reine. The King's aunts, Mesdames, followed her example in the Hameau of their château of Bellevue. The architect Bélanger included rustic pavilions at Santeny and in the gardens of his wantonly extravagant patron, Claude Baudard de Saint-James, which adjoined the grounds of Bagatelle.

The Antique

Above all, French garden architecture – like French dwellings – was expected to demonstrate an antique pedigree. There was still abundant evidence of the Roman presence on French soil, such as the Maison Carrée at Nimes, the subject of one of Hubert Robert's canvases. Its columned portico reappeared in altered form as the Temple of Friendship in the Princesse de Monaco's garden at Bctz,[10] and the Duc d'Orléans' Palladian theatre in the gardens of the Hôtel de Montesson.

Temples proliferated in French gardens, and they all looked back to examples from the ancient world such as the Temple of Vesta in Rome, the Temple of the Sibyl at Tivoli, or Varro's Aviary. The architect P.-A. Paris reinterpreted the famous Aviary as a veritable tholos for the garden, and it appeared in the ephemeral festival architecture

Hubert Robert, 'Monks at a Circular Temple, ?1775. In 1759 Robert was in Italy with his friend and fellow student Fragonard and when they returned to France they were constantly inspired by memories of Italy. Here Robert has drawn upon the circular Roman Temple of Vesta and the Temple of the Sibyl at Tivoli. In the last quarter of the eighteenth century ruins were more interesting to artists and garden designers than intact buildings, for they evoked the grandeur of the past. Here a group of monks sit beside a ruined temple. The base of cut stones has opened up to form a sort of stage as a dark-robed priest descends the stairs. This is an example of the type of caprice ruin picture for which Robert became famous

that he designed for the Queen's parties.

The most appealing antique example was apparently the Temple of the Sibyl (1st century B.C.). Celebrated by artists like Vernet, Fragonard, and Hubert Robert, the round Temple surrounded by a screen of columns was transformed into a garden *fabrique*. It provided the right poetic, artistic, archaeological touch demanded by the theorists, it was equally attractive from all sides, and its hollow centre could be dramatically used to set off a piece of sculpture.

Richard Mique's Temple of Love for Marie-Antoinette's garden was its most celebrated version, a project in which Hubert Robert may have collaborated. The painter/landscape designer modelled many of his garden ornaments upon its unassailable dignity, including the decorous temples of Méréville and Ermenonville, which might be considered the French response to Stowe. Charles de Wailly had interpreted Tivoli as a Temple of the Arts at Ménars (1770), and at Monceau it became the Temple of White Marble with twelve Corinthian columns. At Hagley it was called the Rotunda, and Bélanger sketched it in his English notebook, a valuable source for the architect's future French garden designs.

The Tivoli Temple even inspired table decorations, which often took the form of a French garden in the last reign of the *ancien régime*. A large monopteral temple with columns laced with greenery figured as an impressive *surtout de table* at Madame Du Barry's famous dinner party for Louis XV at Louveciennes in 1771 (p.165). When the City of Paris celebrated the birth of the Dauphin in January 1782, a garden with three pavilions in temple form and white biscuit statuary was constructed on the top of the royal table (opposite). The association of pavilions with festivals has a long history, an extravagant example of which was the landscaped pavilion constructed entirely of foodstuffs (*cuccagna*) that had been created in 1748 at the court of Parma to honour Louis XV's daughter.

The most astounding application of archaeology to a garden was found at Monsieur de Monville's Désert de Retz near l'Ile-Adam. Here the debonair Monville – a companion of the Duc de Chartres – lived in a gigantic truncated Doric column consisting of a cellar and four storeys. It bore no relationship to human scale, and even today this strange apparition suggests a wierd but fascinating dream.

The Orient

There was a reassuring air of permanence and solidity about garden structures in the form of temples, pantheons, columns and obelisks, whose code of reference was the ancient world, but the confirmed classicists took a dim view of the insubstantial frivolities of oriental decoration. Nevertheless, the taste for *chinoiseries* gained ground, and they were even incongruously juxtaposed with classical dwellings.

The garden of the Marquis de Marigny's hôtel by Soufflot (1769), which brought

Moreau le Jeune, Fête Given for Marie-Antoinette by the City of Paris, 21 January, 1782.
The City of Paris offered several days of fêtes for the Queen to celebrate the Dauphin's birth. The state dinner took place in the huge gallery seen here, designed by the architect P.-L. Moreau-Desproux, and the art of the garden invaded the table. The centrepieces are three monopteral temples of astonishing height, resting upon a lake (mirror). The dome of the largest is surmounted by a Medici vase with flowers, and the domes of all three are supported on flowering, beribboned Ionic colonnettes. The tablescape is arranged like a French formal garden, with the statuettes in Sèvres biscuit so highly favoured by the King. During the meal, people constantly circulated around the table, watching the King and Queen dine. Some of the guests complained that there was such a throng the waiters could not get through, so all they had to eat was butter and radishes

Palladianism to the capital, was graced with a wooden Chinese kiosk. Monsieur Morel's severely classical Paris pavilion – with niches for antique sculpture and pediments supported by fluted columns – was topped by a *treillage* pagoda, symmetrically placed. A jarring note at Ledoux's dignified Hôtel de Montmorency (1775) was the delightful oriental garden house (p.185). Even at Versailles, Marie-Antoinette's insouciant Chinese *jeux de bague* flaunted its bright yellow and vermilion painted dragons under the windows of Gabriel's impeccable Petit Trianon of honey-coloured stone.

The oriental influence in French decoration had already been seen in Louis XIV's Trianon de Porcelaine, reflecting the direct contact with China that France enjoyed through its Jesuit missionaries,[11] and *chinoiseries* were perfect complements to the

183

Rococo of Louis XV's day. As the 'beautiful, calculated anti-symmetry'[12] praised by Father Attiret was applied to the gardens of Louis XVI's reign, terrain that had once been arranged geometrically was now set out as a succession of scenes like a Chinese painting, each of which was punctuated by a piece of appropriate architecture.

Imaginative oriental fantasies found their way into some interesting gardens: at Baudard de Saint-James' Paris folly a Chinese kiosk in the middle of a lake; at the neighbouring Bagatelle a Chinese Philosopher's House; at the Duc de Penthièvre's Rambouillet an oriental kiosk; at Choiseul's Chanteloup a tall pagoda; at Monville's Désert de Retz a Chinese House of painted wood; at Bergeret de Grancourt's water garden at Cassan a (now-restored) Chinese pavilion (p.89). Cassan represents yet another marriage of oriental whimsy with classicism, for it rests upon a substructure of eight massive Doric columns.

The Exotic

Besides the numerous structures that were supposedly Chinese, other exoticisms appeared. At the Orléans' Le Raincy was a Russian house; at the Duc de Penthièvre's château of Armainvilliers a Turkish pavilion; at Monceau Tartar and Turkish tents and a den formed of rocks supporting a Minaret. The Turkish mode even swept through the court, where the Queen and the Comte d'Artois ordered Turkish boudoirs. But the most seductive *turquerie* of all was conceived for the Paris hôtel of Monsieur de Monville. Lighted from above, its walls were completely mirrored, a luxuriously thick Turkish rug covered the floor, and disposed around the entire room were crimson velvet divans smothered in Italian silk cushions.

Twenty years before Napoleon's campaign, Egypt was evoked by obelisks in the gardens of Monceau, Bagatelle, the Désert de Retz, and Betz, where Hubert Robert and the Duc d'Harcourt composed a Pharaoh's Tomb for the Princesse de Monaco's Valley of Tombs, planting it with the pines and cypresses associated with tragedy. At Mauperthuis, the Marquis de Montesquieu engaged the Orléans architect Brongniart to design most of the garden monuments, one of which he conceived as an enormous ruined Egyptian pyramid with four heavy columns marking the entrance. But it suggested the Mausoleum of Halicarnassus rather than a monument from the Valley of the Kings.

At Monceau's Valley of Tombs, the principal one was Egyptian with caryatids marking each side of the entrance, and granite columns with Egyptian capitals for the interior. Here the association was masonic and sinister, for the Duc de Chartres was attracted to the ancient rites of freemasonry and the occult practices of the Italian doctor Giuseppe Cagliostro, who claimed to be Egyptian.

This aspect of garden décor was related to the theorists' demand for wastelands, deserts, symbolic and visionary landscapes, where the garden was not so much decorated as haunted by phantasmagoric visions that were far from the primitive Eden. The British architect, William Chambers, prescribed rotting or petrified trees, decayed stumps, wastelands, and rushing torrents.

One entered the Désert de Retz through a dark, mysterious grotto lit by flickering torches held aloft by none-too-reassuring satyrs at either side, and at Méréville, a gigantic rock formation of huge boulders seemed ready to fall upon the visitor, who was deafened by the thundering cataracts that tumbled down beside it. These mysterious, threatening, awe-inspiring features attracted garden builders like Chartres and Montesquieu, but they never appealed to the Queen.

A.-P. Guyot, 'Moulin de la Folie Beaujon en 1827'.
Nicolas Beaujon (1708-1766), amassed a fortune from speculation in grain. In 1773 he bought the splendid Hôtel d'Evreux (today the Elysée). Tiring of metropolitan luxury, he commissioned his architect to build a sort of Dutch farmhouse on a hillside near the Etoile. Here was Beaujon's famous bedroom that resembled a garden bosquet, with the bed – a basket of flowers – suspended from the leafy ceiling, protected by trees at each corner. Commensurate with his eclectic taste, the gardens weere filled with statues, vases, busts and a variety of pavilions, including this pre-Romantic Gothic windmill that stood upon a rocky eminence and delivered water to the gardens. Although its pointed arches evoke the Gothic age, the peculiar masks placed around the tower under the upper platform seem to derive from the Renaissance

Janinet, Chinese Pavilion, Montmorency.
The Hôtel de Montmorency on the Chaussée d'Antin was designed by the sought-after architect C.-N. Ledoux (1771), who built such famous landmarks as the nearby pavilion for Mademoiselle Guimard, the Hôtels d'Hallwyl and Thélusson, and Madame Du Barry's pavilion of Louveciennes. Despite the insistently classical character of the town house, the gardens featured oriental fabrications like this Chinese pavilion

Moreau le Jeune, 'Le Souper Intime'.
Appointed Engraver to the Cabinet du Roi, Moreau le Jeune recorded many of the official occasions of the reign. He also portrayed the joys of pavilion life and la vie intime *in his* Monument du Costume, *in which this engraving and the 'La Partie de Wisch' (opposite) appeared. 'Le Souper Intime' portrays two of* les grands *dining with ladies of equivocal character. The décor, centrepiece with Three Graces, and chairs with legs of swirled fluting are Neo-classical, but the small tables that hold the chilling wine bottles and plates are still Rococo, and so is the sentiment*

Tents

One type of pavilion that Marie-Antoinette especially favoured was the tent, for light tents made of ticking could be put up easily and quickly for her garden fêtes. It was a taste she shared with her brother-in-law, the Comte d' Artois, whose Bagatelle bedchamber assumed a tent form (see p.270); tents were also seen in his adjoining English garden. At Monceau, in a bosquet bordered by flowers, stood two striped tents – one red and white, the other blue and white – both with gilded ornaments. The Marquis de Marigny's Paris garden designed by Soufflot (with the Chinese kiosk) featured a tent of painted ticking, probably for the cold collation.

The Gothic

It was inevitable that some of these garden creations take Gothic form – or more properly 'Gothick' to denote a revival. Like the Rococo, the Gothic had been born on French soil, so it naturally reappeared in the eclectic architecture of the new gardens. Gothic decoration was applied to the prominent windmill at the Folie Beaujon (p.185); a ruined Gothic château was erected in the park of Mauperthuis; in the country garden of Thierry de Ville d'Avray (Director of the Garde-Meuble) stood a Gothic chapel and, as we have already seen, in the garden of Mesdames at Bellevue stood a the neo-Gothic 'tower of Marlborough' (p.181).

The Gothic revival in England interested that dedicated pavilion-builder, Bélanger, for his English notebooks reveal sketches of Gothic furniture as well as the Gothic Temple at Cobham. It may have been a source for the first project he presented to the Marquis de Laborde for the Gothic windmill at Méréville.

When Bélanger was asked to plan Caron de Beaumarchais' famous garden in Paris, he wanted to include a Gothic décor. But instead of designing a pavilion that evoked the Middle Ages, the architect hit upon the notion of using a pre-existing, authentic Gothic monument – namely, the fourteenth-century Bastille that could be seen from the garden. So he ordered that the trees be planted in such a way as to make the nearby fortress a target of attention. Bélanger's excursions into the Gothic mode were short lived, for Monsieur de Laborde was not impressed by the architect's Gothic concept for the Méréville windmill, and the Bastille was destroyed the year after Beaumarchais' garden was planted.

Innovative gardens like Beaumarchais' were springing up all over Paris and its environs, for as Marie-Antoinette's secretary, Madame Campan, put it: 'Le foyer de l'esprit et des lumières était à Paris'.[13] The capital had already become the emporium for the arts during the Regency and even during Louis XIV's lifetime some of the more adventurous members of the court had owned town houses surrounded by gardens. Maximilien Titon's ambitious Folie Titon was decorated by major painters such as Jean Jouvenet and Charles de la Fosse, and was preceded by a vast formal garden terminated by a perspective painted by Rousseau. Mademoiselle de Charolais' famous suppers took place in the dependencies of the Renaissance château de Madrid in the Bois de

Boulogne, and the nearby pavilion of the Maréchale d'Estrées known as Bagatelle.[14] The Regent's wife owned two pavilions at Bagnolet, and the Duchesse du Maine (the Queen of Sceaux) had the enormously inventive architect, Boffrand, build one for her after 1729 in the garden of the Arsenal on the river.

Once *les élégants* had experienced the sheer delight of Regency abandon, the relaxed intimacy and physical comfort so prized by Louis XV, the court and its immediate circle never again recovered that singularity of purpose and dignity that had marked the Sun King's long reign. Once having tasted *la vie intime* afforded by a little house secluded in greenery, they were unwilling to give it up. In the 1770s a new generation of princes began to reclaim the plains of Vaugirard and Sèvres, Passy, the fields near the Champs Elysées, the swamps of the Chausée d'Antin, the forests of Neuilly, the quarter of Les Porcherons, even islands in the Seine, to transform them into delicious gardens as settings for small masterpieces by the foremost architects, decorated by the leading artists, with furnishings and appointments by the finest cabinetmakers and bronze workers.

A discussion of the interiors of these architectural gems is beyond the scope of this study, but many a pavilion was commissioned to house a fine painting collection, a choice suite of furniture, a distinguished *cabinet de curiosité*, a connoisseur's library, a diminutive theatre for concerts and theatricals, or a *salon de jeux* for the English game of whist.

Moreau le Jeune, 'La Partie de Wisch'.
Whist became a popular game on the Continent and a feature of pavilion life. The table has been placed in the open door of a small gaming pavilion, and across the courtyard stands another with Doric peristyle and classical festoons and swags in low relief. Carmontelle's preface to his Jardin de Monceau *(1779) states that in spite of the charms of nature, the gregarious Frenchman required something more – the pleasures of hunting, concerts, spectacles and games*

Each one had to be furnished with distinction, and this is one reason they were so excessively expensive. Superbly orchestrated in every detail, the furniture, paintings, sculpture, porcelains and other appointments consummated the union between interior and exterior. It is a paradox of Marie-Antoinette's age that, the more hedonistic and worldly society became, the more refined became the framework for its life.

Ceilings were gold and white, or painted like domed trelliswork with a blue sky and fleecy clouds beyond, from which depended chandeliers of ormolu in classical form, or bird cages with porcelain flowers. Walls were dissolved by mirrors, with numerous windows giving upon gardens, cancelling the divisions between inside and outside space. Sometimes they were opened up with exhilarating Hubert Robert paintings of Roman ruins under an eternal sky, or overgrown gardens with marble staircases that became lost in a profusion of verdure. At other times the wall disappeared altogether in a *trompe-l'oeil* representation of the garden itself, or the panels would be sculpted in gilt arabesques and antique forms on a white ground. White marble chimneypieces held garnitures of ormolu clocks and Sèvres porcelain to match the sinfully expensive silk lampas used for hangings and the furniture's upholstery.

Colour schemes were never obvious, but offered imaginative and subtle combinations, such as the sulphur and lilac silk draping the Duc d'Orléans' bed. Or the sophisticated lilac and white furniture that Georges Jacob made for the Comtesse de Balbi, covered with periwinkle blue silk woven with garlands and mythological figures.

Especially dear to their Greek hearts was the mahogany introduced with the English taste, for it could be shaped into tripods, or chairs with sabre or curule legs, reinterpreting the bronzes that had been excavated at Pompeii. Bélanger ordered mahogany furniture from Georges Jacob for Mademoiselle Dervieux's hôtel, which so impressed the Baronne d'Oberkirch that she remarked 'the furniture alone was worth a King's ransom'.[15] One of the finest manifestations of the late Louis XVI style was Jacob's coldly classical, austere mahogany suite for Marie-Antoinette's Rambouillet Laiterie.

It is difficult today to understand that in the late eighteenth century one's very identity was embodied in the way one lived. Novelists of the time describe in loving detail the attractions of these small houses that were the essence of chic, and a great deal of their owners' conversations were concerned with the correctness of a cornice, the proportions of a chair, the depth of a niche. But, as Mario Praz has suggested, it would not be until the nineteenth century that the décor would exert an emotive effect upon the heroine, as it did on Flaubert's Madame Bovary.

A fine dwelling surrounded by gardens, however, was no longer simply the privilege of royalty and their princely cousins, for now there occurred a levelling of society. As art patronage passed to the bourgeoisie, some of its most notable achievements were carried out for actresses, architects, writers, financiers, contractors and tax farmers (or farmers-general who 'farmed' certain indirect taxes for the royal treasury). This new, often polished clientele included many women, and the Queen's painter, Elisabeth Vigée-Lebrun, pointed out in her memoirs (written after the Revolution) that women reigned in the late eighteenth century, but were dethroned by the Revolution.

Among them were actresses and singers, who were admitted on even footing with other leaders of society. They were respected, even idolised, for their talents, and were 'protected' by royalty and princes. Their Paris hôtels by the best architects were really large pavilions, not only by virtue of size, but because of their intimate association with gardens. The point of owning a little house, after all, was its being hidden away in a bower of foliage.

The hôtels of Mesdemoiselles Guimard and de Saint-Germain, of Mesdames Thélusson and Valentenois were designed by Ledoux; those of Mademoiselles de Langeac and Dervieux, and Orléans' friend, Madame de Montesson, by Brongniart. But the star performer was Bélanger, who built so many that he was known as 'le constructeur des folies', the most famous of which was Bagatelle. His decoration of Mademoiselle Dervieux' house and gardens were as renowned for this period as were Madame Récamier's for the Directoire, and Bélanger designed the Folie Saint-James, with the most extravagant grotto in Paris – an enormous rock formation arranged to shelter a Doric temple.

Between the completion of the Petit Trianon in 1764 and Bagatelle's inauguration in 1778, over one hundred pavilions were built in and around Paris for a society teetering upon the brink of destruction. The year 1778 was a banner year, for in addition to the Folie Saint-James, the Folie Beaujon was completed, with windmills, *fabriques,* grottoes, and a carnival atmosphere generated by the Ruggieri family who specialised in fireworks. Above all, that year saw the termination of two highly significant gardens built by members of the royal family – the King's Orléans cousin, the Duc de Chartres, and his younger brother, the Comte d'Artois.

Chartres' Monceau and d'Artois' Bagatelle marked the apogee of the feverish pavilion building taking place around Paris. Monceau preceded the Queen's garden, and Bagatelle was begun after two of her pavilions were finished, so they stand as attractive parentheses to Marie-Antoinette's garden experiments at the Petit Trianon of Versailles.

CHAPTER 16

PAVILIONS BUILT BY THE HOUSE OF ORLÉANS

Louis-Philippe-Joseph d'Orléans, Duc de Chartres and future Philippe Egalité (1747-93), embodied some of the finer qualities of the *ancien régime* along with its worst abuses. Heir to the privileges of a prince of the blood, he understood that patronage was implicit therein, and he engaged the outstanding architects, garden builders, artists and sculptors of the realm to create some of the finest achievements in the second half of the century.

On the other hand, Chartres was irresponsible, profligate, hypocritical and

Louis Carrogis, called Carmontelle, 'The Duke de Chartres Receiving the Keys to Monceau'.
The artist, left, hands over the keys to Monceau to his patron the Duke de Chartres. Although Chartres was a confirmed Anglophile, Monceau was not intended to be principally an English garden, but a fantasy where were united at one site 'all times and all places', as Carmontelle pointed out in Le Jardin de Monceau (1779). In it he describes the scene: 'One sees at left the bridge of an ancient ruined fort attached to an aged tower also in ruins, and a crenellated, square brick building which serves as a watermill. Next comes a brick and limestone bridge with three arches . . . Above the bridge one can make out . . . the Dutch windmill, the tall minaret . . . a rock formation and the ruins of the Temple of Mars'

represented the decadence of a society whose principal aim in life was to make it agreeable for each other. It was an unsettling paradox of the age that it reached a zenith of artistic refinement at the same time that it plumbed the depths of moral depravity, and the Duc de Chartres might well stand as its symbol.

At court, Chartres' influence was anything but salutary, for he exerted a malignant influence upon his cousin, the Comte d'Artois, who was ten years his junior. He would take the impressionable d'Artois to the most licentious cabarets, and introduced him to women of the night at the Orléans' Paris establishment, the Palais Royal, which became a centre of relentless antipathy to the Crown. Built by Cardinal Richelieu as his Paris town house (then the Palais Cardinal), it had passed in time to Louis XIV's brother, Monsieur, thence to his son the Regent, and in 1780 to Chartres himself.

With his liberal ideas and flexible life-style, Chartres was not kindly regarded at court, for the King was disturbed by his liaison with his younger brother. The Queen only gradually realised the dangers of associating with this spoiled prince with an elastic conscience who was taken with illuminism and subscribed to the works of scurrilous pamphleteers. Although she attended one of Chartres' parties at the Palais Royal in 1777, and shared the Opéra loge of his father, the Duc d'Orléans, she studiously avoided any potentially compromising situations, eventually saw that she was playing with fire, and began to avoid both of them. When Marie-Antoinette gave birth to a Dauphin in October 1781, making an Orléans accession even more remote, tension between the sovereigns and the Orléans was further exacerbated, and by 1784 relations had become so strained that members of the court's inner circle were compelled to choose sides.

Unfortunately, the heir to the Orléans fortune appealed to women: 'Le sombre éclat de ses yeux bleus et languides jetait le trouble dans le coeur des femmes' remarked one of Chartres' friends.[1] One of these ladies upon whom Chartres cast his languid blue eyes was Louise-Marie-Adelaide de Bourbon-Penthièvre, only surviving child of the Duc de Penthièvre. One of the redeeming figures of the eighteenth century (Louis XV called him the finest man in his kingdom), Penthièvre was father-in-law of Marie-Antoinette's favourite, the Princesse de Lamballe, to whom Penthièvre offered one of the most unusual *folies* of the period.

Penthièvre's daughter, Adelaide, was probably the richest princess in France, if not in Europe, and in 1769 she married her libertine cousin, Chartres. For his daughter's wedding, the Duc de Penthièvre provided a *souper intime* (at least two hundred guests) in his beautiful town house, the celebrated Hôtel de Toulouse, now the Bank of France. With Bourbon affluence added to Orléans fortune, the Duc de Chartres became the major landowner in France, as well as the father of six children, one of whom would become the much-maligned Louis-Philippe.

Another alarming aspect of Chartres' character was his interest in freemasonry, into which he introduced the young d'Artois, for Chartres was a powerful figure among the freethinkers who rejected historical Christianity. He was Grand Master of French Freemasonry, and founded his own lodge in September 1774, calling it St. Jean de Chartres à l'Orient de Mouceaux [Monceau]. The clandestine rites that took place in the principal pavilion at Monceau were accompanied by theatrical effects – blindfolded initiates, thunder, and lightning. Freemasonry accounted in large measure for the philosophical presuppositions of a tottering society, and found tangible expression in such garden ornaments as the obelisks, pyramids and columns that recur with

Louis Carrogis, called Carmontelle (1717-1809), self-portrait. When the peace that ended the Seven Years' War was signed in 1763, Carmontelle became Reader to Chartres' father, the Duc d'Orléans (1725-85), a post that also entailed writing, portraiture, organising fêtes and plays, and creating stage scenery. So versatile was he that the author Philippe Jullian called him 'the Sacha Guitry of his time'. In almost all the portraits he painted, his sitters are presented in profile. Besides the Orléans, others he portrayed were the Duc de Penthièvre, Princesse de Lamballe, the Duchesse de Polignac, and celebrities like Mozart, Bachaumont, and Benjamin Franklin

monotonous regularity in the landscape garden, particularly at Monceau.

Freemasonry was essentially aristocratic, and attracted some of most illustrious men of the realm: Louis XV's valet de chambre, his father-in-law Stanislas, the Comte de Mailly, the Duc de Richelieu of course, the Prince de Conti, the secretaries of state Maurepas and Saint-Florentin, and the Duc d'Antin, a peer of France and – significantly – the Orléans' tutor.

These influential figures were patrons of the most accomplished artists, most of whom were members of masonic lodges themselves: painters such as Hubert Robert and J.-B. Greuze, the sculptors Clodion, Pajou and Houdon, the engraver Moreau le Jeune, the architects Charles De Wailly and Chalgrin. Among members in salon circles were Benjamin Franklin and the enormously influential writers d'Alembert and Voltaire.

Hubert Robert's biographer, Jean Cayeux, noted that it was safe to say that almost everyone in France was a mason in the years just before the Revolution.[2] Hubert Robert himself was a prominent mason whose clientele ranged from the royal family to the rich bourgeoisie, which played a key role in art patronage. He enjoyed a personal friendship with the King and Queen, and at least two of his Mason friends moved in court circles: the Comte de Caraman, who planned the Queen's garden, and the artist Joseph Vernet, who had painted the famous series of French seaports for Louis XV.

Cardinal Fleury, to whom Louis XV as an orphan child was close, fought valiantly against these secret societies, but Fleury's death in 1743 ended most official opposition to them. Bernard Faÿ believed that the decline of Louis XV corresponded exactly with the triumph of freemasonry, which quietly put a minister into an important post, operated in back corridors, and manipulated politics to its own interests. Since Chartres stood at the apex of French freemasonry, it is not surprising to find masonic imagery abounding at Monceau.

Monceau

For the design of Monceau, Chartres turned not to an architect, but to a playwright who since 1763 had been *amuseur attitré* to his father, the Duc d'Orléans: Louis Carrogis, known as Carmontelle. His duties required that he arrange the Duke's fêtes at the Palais Royal, compose theatre pieces to be played in the Orléans' private theatre, design the garden buildings, accompany his patron to the cascades of Saint

The Egyptian Tomb in the Woodland of Tombs at Monceau.
Death was robbed of its significance and tombs exploited as decorative devices in Monceau's Woodland of Tombs. Here tombs of all sorts were scattered among suitably funereal trees, this pyramidal form being the principal feature and suggesting Egypt

The Naumachie, Parc Monceau.
Named for the Roman naumachia, a place for mock sea battles and spectacles, the Naumachie was a lake with a half-circle of ruined capitals. In Chartres' day it was favoured as a pleasure and boating area

Duc d'Orléans and his son Louis-Philippe, Duc de Chartres.
The fat Duc d'Orléans sits with his son, the Duc de Chartres age twelve, probably watching a play or an early version of a magic lantern or transparency show, with which invention Madame de Genlis credited Carmontelle. Scenes were painted on a band of Chinese paper or vellum bound at top and bottom by a black galloon to prevent tearing, then passed before a sunlit window, giving the effect of an ever-changing panorama. On these bands Carmontelle, the Duke's master of entertainment, painted scenes of the seigneurial life in parks and châteaux: hunts and fishing parties, evening balls, châteaux with windows lighted at night, fires, and strollers in the Orléans gardens

Cloud to escape the air of Paris, hunt with the family at the château of Villers-Cotterêts, and participate in the pleasures of Le Raincy's model farm, where he would sit, crayon in hand, transforming the guests into harlequins, Turks, or Romans. For Carmontelle wore his sketching pad on his sleeve, and has left us portraits of the major part of eighteenth-century high society, twenty-seven of which Catherine the Great ordered Baron Grimm, her agent, to have engraved for her.

Madame de Genlis, of whom more later, was instrumental in the publication of twenty volumes of Carmontelle's plays, and she credited him with having conceived the idea of constructing the magic lantern that became a popular amusement. This forerunner of motion pictures she described as a strip of transparent paper upon which the artist had painted a series of landscape scenes, some of which are extant. The long rolls were then passed before a light, which gave the viewers an impression of visiting the gardens Carmontelle had depicted.

This is exactly the way that Carmontelle conceived of Monceau (or Mousseaux) – like the painted paper that passed before the magic lantern, but in three dimensions. For the playwright naturally thought in theatrical terms, and his aim at Monceau was to create a garden that represented 'the shifting scenes of an opera', as he stated in the preface to his publication *Le Jardin de Monceau*.

In 1769 Chartres had created a small *jardin français* on a large piece of property on the edge of Paris bordering the vast plain of Monceau, and at its centre stood a pavilion by Louis-Marie Colignon. In 1773 Carmontelle took over, and during the next five years he transformed Chartres' terrain into the type of garden that had triumphed at Moulin-Joli, Ermenonville, Chantilly, and was just beginning to take shape in the Queen's landscape ventures at Versailles. The aim, he wrote, was 'to embellish the countryside with taste and talent.'

Here the heir to the Orléans forturne could indulge his mania for collecting on a grand scale, for Chartres was a graphic example of the encyclopaedic interests of his class – and its escapist mentality. So, into the fantastic topography of this land of illusion, his designer scattered copies of Greek and Roman statues executed by the best sculptors. Among them were Bouchardon, Pigalle and Houdon, who provided the figure of a bather with her attendant for the Naumachie, a lake with half-circle of columns. The terrain featured every conceivable type of *folie*, placed like objects in a

Louis Carrogis, called Carmontelle, view of the Wooden Bridge at Monceau.
The path that passes over the Wooden Bridge leads to the Naumachie. In the middle of the vast oval
basin of the Naumachie stood a rock formation with a granite obelisk carved with hieroglyphs, symbol of
the Orient and no doubt a reference to freemasonry. The obelisk was a highly exploited device, having
been used by both Papal and Imperial Rome

vitrine, and they provided emphasis to the dramatic sequences of the park as they unfolded before the stroller's eyes.

For erudite visitors they could be read as a lesson in architecture, for members of Chartres' class delighted in building, and commissioned some of the outstanding town houses of Europe. Voltaire described them in a classic passage: 'A young nobleman of fortunate birth is neither painter, nor musician, neither architect, nor sculptor; but he makes all these arts flourish through his munificence, for it is probably more valuable to *support* them than to practise them. It is enough for my lord to have taste, and only right for the artists to work for him . . . persons of quality . . . know everything without having learnt anything, because they genuinely know how to appreciate all the things which they commission and pay for.'

One entered the grounds of Monceau via a Chinese gate beside a small Gothic building that housed the chemistry laboratory. The principal pavilion, which served as Chartres' residence, was conceived on a central plan, of two storeys, and elongated at each of the four angles by four galleries crowned with antique balusters. Monumental pilasters surrounded the central edifice, with the basement of stone horizontally rusticated, and enriched with precious materials: yellow Siennese marbles alternating with *rouge du Languedoc* marble (like the Grand Trianon), and gilt bronze garlands adorning the capitals, cornices, and grillework.

From the main dwelling, the visitor moved from marvel to marvel, beginning with the Jeu de Bague, a game popular with such perpetual adolescents as Chartres and d'Artois. It was covered by a large Chinese parasol decorated with bells, the platform supported by three oriental figures, a fashion that would be reflected in Marie-Antoinette's merry-go-round at the Petit Trianon.

Then the path skirted a lake with an island of poplars, reminiscent of those that guarded Rousseau's tomb on the island at Ermenonville. This introduced the visitor to one of the cerebral pleasures of the picturesque garden – ruins, which recalled the antique glory that had passed away. Although not as grand as the spectacular ruins that Hubert Robert composed for the Princesse de Monaco at Betz, there were fragmented moss-covered bridges, remnants of 'Gothic' buildings that sprouted trees, an abandoned Temple of Mars with a mutilated statue of the god at the centre, and truncated columns imbued with masonic imagery.

Columns invariably played a major role in the decoration of an English garden, but

Louis Carrogis, called Carmontelle, view of Principal Pavilion and Jeu de Bague at Monceau.
The principal pavilion, occupied by Chartres, was described by Carmontelle as having been painted to resemble rustications of yellow Siennese marble with bronze garlands, and pilasters encircling the entire building. The capitals, bases and ornaments were of antique bronze and it was furnished in the English taste. Carmontelle described the Jeu de Bague as a Chinese parasol with a border decorated with small bells and supported by three Chinese figures. The ladies' seats are held by Chinese personages, and four lanterns hold the rings that are presented as the riders pass

in this matter Chartres was upstaged by his admired friend, Monsieur de Monville, who had bought a property near Marly, which he was transforming into a garden that rivalled Monceau. At the Désert de Retz stood the most impressive column in garden history – a gigantic fragment of four storeys like a piece of sculpture to be inhabited (see Chapter 17). In fact it *was* lived in, for Monville fitted up the interior as an elegant folly, and Thomas Blaikie, the Scottish gardener who was engaged at Monceau about 1781, thought the Retz column was 'meant to emitate [sic] the tower of Babel.' The cantankerous Scot often encountered de Monville with the Orléans clan at Le Raincy or Monceau, and considered this quintessential French *amateur* to be 'a Pretended Connoisseur in everything'.[3]

If Monville's column was the largest, the highest must have belonged to the proprietor of the the Maison Deshayes (1781-2) at the corner of the Boulevard de la Madeleine and Rue Caumartin in Paris. This fascinating hôtel featured an Anglo-Chinese garden on its roof, complete with pyramids, triumphal arches, Chinese bridges over artificial rivulets, a large oriental pavilion over the entrance visible from the street below, sham ruins, and airborne truncated columns.

The eighteenth century's appreciation for ruins was interpreted by Mario Praz as 'an outspoken refusal to see architecture as the expression of a permanent law of harmony: instead, it was invested with the capricious character of the English garden, and valued as an expression of the picturesque.'[4] Whether ruins were to be considered as masonic expressions, references to the Tower of Babel, or merely as picturesque, it was apparent that no self-respecting English garden could be without them. In the same melancholy (and sinister) vein was a Woodland of Tombs at Monceau, with the principal tomb in pyramidal form to suggest Egypt. It recalled Mozart's *The Magic Flute* and referred to the association of freemasonry with the Orient (p.192).

In Monceau's Woodland of Tombs, death was robbed of its significance and exploited as a decorative device, for tombs of all sorts were scattered among groves of cypresses, poplars and sycamores to induce the proper mood. Funerary monuments were so popular that P.-A. Paris, the architect who designed fêtes for the Queen, sketched a project for a nymphaeum with coupled cenotaphs to commemorate departed friends, leaving spaces for those yet to die. Apparently he hoped they'd go in pairs so as not to

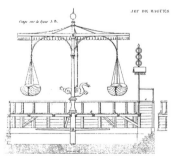

Georges Le Rouge, model of a jeu de bague.
Usually the jeux de bague were turned by men in an underground chamber, and as the riders circled around, they attempted to put pegs into the rings as they passed

Gabriel de Saint-Aubin (1724-1780), 'The Naumachie at Parc Monceau, 1778'. Saint-Aubin is remembered as a charming and remarkably prolific watercolourist. In his painting of the Naumachie, he takes a romantic view of the architectural ruins being sketched by the seated artists at right

spoil the symmetry. And the playwright and supplier-of-arms to the rebel American colonies, Caron de Beaumarchais, introduced a tomb into the elaborate gardens of his Paris house, to mark the spot where he intended to be buried.

Monceau boasted not only architectural exoticism, but botanical and animal as well, to create the illusion of distant lands. Thomas Blaikie described the Orléans collection of choice botanical specimens as 'a Botanic school where the Duke and sometimes his children came to learn plants.'[5] There were camels with keepers in Tartar costume, presumably occupants of the gaily striped tents trimmed with gilt fringe. Freshly groomed sheep and cows wandered freely among the strollers to lend a pastoral note, and a picturesquely dressed farmer presided over the immaculate farm with its story-book domestic animals – Beatrix Potter *avant la lettre*. Blaikie, in fact, described the Orléans château of Le Raincy with its romantic log huts as 'an English colony'.

Beyond Monceau's Ile des Rochers stood a Dutch windmill, and behind it an impeccable laiterie, its interior walls clad with marble revetments. The dairy was appointed with porcelain vases, and a porcelain service for dispensing fruits, milk and cheese upon marble tables. Elegant tableware had been an Orléans tradition since the days of Monsieur, patron of the renowned St. Cloud manufacture of soft paste porcelain and faïence. Their Le Raincy dairy boasted Wedgwood pottery in the latest taste, for the Orléans were among the foremost enthusiasts for the English vogue. Chartres perpetuated the family's patronage for ceramics, and he even established a glassworks at their château of Villers-Cotterêts.

A favourite spot at Monceau for those given to boating – and nostalgia for the Roman past – was the Naumachie, which took its name from the mock naval battles of antiquity. It consists of a lake bordered by a circular screen of columns brought from a chapel which Catherine de' Medicis had begun to construct at the north of the basilica of Saint Denis as a tomb for Henri II and then her own.

Characteristic of the period (and the Orléans family), elements destined to serve a sacred purpose were appropriated for a secular one, and to reinforce the concept, the basin and columns of the Naumachie were installed to invoke the spirit of pagan nymphaea. The Naumachie is extant in the Park Monceau (p.192). Another feature of the park based on a sacred building but intended to serve as a secular one was the Temple of White Marble, a favourite spot for secluded conversation, reading or concerts.

Louis Carrogis, called Carmontelle, view of Temple of White Marble, Monceau. The Temple, almost hidden by trees and low shrubbery, offered a shelter for secluded conversation, reading, or concerts. In the form of a rotunda with cupola, it was later transported by order of Louis-Philippe to the Island of La Grande Jatte, immortalised in Seurat's painting

The park's primary purpose was for convivial gatherings, for the gregarious Frenchman was 'not sufficient unto himself', in Carmontelle's view, but motivated by a 'desire to please, to love and be loved', and this – he argued – was best accomplished in the country. When he wrote: 'C'est dans la campagne qu'on gôute mieux la douceur d'être ensemble' he voiced the opinion of an entire society.

One delectable hideaway for the Duke's special guests was the Winter Garden. It was hidden by trees, its entrance marked by a faun holding two lighted torches, with a grotto and cascade beside it, similar to the entrance to his friend Monville's Désert de Retz. Access was gained by pushing a button beside a mirrored door that swung open to reveal a vaulted cavern, from whose coloured sand floor sprang tropical plants – bananas, palms, Judas trees, Indian walnuts, coffee, and cane sugar. At the bottom of the cavern, there were three steps, another door, and beyond it a pavilion in the form of an 'antique tent' hung entirely in white cotton embroidered with pearls. Here the Duke entertained his guests at dinner with the most exquisite dishes, serenaded by his orchestra concealed in a space above. Whereas the walls of the Prince de Condé's Hameau had been painted in *trompe-l'oeil* to represent a forest glade, in Chartres' cavern, naturally coloured trees were sculpted in relief, their branches arching over the ceiling from which crystal lanterns were suspended.

The *vie galante* was served on every hand: intimate suppers lighted by flickering candles in an underground grotto; rendezvous on cosy ottomans in striped tents with serenades by hidden musicians; reading on benches in white marble temples where one took refuge from the rain; lolling on mossy banks beside rushing cascades. His inclination for the *vie galante* Chartres inherited from his father, for both would have heartily agreed with Carmontelle, who declared in the preface to *Le Jardin de Monceau*: 'On s'occupe de plaire aux femmes; ce sont elles qui font les délices de la société'.

The Palais Royal

Although Monceau was principally intended for the delectation of the Duc de Chartres and his guests, he opened it up to the public with admission tickets. It was, as Carmontelle indicated, like going to the opera, except that the 'audience' was able to enter the three-dimensional settings themselves.

Chartres' fascination with the stage must have begun as a child, for his father's court at Villers-Cotterêts, Le Raincy, Saint Cloud, and the Palais Royal resonated with the sounds of rehearsals for Carmontelle's *proverbes*, comedies, or revivals of Molière. After the peace of 1763, Carmontelle staged *Le Bourgeois Gentilhomme* for Chartres' father

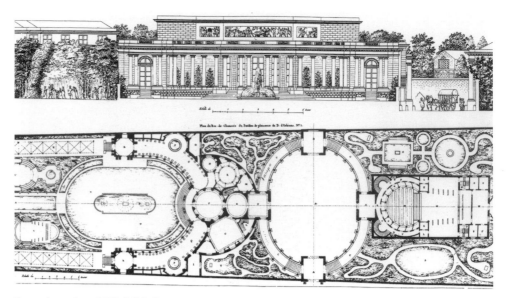

Brongniart, plan of Hôtel d'Orléans.
The pavilion in which the Duc d'Orléans lived in the midst of gardens features a round salon (centre) with curving steps leading down to the oval tapis vert with a long basin at its centre. North and south of the basin are two small octagonal outdoor salons for concerts or meals. The round salon joins an oval then a rectangular anctechamber, from which one descends to a huge oval court defined by trelliswork. Across it is the theatre (right), its large curving pit surrounded by loges with two circular stairs in the corners and set in an English garden

(the Duc d'Orléans) in the grand salon of Villers-Cotterêts. Of course, the fat duke and his son Chartres also patronised the three highly respected Paris theatres subsidised by the King – the Opéra (Académie Royale de Musique), the Comédie-Française, and the Comédie Italienne – the last of which had been restored to France by the Duc d'Orléans' grandfather, the Regent. The Queen, whose attachment to the theatre contributed to her undoing, sometimes shared the Orléans loge in the early days of her marriage. She would often be accompanied by her brother-in-law, the heedless Comte d'Artois, who is known to have written verses for satirical popular songs that found their way into some of the most aristocratic establishments.

In an age preoccupied with the stage – and which made idols of those who performed upon it – it was considered modish to include a theatre in one's town house or in the garden. This is precisely what happened at the luxurious enclave that the Duc d'Orléans shared with a lady whose private theatricals were among the most renowned in Paris.

Just before Chartres began Monceau, his father fell in love with a virtuous and accomplished widow, the Marquise de Montesson. With a handsome inheritance from her rich husband, the Marquise engaged the Duke's architect, Alexandre Brongniart, to design a delectable pavilion for her at the corner of the Rue de Provence and the Chaussée-d'Antin, which was finished in May 1771.

It was a model of Brongniart's restrained classicism: the garden elevation with tall windows and doors surmounted by delicate plaques with low-relief decoration, and enframed by two *treillage* pavilions. The same architect also gave projects for Madame de Montesson's famous theatre, to which invitations were eagerly sought by the *beau monde* of Paris.

In 1773 or 1775, she married the Duc d'Orléans, a union that Louis XV permitted on condition that Madame de Montesson never appear at court, nor assume the Orléans name, nor live under the Duc d'Orléans' roof. So the Duke forfeited his apartments in the Palais Royal, and in 1773 engaged Brongniart to construct his own pavilion on the Rue de Provence adjacent to Madame de Montesson's hôtel with which it shared the extensive gardens. Madame de Latour du Pin remarked that 'the Duc d'Orléans had his

Ledoux, Hôtel Guimard.
The façade of Mademoiselle Guimard's town house focuses upon Félix Lecomte's central sculptural celebration of the Triumph of Terpsichore, muse of dancing and choral song, and the low-relief panel over the doorway enlarges upon the Terpsichorean theme. Composed in austere geometrical terms like Louveciennes, the entrance is also marked by four fluted Ionic columns, and the unframed openings by voussoirs with panels above them

own entrance in the Rue de Provence, with a porter in his livery, and Madame de Montesson had hers with a porter in grey livery. But they shared the same courtyard.'[6]

Although greatly altered later by the architect Henri Pietre, the circular lines of the Duke's pavilion gave the impression of a huge spiral shell, its lines echoed in elliptical courtyards. One room was painted to simulate a garden bosquet, and the round salon exuded an 'aquatic freshness',[7] perpetrating the garden theme in wall reliefs, cornices of children bearing garlands, and a view of the long *tapis vert*. Hidden away from the boulevard and communicating with the Hôtel de Montesson via the garden, it suggested a Roman villa in a landscape garden of great depth and unlimited perspectives.

In 1774 the pavilion that housed the theatre was added, with Palladian façade and mechanical stage, approached through a colonnade of *treillage*. Heroic columns embraced a two-storey gallery, and among those who occupied the boxes were the brilliant diplomat Talleyrand (Napoleon's future minister), and Voltaire. There were two or three performances weekly, followed by fireworks bursting into polychrome bouquets over the boulevard and illuminating the deepest recesses of the gardens.

Chartres must have attended his father's and Madame de Montesson's spectacles, when he was not otherwise engaged at an even more famous private theatre further along the Chausée-d'Antin. This was the splendid Hôtel Guimard, which Ledoux had begun in 1770 for the infamous Opéra dancer, Mademoiselle Guimard, at the same time that Brongniart was pushing forward the Hôtel de Montesson. Although the plays chosen for the dancer's stage were described as 'd'agréables ordures', the setting was – appropriately – a veritable boudoir, the loges hung with pink taffeta trimmed in silver fringe, and four decorative paintings – probably set within the *boiseries* – by the most exciting and in many ways the most original painter in Paris at the moment, Jean-Honoré Fragonard. The Duc de Chartres – with d'Artois in tow - was often to be seen at the Temple of Terpsichore – as the pavilion of the 'belle damnée' was called – and the cast for Mademoiselle Guimard's extravagant performances was so extensive that the dignified Opéra sometimes had to close its doors.

The names of Chartres and d'Artois also figured prominently in the guest list of an unusually decadent evening planned by the first singer of the Opéra, Sophie Arnould, and Mademoiselle Dervieux.[8] Sophie was 'protected' by Bélanger, the Comte d'Artois, Monsieur de Monville, and the Comte de Lauraguais, Duc de Brancas – presumably in succession. When Sophie grew tired of Lauraguais, she called one day at the door of his

The Palais Royal, c.1780.
The galleries of the Palais Royal were erected by Victor Louis between 1781 and 1784. To replace the Opéra that burned in 1781 the new Duc d'Orléans in 1786 had a vast salle de spectacle built in the middle of the garden. The building above ground looked like a vast pavilion covered with treillage. Below ground was a place that all foreign visitors wanted to see first in Paris, because it offered a variety of entertainments – exhibitions, operas, plays and balls – and was the centre of Paris life

wife, the Duchesse de Brancas, saying that she wanted to leave some things the Duke had given her that she no longer wanted – a casket of jewels and a basket of babies. The two infants would certainly have fared better with the Duchesse de Brancas, and perhaps they played in the beautiful bath house pavilion that Bélanger designed for the garden.

In 1780 the Duc d'Orléans handed over the Palais Royal to his son,[9] and it came at a propitious moment, for Chartres had just spent considerable sums on Monceau. His ambitions always ran ahead of the cash in hand, however, and to support his prodigal manner of living, he seized an opportunity to turn the gardens and surroundings of the family town house to commercial profit.

The idea of speculation in the environs of an historical landmark that served as the town house of princes of the blood was a shocking idea. For generations one had been conditioned to think of the 'Parisian hôtel [as a] closed and secret oasis',[10] where the family and its friends shared the genteel pleasures of a dinner, a game of cards, a concert, or a play in the gardens.

But the Duc de Chartres flouted tradition, and the grand old Palais Royal that stood at the heart of Paris, a venerable monument since the time of Cardinal Richelieu, was soon engulfed in the scaffolding, dust, and noisy reconstruction that eventually turned it into 'the most spectacular habitat for pleasure and politics in Europe.'[11] Erected alongside the Palais was a wooden gallery that Parisians called 'le camp des tartares', a veritable side-show with such curiosities as a beautiful woman who had been dead for two hundred years (made of wax). The fine old trees were felled in the wondrous gardens, that *most* 'secret oasis' of all, which were now frequented by thieves and prostitutes. The Palais Royal soon became a centre of opposition to the monarchy, too, and in July 1789 Camille Desmoulins' irresponsible and inflammatory speech in the gardens would make him an instant hero of the mob.

Yet there was another garden attraction at the Palais Royal that counted as one of the architectural triumphs of Paris. It was a singular *salle de spectacle* in the form of an underground circus, an idea which may have derived from Chartres' predilection for subterranean garden structures – like the winter garden at Monceau – combined with the mania for theatre inherited from his forebears. The architect he chose for this interesting project was Victor Louis, fresh from inaugurating a new era in theatre design in his recent theatre at Bordeaux (1775-80). Beginning late in 1781 (Moreau's Opéra at the Palais Royal had burned in July), Louis enclosed three sides of the garden with arcaded galleries to create a covered promenade adjoining shops on the ground floor. Each side was articulated by heroic pilasters with Corinthian capitals that enframed segmental openings on the ground floor and rectangular ones on the first floor.

This subtle cadence of pilasters marching around the sides formed a sympathetic framework for the long, low pavilion that the architect designed for the middle of the garden in 1786 to shelter the underground circus. Covered with *treillage,* its design was intimately related to the surrounding galleries, for the openings echoed the window shapes above the arcade, and the enframing columns found their responds in the pilasters. Victor Louis equipped his trelliswork pavilion with a glass roof running its entire length, permitting light to flood into the Duke's underground theatre for equestrian exhibitions, operas, plays, and balls. Sebastien Mercier, that inveterate eighteenth-century guide considered it 'the most original architectural monument . . . found in Paris.'

This ambitious project could be completed because Chartres' father had died in 1785, making him Duc d'Orléans and First Prince of the Blood. With his new title came the necessary funds for the completion of Le Cirque which brought 'raw . . . Rabelaisian popular culture right into the heart of royal and aristocratic Paris'.[12] Probably the new Duc d'Orléans (as Chartres was now called) did more than anyone else to amalgamate aristocratic theatre with popular theatre – of the bawdy sort seen in the Saint-Laurent and Saint-Germain fairs.

But one salon for spectacles at the Palais Royal was not enough to satisfy its energetic owner, who in 1785 had persuaded the Théatre des Variétés Amusantes to move from the boulevards to the Palais Royal, where it occupied a large wooden pavilion alongside the palace. An engraving of 1786 shows the theatre's interior to be much like those *pavillons de verdure* for the Sun King's garden parties, for branches rise from the

The Subterranean Circus, the Palais Royal.
Le Cirque, as it was called, was lit by glass panes in the roof of the treillage *building above. Galleries with balustrades for the spectators, supported by Doric columns, ran around the sides of the huge space for spectacles such as the 'equestrian exhibitions' that Thomas Jefferson noted*

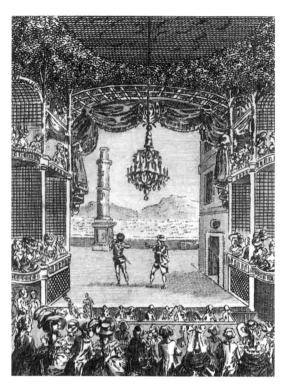

Théatre des Variétés Amusantes, Palais Royal. The theatre moved in 1785 from the boulevards to the Palais Royal where it was housed in a large wooden structure next to the palace. The entire interior was lined with treillage, *with two tiers of boxes, foliage springing from the tree trunks that divide the upper tier. It was lit by a splendid Louis XV lustre*

upper loges to form a foliage canopy, and the entire structure is lined with *treillage*.

Behind the gardens stood yet another theatre – the Théatre de Beaujolais (named for Chartres' brother) – where child actors and three-foot-tall Italian marionettes performed. Traditions persist in France, for today it is the Théatre du Palais Royal, one of the few stages upon which vaudeville is still played.

Almost immediately after excavations for the circus were begun, the Duke set Victor Louis to work on the Théatre Français adjoining the Palais Royal – and known today as the famous colonnaded Comédie-Française in the Rue de Richelieu. With its four theatres, numerous cafés, the Curtius waxworks, strolling guitar players, billiards, the most enticing boutiques in town, and side shows of doubtful reputation, the Palais Royal was turned into an urban resort that Mercier called 'the capital of Paris'.

It attracted Parisians of all classes as well as foreigners. On 13 September, 1788 the Duchesse d'Orléans received in the underground circus under the *treillage* pavilion the exotic emissaries of Tipoo-Sahib, Sultan of Mysore. Americans especially loved the Palais Royal, and Thomas Jefferson's first residence in Paris – where he served as the American minister (1785-9) – was nearby. He attended performances in the Théatre des Variétés Amusantes adjoining the palace, bought mementoes in the boutiques, and had his profile traced by Edmé Quenedey, who exploited for the purpose the newly invented mechanical device, the *physionotrace*.

As a visiting minister and friend of many prominent French people such as the Comtesse de Tessé (Lafayette's aunt), Jefferson was able to visit the interior of the renowned Orléans town house. The Virginian admired the marvellous art gallery (a tradition of the Palais Royal since Richelieu's day), the natural history cabinet which was *de rigueur* for people of the Orléans' class, and the Duke's famous medal cabinet that he would soon be forced to sell. The future builder of Monticello and gentleman farmer took a special interest in the scale models of machines and tools that were constructed after plates in the *Encyclopédie* for the instruction of the Orléans children.

The Pavilion at Bellechasse

The education of princely families was a serious matter, especially when it concerned those who were eligible to mount the throne, and Chartres' children were in that class. Besides his daughters, there were the future Louis-Philippe (1773-1850), the Duc de Montpensier (1775-1807), and the Comte de Beaujolais (1779-1808). Since the surroundings of the Palais Royal had been converted through Orléans' speculations into a 'carnival of the appetites',[13] and the gardens overrun with too many inebriated 'honest citizens', the town house was no longer considered a proper place to bring up the children.

Although the young princes slept at the Palais Royal, during the day they were sometimes spirited away to Saint Cloud to watch the construction of the glorious cascades at the Orléans château; to Monceau with their tutor, Madame de Genlis, to tend her herb garden and memorise the names of Thomas Blaikie's botanical specimens; or to the Orléans properties at Le Raincy to see the model farm and study

Bernard Poyet, 'Le Pavillon de Bellechasse', 1778.
Within the confines of the Convent of Bellechasse, far from the noise of the Palais Royal, the Duc de Chartres built this austere pavilion in 1778 for his twin daughters, confiding their care to Madame de Genlis. She left her husband (later reproaching herself for it) to take up her post at Bellechasse. Poyet's watercolour shows Madame de Genlis in her famous hat standing at the top of the stairs, watching the little girls learning to walk in the garden below. One twin would die very young, but the other became Madame Adelaide, the highly visible and wise counsellor to her brother when he came to the throne in 1830

the latest agricultural methods. As Madame de Genlis' friend, Henriette-Lucy de Latour du Pin put it, their outings were 'devoted . . . to everything improving and instructive. They knew something of the various trades, of machines, libraries . . . public monuments and the arts.' Quite a contrast with the Comte d'Artois' two children who 'were never seen, and knew as little of France as if they had been heirs to the throne of China'.[14]

Usually, however, Chartres' children were driven to the Convent of Bellechasse, not far from the centre of the city, where their sister, Adelaide, lived in a pavilion with Madame de Genlis and an English girl of mysterious origin named Pamela.[15] The boys arrived early in the morning, were given their lessons during the day, and stayed until after supper, when they were taken back by their assistant-tutor to the Palais Royal.

Bellechasse was west of Paris where there were still open fields, and in 1778 Chartres commissioned the architect Bernard Poyet (1742-1824) to put up a rusticated pavilion to serve as classrooms, adjoining the large enclosed garden of the Augustan Dames' convent on the Rue Saint-Dominique. In her memoirs Madame de Genlis claims to have had a hand in its design, but she may have been referring only to the interior arrangements. The nuns kept the keys to the gate of the secluded garden, and it was opened only at specific times, and (theoretically) only to ladies and members of the nobility.[16]

A watercolour in the Carnavalet Museum in Paris preserves the image of Poyet's small convent-pavilion, an exercise in the reductive, obsessive geometry beloved of Ledoux's generation. Its sombre, rectangular severity is relieved by a reticent decoration – walls articulated with rustications that break out into voussoirs over the windows.

The radical austerity of the Bellechasse pavilion's design was matched only by the life the governess imposed upon her charges, as Madame de Latour du Pin observed, and Louis-Philippe recalled in his memoirs. Heir to the greatest fortune in France, he was

Stephanie Félicité DUCREST
ci-devant Csse de Genlis
de S.A.S. Monsgr.

Marquise de SILLERY
Gouvernante des Enfaus
Le Duc d'Orleans.

Vertus, graces, talens, esprit juste
enchanteur,
Elle a tout ce qu'il faut pour embelir
la vie,

C'est le charme des yeux, de
l'oreille du cœur,
Et le desespoir de l'envie.

Tirie pinx.

Par Mr de Sauvigny

Copiet sculp

Madame de Genlis.
Félicité de Genlis, who had been educated by the
famous salon leader Madame Tencin, sits at her
desk in her enormous hat, every inch the pedant.
Horace Walpole wrote that she was an
extraordinary lady who possessed more common
sense than anyone he had ever met, and an
uncanny ability to discern another's character
immediately. He added that she had little taste
and did not know how to present herself, but a
redeeming feature was the protection she accorded
to artists and writers

accustomed to dining upon silver, but Madame de Genlis had the shockingly frugal meals of watered-down soup and dry bread served upon heavy, brown faïence. In a curious reversal, a century before Madame de Maintenon had invited peasant girls to 'dine like princesses' on plates of silver.

It is apparent from her memoirs that Madame de Genlis governed with a tight rein. She remarked that her bedroom was separated from the princesses' room by a glass door 'so that I could see from my bed what they were up to'. The cupboards that held her many manuscripts contained her natural history collection.

The governess was perpetually at her desk, turning out volume after volume on the education of children, and she was responsible for the all-pervasive English influence upon life in the Bellechasse pavilion. There was a pack of hounds for the little princes, and English was spoken with the students by Pamela and Madame de Genlis, who managed quite well, if Thomas Blaikie is to be believed.

But life in the 'charming pavilion' (Madame de Genlis' words) was not as genteel as it appeared, for this officious person in charge of the childrens' education was none other than the mistress of their father.

The association of Félicité de Genlis with Chartres' family seems to have begun around 1772, when her husband, Charles-Alexis Brulart de Sillery, Comte de Genlis, was captain of Chartres' guards. Charles and Félicité insinuated themselves into the Palais Royal through the good graces of Félicité's aunt, the Marquise de Montesson, whom we have seen as the Maintenon of the Duc d'Orléans.

Félicité was genteel, bright, indefatigable, and it was due to her perseverance that twenty volumes of Carmontelle's comedies were published. A private collection in Paris contains a portrait of her in the costume she wore at an Opéra ball in 1768 for a quadrille of *Proverbes* – as Carmontelle's theatre pieces were sometimes called – in which she illustrated 'Contentment surpasses riches'.

Then, there was the added attraction of her poverty. For the Duchesse de Chartres' passion was charity, and like her father (the venerable Duc de Penthièvre) she welcomed any opportunity to assist the less fortunate. But the Duchesses' charity was sadly misplaced, for in 1772 she invited the impoverished young Comtesse de Genlis to accompany her and her husband on a voyage to Forges-les-Eaux, where the Duchess took the curative waters in hopes of conceiving an heir.

A year later Louis-Philippe was born, but the Duchess had lost her husband, for during their stay at Forges, Chartres became Félicité de Genlis' 'protector' (*entreteneur en titre*), a fact to which the Duke's wife seems to have been oblivious for another thirteen years. For a decade the Chartres' establishment appeared to be the most congenial imaginable, with cordial relationships among the three protagonists, for the Duchess did not suspect that their domestic arrangement was a *ménage à trois*. What is more, the credulous lady gave her blessing to the highly unusual arrangement (for that day) whereby Madame de Genlis, a woman and a writer, was appointed governess to her children, princes in line of succession to the throne.

The governess was well-known in Paris, and disliked for several reasons. The first was public disapproval of her position as governess, another was that the books she wrote assumed (ironically) a moralising tone which irritated a society bent upon pleasure. And – more seriously, from the French point of view – Félicité had abandoned a woman's prerogative and obligation to make herself as attractive as possible, for she gave up all coquetry and wore a plain but offensive hat 'as large as an umbrella'. On 10 April, 1782 both Chartres and his father were attending a play entitled *Les Femmes Savantes* at the new Théatre-Français on the Rue de Vaugirard. Chartres' party arrived early, with Félicité in her trademark hat, followed by her young charges. But when the governess slipped into her box, the audience openly expressed its disapproval.

Before the hissing had quieted down, the corpulent Duc d'Orléans appeared in the opposite loge with Félicité's aunt, Madame de Montesson, and the fickle audience broke into applause.[17] The old Duke was popular in Paris, and everyone knew that Madame de Montesson – a lady of strict morality and devotee of theatricals – brought the best society to the Orléans court. In the years just preceding the Revolution, the theatre was not only a beautifully designed monument for spectacles, but its audience was a reliable barometer of public opinion.

Le Raincy

At the time that the Palais Royal circus was being built, Chartres (now Orléans) inherited another property, the château of Le Raincy, so he took Thomas Blaikie out to consult him about further embellishments to the garden. During his father's lifetime, it had already acquired a grotto in the English taste, cascades, and a temple. In 1773, when Madame de Montesson was travelling in Holland, she visited a landscape garden near La Haye that she wanted to have copied at Le Raincy. So an artificial river was excavated, trees were planted along its winding course, and English lawns installed. Dezallier d'Argenville described it as a 'delicate marriage between water and vegetation',[18] and it was praised by the poet, the Abbé Delille, whose words were often inscribed upon huge boulders in French picturesque gardens.

In 1786 Orléans – no doubt anticipating profits from the Palais Royal – decided to make even more radical improvements at Raincy, so he commissioned Blaikie to abolish every straight line in the park. The Scotsman's team of gardeners was mostly English, with a French nurseryman named Gérard, who was 'more an English man than any of the English'.[19] They completely transformed it into a model *parc à l'anglaise*, with pavilions scattered at random, topping little hills, and nestling in dense shrubbery beside refreshing springs. There was a Hermitage with Chinese bell tower, a Hameau with a flock of sheep and hens, an English farm, a fortress with four towers, and naive log cabins known as *maisons Russes*. The village at Le Raincy was

Louis Carrogis, called Carmontelle, the Iron Bridge in the Park of Le Raincy.
Here Carmontelle depicts a rare moment when the Duke and Duchess were together, strolling in the park
at Le Raincy, followed by one of the dogs used in the English hunts popularised through the Anglomania
that originated with highly-placed Frenchmen like the Duc d'Orléans and his friend de Monville. The
Duchess holds a walking stick and the Duke is behind her with his page Narcisse. On the far right are
either the buildings of the Hameau or the English village conceived by Blaikie, with houses of wood and
plaster painted to resemble brick. These were dwellings for workers on the estate

different from others of its type, for the garden buildings were not just fantastic constructions designed to produce a pictorial effect, as at Monceau, but durable buildings covered with sturdy slate roofs to serve a utilitarian purpose – as habitations for the large Orléans staff.

Blaikie's diary reveals that the Duke brought over an English gamekeeper and 'a great many fancy Deer and . . . Monkies and Birds of different sorts'. Le Raincy was 'allmost an English colony [with] one Mr. Farrer as a sort of governor . . . to conduct the farm à l'Anglaise'. There was riding to hounds in English tweeds, and it was probably at the Le Raincy hunt that Blaikie admired the prowess of the Duke's eccentric and gifted friend, Monsieur de Monville of the Désert de Retz, who was generally considered the finest archer in Europe. Blaikie observed him '[shooting] with his Bow and Arrow Phessants flying and many other things equally dextereuss'.[20]

As Philippe Egalité, Chartres espoused the Revolutionists' cause, became the crown's deadly enemy, possibly instigated the march on Versailles, and voted for the death of his cousin, Louis XVI. It was all to no avail, for instead of mounting the steps of the throne, he was forced to climb those that led to the scaffold. His sister Bathilde, the Duchesse de Bourbon-Condé, assumed the name of citizen Verité, and turned her famous Paris town house into a principal meeting place for the militant Jacobins.

Chartres' Anglomania took root in his ineffectual son, Louis-Philippe, whose foreign policy embraced an English alliance. When another Revolution broke out in 1848, the unpopular King collapsed in senile resignation, fleeing to the country he loved, where he undoubtedly became – to borrow Blaikie's phrase – 'more an English man than any of the English'.[21]

Vue Perspective de la Colonne

Sparsholt College Library
Sparsholt, Winchester
Hants. SO21 2NF

CHAPTER 17

MONSIEUR DE MONVILLE AND THE DESERT DE RETZ

On a stormy June day in the 1940s, the French writer Colette pushed her way through a 'No Entry' sign on the edge of the forest of Marly, and forged through heavy undergrowth in hopes of finding the remains of what André Malraux called some of the most important monuments of the eighteenth century, and 'the only place in Europe where such creations exist'. The garden to which Malraux referred, and which Colette sought on that stormy day was one of the strangest landscapes created during the eighteenth century, the legendary Désert de Retz.

The Désert – a word that suggests Molière's idea of a refuge – had been created in a picturesque woodland of some one hundred acres between 1774 and 1786, and even before all pavilions had been completed, this unusual garden had attracted the French court and illustrious visitors from all over the world.

Who was responsible for this unusual combination of landscape garden (*jardin anglais*) and ornamental farm (*ferme ornée*) that was established in the neighbourhood of Louis XIV's once-renowned collection of pavilions at Marly? It was not one of the royal family nor even one of the princes of the blood, but an unconventional dilettante who epitomised his age: François-Nicolas Henry Racine du Jonquoy, better known as Monsieur de Monville (c.1730-97). Although never a member of the immediate court circle, he cavorted about Paris with many who were, becoming an *habitué* of the Orléans clique, for he was a fellow freemason and comrade-in-pleasure of the Duc de Chartres.

De Monville was the scion of a family of financiers recently allied with the nobility, and he inherited a large fortune from his maternal grandfather, the tax farmer Thomas Le Monnier. In 1757 François-Nicolas received the title of Grand Master of Waters and Forests at Rouen, and during the eight years that he occupied the post he demonstrated a genuine passion for botany and the cultivation of unusual trees and flowers. Evidence of his continued interest in the subject was to be found in his

Georges Le Rouge, perspective view of the Column House, Désert de Retz.
In its day the Column House attracted visitors from all over Europe as well as the American Thomas Jefferson, who wrote to Maria Cosway: 'How grand the idea excited by the remains of such a column'

Jean-François Janinet, garden façade of the Hôtel de Monville, after 1764.
The architect of the Hôtel de Monville in the Rue de la Ville-l'Evêque was
Etiènne-Louis Boullée (1728-1799), a pupil of the celebrated teacher of
architecture Jacques-François Blondel. Typical of the revolutionary generation
of French architects, Boullée has composed Monville's hôtel in starkly
geometrical terms: elongated rectangle surmounted by another for the attic, which
is surmounted and flanked by figures. The openings across the garden front are
unembellished, and the building's austerity is relieved only by panels of low-relief
sculpture and six Ionic columns. The restrained exterior contrasted dramatically with the
voluptuous interiors created for the debonair Monsieur de Monville

impressive library at the Désert de Retz, as well as the extensive plantations of rare specimens that adorned its park.

In 1750 the twenty-year-old de Monville was residing in Paris at his grandfather's hôtel, enjoying the life of a *bon vivant* in the company of actresses from the Italian Comedy. By 1761 he was often seen with the eighteen-year-old beauty, Jeanne Bécu. She caught the eye of all the *grands amateurs,* and would soon step from Labille's establishment into the world of the salons, and thence to the court at Versailles as Madame Du Barry.

De Monville was naturally drawn to the fashionable hôtel of Sophie Arnould, leading singer of the Opéra. Here he would have met the German composer Gluck, who – under the Queen's patronage – was introducing a new kind of opera into Paris, his success further insured by Sophie's endorsement. There was also the architect François-Joseph Bélanger, who proposed a project for Sophie's town house in 1773, and who would design pavilions for members of the Queen's circle such as the Comte d'Artois, the Prince de Ligne, and the Comte de Lauraguais, for whom the architect devised the splendid garden pavilion at the Hôtel de Brancas.

De Monville's singular appearance impressed everyone who met him. The suave Dufort de Cheverny, official Greeter of Foreign Ambassadors, reported that Monsieur de Monville was one of the handsomest *cavaliers* in Paris, with the face and figure of a model. He was often noted in the Orléans entourage, and we find him hunting with the Duc de Chartres at the Orléans châteaux. For de Monville was considered the best archer in Europe, able to bring down a pheasant with only one arrow from his elegant steel and black velvet bow. He cut a fine figure on horseback, too, and was a renowned tennis player.

What counted most in Paris society, however, were de Monville's social accomplishments, and as a superior dancer, he was invited to all the balls. Monsieur de Montclos remarked: 'Ses dons de société exceptionels lui valurent les faveurs de la mode'.[1]

Not only was de Monville appreciated by *le beau monde,* but his musical abilities were such that he was respected by professional performers and leading composers. Besides being a gifted dancer, François-Nicolas was an accomplished musician in his own right, excelling in both flute and harp. Considered to be the first male harp player in France, he studied – along with Madame de Genlis – with Monsieur Gaiffre, who transformed this instrument by adding the pedals.

De Monville became so proficient that he even performed with professionals, and twice a week he would join in concerts arranged by Félicité de Genlis at the pavilion

Georges Le Rouge, the Ice House, Désert de Retz.
Monsieur de Monville's pyramidal ice house was engraved for Le Rouge's eighth Cahier des Jardins anglo-chinois with some artistic licence concerning the materials used for the lower part of the structure. The engraving shows a central door at its base leading into the underground chamber where the ice was kept, and stairs mounting at either side of the door to reach a shallow platform running around the sides. Strangely, in the engraving it is encircled by small trees, which would have been unusual, for glacières were normally placed in a dense woodland for protection against the sun

of Bellechasse, where — as we have seen — she reigned as governess of Chartres' children. Here François-Nicolas played his flute with the best violinist of the day, Jarnovitz, accompanied by Gluck himself and Monsigny, who sang airs from their latest operas. And attached to Monville's own luxurious establishment in Paris (he owned two hôtels, a larger and smaller) was a private orchestra.

Just when the Hôtel de Monville was begun is not known, but it was some time after 1764. For this project, the owner summoned the avant-garde architect, Etiènne-Louis Boullée, who conceived the building in terms of pure geometry. The classical reticence of the exterior hardly prepared the visitor for the unbridled opulence of the interior.

One entered an antechamber decorated in stucco relief, heated by a splendid faïence stove in Neo-classical form. The antechamber that followed was entirely gilt, lighted by a chandelier of eight branches and six pairs of wall lights, and at the back stood a superb buffet. As the visitor passed into the first salon adorned with free-standing columns illuminated by hidden light sources, out of the wall panelling emerged the sounds of an air by Rameau. Next came a seductive bedroom in crimson velvet with gold fringe, and beyond it was Monsieur de Monville's study, where he worked at a desk covered with porcelain plaques, and warmed so efficiently by ornamental faïence stoves that it seemed always like midsummer.

Especially renowned was the Turkish salon with mirrored walls, thick Turkish carpets and, disposed around the walls, ottomans of scarlet velvet smothered

The restored Ice House or glacière, Désert de Retz.
The pyramidal form of the ice house was probably chosen by de Monville because of its associations with freemasonry, de Monville being a fellow freemason and comrade-in-pleasure of the Duc de Chartres

Rock formation with satyrs, Désert de Retz.
Shadowy grottoes with overgrown foliage and mosses, a suggestion of the wildness of nature, were used in the picturesque garden to contrast with formal components like temples or columns that represented at once civilisation and the ancient world. In the Désert de Retz, the tone was set from the start, for the visitor entered from the forest of Marly via this unusually theatrical grotto of huge boulders, with satyrs holding aloft blazing torches. Further along the path, they encountered the world of antiquity in the form of the Column House, temples, and pyramids

in Italian silk pillows, like the palaces in *The Thousand and One Nights*. Concealed in the ceiling was de Monville's six-piece orchestra consisting of stringed instruments, a fashion that was introduced from Germany in the 1770s.

In September 1774 de Monville bought the wooded property augmented with several ponds situated at Retz in the parish of Chambourcy. Over the next ten years he constructed an English garden that became a veritable model of its type and that soon enjoyed international renown. North of de Monville's domain a wall enclosed the royal forests, and the courtiers of Versailles entered the park via a gateway that appeared to be the upper portion of an immense doorway enframed by gargantuan rustications. It was an example of the 'buried architecture' so dear to Boullée, the architect of de Monville's Paris residences, who once designed an entrance for a cemetery in the form of a gigantic pediment rising from the ground.

Having pushed open the heavy wooden doors incised with lozenges, visitors found the opposite side of the gate embellished with a large rock formation covered with vines and shrubs, suggesting an immense grotto. The theatrical entrance to the gloomy cavern was enhanced by a pair of painted tole satyrs who stood upon rocks, holding aloft lighted torches to provide a touch of drama – and classical antiquity – to the mysterious realm. This popular feature of the landscape garden – a rugged grotto – was seen in the Queen's gardens nearby, while the enormous aperture of the grotto in Madame Thélusson's Paris garden attracted all Paris, with tickets to gain admission.

From the Désert de Retz *rocher* a wide path led down the slope, past an ice house in the pyramidal form favoured by freemasonry (see previous page), and thence to the *pièce de la résistance* of theatrical extremes that served as principal residence of the owner. This was an immense Tuscan column extrapolated from a Doric temple of Piranesian proportions, and its imposing girth – fifteen metres in diameter – suggests

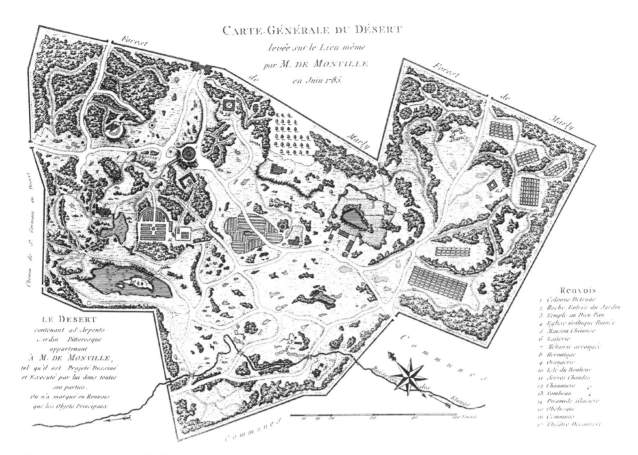

CARTE·GÉNÉRALE·DU·DÉSERT
levée sur le Lieu même
par M. DE MONVILLE
en Juin 1785.

LE DESERT
contenant 95 Arpents
Jardin Pittoresque
appartenant
À M. DE MONVILLE,
tel qu'il est Projeté Dessiné
et Exécuté par lui dans toutes
ses parties.
On n'a marqué en Renvois
que les Objets Principaux

Renvois
1 Colonne Détruite
2 Roche Entrée du Jardin
3 Temple au Dieu Pan
4 Église Gothique Ruinée
5 Maison Chinoise
6 Laiterie
7 Metairie arrangée
8 Hermitage
9 Orangerie
10 Isle du Bonheur
11 Serres Chaudes
12 Chaumière
13 Tombeau
14 Piramide Glacière
15 Obelisque
16 Communs
17 Théâtre Découvert

Georges Le Rouge, plan of the Désert de Retz.
The plan shows the winding paths that connect the different parts of the garden, leading the stroller past the various fabriques, the Ice House, Column House, Temple of Repose, Temple of Pan, the Chinese House by the lake, and the Turkish and Tartar Tents. The plan of the Désert fuses the two great enthusiasms of the late eighteenth century – pavilions and picturesque gardens

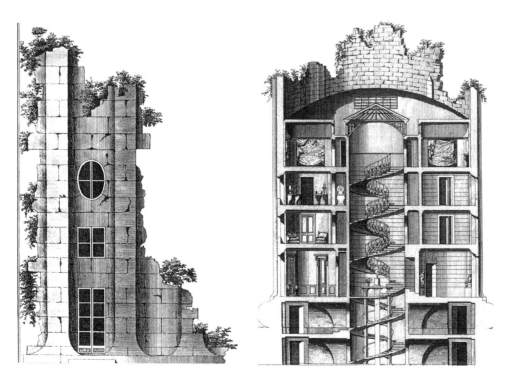

Far left: Georges Le Rouge, elevation of the Column House, Désert de Retz.
The alternating bays of the stone Column House, giving a ribbed effect, are articulated with rectangular, square, and oval openings, providing light to the rooms surrounding the staircase on each floor

Left: Georges Le Rouge, view of the interior of the Column House, Désert de Retz.
The kitchens were not in the basement, as Le Rouge indicates, but in a cottage next door connected to the basement by a tunnel. Each storey contained four rooms ranged around the staircase. On the top floor were servants' quarters, storage room, and a studio connected by a private staircase to de Monville's laboratory

211

The Column House, Désert de Retz.
The Column House is unusual in at least two ways: its immense size – fifteen meters in diameter, and the fact that it was intended for habitation. Windows were cut into the giant fluting and the four floors of rooms were used for elegant living. At the centre of the building was a spiral staircase where Monsieur de Monville placed flowering plants that received sunlight from the opening above, for he was an excellent botanist

that de Monville may have consulted his architect, Etienne-Louis Boullée, for the design, although there is no proof. The column was truncated at the top to suggest decomposition, and would have attained a height of 120 metres if it had not been a 'ruin'. Since it consciously evoked ideas common to all cultivated eighteenth-century people, there was no need for it to be terminated, for de Monville's friends – connoisseurs like himself – could complete it in their imaginations. To the Prince de Ligne it looked like the remains of a gigantic temple upon whose arrogant proportions the wrath of God had been invoked.

For Monsieur de Monville, the Column House became an unusual and highly refined summer residence, for when the first warm days arrived, he left Paris for this private paradise in the country. It was ingeniously lighted by window/doors on the ground floor, square windows on the *premier étage*, and oval ones on the top. Rooms were arranged around the central staircase which was illuminated by an opening in the top of the column.

The light that flooded down from above allowed the stairwell to become a kind of spiral greenhouse, for between each balustrade was placed a faïence vase filled with green plants or flowers – geraniums, heliotropes, periwinkles, carnations. These fine specimens came from the owner's greenhouses, which were so well-known that plants were taken from the Retz to the Museum of Natural History in Paris in the midst of the Revolution – exotic Farnese acacias, Barbary figs, American roses, orange trees, pomegranates, currants from Buenos Aires, jasmines from the Azores, myrtle and cinerarias.

On the ground floor of the Column House was a vestibule, dining room, salon, and bedroom, with more living quarters on the next floor, and de Monville's laboratory and atelier at the top. Here he painted, laboured at his workbench, and arranged his collections of plans and architectural models, some by the architect François Barbier, who assisted the owner as a draughtsman in the realisation of the garden buildings, notably the Chinese House.

In keeping with the antique world invoked by the Column House itself, its interior appointments were of Neo-classical design: white marble fireplaces sculpted with acanthus leaves, ormolu firedogs and wall lights in pomegranate form, and mahogany furniture, whose highly-polished surfaces imitated the patina of ancient bronzes. On mantelpieces, commodes, tables, and desks stood Sèvres biscuit figures (the classical world was thought to be white), the small bronzes so prized by collectors, and terracotta figures whose subjects suggest some of Clodion's more licentious models.

Mirrors augmented the illusion of space and reflected the gardens, and on the walls hung engravings, and paintings by such popular artists as Lagrenée, Van Loo, and Hubert Robert, whom it is tempting to think de Monville consulted in laying out his gardens.

The Column House, Désert de Retz, in its landscape setting.
Evocative of the great classical past in so many landscape gardens, scholars believe the building is related to Piranesi's celebrated views of decaying antiquity that were taken up and copied as residences

Even Alexandre de Laborde, who was so critical of the Chinese House, praised de Monville's ability to create the chiaroscuro of Dutch landscapes – or the more classical ones of Poussin – through his choice of trees, shrubs, and judiciously placed bodies of water reflecting the enticing morsels of architecture that enlivened the landscape garden.

The evocative power of the Column House, an element lifted from the Graeco-Roman tradition, appealed to the aesthetic and archaeological interest in ruins characteristic of the period. Its astonishing precocity made it one of the most widely-discussed garden monuments of a century that abounded in surprises, if not absurdities, like the huge garden *fabrique* in bovine form by the architect Jacques Lequeu. Here the 'speaking architecture' prized by the late eighteenth century becomes zoomorphic. An enormous cow wearing an 'oriental' robe supports a vase with bull's-eye opening through which light streams into the hayloft. This and the other animals of the park were make of limestone combined with sulphur which, when rubbed, exuded odours of the barnyard. 'The nonsense which the eighteenth century required', observed Kenneth Clark, 'was some escape from its own oppressive rationalism'.[2]

A nearby monument that functioned as a 'ruin' was the thirteenth-century chapel of Retz, whose ivy-covered walls de Monville incorporated (1777) into his garden as an authentic vestige of the medieval age. This robbed the church of its original meaning and function, but it was precisely what Chartres had done at Monceau where he appropriated a screen of columns that had been intended for a Valois sepulchre as backdrop for the Naumachie.

In the southern part of the Désert de Retz gardens the proprietor established his model farm, with dairy and *métairie* (farmer's house) of utilitarian form, a thatched-roof *chaumière*, orangery, and greenhouses. There was the usual romantic hermitage, a tomb that resembled the base of a pyramid with classical frieze, a Temple of the God Pan, a Temple of Repose, and the obelisk (of painted tole) that was *de rigueur* for an owner whose friends were freemasons. Like Parc Monceau, the Retz featured tents and an ice house, united to the other *fabriques* by meandering walks, and the picturesque Pompeiian red service buildings of the Column House were reached by an underground passage.

One of the most widely acclaimed of the Désert's pavilions was the Chinese House, among the first of this type built in France, and the 'unique example in Europe of a bourgeoise habitation of this type'.[3] The Prince de Ligne, whose own property in Belgium boasted a charming oriental pagoda, thought that de Monville's was so ingeniously conceived that it would have pleased the Emperor of China himself.

It was constructed of teak resting on a stone base. From its base flowed a spring that formed a rushing brook which tumbled into a pond with two little islands, surrounded by luxuriant trees. Its exterior resembled bamboo, with geometrical panels painted red and violet, and cartouches containing Chinese ideograms. Lanterns of *bombé* glass hung from the corbels, and the curving slate roofs were of fish-scale

The Chinese House, Désert de Retz.
The Pavillon Chinoise is no doubt the most elaborate built on French soil. Originally there was a garden in front of the house. At its base a small spring flowed down to form a pretty brook with two small islands, then a flat pool as an ornament in a small French formal garden. In this engraving, which dates from the early years of the nineteenth century, the garden has disappeared, but the Chinese House, with its orange-red and violet panels reflected in the still waters, is still intact

design, surmounted by a flat area with a Chinese lattice rail where two Chinese figures stood, one holding a lantern, the other a parasol of gilt copper with tinkling bells. Two painted tole Chinese vases on the roof were really chimneys from which the smoke from de Monville's glazed terracotta stove escaped.

The interior was fitted with oriental alcoves, a salon with flowered wallpaper, beds and chairs covered in toile-de-Jouy of Persian design. The salon walls were solid mahogany sculpted in the Neo-classical style, which must have appeared strangely incongruous with the Chinese designs decorating the upper part of the room. De Monville shared Marie-Antoinette's taste for oriental lacquers and porphyry vases, luxury wares that he doubtless acquired from the *marchands-merciers* in Paris who specialised in such items. But he served tea and coffee to his guests in authentic Chinese porcelain cups and saucers rather than Sèvres.

When she was planning her own Hameau at Versailles, the Queen came over to see the layout of de Monville's gardens and farm, and studied the unusual *fabriques*. So did her witty and knowledgeable adviser, the Prince de Ligne, as well as one of her pages, the handsome Alexandre de Tilly, who found this place 'ornamented by Art and Nature' a tribute to the 'exquisite taste of its owner'.[4]

In 1784 Gustavus III of Sweden was travelling in France, extravagantly fêted by the Queen at Trianon, the Condé family at Chantilly, and Madame Du Barry at

Georges Le Rouge, Chinese House, Désert de Retz.
The two-storey Chinese House was of Indian teak, its façade of carved and trelliswork panels trimmed in vermilion and violet. On the ground floor was a salon, antechamber and office, and on the second floor a library panelled entirely in mahogany, following the English taste

Georges Le Rouge, treillage *at Désert de Retz.*
The exact location of this treillage construction at the Désert de Retz is not certain. It must have functioned like the 'perspectives' noted in seventeenth-century gardens, and it provides a backdrop for the sculpture

Louveciennes. This Francophile King took a particular interest in de Monville's property, for he was making improvements at his own Châteaux de Haga and Drottningholm, where he put up a tole pavilion simulating a striped cotton tent and an oriental house, both types that figured among the twenty-odd garden structures at the Désert de Retz.

During the summer of 1786 Thomas Jefferson took Maria Cosway out to see the Désert de Retz, taking particular notice of the Column House. He was impressed by the variously shaped rooms (some oval) that were artfully arranged around the central spiral staircase. The concept of ovals contained within a circle apparently inspired Jefferson's later plan for the University of Virginia, where he incorporated into his famous Pantheon a fine suite of oval rooms.

A frequent visitor to the Désert was Chartres – now the Duc d'Orléans – who came for card games in de Monville's delightful retreat. But as Alexandre de Tilly noted, it was highly imprudent for the owner of the Désert to persist in his liaison with a man who was playing such a treacherous political role in the 1780s. As the situation deteriorated and people of his class began to think of emigrating, Monsieur de Monville was advised by a banker friend to sell both of his hôtels in Paris as well as the Désert de Retz. The sale took place just in time – 20 and 21 July, 1792 – for only four days afterwards, the Duke of Brunswick, chief of the coalition armies, delivered his famous manifesto to the French. He threatened Paris with severe measures – complete subversion and military execution – if any harm came to the royal family.

With the *sang-froid* that was typical of his race and class, de Monville accepted these reverses and lingered in Paris, although the King was executed on the Place Louis XV in January 1793. Nevertheless, on 6 April we find the heedless Monsieur de Monville with the Duc d'Orléans in the grand old Palais Royal, at yet another game of cards. The famous account of that scene has come down to us from the Duc de Lauzun, who had it from the Abbé de Montgaillard.

They had been playing for some time when Monsieur de Monville observed that the dinner hour had sounded long ago. So they were served right on the gaming table, course by course. During this dinner, the Convention was in the actual process of deciding the fate of the Duc d'Orléans, and Merlin de Douai came to announce to him the dreadful news of his imminent arrest and the death warrant.

'Is it *possible*?' Orléans cried. 'After the proofs of patriotism that I have given, after all the sacrifices I have made, to strike me with such a decree! What horrible ingratitude! What do you say, de Monville?'

De Monville was in the process of squeezing lemon juice over the sole, and without

The reconstructed Turkish Tent, Désert de Retz. Tents were practical and picturesque features of every self-respecting French garden in the second half of the eighteenth century. The Queen and her ladies viewed the balloon ascent at Versailles from a terrace, protected by a large white tent, and she used tents frequently for the court fêtes. Among the most elaborate of all were Monceau's Tartar tents in red and blue with gold ornaments. Le Rouge's engraving of de Monville's tent in his Cahiers des Jardins anglo-chinois *shows it to have been of striped material (or possibly painted tole) with cords holding open the doorway, and a spirited little flag flying from the top*

interrupting what he was doing he replied 'It is frightful, Monseigneur, but what do you expect? They treat your Highness as I treat this lemon', and with that he threw the lemon into the fireplace, observing to the Prince that sole should be eaten piping hot.[5]

In November 1793, the Duc d'Orléans (known to history as Philippe Egalité) perished on the scaffold, but Monsieur de Monville died in his bed in April 1797.

After the Revolution, the Désert de Retz passed through a succession of owners. Assaulted by undergrowth and brambles, its gardens were gradually effaced, and the tantalising collection of *folies* began to give way to the ravages of time. But just as the abandoned Pavillon de l'Aurore fascinated novelists (Alain Fournier) and photographers (Eugène Atget), so the poetic atmosphere surrounding the relics of the Désert de Retz haunted the Surrealist imagination of André Breton, and the ravaged Column House in which de Monville had received his stylish friends was exploited as the décor for his film *Au Secours.*

By the early 1930s, nature – abetted by human indifference – had taken over the Désert de Retz, and its fantastic *folies* were threatened with total ruin, as Colette discovered when she pushed through the gate on that gloomy day in the 1940s. 'Certainly', she wrote in *Paradis Terrestre*, 'the rare spirit expressed by such audacious architecture and the magnificent . . . specimen trees in the park are entitled to endure . . . A little longer, and the Désert de Retz will be no more than a poem in the style of an epoch. And yet, is it not beautiful that from an epoch one saves a poem?'

It would be another fifty years (1986) before the legendary terrain acquired an owner with the requisite knowledge, taste, vision, and perseverance to begin its careful restoration. Today, debris has been cleared away, the farm has regained its *potager*, the entrance from the Marly forest is being opened up, the Temple of Repose reconstructed, the striped tole tent stands again beside a pond, and the refurbished Column House rises from carefully clipped lawns. Refurnished and heated, it is inhabited once again. The latest owner of the Désert de Retz has managed to save the poem.

CHAPTER 18

LOUIS-JOSEPH DE BOURBON-CONDÉ
AND CHANTILLY

When we last saw Chantilly, that Versailles of the Condés north-east of Paris, Louis XV was being entertained by Monsieur le Duc. At his death in 1740, Monsieur le Duc was succeeded at by his four-year-old son, Louis-Joseph de Bourbon-Condé (1736-1818), who was reared in Paris and at Saint-Maur, and at ten became Master of the King's Household. This position implied a surpassing knowledge of protocol, for the Master was required to solve such pressing questions as the right to a *tabouret* (folding stool), and whether a certain ambassador would be granted a *cadenas* (locked silver casket for cutlery). At twelve, the new Prince de Condé was taken up to Chantilly for the presentation of his vassals. Affectionate ties existed between the town and the château, and its master was honoured by the villagers at an annual festival for forty years.

That indefatigable guide, Sébastien Mercier, remarked that Chantilly was memorable for its marriage of nature with art. No wonder, for at Monsieur le Duc's death, the Grande Singerie — a salon delicately painted by Christophe Huet with monkeys and oriental figures — had just been completed. Monsieur le Duc's manufacture of Chantilly porcelain, which contributed so much to France's reputation for soft-pastes, was flourishing; the painting collection had been enriched by his numerous acquisitions; and the glorious stables, with the hippodrome facing the vast lawns, formed a world of its own. The stables were a decorous prelude to the château and — like the Orangerie at Versailles — became a favourite rendezvous for fêtes.

Usually gifted, sometimes eccentric, and invariably lavish, the Condés of each generation were noted for their extravagant *divertissements*, and Louis Joseph — the essence of courtly civility — was no exception. Especially in the good months, an army

Pediment of the west portal of the Chantilly stables.
The triangular pediment with culminating moment of the hunt is played off against the monumental segmental pediment of the doorway that dominates the façade facing the lawns (p.106). Diana with her stag is on the left, and Cyparisse on the right

Louis-Joseph de Bourbon, Prince de Condé.
Louis-Joseph de Bourbon inherited the title of Prince de Condé and the château of Chantilly, among other properties, from his father Monsieur le Duc. When the monarchy was humiliated in the events of July 1789, Condé found it insupportable. So he, the Comte d'Artois, the Prince de Conti, the Polignacs, and the Queen's adviser, the Abbé Vermond, left Versailles for the frontier. The Prince de Condé became head of the army of emigrés, numbering about four thousand, and established his quarters at Coblenz

of distinguished guests would descend upon Chantilly, each bringing at least three domestics. A foreign monarch was usually accompanied by about ninety, and when the King made pilgrimages to the royal châteaux (or was entertained by the princes of the blood and the nobility), five hundred attendants were to be expected.

This would have been the case when Louis XV and his entourage went to meet Marie-Antoinette at Compiègne in 1770, and broke the journey back to Versailles by stopping at Chantilly. The King was completely taken by the vivacious young Dauphine, but Louis-Joseph's attention – as might be imagined – was concentrated upon Madame Du Barry. Louis XV and the favourite visited Chantilly again informally while her pavilion of Louveciennes was underway.

Louis-Joseph managed to accommodate his numerous guests with the services of a professional entrepreneur, and the assistance of some two thousand employees. In spite of the renowned parties that Berain had designed when Condé received Louis XIV, or those staged by Monsieur le Duc for the young Louis XV, these affairs paled before the explosion of riches, the luxurious inventions of the pavilion parties conjured up by the new master of Chantilly.

Fortunately, Louis-Joseph was able to entertain with panache, for he inherited his father's fortune, which was doubled when he married (for love) Charlotte de Rohan-Soubise. Drouais painted the couple as gardeners in 1757, but she died in 1760, leaving the prince a widower at twenty-three. By 1770 the Princesse de Monaco was installed at Chantilly, and Condé married her in 1808.

The anniversaries of Louis-Joseph and his first wife were celebrated in grand style, often with collations in the magnificent Laiterie. When an heir was born, even the articulate Duc de Croÿ was hard put to describe the astonishing illuminations and water displays, the spectacular fireworks in the Condé colours bursting over the Grand Canal, and the cold collations at the Maison de Sylvie.[1] Although there was no Molière or Lully as in the days of the Grand Condé, for sheer invention and imagination Louis-Joseph's parties were unparalleled, and under his aegis Chantilly reached its apogee, to the undying frustration of his Orléans rivals.

The animosity between the Condés and Orléans was exacerbated by the fact that both Louis-Joseph and the Duc d'Orléans (Chartres' father) wanted Louise-Adelaide de Penthièvre as a bride for their sons. In the end, as we know, Chartres won, and Louise-Adelaide, as the Duchesse de Chartres, became one of the most miserable women in France.

When Monsieur le Duc had been master of Chantilly, he respected Le Nôtre's carefully coiffed parterres, but Louis-Joseph's generation was bored by the strict formality of its ancestors' parks. What *he* envisioned for Chantilly was the kind of garden inspired by the Anglomania that had seized the Orléans – the natural garden that Rousseau prescribed for people of 'simple' manners who desired to live intimately with nature. So in the autumn of 1772,[2] as Louis-Joseph was walking in

Pavillon de Venus, Chantilly.
One of the compelling attractions of the Pavilion of Venus built in 1765 was its situation on the Island of Love, its amorous theme carried out in the interior decoration. One contemporary said of Chantilly that it was a beautiful and grand kingdom hidden away in greenery and animated by rushing waters

the marsh between the parterres and the head of the Grand Canal with his architect, J.-F. Leroy (1729–91), he suddenly decided that the time had come to augment the formal gardens with an irregular one as a dramatic setting for his lavish garden parties.

Leroy was intimately associated with the Condés, having been born at Chantilly, and involved in architectural projects at both the Palais Bourbon and the château, where he built (1769) the small Italianate Château d'Enghien, which was often used as a hunting pavilion.

Louis-Joseph's second wife, the Princesse de Monaco, engaged Leroy for *fabriques* in the nearby gardens of Betz-en-Multien designed for her by the Duc d'Harcourt and Hubert Robert, with a Valley of Tombs accented by pines and tragic cypresses, and Robert's remarkable ruins with statues at their base. At Betz, Leroy produced a Pavilion of Repose (perpetual pleasure is exhausting), and in deference to antiquity, one of the most perfect temples of the age – the extant Temple of Friendship with peristyle of Ionic order. In niches stood statues of Castor and Pollux, with pines at either side as their vegetal response.

Leroy must have started work on Louis-Joseph's English garden immediately, for it was apparently finished by 1773. The architect's task at Chantilly was facilitated by the abundant natural water sources which were channelled into rushing brooks, lakes with islands, and cascades enhanced by rock formations. With its completion, Louis-Joseph had achieved the backdrop he desired for the theatrical diversions invented by his *animateur* Monsieur Laujon.

The park was already endowed with a plethora of architectural delights, and even before the new garden was begun, Louis-Joseph had added (1765) to the l'Ile d'Amour the Pavilion of Venus by Babel, who executed it entirely in Rococo *treillage* with vases of flowers on the skyline (above and p.220). The interior walls were mirrored to reflect the candlelight and waters, for the prince's *fontanieri* channelled the water up into multi-branched chandeliers before it tumbled into marble basins. A *féerique* quality was imparted to the soirées and receptions at Chantilly by means of the lighted cascades and jets of water which were made possible by a hydraulic machine constructed by the architect de Mause between 1679 and 1680. Housed in a pavilion with a dome and

PLAN ELEVATION ET COUPE DU PAVILLON DE VENUS
DANS L'ISLE D'AMOUR

Elevation Interieur
du Coté du Canal St Jean

Coupe Interieur sur la ligne A B.

Elevation Interieur
du Coté de la Porte d'Entrée

Elevation de la Face
du Coté du Canal St Jean

Elevation de la Face Exterieur
du Coté des Petites Cascades

Elevation de la Porte
d'Entrée

Plan du Pavillon de Venus

B

Canal   St Jean

Prairie

A

Chambé, Pavillon de Venus, Chantilly.
A precious unpublished album, known as the Atlas du Comte du Nord, *was executed for the Russian court in 1784 by someone known only as Chambé — possibly an architect in Condé's employ. In 1922 the album was acquired by the Musée Conde, Chantilly. It contains valuable sketches of the various fabriques in the Chantilly gardens when Louis-Joseph de Condé was master. This is Chambé's sketch of the neo-Grecian Pavilion of Venus, the exterior covered with fashionable* treillage, *the interior walls painted with scenes of pastoral flirtation by J.-C. Cardin after Boucher cartoons, and the ceiling with Venus surrounded by the Graces. The Revolutionists wantonly destroyed it*

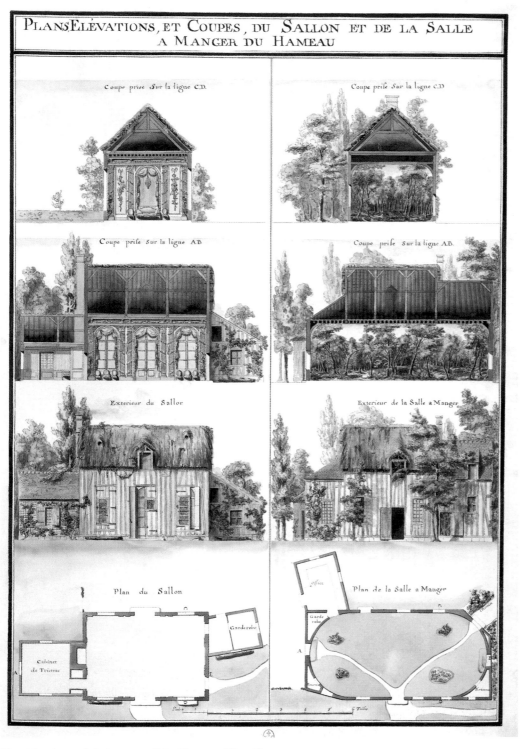

Coupe prise sur la ligne C.D.

Coupe prise sur la ligne C.D.

Coupe prise sur la ligne A.B.

Coupe prise sur la ligne A.B.

Exterieur du Sallon

Exterieur de la Salle a Manger

Plan du Sallon

Plan de la Salle a Manger

Cabinet de Trictrac

Garderobe

office

Garde robe

Chambé, salon and dining room of the Hameau, Chantilly.
The Hameau was inaugurated in April 1775, and became a major attraction of the Chantilly gardens.
The interiors were a great surprise, for the salon was painted white, decorated with bucolic attributes and pilasters entwined with garlands, with a suite of furniture covered in materials matching the curtains. The dining room walls were of canvas painted to resemble a forest, and one guest noted that the illusion was so perfect that one could hardly tell any difference between the interior and the woodlands outside. Even the window panes were painted like foliage, and garlands of lilies and roses fell from the curving branches of trees overhead, holding the chandeliers. The seats were made of tree trunks, and the floor was scattered with tufts of grass and flowers. The pavilion housing the billiard room was hung with toile-de-Jouy, and the reading pavilion lined with Chinese wallpaper

221

segmental windows, it is still there today. Many of the garden structures at Chantilly are illustrated in an album by one Chambé, the pretext for which was the visit to Chantilly in 1782 of the Grand Duke Paul of Russia, the future Tsar Paul I who, with his wife the Grand Duchess Marie, travelled as the Comte and Comtesse du Nord.

In 1767 a delightful theatre was built, its walls and ceiling decorated by Piat-Joseph Sauvage, who would paint in *trompe-l'oeil* the interior of Louis XVI's Pavillon de Chasse at Rambouillet. In the Chantilly theatre, this master of grisaille created a vault of leafy branches supported by palms that enframed the loges. The ceiling represented the sky in which flew dimpled putti bearing garlands. By a mechanical device, the back of the stage could be opened to reveal a grotto and a statue of Thetis, with cascades and jets of water lit by fifteen hundred candles. During the Grand Duke Paul's visit, one of his entourage reported that the plays given here had no rivals in any other court.

Among the first to popularise chinoiseries for garden buildings, the Prince de Condé added a Chinese kiosk (1770). Its walls were yellow and blue with red vertical bands, and the ceiling was adorned with birds in flight, a memory of those suggesting leafy pavilions painted on the ceilings of Italian Renaissance *cassine*.

Capitalising on the abundant waters, Louis-Joseph planned the suppers for his fêtes on an island, for which he ordered rotundas made of cloth in bulb form, the roofs supported by caryatids of painted wood holding *torchères* from which depended coloured lights. The interior vaults foliated in *trompe-l'oeil* trees, and guests arrived at the tiny port in barques, serenaded by the Prince's musicians. The brilliant illumination of the park was achieved by placing three thousand candles in containers of coloured glass.

Each of two so-called Roman pavilions (of which one remains) was composed of a large rectangular room decorated with gilt *treillage* ornamented with flowers and fruits, terminating in a salon. Niches held fountains in the shape of mushrooms from which sprays of water fell into a shell held by nymphs.

The true focal point of Louis-Joseph's new garden, however, was a group of buildings that would be of seminal importance to one of Marie-Antoinette's most ambitious garden complexes – the Hameau at Versailles. This was the Prince's Hameau, consisting of seven peasant cottages made of plaster and timber, with thatched roofs (previous page). They evoked the imagery of pastoral revels, and were ranged around a village green shaded by a large elm. The Hameau was inaugurated in April 1775, and provided an early example of that strange architectural deception that provides a window into the psychology of the age.

In startling contrast to the rustic exterior, the interior of the *grange* (barn) contained a splendid salon with coupled Corinthian pilasters, a richly embellished frieze, mirrored walls, all hung in pink taffeta. The open air dining room was painted to resemble a forest, the window panes etched with leaves. Garlands of lilies and roses fell from the tree branches to support the chandeliers, and the seats took the form of tree trunks, while the grass floor was scattered with tufts of field flowers.

A favourite feature of the Prince's Hameau was the Laiterie where guests were served ices, fresh fruits from the farm, and dairy products from the estate. Like other Laiteries (including the Queen's), it was equipped with a large marble table at the centre, and a buffet of stone running along the sides of the room for setting out the dairy products and fruit to be served to guests. The buffet featured Neo-classical rams' heads at the corners that spouted water into shells, then overflowed into channels grooved into the buffet. It was all part of the 'peasant life' sought by those of Condé's class, for the peaceful countryside offered a refuge from responsibilities, and in games of make-believe even a Condé could momentarily lose his identity.

Chambé, the Chinese kiosk, Chantilly.
The Chinese kiosk was in octagonal form, with semi-circular niches occupied by sofa beds, alternating with painted panels representing Chinese amusements. The ceiling evoked a sky in which colourful birds were flying, one holding in his beak the cord from which a chandelier of enamelled flowers hung. The exterior was painted with 'Chinese' characters

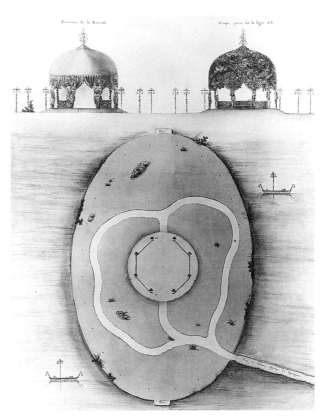

Chambé, toile rotundas, Chantilly.
Chambé's notations indicate that these charming toile tents were put up on the banks of the island at the spring of mineral waters, where Mademoiselle de Clermont's pavilion still stood. Three thousand candles and coloured lights illuminated the receptions and suppers given there. The Prince of Brunswick remarked that the interiors were more authentic than nature itself, for the vaults were painted in trompe-l'oeil *foliage*

In 1777 the Prince offered a party in the form of a movable feast, for the guests assembled at the *rocher*, proceeded to the Port of Pirogues, thence to a cavern, the windmill, dining room, billiard house and library. At several of the rendezvous, abundant cold collations were offered, with songs by shepherds and *ingénue* shepherdesses during the meals. The festivities terminated on the village green under the elm, where peasants danced for the company, the choreography and songs no doubt composed by Monsieur Laujon. They were by no means always innocent pastorals, for they often contained words and phrases of *double entendre*.

The frailest excuse would suffice for a party at Chantilly, and on 3 and 4 June, 1777 the Hameau was the scene of a fête to honour the Prince's daughter, Mademoiselle de Condé. She was always called Mademoiselle, because a marriage had been projected with the Comte d'Artois when the two were children, but Louis XV disapproved of it, so (fortunately for Mademoiselle) it was called off. From the Hameau, the party moved to the Grandes Écuries, where they found supper laid out around the central fountain under the dome of the salon which was decorated like a tent.

In the summer of 1782 the big news in Paris and at court was the arrival of the Comte and Comtesse du Nord, the future Tsar Paul I of Russia and his wife Marie. It was politically expedient to receive them graciously, but their appearance also helped to fill the vacuum left when the younger nobility departed with the French army to fight in the American war. The Russian imperial couple were entertained by Marie-Antoinette in her new gardens at Trianon, and the Galerie des Glaces came to life again with a magnificent fête. The Baronne d'Oberkirch, a childhood friend of the future Tsarina, the Grand Duchess Marie, was overwhelmed, and recorded the events in her diary. She noted that Versailles blazed with the light from a thousand candelabra and girandoles, and the Queen, 'beautiful as the day, animated everything with her *éclat*.' Claude Manceron described the baroness as 'all huge eyes, tiny squeaks, always occupied with her coiffure and migraines . . . a faithful witness to the fêtes, but totally devoid of a critical spirit.'[3] At the ball, the Grand Duchess Marie wore her chalcedonies, the finest in Europe, and the tactful Queen, noting her near-sightedness, presented her with a lorgnette enriched with diamonds concealed in a fan.

In Paris the visitors were taken over by the Orléans at the Palais Royal, but despite their best efforts, they would be entirely upstaged by the Condés, for the week that the travellers spent at Chantilly was discussed at the Russian court for years to come. They arrived on 10 June with their entourage of eighty-nine people – insignificant by Condé standards – and the old family retainers sniffed at such an impoverished display.

The party was conducted through tunnels of greenery decorated with fresh flowers to the façade of the château where the arms of the Comte and Comtesse du Nord were displayed in lights. Supper was served on the l'Ile d'Amour in the artificial lake created by the waters of the Nonette, an island that had by now become an elegant amusement park for royalty with its jeux de bague, swings, and ballroom under the stars. The play presented in the Prince's theatre was almost forgotten in the audience's fascination with the stage, for the setting opened to reveal living water that descended in eight tiers with a magical effect.

The absence of the King and Queen was noted, though the truth was that Louis XVI would not permit the Queen to go, for he did not approve of Louis-Joseph's son, a companion in debauchery of d'Artois and the Duc de Chartres.

On 12 June the Russian visitors were driven in a *calèche* through the park to admire the illuminated Maison de Sylvie, the mirrored Pavilion of Venus, and the Roman pavilions. In open-air rooms made of greenery there were dances, followed by a late supper in the Hameau's oval salon – a 'peasant's meal' consisting of six soups, twelve entrées, twelve kinds of fish, three roasts, six poultry dishes, entremêts, and a table laden with oriental delicacies. Afterwards, the company was conducted to a pavilion hidden in the woods not seen before, where they flung themselves down upon silken divans, serenaded by the prince's musicians who were concealed in a room in the ceiling. The hunt was to begin at dawn . . .

Those who managed to get to bed (the Prince de Condé was not among them) were awakened the next morning by fanfares that sounded like thunderstorms in the park. The ritual of the chase, as carefully choreographed as a ballet, was played out in the deep forests of Chantilly. When the stag was finally killed, the Prince presented the four teeth to the Comtesse du Nord, who later had them mounted, surrounded with diamonds.

By the final day the guests were waxing eloquent with superlatives. 'The youngest, prettiest ladies of Paris and the most amiable cavaliers attended the fêtes at Chantilly . . . the Ménagerie is more numerous [contains a larger number of species] than the King's and was better maintained. As for the Écuries, all the world knows that one can drive through them with the greatest of ease in a carriage with four horses abreast.'[4]

It was all an immense success, and even the royal manifestations were no match for those at Chantilly. Soon the word was circulating around Paris, to the detriment of both the Palais Royal and Versailles: 'The King received the Comte du Nord as a friend; the Orléans received him as a bourgeois; but Monsieur le Prince de Condé as a sovereign.'[5]

CHAPTER 19

PREPARATIONS FOR MARIE-ANTOINETTE'S GARDEN AT VERSAILLES

At Maria-Theresa's court in Vienna the performing arts were appreciated and encouraged. Mozart and Gluck perfomed at Schönbrunn, and Gluck gave harpsichord lessons to the Empress' daughter, Marie-Antoinette. The young Archduchess played the harp as well, and appeared in ballets with her brothers, one of whom – the future Joseph II – was not only a pianist, but a first-class performer on the violincello. So it is not surprising that the vivacious, socially accomplished young Dauphine loved music, dancing, and the stage. When she became Queen, Marie-Antoinette's personality inevitably found expression in art forms such as theatre, fêtes, balls, interior décor, gardens, pavilions, and fashion, and she proved to be the couturiers' ideal model.

Not long after her arrival in France, however, she began to understand that the spontaniety, informality, and warm intimacy of life in the large family that she had known at her mother's court in Vienna were impossible within the confines of Versailles, for here the slightest error of *mesure* might provoke grave consequences for

Krantzinger, Marie-Antoinette.
The arrival of Marie-Antoinette in France gave real impetus to the art of the couturier, for the fashion designers delighted in her perfect figure, her natural dignity enhanced by the lilting walk of a ballerina, her flawless skin, 'without shadows', as Vigée-Lebrun put it, and her gift for wearing the robe à la française with conspicuous distinction. Although criticised by her enemies for extravagance, it it forgotten that she was expected to wear morning, afternoon, and evening dresses of the latest designs and finest materials to promote the fashion industry. The long tradition of sending dolls dressed in the latest Paris fashions to all European courts was continued, but now the silk weavers, designers, lace and passementerie makers appreciated a Queen who displayed their art to its best advantage

the prestige of the royal family. From 1778, she drew indignant criticism when she began to walk in the Versailles gardens in the evening, for they were opened to the public. A Queen's life was governed by inflexible protocol – a cult of civility established by the Sun King, the expectations of a people whose identity was bound to its sovereign, and the rules of succession that often created unbearable tension between the rulers and those eligible to ascend.

Most frustrating of all was the absence of privacy, for 450 people were attached to the Maison de la Reine alone. Furthermore, their ranks and privileges (a word devoid of emotion before the philosophes appeared) were expected to be upheld, and the consequences of the inherited system were sometimes more than the Queen could bear. The articulate Comte de Ségur, an habitué of Madame Du Deffand's Paris salon and intimate of the Empress Catherine, remarked that Marie-Antoinette dreamed of simplicity while wearing the diadem of France.

To complicate matters further, the independent, lively Queen chose the members of her immediate suite unwisely. Although there were notable exceptions – such as her devout (and devoted) sister-in-law, Madame Elisabeth and the loyal Princesse de Lamballe – Marie-Antoinette damaged her reputation by imprudently patronising the Polignacs, who were satirised by the Revolutionists as symbols of greed.[1] Then there were her sorties with her brother-in-law, the Comte d'Artois, and a clan that included the wild, adventurous Duc de Lauzun; the disturbingly attractive Comte de Vaudreuil; 'the old Celadon' Baron de Besenval of dubious character; the Comte de Lauraguais, a natural son of Louis XV and a 'protector' of Sophie Arnould; and the unscrupulous Duc de Chartres.

The Queen's casual manner and high spirits were misleading, for the Prince de Ligne assures us that her charming obtuseness kept all lovers at a distance. The Austrian Ambassador, Comte de Mercy Argenteau, who promptly reported any real or imagined impropriety on the Queen's part to his sovereign, Maria-Theresa, declared that Marie-Antoinette was very reserved with men. The Comte de la Marck insisted that she was infinitely superior to her entourage, and another commentator maintained that she was one of the purest of human beings. It is known that she drank no wine (only water), and was so modest that she bathed in a flannel gown in the presence of her ladies. The most touching tribute to her character came from Louis XVI himself at the end: 'If only the people could know her as I know her'.

Naturally drawn to the sights of Paris, and especially the Opéra balls, Marie-Antoinette became too Parisienne for her own good, for her frequent presence there meant Paris had to share honours with Versailles. According to Mercy, she went to the capital every week during the first years of the reign, where she attended the painting salon, examined the gallery of plans at the Louvre, the merchants' boutiques, the Saint-Ovide fair, and looked over the precious objects offered by *marchands-merciers* like Lazare Duvaux and Dominique Daguerre in the Saint-Honoré quarter, to whose shops she had been taken while she was still Dauphine. She was seen at one of the Comte d'Artois' Paris residences, the Temple, and in 1776 she dined in a Paris house that belonged to the Duc de Chartres ('that monster' as Madame de Latour du Pin called him). He gave a supper followed by a ball in Marie-Antoinette's honour on 24 January, 1777, and she did not refuse the invitation to attend.

Although so young when she became Queen, Marie-Antoinette quickly began to assume a role that perhaps no Queen of France had ever adopted. She gave an

Grand Salon of the Petit Trianon today. Although the Petit Trianon was probably begun as early as 1762, during Madame de Pompadour's lifetime, it was one of the first interiors to reflect the antique style. So the two commodes flanking the fireplace, the splendid ormolu 'appliqués' on each side of the mirror that reflects the Queen's bust – all in the Louis XVI manner – are appropriate to it now, and at least suggest its appearance when Marie-Antoinette lived there. The expertly carved panelling was a very pale bluish green picked out in white and gold with branches of lilies surrounded by classical laurel

unprecedented number of orders for refurbishing the private apartments at Versailles, Fontainebleau, and later Saint Cloud, and left such an imprint upon taste that the Neo-classical mode prevailing during (and even before) her reign should properly be called 'the Marie-Antoinette style.'

She owned her own porcelain factory on the Rue Thiroux in Paris, while the King faithfully patronised Sèvres. The décors she commissioned, such as the silvery gold boudoir with arabesques at Fontainebleau, were among the most refined in the history of the interior. The furniture she ordered, especially from the master cabinetmaker J.-H. Riesener, represented the summit of the art of the *ébéniste*. Her rooms were appointed with ravishingly beautiful gilt bronzes by the great *ciseleurs*, magnificent hardstone vases mounted in gold or ormolu sent from the sale of the Duc d'Aumont, and tasteful oriental lacquers.

She was especially fond of fêtes, and with the collaboration of the architect of the Menus-Plaisirs, P.-A. Paris, she devised numerous imaginative and original *divertissements* for distinguished visitors and members of the royal family. Some of the most memorable were those she arranged in the gardens of Versailles – not in the Sun King's expansive formal gardens, but in her own domain.

It was in June 1774, according to Mercy, that the opportunity came for Marie-Antoinette to have a place for herself. 'Since you love flowers', Louis XVI is supposed to have said to her, 'I have a bouquet to offer you – it is Trianon'. Along with this

The Queen's Boudoir, Petit Trianon.
Although she made few changes to the interior of the Petit Trianon when she acquired it, Marie-Antoinette introduced as much light as possible into her apartments, in contrast to the dark and dull interior of the château of Versailles. She hung diaphanous fabrics in her boudoir that looked out upon the gardens, and installed mirrors to reflect wall lights and chandeliers. In the spring of 1779 she lay ill with measles in this room and was ordered by the doctors to leave Versailles

Panelling in the Queen's Boudoir, Petit Trianon.
The new pale blue-and-white panelling for Marie-Antoinette's boudoir installed in 1787 is of unusual refinement, delicately carved with garlands of jasmine and roses interspersed with doves, crowns, quivers, lyres and fleurs-de-lis. There was no such thing as 'gris de Trianon', a nineteenth-century invention, but the Queen liked pure white, lilac, soft blue, and a subtle green. Her bedroom in the Petit Trianon was decorated in trelliswork

atypical flowery speech came a key adorned with 531 diamonds Louis had ordered from the jeweller of the Menus-Plaisirs as pass key to the Queen's own dominion.

The new proprietor of the Petit Trianon was ecstatic, for it meant that she could escape some of the iron-clad etiquette of the court as well as the sombre apartments she occupied at Versailles. Although she was decorating the Versailles apartments to her own taste, they were depressingly dark, whereas Louis XV's pavilion was flooded with the light she craved. To capture as much sunlight as possible, she added diaphanous *mousselines* to the boudoir that looked out upon the garden, and ordered from the mechanic, Mercklein, a system of mirrors that ascended from the basement to cover the boudoir windows, reflecting the wall lights and chandelier at night (as in her Turkish boudoir at Fontainebleau).

Marie-Antoinette made few changes to the interior of Louis XV's Trianon, and Madame Campan claimed that she was even parsimonous, although her boudoir acquired new panelling in 1787 with arabesques and flowers in relief, and her bedroom was decorated with trelliswork, to accord with the spirit of the place. The extant chairs in the bedroom by the great *ébéniste*, Georges Jacob, echo the garden theme, for they are adorned with polychrome jasmine, lilies-of-the-valley, and basketwork. In her chamber hung a pair of portraits sent by her mother, Maria-Theresa, of her performance with her brothers in a ballet.

Another delight of Trianon was the prospect of cultivating her own flowers, and Marie-Antoinette's name is always associated with flowers. Floral motifs were embroidered or woven into the materials for her clothing and the lampas covering her furniture, carved in mirror and picture frames, painted on the Bélvèdere *boiseries*, sculpted upon the backs and legs of chairs, enwreathed in overdoor motifs, or wrought in ormolu for the mounts of her tables and desks.

The King gave her *carte blanche* in this delicious realm removed from the château, so she soon began to think of converting the land north-east of Trianon – where Louis

Georges Jacob (1739-1814), chair for Marie-Antoinette's trelliswork bedroom at the Petit Trianon, 1787-8.
The garden theme of Trianon was perpetuated in the trelliswork bedroom, and these chairs with polychrome carvings of lilies-of-the-valley and jasmine created for the room by the renowned ébéniste, Georges Jacob, are extant. The Queen appreciated his ingenuity, and these extraordinary chairs (which have miraculously kept their original upholstery) were part of a suite which included a bed, low-backed armchair for dressing, firescreen, footstool, and armchairs. Jacob enjoyed the favour of the King's brothers, the Comtes d'Artois and Provence, the Prince de Condé, and foreign royalty such as Gustavus III and the future George IV of England, whose Carlton House owed much to French ébénistes

XV's hothouses stood — into a fashionable new picturesque garden. Her ideas on garden building would have been brought into focus by several publications that appeared at the time of her ascension, such as Watelet's *Essai sur les Jardins* (1774). She even went out to see Watelet's garden on the island at Moulin-Joli, in which Hubert Robert and François Boucher had a hand, and whose plan blended the formal with the natural. This would have been of particular interest to the Queen, for her own Arcadia at Trianon would have to exist on the fringes of Le Nôtre's cohesive formal plan.

In 1775 came the publication of Duchesne's *Sur la formation des Jardins,* which gave further impetus to the popularity of natural gardens, and the following year Jean-Marie Morel published his *Théorie des Jardins,* a volume found in Marie-Antoinette's library. Morel was architect of the Prince de Conti's park at l'Ile-Adam, and he worked at Ermenonville, a garden that enchanted the Queen.

Besides the landscape gardens in the country, there were several in Paris that were praised by her friends, such as the Maréchal-Duc de Biron's, which had become one of the curiosities of the capital. It combined a formal garden with a new picturesque garden, for the *parterres à la française* were kept near the dwelling, with the irregular garden created beyond the parterres, much like the Comte de Caraman's garden in the Rue Saint-Dominique.

Even though the Queen's contemporaries championed the natural garden, there was a member of the older generation whose opinion weighed heavily with her. It was Charles-Joseph, Prince de Ligne (1735-1814) the very incarnation of a cosmopolite, and described by Leigh Ashton as a man who was able to gather around himself 'more . . . friends of note than any other man of historical insignificance who has ever lived.' The Prince de Ligne was Austrian like the Queen but born in Brussels, and he was devoted to her brother, the Emperor Joseph II. An excellent gardener, Ligne was consulted by connoisseurs of the landscape garden, such as the Duc de Chartres (at Monceau) and his companion, Monsieur de Monville at the Désert de Retz. Ligne enthusiastically encouraged the Queen in her design, pointing out that it was she who must show the way in France in this important matter of gardens.

Ligne knew what he was about, for he had the wit to engage the popular architect Bélanger to design pavilions for his celebrated garden at Beloeil that made it a model of its type. One looked like a mosque, with minarets serving as pigeon roosts and a dairy inside. Another was a Temple of Morpheus, planted appropriately in a field of poppies, and decorated with pilasters and ornaments in blue and yellow stucco. Inside were immense round divans where 'twenty weary guests could rest and restore their strength.'[2]

The Queen would certainly have consulted Bélanger, for she already knew him in another context – as the designer of superb furniture, such as the magnificent table with Gouthière bronzes for the Duc d'Aumont's daughter-in-law, the Duchesse de Mazarin (Frick Collection). The architect had entered the office of the Menus-Plaisirs upon his return from England in 1767, and had conceived the magnificent jewel cabinet – again with Gouthière bronzes – the Duc d'Aumont ordered as a gift to Marie-Antoinette on the day of her marriage.

With the support and encouragement of the Duc d'Aumont, Bélanger opened an atelier for making marbles, jasper and porphyry objects, many of which were destined for d'Aumont's renowned Paris hôtel. Especially sumptuous were the vases Bélanger designed for the Duke, sculpted by Bocciardi (who executed the Queen's jeu de bague), with mounts by Pierre Gouthière. They were so appealing that the Queen bought a number at the sale following the Duke's death.

There were two other members of the royal family living at court, the Comte and Comtesse de Provence (Monsieur and Madame), whose architectural projects the Queen would have known. Provence gave a party in the Queen's honour at his château of Brunoy – with its usual accompaniment of garden pavilions – which has often been cited as the most remarkable fête of the reign. Monsieur's architect was the talented J.-F. Chalgrin (1739-1811), who had designed a gallery for the Queen's marriage, and the pavilion within the precincts of Versailles for Monsieur's mistress, Madame de Balbi. But it was hardly a match for the superb little Pavillon de Musique de Madame nearby that the same architect devised in 1784 for Provence's wife, Marie-Josèphine de Savoie. Its vestibule is painted like a flower garden under a blue sky, and the salon – with superb stucco enrichments of cherubs bearing garlands – gives the illusion of great space, with mirrored walls and windows opening upon the garden.

Both Provence and d'Artois were garden-builders, so it is not inappropriate that the two royal brothers, costumed as *jardiniers galants,* had their portraits painted by François Drouais. It was no misnomer in either case, for the term *vie galante* was merely an eighteenth-century euphemism for adultery.

Also known to the Queen was the vast range of garden architecture commissioned – inevitably – by the rich Orléans, who were always to be found in the avant-garde. In fact, Alexandre de Laborde, writing in 1804, considered the park of their château Le Raincy (1763-83) to be the first to break with the French classical tradition. Possibly the Queen went out to Le Raincy to see the model farm, and the Hameau that Blaikie intended to be seen *beyond* an irregular pond decorated with floating swans, in exactly the way that the Queen's Hameau was designed to be viewed from Trianon.

The painter, Hubert Robert, also figured prominently in the Queen's plans, and enjoyed a personal friendship with the royal family. Her portraitist, Vigée-Lebrun, painted Robert at Moulin-Joli in 1788, and many of her friends – Vaudreuil, Vigée, d'Artois, Choiseul, Besenval, Lalive de Jully, the Prince de Ligne – were Robert's patrons. Louis XVI ordered from him two paintings depicting the Versailles gardens at the moment when the large trees were being taken down, and they were exhibited at the 1777 Salon. The Queen is seen bending over to speak to two small girls, possibly Louis' sisters, and the King is chatting with his Directeur des Bâtiments, the Comte d'Angivillers. Louis XVI was evidently pleased with the canvases, for the following year Hubert Robert was appointed Designer of the King's Gardens and Keeper of the King's Paintings.

One wonders if Hubert Robert had first been presented to the Queen at Moulin-

Hubert Robert, Marie-Antoinette and Louis XVI promenading in the Versailles gardens (detail).
The detail from one of the two paintings Hubert Robert exhibited at the 1777 Salon shows Marie-Antoinette in a white dress with little round hat, bending over two small girls, possibly the King's sisters, Mesdames Clotilde and Elisabeth, who would have been about twelve and seventeen; although they look much younger than this, the contrast in size may be artistic licence to enhance the Queen. The King wears a red coat with a tricorn under his arm, and is talking with a man who is probably the Comte d'Angivillers, his Director of Buildings. The overgrown trees planted in the Sun King's day are being felled, and the famous Puget statue of 'Milo of Cretona' is seen in the background

Joli. Although she does not seem to have been particularly impressed by its site, the rustic dairy and watermill must be seen as precursors of the Queen's own Hameau, which was conceived by Hubert Robert, and whose ideas were incorporated into Richard Mique's plans of 1780. It is certain that she visited another garden in which Robert collaborated – the Marquis de Girardin's park at Ermenonville. This unceremonious visit was recorded by Blaikie: 'All the Court was there except for the King. The Queen, Madame Elisabeth, the Comtesse d'Artois rode upon asses with all their suites following – a noble procession'.[3]

In the spring of 1774 the Queen began to look at the garden proposals presented to her by the court gardener, Antoine Richard, who had studied the *anglo-chinois* mode in England. He was the son of Claude Richard, who had been in charge under the Bien-Aimé, and who continued to work with Antoine until he retired in 1782. Antoine Richard was an exponent of the school that favoured a garden like Wanstead with Gothic forts and ramparts, or even Stowe and Monceau, where every element found in nature and all kinds of pavilions were crammed into a given space. To the Queen's credit, she rejected the idea, and although she courteously consulted Gabriel for projects in July 1774, the architect of the Petit Trianon (then sixty-four) asked to be excused.

On the advice of the Princesse de Beauvau (a friend of the Duc de Choiseul), the Queen next turned to the Comte de Caraman, a true student of gardening. His country property at Roissy was planted as an English park, and the garden behind his Paris hôtel on the Rue Saint-Dominique was reputed to be a model of the irregular genre. The Queen went to see it on 22 July, 1774, and Caraman's account of her visit accompanies his sketch of the occasion:

> Due to the short notice and extreme drought, I was ill prepared for the royal visit. Furthermore, the house was not inhabited during the summer, so the garden was somewhat neglected. But my team of gardeners and concerned neighbours rallied round, getting the withered lawns into shape, placing flowering shrubs borrowed from families in the quarter among my barren ones. The result was that roses emerged from syringas, and snapdragons from lilac bushes.
>
> A lovely tent was erected upon a grassy knoll, its cords of flowery garlands, and a moat of blossoms – orange trees, laurels, Spanish jasmines – encircling it. For the cold collation and ices, a round table was put up inside, laden with huge baskets of fresh flowers, with plates and flatware of vermeil. All of the parterres burgeoned forth with summer flowers, again lent by neighbours, as well as the interior of the hôtel and small pavilion at the bottom of the garden
>
> The day of the Queen's arrival, the heavens opened up and the rain descended, stopping only an hour before the Queen stepped from her carriage, with the happy effect that all of the lawns regained their freshness. Since the Queen was in mourning, there could be no music in the garden, but two orchestras, discreetly muffled, played in the Palais Royal across the street. When she alighted at the door, the Queen was met by my pretty little girls with flowers in their hair, who presented her a bouquet and sang a trio from *Zémire et Azor* . . . The Queen stayed more than two hours, taking ices and talking with Madame de Caraman, who had come from Roissy.

Before the Queen left, she had conferred upon the Comte de Caraman the task of reconstructing the Trianon park. As the royal carriage rolled away, the people of the

Comte de Caraman, sketch of Marie-Antoinette's visit.
The town house of the Comte de Caraman stood on the Rue Saint-Dominique in Paris, and this is his naïve sketch of the Queen's visit of 22 July, 1774. The hand-written caption notes that the Queen accepted a collation in his garden and treated all his family with the greatest kindness. The tent on the rising ground in the background, encircled with Spanish jasmine and roses, is decorated with flowers running from the summit, which is crowned by a 'bouquet' like those that trimmed French beds. The Queen in left foreground receives flowers from the Count's young granddaughters

quarter who had rallied around their neighbour in his time of need, breathed a sigh of relief, and came to congratulate him upon his brilliant improvisations and his exalted new position as Director of the Queen's Gardens. The very next day he presented himself at Versailles to discuss his plan with Richard Mique.

Unfortunately, the new Trianon garden necessited the sacrifice of Louis XV's wonderful botanical garden, probably the finest, costliest, most sophisticated in Europe. The plants were all saved, though, being sent to Paris to the Jardin des Plantes, under the direction of the Richards. This loss was deeply regretted by the Duc de Croÿ, old friend of the Bien-Aimé, who (after the initial phase of the work had been completed) noted in his journal on 21 April, 1780: 'In place of the great hothouse, now there are rather tall hills, a huge rock formation and a river. Never did two *arpents* of land change so much or cost so much money.'[4]

Thomas Blaikie, who went out to Versailles in 1776 to see what was going on, commiserated with the Richards, father and son. 'Monsr. Richard . . . showed us . . . the gardins which formerly was one of the first Botanick gardens in Europe; there is stil a great many rare and curiouss plants but, as this belongs to the Queen who is not fond of plants, they are turning it into a sort of English garden . . . what a pity such a valuable collection should be destroyed! This seems much to affect old Mr. Richard'.[5]

Besides his grammatical errors, the dour old Scotsman was mistaken in accusing the Queen of a distaste for flowers, for her cutting garden was a compelling attraction of Trianon. She would snip them herself with little gold scissors and arrange them in crystal vases, placed on tables laden with bibelots and family portraits. What Blaikie apparently meant was that she was not interested – as the Empress Josephine would be – in their scientific classification.

The Comte de Caraman's plan for Marie-Antoinette's garden showed that he understood perspective and the natural landscape. Carried out under the direction of the Queen's architect, Richard Mique, it was of a happy simplicity, conserving the best aspects of the *jardin anglais* without its abuses, and incorporating some of nature's wildness and yet domesticating it. Above all, he understood how to take advantage of

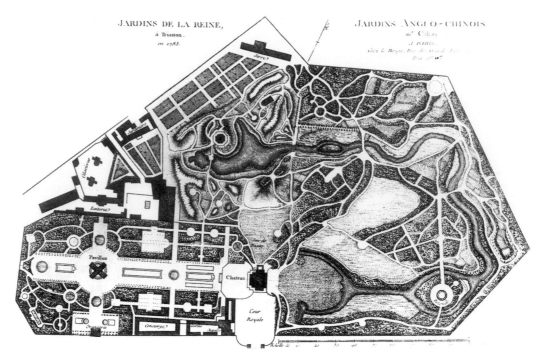

JARDINS DE LA REINE,
à Trianon.
en 1783.

JARDINS ANGLO-CHINOIS
... Cahier
A PARIS
Chez le Rouge, Rue des Grands Aug...
...

Georges Le Rouge, plan of Queen's garden, Petit Trianon.
In 1776 Le Rouge began to publish his Détails de Nouveaux Jardins à la Mode *which dealt with European gardens, and the Queen's garden as it was in 1783 was naturally included. Louis XV's garden with the Pavillon Français at the centre is still to be seen at lower left, but the valuable plants of his botanical gardens situated on the opposite side of the Petit Trianon have been removed to Paris. The land on which they once stood is now rolling meadows with a meandering river that flows down to the island upon which the Temple of Love sits at lower right. The Belvédère rests upon a knoll overlooking the lake above the Trianon, and in the top right corner are the buildings of the Hameau, the last stage in the reconstruction of the royal domain*

the topography, emphasising its assets and masking its faults.

As in Caraman's park at Roissy, a river formed the principal motif of his project, descending from the highest point, and tumbling over rocks to form cascades, 'pour nous parler et nos faire rêver', in the manner that the influential authority on architecture, Père Marc-Antoine Laugier had prescribed. The river wound its way among trees and meadows, and gave birth to a lake where two islands would soon be added. This feature invited bridges, an essential feature of the landscape garden, and the Queen capitalised upon the curving spans, banking them with scarlet tulips for a fête, with the colours picked up in her footmen's livery of cardinal and silver. Hubert Robert was consulted regarding the placement of rocks, trees and pools, and the Richards' advice was sought concerning the plant material, especially the numerous trees required for the *paysage*.

Eight hundred species of trees – the rarest varieties – were planted in an utterly capricious manner, some of them brought from the Alps by the Richards and acclimatised at Trianon. Flowers were banked close to the little château and sprinkled casually about the meadow. The terrain was made to mount and descend, and from it sprang massive boulders to form a cavernous grotto, while a 'natural' spring flowed from its mouth as a cascade to water the gardens.

Athough it had been built for Madame de Pompadour and was enjoyed by Madame Du Barry, the Petit Trianon is embued with the spirit of Marie-Antoinette. It is here that one may almost hear her 'pearly, crystalline laughter that was so close to tears', as the Prince de Ligne remembered it. Pierre Verlet called Trianon 'the symbol of her taste, the abyss of her expenditures, the source of her legend'. And Camille Mauclair believed that the Petit Trianon was the very soul of the Queen, 'embaumé par sa royal présence.'

CHAPTER 20

THE PAVILIONS OF MARIE-ANTOINETTE
AT VERSAILLES

It is a curious aspect of Marie-Antoinette's history that the first reception offered to her just before she stepped onto French soil took place in a pavilion. Shortly before Easter in 1770 the youthful Austrian Archduchess was conducted by a huge cavalcade from the House of Habsburg in Vienna to the Bourbon court in France to become the new Dauphine. At Kehl, on a small island in the Rhine − a piece of neutral territory which divides Germany from France − had been erected a large wooden pavilion hung with some of Strasbourg's costliest tapestries (p.243). Here the future Queen was divested of her Austrian garments and clothed entirely in French ones, an ancient tradition observed when a royal bride was brought from a foreign country.[1]

The Provisional Structures

When Marie-Antoinette arrived at Europe's leading court, she began to discover that she could not indulge her proclivities for theatre, music, dancing, billiards and fêtes in the way she had envisioned. True, the splendid state apartments were of ample proportions, and Gabriel's elegant Opéra with its mechanical stage had been inaugurated for her marriage, but the layout of the public salons *en enfilade* was not (in her view) suitably disposed to stage effectively the balls, theatrical performances, innovative diversions, cold collations and billiard games that were her delight.

When she became Queen, a solution to the problem was found, and perhaps she took her cue from the wooden pavilion in which she had been greeted at Kehl. There soon appeared in the Versailles gardens and courtyards provisional wooden structures that could accommodate the large number of guests who were invited to both the official and private fêtes and ceremonies. These temporary buildings became an institution under Marie-Antoinette, and besides the additional space they afforded, they could be arranged in such a manner as to provide the mobility required for various phases of the imaginative *divertissements* designed by the Queen's architects and artists. The unceremonious exteriors of these barracks − which sharply contrasted with the exterior of the formidable château − were misleading, for the interiors were ingeniously transformed by the architects of the Menus-Plaisirs and their teams of artisans into palatial settings that carried out themes appropriate to a particular occasion.

The older courtiers grumbled that the peculiar physiognomy of the barracks disfigured the majestic approach from the town and cluttered up the gardens (the greatest outdoor sculpture museum in the world). But the Queen was − perhaps unwittingly − following a tradition. The King's grandfather, Louis XV, had seen fit to put up small wooden houses at Compiègne, at the nearby château/hunting lodge of Saint-Hubert, and even for his military campaigns.

It may have been one of the Bien-Aimé's temporary wooden buildings that Marie-Antoinette ordered to be brought over from Saint-Hubert to Compiègne, during the court's sojourn there in 1774. She had it fitted up as a billiard room, a game that was always associated with the Bourbon court, and which she particularly favoured.

One can understand why she sought a gentler diversion than that for which this royal château was renowned, for she was repelled by hunting, and the vivid impression that it made on her is evident from the letter she wrote from Compiègne on 26 August, 1772 to her sister, Marie-Christine:

> M. le Dauphin hunts a great deal and I was there for the frightening massacres in the courtyard of the château by the light of torches. They would laugh at me if I said in a loud voice that these so-called pleasures were simply unadulterated cruelties; the dogs unleashed [upon their prey] made me think of the remains of Jezebel . . .[2]

In December 1774, Marie-Antoinette inaugurated her court balls, and one can imagine the room's décor (designed by Louis-René Boquet) from the costumes she stipulated for the courtiers: blue velvet for the men, and white dominoes for the ladies.

During January and February of the following year, the balls took place in a temporary house erected in the Court of the Princes and in the beautiful Hercules Salon – with its heroic marble pilasters, gilt enriched cornice, and the finest illusionistic ceiling of the day. One would have thought that a room created by the architect Robert de Cotte, the sculptor Antoine Vassé, and the painter François Lemoyne – a veritable milestone in the art of the interior – would have satisfied the most discriminating taste.

But the Queen ordered a décor that evoked the age of Henri IV and Marie de' Medicis, with instructions that the guests appear in festive court costumes from the precocious age of the Sun King's colourful grandfather.

If she found the official residence of the monarchy too restrictive, she quickly perceived that the pavilion complex at Marly lent itself nicely to her purposes. So in April 1775 – when the Prince de Condé was offering a fête to inaugurate his new pavilions at the Chantilly Hameau – the artists attached to the Menus-Plaisirs organised a Chinese fête at Marly for the Queen.

In 1778 she ordered a provisional theatre for one of the Marly bosquets, its interior much like the décor created for her balls in the state apartments at Versailles, which usually featured sky-blue draperies edged with gold fringe. The carpenter Francastel specialised in the framework for these structures, which were then covered with a heavy canvas to which was glued paper that had been painted to suggest the materials of permanent architecture. This theatre in the delightful bosquet so pleased the Queen that she had it enlarged, further embellished, and covered with a slate roof in the spring of 1779.

One great advantage of Marly was its layout (p.54): the royal house at the head of the central reflecting pool, whose salon with high ceiling and giant pilasters made a perfect supper pavilion; the series of smaller pavilions at either side of the principal body of water that could be used for different courses; the dramatic bosquets with foliate niches for sculpture and walls of clipped shrubbery that functioned as outdoor rooms; the tunnels of greenery through which the guests could pass from one stage of the fête to another; above all, the exploitation of the abundant water supply in the huge *pièce d'eau*, cascades and fountains, enhanced with statuary by leading sculptors of the Versailles school.

This dramatic ensemble, realised for the Sun King one hundred years before, provided the perfect setting for the unsurpassed fêtes staged there during the court's sojourn from 22 April to 20 May in 1781.[3] Before examining them in greater detail, it must be pointed out that the distinctive character of these lavish affairs was due largely to the architect who had been named in 1778 Designer of the Menus-Plaisirs, Pierre-Adrien Paris (1747-1819).

Indirectly, it was really the Duc d'Aumont who was reponsible, for this perspicacious First Gentleman of the King's Bedchamber discovered Paris' talent in the first place, and he had the promising young architect named to this important post. The Queen had known the Duc d'Aumont since her arrival in France, for it was he who had commissioned Bélanger to design her famous (lost) jewel cabinet when she was still Dauphine. (It was adorned with an Apollo head by Houdon executed by Gouthière, and held gifts — watches, fans, snuff boxes — that the Dauphine passed out to members of the court.)

For the decoration of his own hôtel on the Place Louis XV in 1774, the Duke had turned to P.-A. Paris, and the architect produced a masterpiece of cold, sombre brilliance of seminal importance to the marvellously wrought interiors in the Etruscan style characteristic of the latter years of the reign. In d'Aumont's hôtel there were no paintings, but columns, tables, chandeliers, marbles, porphyry, granite and jaspers of an outrageous price.

D'Aumont acted as intermediary between the designer and sovereigns, and given the Queen's abiding interest in every detail contributing to the effectiveness of her fêtes, it is certain that she worked closely with d'Aumont and the architect Paris. There is a thin red line between architecture, décor and the settings for fêtes, and one can almost catch glimpses of the Hôtel d'Aumont in some of Paris' designs for the Queen's provisional ballrooms.

One is the setting that Paris devised for one of the Queen's balls where false marble proliferates in walls, dado and in fluted Ionic columns imitating porphyry or marble. They enframe a mirror in the form of a triumphal arch, reflecting a crystal chandelier suspended from a garland of fresh flowers (p.242 top). That the entire confection Paris conjured up for a ball — painted ceiling and marbled walls, chandeliers roped with flowers — would all disappear within a few hours only enhanced its magic.

Yet, details of these fragile décors for the Queen's fêtes — and others — found their way into actual interiors, an art form that reached a pinnacle of refinement under the aegis of Marie-Antoinette. A design by Chalgrin for the fêtes celebrating the Queen's marriage was emulated by Brongniart for the hôtel of Madame de Montesson, wife of the Duc d'Orléans, and Chalgrin's festival designs inspired Ledoux in his design for Madame Du Barry's pavilion of Louveciennes. Before the Eglise Sainte-Geneviève (Panthéon) was constructed, Soufflot put up a wood and papier mâché model for Louis XV to judge, and a painting in the Musée Carnavalet, Paris, records the festive occasion.

In addition to the relentless demands of the Menus-Plaisirs upon Pierre-Adrien Paris' talents, he designed pavilions at the Folie Beaujon in Paris, settings for the Opéra, and fêtes for the Duc d'Aumont and the Comte d'Artois. The last two were demanding, affluent and discriminating patrons (in the case of d'Artois, it was largely thanks to the Comte de Vaudreuil, his artistic adviser).

With Paris' designs for the Queen, we approach a signal moment in an evanescent art form which reached its finest manifestation after she assumed the throne. For one occasion — possibly the visit of her brother Joseph II in July 1781 — Paris composed an enormous salon for the ball and banquet at Marly, placing it between a pool from which issued sprays of water (known as des Gerbes, or sheaves) and the large reflecting pool. The salon was shaped to conform to the semicircular edge of the great basin, its rustic substructure pierced by staircases that led to a balustraded terrace (p.242).

Following the tradition for foliage pavilions that dated back to the Middle Ages and that was perpetuated during the French Renaissance, Paris covered the huge room with greenery so that it appeared to be a clipped bosquet. The custom looked back to an even more remote history, for the Jews of Moses' day lived in booths made of branches to celebrate the Feast of the Tabernacles.

Emerging at the centre of the green ballroom at Marly was a circular pavilion of Ionic order ornamented with gilt trelliswork, and gilt statues on the entablature and balustrade. Arcades made of foliage featured trunks of trees, the bases of which were adorned with great baskets of multicoloured flowers. Ranged at each side of the salon were ravishing galleries made of crimson and gold curtains that fell in large cascades, connecting the provisional salon to the *treillage* separating the twelve courtiers' pavilions facing the large central basin.

Passionately fond of Italian villas (particularly the Villa Albani at Rome and Caprarola), Paris formed the structure for launching the fireworks as a hemicycle representing an ancient nymphaeum. It stood opposite the provisional salon at the other end of the reflecting pool, and was adorned with river gods and goddesses reclining upon a large rock formation. Behind it stood a monumental obelisk with four lions' heads from whose mouths water flowed into a basin, then cascaded over rocks, and finally emptied into the central pool. So artfully was it composed that the temporary structures of obelisk and nymphaeum seemed to be permanent features of Marly's reflecting pool, and from them were launched the fireworks whose flaming *bouquets* were reproduced in the shimmering waters.

During the Carnival season of 1786 at Versailles, people alighting from their carriages were shocked to come upon a wooden structure standing right in front of the château, as jarring as it was absurd. But it had been ordered by the Queen to accommodate the annual events of Carnival, and she chose this position in order to use the old Salle de la Comédie nearby as a ballroom.

The following year, a fantastic construction that could house five hundred people for the Carnival events appeared on the south terrace, access to which was obtained by the vaulted (and inevitably cold) passage that led from the royal courtyard back to the terrace. The pavilion was composed of three parts: near the south wing of the château stood the entrance and promenade, with the Billiard Salon; then came the Game Salon, with a separate one for the King's entourage; and at the centre stood the Ballroom, with a hemicycle towards the Orangerie below, in which was placed the elaborate buffet, with fountains playing around it. To give the appearance of greater space, large mirrors were installed at strategic points, one of which was placed so as to give the illusion of a rotunda. It was heated with faïence stoves in classical shapes, serviced from behind so that their antique forms remained undisturbed.

This memorable and expensive Carnival of 1787 was the last ever held at the royal château, ending a long tradition that had been established by the Sun King. Never again would there be the extravagant, even hilarious costumes (a head-dress with five faces) that Jean Berain had invented for the Grand Dauphin, or the beribboned and feathered ball gowns created by Rose Bertin for the vivacious, blonde Queen. Gone were the vital and imaginative décors whereby the architects of the Menus-Plaisirs converted unsightly wooden sheds into mirrored fairylands that reflected crystal fountains, blue silk curtains, and glistening chandeliers entwined with flowers.

The *maisons de bois* were not used exclusively for court parties, however, but for serious official affairs. Since Louis XV's day, it had been customary for solemn assemblies of Parlement (*lits de justice*) to take place at Versailles, as well as meetings of deputations from the various provinces. The deputations met in a wooden structure decorated for the occasion, and afterwards the King would entertain the visitors by having the waters play in the gardens. Then they would be taken to three of the Sun King's pavilions: by gondola to the south end of the Grand Canal to see the Ménagerie, with its camels, dromedaries, lions, tigers, all sorts of birds, an elephant and a rhinoceros; thence to the north end of the Canal, where they mounted the steps to the Grand Trianon. Afterwards, they all piled into carriages to be driven off to Marly, the Kingdom of Water.

By December 1786, the national economy had reached a critical state, so in an effort to resolve the crisis, Louis XVI summoned the Assembly of Notables (about 150 distinguished men) to Versailles for a meeting on 22 February, 1787. It was to take place in the scenery storehouse of the Menus-Plaisirs in the Avenue de Paris near the château. Pierre-Adrien Paris was quickly summoned again to provide a suitable stage for the auspicious occasion, and the King ordered Jean-Michel Moreau (Moreau le Jeune) to make a drawing of it, which was exhibited in the Salon of 1787.

The martial décor is almost a metaphor for the glorification of royal power. The King is seated upon a throne under a dais topped with a panache of plumes, like the state bed. Along the walls hang six Gobelins tapestries of Van der Meulen battle scenes (1665-77), the famous 'L'histoire du roi', enframed with a bas-relief of laurels and separated by trophies. The walls are joined to the flat ceiling (painted to suggest a blue sky with white clouds) by means of coffering above the entablature which features helmets and bucrania in the metopes. The result of Paris' artistry shocked the public, who considered it too elaborate in view of the budget deficit, so for the meeting that followed the King warned the architect that a much more circumspect setting must be arranged.

Austerity became the keynote thereafter, when a few months later – 4-5 May, 1789 – Louis called the meeting of the Estates-General, ironically signing the 'monarchy's own death warrant'.[4] Paris' first design for the Notables influenced the new, larger provisional structure to be put up in the same place, this time to accommodate a thousand representatives.

Again the architect of the Menus-Plaisirs, aided by Papillon de la Ferte, frantically searched through the scenery stored at Versailles, for the assembly room had to be finished without delay. Paris used columns from the Queen's balls of 1785 and 1786, and the throne, dais, benches and rug from the Coronation ceremony. His design was a hall inspired by antique basilicas, a form he had used for fêtes during the past twenty-five years, and it was again recorded by Moreau le Jeune. The King and Queen sit under an elaborate, heavy dais, with the entire wall draped with taffeta to hide the carpentry needed to support it. Colonnades of baseless Doric columns separate the main area from the lateral aisles where spectators sit. The barrel-vaulted ceiling is painted with *trompe-l'oeil* coffering, and light floods through thermal windows and an oculus.

The opening of the Estates-General was, as Pierre Verlet wrote, the last great spectacle given by the monarchy of the *ancien régime*. This gloomy presentiment of the culminating, tragic events of the reign also marked the last official public appearance of the Queen, who is seen in the Moreau drawing (overleaf) seated next to the King on his throne, wearing flowers in her hair. As she walked in, the American, Gouverneur Morris, nudged his neighbour and whispered, 'Voila la victime'.

Moreau le Jeune, opening of the Estates-General, 1789.
As Engraver to the King's Cabinet, Moreau le Jeune recorded the opening ceremony for the meeting of the Estates-General on 4 and 5 May, 1789. Since the last meeting had occurred in 1614-5, it was not easy to determine the proper décor for such a solemn occasion, so the difficult task was given to Papillon de la Ferte, a man of vast culture who had been ably serving the King as his Director of the Menus-Plaisirs. The huge room carried out by P.-A. Paris and his team followed the form of antique basilicas, a central nave separated from the aisles by deeply fluted Doric columns without bases, with the upper part ornamented as it had been for the Assembly of Notables in 1787, except that the roof was pierced to receive light. The Paris gazettes praised the ingenuity and taste of the Menus-Plaisirs for the sophisticated lighting, the elegant colours, false marbles, and superb textiles

It was also the last time that elements from the ephemeral structures for Marie-Antoinette's balls and Coronation were used for a public occasion. Alain Gruber regarded the room for the Estates-General as:

> The final great achievement of the Menus-Plaisirs. It was with elegance and distinction that they brought to an end a mission which had lasted a century and, through the royal fêtes, had been largely responsible for spreading a sumptuous and original art.[5]

The Jeu de Bague

The preparation of the ground for the Queen's gardens had already begun during the summer of 1774 with a new enclosing wall, and the sculptor Deschamps from Augustin Pajou's atelier presented models of the proposed garden for the Queen's approval. The operation was directed by her architect Richard Mique, and Louis XV's gardener, Antoine Richard (helped by Belleville), was there to advise upon the excavations and terracing required to create the river and island.

The year 1776 marked the high watermark of the Queen's pleasures. She went into Paris for the races, presided over the games at Versailles, surveyed the progress of her gardens, and on 26 September the mobile Jeu de Bague was christened. It was at this time that she became particularly interested in oriental objects: Chinese porcelains, lacquers, bamboo boxes and birds. As we have seen, a Chinese fête had been organised at Marly the year before, and this initial pavilion for the Trianon gardens –

The Jeu de Bague at the Petit Trianon. The Queen is said to have been impressed by the Jeu de Bague at Monceau. In 1775 she had already become fascinated by chinoiseries, and had attended a fête with Chinese motifs at Marly in April of that year. The mechanism was hidden in a ditch and was turned by three men

the Jeu de Bague, evoked the Orient, and was similar to the one that stood in the Duc de Chartres' Jardin de Monceau in Paris.

Connected to Trianon via an underground passage, the Jeu de Bague looked like a Chinese pagoda in motion, for it was topped by a huge fixed parasol with a weathervane of two gilt dragons, and bells that tinkled as it moved. The parasol sheltered a platform on which were placed seats in dragon form for the men, peacocks for the ladies. These figures were sculpted in oak from the Vosges and Holland by Augustin Bocciardi, whom the Duc d'Aumont had brought to the Menus-Plaisirs in 1766, while the gilding was done by Dutemps. The idea was to tent-peg the rings that hung from the periphery of the parasol as the platform whirled around. But the incessant clamour of the bells tired the Queen, so her German mechanic, Mercklein, suggested a 'jeu de balles' which he assured was also Chinese.[6]

Like Louis XV, Marie-Antoinette was constantly adding something new to the gardens. On 2 August, 1781 the Queen visited the popular Redoute Chinoise in the Saint-Laurent fair which had been opened on 28 June with a gala designed by P.-.A. Paris.[7] The playground consisted of an exotic garden with pagoda, oriental swing, and jeux de bague – three pavilions joined by a circular gallery. They were painted in brilliant colours with gilt reliefs, and with garlands, tassels, and bells hanging from a glittering fish-scale roof.

The gallery that the Queen added to her own Jeu de Bague assumed the form of a half circle uniting three pagodas painted in yellow, green, azure blue, and vermilion picked out with gold. This new feature sheltered the spectators who watched the games and applauded the ladies' success in pegging the rings.

The arrangement apparently gave her ideas for further *divertissements*, for one of which she put up a large oval tent close to the Pavillon Français for a ball. It was so constructed that guests could pass from Trianon through a subterranean passage to the Chinese gallery, through other cloth-covered passages to the oval ballroom in tent form, and afterwards to the theatre. The fact that people could move from one pavilion to another, each in a different material and of contrasting moods and shapes, added zest, novelty – and expense – to the Trianon fêtes.

The Queen's expenditures seemed almost insignificant, as

Claude-Louis Châtelet, Redoute Chinoise.
The Queen's visit in August 1781 to one of the most popular amusements in Paris, the Redoute Chinoise, apparently gave her the idea for the semicircular gallery composed of three pagodas that she added to the Jeu de Bague

Pierre-Adrien Paris, interior of pavilion for one of the Queen's fêtes, Versailles.
The walls are painted in faux bois with delicate frieze in the entablature above; the doors and plaques above them are embellished with arabesques and motifs from the classical repertoire. Two free-standing false marble columns with Ionic capitals flank a mirror against which is suspended a crystal lustre, with garlands of fresh flowers. The light is multiplied by crystal wall lights at each side of the mirror, and an altar with festoons and swags supports an antique vase. These accomplished décors were created in the ateliers of the Menus-Plaisirs in Paris or Versailles

Exterior of Foliage Pavilion at Marly.
The date of the fêtes at Marly is uncertain. If they occurred during the July 1781 visit of the Queen's brother, Joseph II of Austria, they could have honoured her pregnancy, for she gave birth to the Dauphin in October. This large room covered with greenery was erected before the enormous reflecting pool, and looked like a marvellous bosquet clipped and richly decorated. At its centre emerged a circular pavilion ornamented with gilt treillage of Ionic order, the entablature and balustrade heightened with gilt statues. It was encircled by a suite of arcades of feuillage, each column made of a birch trunk, the vases of which were embellished with multicoloured flowers. This highly original invention by P.-A. Paris is part of a tradition that began in the Middle Ages and looks forward to the winter gardens of the Second Empire. It was so firmly entrenched in the French psyche that the same pavilion of greenery, albeit less sophisticated than the Marly example, reappeared in the New World as the pièce de résistance *for the French army's celebration of the Dauphin's birth (p.303)*

Verlet pointed out, compared to the immense cost of operating Versailles itself, and by 1787 the royal treasury was almost bankrupt as a result of the French contribution to the American Revolution. Monsieur Necker was already concerned in 1777, but this was the summer when the Queen transformed the entire garden into a village of pavilions representing merchants' boutiques, and she herself poured the lemonade.

Claude-Louis Châtelet, Jeu de Bague, Petit Trianon.
The Queen was so pleased with her gardens and the new fabriques that she ordered views of them, and Claude-Louis Châtelet was put in charge of carrying out the drawings. They were bound into albums with gilt-embossed leather bindings and covers lined with rich silk to be given to visiting royalty to whom the Queen offered fêtes in the Trianon gardens. Three are known to have survived, one in the Royal Library in Stockholm, another in a private collection, and a third in the Biblioteca Estense, Modena

Simplicity was chic among members of the princely class, and the sentiment evoked by a fête like the Queen's was akin to the ones in the Hameau of Chantilly where sentimental homage was paid to the Bon Seigneur. In the same year (1777), Elie de Beaumont at Canon instituted a *fête des bonnes gens* with medals struck for the occasion. The most ridiculous was the fête reported by the *Mercure de France* in February 1778: a *fête des bonnes gens* under the patronage – of all people – the depraved Comte d'Artois! It was part and parcel of a sudden 'love for humanity', and it reminds us of the Marquis de Mirabeau, 'a "friend of man" who loved humanity, and hated his own family.'[8]

This is not to suggest that there was anything hypocritical in the Queen's gesture, for it is common knowledge that she was a consistently kind and gracious person. It was an innocent and thoughtless game, but it contributed to a loss of respect for the Crown that came to be resented.

In juxtaposition to the dignified purity of the Petit Trianon, the Jeu de Bague must have looked somewhat vulgar. But this and the carnival atmosphere of certain fêtes were not the only examples of questionable taste at Trianon. For the Queen had lanterns garnished with porcelain flowers placed about the garden, benches painted green accented with vermilion, and there was a see-saw in front of her house at the Hameau in 1783, but it was probably for the children.

Section of embroidery for Marie Antoinette's Pavilion at Kehl.
Marie-Antoinette's solemn entry to France on 7 May, 1770 took place on an island in the Rhine, upon which a wooden pavilion painted in tromp-l'oeil to resemble cut stone had been erected for the ceremony of her arrival. It consisted of an enfilade of salons, one side for Austrians, the other for the French. The embroideries have been reattached to a modern fabric; how they were used on the occasion of Marie-Antoinette's arrival have not yet been determined

The Temple of Love

The Queen's boudoir and bedchamber were on the ground floor of Trianon, and from it she could pass directly into the gardens which became her private world. A prominent feature was the river, and she must have been contemplating an ornament for the island shortly after the Jeu de Bague was finished.

In stark contrast to this garish toy, the next pavilion to appear (1777-8) was of a classical sobriety totally commensurate with the character of Gabriel's small château, and in perfect scale. It was a structure that would not be used for meals or games, but a Neo-classical temple by Richard Mique to shelter the famous statue by Edmé Bouchardon that had already been exhibited at the Louvre: 'Cupid Shaping his Bow into the Club of Hercules' (1746).

The round temple that rose upon the island was a touch of Hellenic perfection, dedicated to the god of the century, for it was called the Temple de l'Amour. It was an appropriate gesture, for it could have symbolised the conjugal fidelity of Marie-Antoinette and her husband, both of whom displayed an exemplary loyalty in the terrible days that came later.

According to the Prince de Ligne, temples inspired voluptuousness. Whatever this one evoked, it is of unquestionable propriety in its reference to antiquity, with a circular colonnade of twelve Corinthian columns in white marble supporting an entablature of flowering rinceaux, and a cupola of Conflans stone (p.246). In relationship to the Petit Trianon, it was instinctively right, although there was nothing unusual about an antique temple that resembled the one at Tivoli. Among Mique's belongings were found two undated drawings of the cascades of Tivoli, and the Temple of the Sibyl was invariably visited by landscape artists such as J.-F. Hue, Hubert Robert, and Fragonard, all of whom painted views of it. The Sibyl Shrine became a cherished motif for the landscape garden, for a Temple of Flora stood on an island of lawns and flowers at the Prince de Ligne's Beloeil, and a similar one appeared on an island at Méréville in the Marquis de Laborde's gardens, enclosing a sculpture by Pajou.

The Temple de l'Amour was surrounded with a variety of fragrant shrubs, roses, trees chosen for their graceful forms, and united to the mainland with bridges garnished with flowers in boxes. Flowers abounded at Trianon – on the island, around the Belvédère, in the borders and hothouses, in the kitchen garden of the Hameau, and even in faïence pots (1,232 of them with the Queen's monogram) placed upon the winding stairs of the Queen's House at the Hameau. Her botanical interests lay in ornamental plants rather in classified botanical gardens, and Trianon again became almost as important a centre for horticulture – though for a different reason – as it had been under Louis XV.

The chaste white tholos on the island which paid tribute to the French classical tradition was admired by almost everyone, including such connoisseurs as the Duc de Croÿ. He saw it in April 1780 and described it in his journal as 'le superbe palais de l'Amour en rotonde, de la plus riche architecture grecque'.[9] Even today its graceful marble form speaks to us as it did to the Prince de Ligne, who called it 'le comble de la perfection de goût et de la ciselure'.[10] The Prince, who always had an eye for trees, went on to praise the park with its impressive specimen collection which made it seem ten times larger than it really was.

The Queen's party of 3 September, 1777, when she poured lemonade, and the court ladies pretended to be shopgirls selling alluring wares in boutiques, transformed

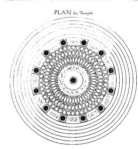

PLAN du Temple

Section and plan of Temple of Love, Petit Trianon.
Stendhal observed that the Pantheon in Rome was the first monument of non-useful architecture. Like the Pantheon, the Temple of Love serves no practical purpose except to embellish the garden and provide an exquisite setting for a piece of sculpture. Like the Pantheon, its dome is coffered, and it is supported by twelve Corinthian columns, an order that its architect, Richard Mique, must have considered appropriate to the discerning patron who commissioned it, Marie-Antoinette

the gardens into a fair and inaugurated the Temple of Love and her new English garden. The lawns were turned into a public square with bakers' shops and rôtisseries, and in another part of the garden a small inn was flanked by twenty-one arcades of *treillage,* each bearing the name of one of the royal houses.

Further on, a theatre had been erected, its façade decorated with various architectural motifs. Garlands of fresh flowers were strung from one *fabrique* to another, and in the middle of the garden, resting upon a pink marble base, was raised a pavilion from which one could see the entire village at a glance. Entertainment was provided by the celebrated harlequin of the Italian Comedy and Mademoiselle Dugazon of the French Comedy, who performed in a bird-catcher's boutique. The Jeu de Bague was encircled by a lighted amphitheatre, on the tiers of which were placed forty large 'porcelain' vases decorated with flowers, while the musicians of the guard, wearing Chinese costumes, played oriental tunes.

When news of this event reached the Empress Maria-Theresa, the Queen's mother was upset not so much by the juvenile spirit of the party, as by the fact that her daughter had given the party for the King. This reversed a time-honoured tradition, for the Queen derived her authority from her husband.

The Temple of Love became almost a symbol of the Trianon gardens, for when the City of Paris offered a fête in January 1782 for the King and Queen to celebrate the birth of the Dauphin, the table was decorated with three monopteral temples placed on a 'lake' made of mirrors. The central temple reached an amazing height, the columns were made of greenery, the dome surmounted by a Medici vase with flowers, and the two smaller temples were supported by Ionic columns wreathed with flowers and ribbons. They were the central features of the tablescape representing a French garden with green lawns, flowered borders, figurines and statues – probably white biscuit from Sèvres. This municipal fête was also staged in a provisional structure hung with silk festoons and crystal chandeliers suspended by ropes of fresh flowers (see p.183).

The huge gallery with screens of columns and coved enriched cornice was designed by the architect responsible for all Paris ceremonies, P.-L. Moreau-Desproux, and served the same purpose as the Queen's wooden barracks at Versailles. Aside from its practical aspects, it was a manifestation of French philosophy – that life itself was an art. The fragile ballrooms, light toile tents and evanescent jeux de bague were yet another art form whereby the unbounded energy of the Age of Enlightenment expressed itself.

The Belvédère

Although the Temple of Love was a splendid visual addition to the garden, and could be dramatically lighted for evening parties, the Queen wanted an outdoor dining room near the small château that served the same purpose as had the Salon Frais for

Claude-Louis Châtelet, the Temple of Love, Petit Trianon.
The Queen's Temple of Love was the most famous of the period, and its presence in her garden must have owed much to Hubert Robert, who painted just such a temple standing on a high rock formation in an imaginary landscape, and again in a dramatic view of the Temple of the Sibyl at Tivoli. Joseph Vernet also left his own interpretation of the scene. Marie-Antoinette's Temple is more effective by being situated on relatively flat terrain on an island so that it is reflected in tranquil waters

Left: The Temple of Love today.
At the end of the twentieth century, although the crisp modelling characteristic of French sculpture has been dulled by the elements, the graceful marble Temple of Love speaks to us as it did to the Prince de Ligne who called it 'le comble de la perfection de goût et de la ciselure'

Opposite: The Belvédère today.
Even today the Belvédère represents the epitome of that decorative elegance and refinement that gave France the artistic hegemony for centuries, and French artisans the supreme rank

Claude-Louis Châtelet, Rocher and Belvédère
The naturalising of a terrain as prescribed by theorists like Watelet in his Essai sur les Jardins *(1774) is expressed in the Queen's Rocher, the rocky outcrop and grotto above the lake behind the Trianon. The white, octagonal Belvédère nearby — essence of Richard Mique's sophisticated antique manner — was intended as a deliberate contrast to the cavernous grotto on the far left*

Louis XV. So the construction of Mique's enchanting octagonal Belvédère of cut stone was begun in 1778. Placed upon an artificial rocky eminence overlooking a small pond behind Trianon, it was within easy access of the Queen's boudoir.

There was a subtle decorative affinity between the boudoir and the effete elegance of the Belvédère, for the motifs of the boudoir were repeated in the pavilion's interior (p.250). Le Riche painted the walls with musical instruments, garden tools, thyrses, quivers, birdcages, straw hats, and baskets in fresh, natural colours. Jean-Jacques Lagrenée (1740-1821), who specialised in ceilings, executed the Belvédère ceiling with cupids bearing garlands of flowers against a blue sky.

Emphasising and underlining the geometrical character of the pavilion is the floor paved in a mosaic of marble in turquoise blue, rose, and green with white veins. As Baulez has shown, a splendid suite of gilt chairs was designed by the Garde-Meuble architect, Jacques Gondoin, and executed by F. Foliot: sculpted flowers in the cresting, deeply undercut leaves encircling the apron.

The exterior is a suave résumé of the distinguishing traits of French Neo-classicism, with four doors alternating with

The Belvédère, Petit Trianon.
An Englishman, writing about French gardens, stated that the garden buildings were important as objects contributing to the composition of the garden, so that the landscape became a theatre, a sort of fairyland. The theatrical possibilities of the Belvédère were exploited to the full for Marie-Antoinette's evening fêtes. When it was finished in the summer of 1781, on 15 July she offered a supper on the lawns, followed by a theatrical. When Gustave III of Sweden came in the summer of 1784, the fête given for him on 21 July included three hundred guests, one thousand attendants lodged in dependencies, bands of the French and Swiss Guards, with the brilliantly lit Belvédère the brightest spot in the garden. This is how the Belvédère looked in the nineteenth century

four windows in the eight bays, and a crowning balustrade, while the bas-reliefs of the Four Seasons over each window were masterfully modelled by the sculptor Deschamps (p.251). Over the doors, triangular pediments supported on enriched consoles enclose scenes of gardening and hunting. The frieze of festoons is of lead, but so skilfully fixed to the wall and painted to resemble stone that it is indistinguishable from the stone itself.

The Belvédère must be imagined as it was during the Queen's lifetime, when the fragrant plantings of Snowball rose trees and apples of Paradise seemed to invade the room through the tall doors. From the terrace she looked down upon Trianon with the riotous Jeu de Bague before it, the deep green bosquets of the park beyond. To her left ran the river with its sparkling white Temple, flowering shrubs, and tender green trees as foil for the pale stone. These two first creations – the Temple and the Belvédère – displayed a courteous deference to the wonderful small château that Gabriel had put up thirty years before, and when the old architect of the Petit

La Grotte de la Reine, Trianon.
The Queen was presented with seven models of the grotto before she accepted one. Although Marie-Antoinette liked to hide in the grotto, where she felt herself far removed from the court, it also figured prominently as another motif for her garden parties

Trianon saw the Belvédère, he nodded his approval.

Just to the right of the Belvédère, as one looked down towards Trianon, stood the Rocher, begun in 1779 and probably designed by Hubert Robert. This indispensable element for an English garden was intended to bring some of nature's wildness into the park. It held the mysterious grotto, which was entered through a low opening beside which tumbled a cascade feeding the lake, and the dark interior was carpeted with moss.

There was an opening at the top from which the Queen could see anyone approaching, although she herself was hidden. Verlet saw it as symptomatic of her increasing desire to escape, along with the mirrored panels she had installed at Trianon so that the interior could not be seen at night from the outside. This was particularly true after April 1785, when she attended the ceremony at Sainte-Geneviève in Paris to celebrate the birth of the Duc de Normandie in March 1785. After the usual canon salutes from the Invalides, the Place de la Greve, and the Bastille, the crowds in the streets remained silent. The Queen was so shaken by the reception that she closeted herself at Trianon with Madame Elisabeth.

The Rocher became one of her favourite retreats. When the Belvédère was lighted for evening fêtes (p.255), the guests climbed the grassy knoll to the octagonal painted room which would be brilliantly lighted for a cold collation. Then they crossed over the bridge to experience the dramatic contrast of the grotto, shivering deliciously as they entered the damp, mossy cavern. Drawn by the magnet of royalty, most visitors to Trianon were captivated, but the Duc de Croÿ still regretted Louis XV's botanical garden, and found at Trianon 'l'Anglais et la Chine partout'.

The Prince de Ligne, though, thought otherwise, and made flattering comments, exulting (ironically) that here he could breathe 'the air of contentment and of liberty'. It was a delusion, for on 5 August, 1789 – while the Queen was resting within the dark cavern of the grotto – a servant came running from the palace to tell her that Versailles was being invaded by a mob.

Interior of the Belvédère.
The marble mosaic floor is in blue, rose and green, with white veining. Around the walls stood the suite of chairs sculpted with leaves and flowers by the gifted master Foliot. There was a decorative relationship between the Queen's boudoir in the Trianon and the Belvédère, for the motifs of the former were repeated in the Belvédère

Interior of the Belvédère.
Among the few extant examples of Louis XVI interiors is the precious room of the Belvédère painted by Le Riche with typically French cachet and elegance. With trophies suspended by ribbons, garden instruments, straw hats and baskets, it perfectly represents the spirit of Trianon as defined by Marie-Antoinette

Exterior of the Belvédère.
The exterior of the Belvédère is a suave résumé of the distinguishing traits of French Neo-classicism with four doors alternating with four windows in the eight bays and crisply sculpted bas-reliefs over each window. Like Bagatelle, it is guarded by sphinxes

Exterior detail of the Belvédère.
Sphinxes outside the Belvédère. The pavilion was used as a breakfast and music room, and is sometimes referred to as the Pavillon de Musique

Exterior detail of the Belvédère.
The bas-reliefs above each window of the Belvédère are by Duchamps and represent the Four Seasons. The theme relates the Belvédère to the gardens where the gardener Richard had randomly planted a variety of flowers and shrubs. He tried to acclimatise Chinese and American trees, as well as evergreens such as larches, pines, and junipers that he had brought from the Alps

The Theatre

From her first days as Dauphine, Marie-Antoinette had encouraged court theatre, and in August 1770, during the traditional summer stay at Compiègne, she wrote to her mother:

> M. le Dauphin is so polite to me that I am happy; we have from time to time a comedy which is often amusing . . . especially one called Rose and Colas . . . M. le Dauphin had a violin concert presented which charmed me. I would like a little German music, but I do not dare brag about our Gluck . . . but I shall await an occasion.[11]

By 1773 Gluck was in Paris, and the Queen called him to Versailles, and despite his undeniable talent, his work would never have been performed at the Paris Opéra without her patronage. His *Iphégenie* was a triumph, especially at the memorable Opéra performance on 13 January, 1775, when the Queen was at the height of her popularity. The audience rose to join the choir in 'chantons, célébrons notre reine', and cheered for ten minutes, turning towards her box.

Marie-Antoinette maintained her own loge at the Opéra, as well as the Italian and French Comedies. She particularly wanted to promote performances at court, but she found Gabriel's Opéra at Versailles inadequate for the purpose. What she wanted was a small theatre of modest dimensions that could be taken down, so she had one put up in the cage of the staircase Gabriel had begun to construct in the new wing. Its scenery of arabesques was quickly sketched by Hubert Robert on a wooden base covered with canvas. Her own loge was below, and that of the King higher up.

While she was still Dauphine, Marie-Antoinette sang airs by André Grétry, accompanied on the harp by Jeanne Genet, later Madame Campan (1752-1822).[12] Madame Campan credited the Queen with supporting composers of musical comedy, which she claimed reached a pinnacle of perfection at the time.

She also greatly contributed to the vogue for amateur theatricals. The Duchesse de Villequier formed a small band of players at Versailles, and by the summer of 1780 the Queen had created her own company, appearing in the performances herself. A friend of the Prince de Ligne, the well-known actor Joseph Dazincourt (1747-1809), who played in the Comédie Française, was engaged to come out to Trianon to give the Queen's troupe lessons in comedy.

She was completely at ease on the stage, for she had performed a ballet and opera with her brothers and sisters for the marriage of her brother Joseph II, and two paintings by Weichart representing this event hung on the walls of her bedroom at the Petit Trianon. Marie-Antoinette had been trained by the innovative French ballet master, Jean Georges Noverre (1727-1810), whose tutelage no doubt accounted for her famous lilting walk and unusually graceful carriage.

D'Artois was a member of the troupe, often forgetting his lines and cleverly improvising, but the Comte de Vaudreuil's performance was always above reproach, and he was regarded as the best amateur actor in France. The plays sometimes took place in those wooden provisional rooms, and on one occasion the gallery in the Grand Trianon was commandeered for the purpose.

This was not satisfactory, however, so Mique was asked to draw up plans for a private theatre, which he prepared in 1777, submitting to his sovereign a coloured wax model, complete with lighting, sets, and silk curtain. Hubert Robert was again summoned for the decoration, this time far more elaborate, and the painters Jean-Jacques Lagrenée and René-Hyacinthe Deleuze assisted him. The theatre was a happy collaboration between the painter Hubert Robert and his friend Richard Mique, both

Theatre of the Queen, Trianon.
The Queen's small blue and gold theatre in the Trianon gardens, recently restored, was one of the most charming private theatres in Europe. Vigée-Lebrun recalled in her memoirs that when the Queen discovered that Vigée had a nice voice, she rarely granted a sitting without having the artist sing with her several tunes by Grétry, one of her favoured composers. With her English garden, the Trianon theatre in which she herself performed, her innovative fêtes, ballets, musicals and patronage of composers like Gluck, Marie-Antoinette reinvented a new and novel art de vivre

of whom were lodged at the Louvre with the King's other artists.

By the summer of 1778 the Queen's theatre – in the form of a small antique temple – was started, and at the end of June 1779 the sumptuous and very expensive curtain was ready to be hung. Even the mechanical devices for changing the sets were costly, for the Queen insisted upon their operating perfectly. Again it was Deschamps who executed the sculpture, with the oval ceiling painted by Lagrenée the younger: 'Apollo Surrounded by the Graces and Muses'.

Mercy Argenteau, the Austrian Ambassador, compared it to the great Opéra by Gabriel, although it was more amusing than noble, as Verlet pointed out. Like the Opéra it took a U-form, the second balcony was decorated with acanthus leaves, there was abundant gilding with touches of white, with blue silk hangings – *bleu clair* Mercy Argenteau called it. One of the most delightful court theatres in Europe, it has recently recovered its sky blue and gold interior, painted ceiling, and richly embroidered curtain.

In the summer of 1780 were performed Sédaine and Monsigny's *Rose et Colas*, which had inaugurated Bagatelle, and Jean-Jacques Rousseau's *Devin de Village*, with Vaudreuil singing the rôle of the Devin and Marie-Antoinette that of Colette. When the Queen's brother, the Emperor Joseph II, came again to Versailles in 1781, she had Gluck's *Iphégenie* presented in his honour.

Of particular interest to us is the stage set Sageret created for this occasion, for it consisted of pavilions in a garden. There was a Temple of Minerva with Ionic order, a subterranean *fabrique* with bronze doors highlighted in gold, and a Temple of Diana. All were heightened by a backdrop with transparencies to suggest clouds floating across the sky, and a shimmering sea in the distance.

When the guests left the theatre, the gardens were brilliantly illuminated by means of flares, but the brightest spot in the landscape was the Temple of Love, which formed the focal point for the fête – as if to carry the theatre's stage décor into the gardens. The Temple seemed to float upon a lake of flames, which was accomplished by burning thousands of fagots in the ditch behind.

The Queen herself became part of the décor, for she had the wit to choose a simple dress of white muslin cut like a dressing gown (*en déshabille*) to set off her transparent skin. White muslin, linen, or percale – such as the Créole women of Saint-Domingo wore – would be the appropriate attire for Trianon, for which the scarlet/silver livery of the men in her service provided a dramatic foil. This studied simplicity, though, would be costly for the silkworkers of Lyons, and helped to contribute to the Queen's unpopularity.

Comédies de société were the rage of day, and in 1784 the burning question was whether Beaumarchais' *Mariage de Figaro* should be presented, for it had already been read privately in various salons by the author. Some of the nobility, like the Comte de Vaudreuil along with Mesdames de Lamballe and Polignac, gave resonant approval of Figaro's famous monologue attacking the privileges of royalty and their own class. Three months after *Figaro* was to be performed in June 1783 (but cancelled by the King at the last moment), Vaudreuil impetuously staged it in his own house. Naturally d'Artois and Polignac were in the audience, but the Queen stood solidly behind her husband. The breach was irreparable, and Beaumarchais became a symbol of the new age, for he 'brings us to the point at which literature acquires a direct social and political significance'.[13]

Despite the controversial nature of Beaumarchais' work, the Queen rashly summoned Dazincourt to Trianon in the summer of 1785 to teach her the rôle of Rosine in Beaumarchais' *Barbier de Séville*, with the flamboyant d'Artois playing Figaro and the suave Vaudreuil as Count Almaviva. It was played on 19 August, and might be regarded as the first act in the historical and spiritual drama that was about to unroll in France, in which the King and Queen would be the principal actors – and the most illustrious victims.

Nor could the play have come at a more inauspicious moment, for it followed by only four days the arrest of Cardinal de Rohan in the ludicrous 'Affair of the Necklace'. The Queen was the victim of a cruel hoax that centred on her alleged order for a shockingly expensive diamond necklace that interested Madame Du Barry. Although Marie-Antoinette was completely innocent, her imprudent patronage of the jeweller Böhmer in the past militated against her, making her an easy target for her enemies. They quickly seized the opportunity, and manipulated public opinion to their own purposes, so irrevocably damaging her reputation that Napoleon, looking back upon the tragic incident, saw it as the beginning of the French Revolution.

The ill-considered productions at the Queen's private theatre made their own contributions to the disasters of the summer of 1785.

The Queen's Hameau

Few phenomena of social and architectural history have been as curious as the turning of a cultivated society to the construction of small rustic villages upon their country estates. We have seen this plaything of the privileged class at Chantilly, where the Prince de Condé's model Hameau was endowed with houses of plaster and thatched roofs, their interiors a cachet of elegance. A *chaumière* graced the garden of the Duc d'Harcourt, governor of the Dauphin, and at the moment when the Queen's Dairy was going up, Madame instructed Chalgrin to add a hamlet to her pavilion at Montreuil near Versailles (1784). Even Mesdames, the King's aunts (Louis XV's daughters), would later imitate the Queen's Hameau on their Bellevue estate, except that their table service was real wood, not porcelain of *faux bois* like the service for the Queen's dairy at Rambouillet. As Madame Campan put it 'On ne se croyait chez soi que dans les demeures les plus simple'.[14]

These artless dwellings in a rural setting were intended to imply a sense of virtue *à la Rousseau*, and they looked like paintings by J.-B. Greuze (1725-1805) in three dimensions. Diderot urged that painting teach a moral lesson, and Greuze – a protégé of both Louis XV's eminent minister Choiseul, and his influential Director of Buildings the Marquis de Marigny – got the message. He specialised in lachrymose maidens with broken eggs or empty birdcages (symbols of lost virtue), and the *mise-en-scène* that he created for his sentimental stories usually consisted of a tumble-down barn, or the interior of a peasant's cottage with peeling plaster, sagging rafters, and worn floor.

The Belvédère illuminated.
This illumination of the Belvédère may have occurred during the series of fêtes given at Trianon in July 1781, one for the King's brother the Comte de Provence, and then for Marie-Antoinette's brother, the Emperor Joseph II of Austria, travelling under the pseudonym Comte de Falkenstein. A play was performed at the theatre of Trianon on 26 July, 1781, and when the guests came out of the theatre, the Rocher was illuminated and surrounded by transparencies in the shape of rock formations covered with greenery. The highest point of the Belvédère was strung with lighted cords, and lanterns hidden in clusters of artificial reeds threw their reflections into the lake. So that the Belvédère would be silhouetted against a bright light, countless logs were burned in a ditch behind it

This was the type of setting required for Diderot's plays in the bourgeois genre, as well as for certain musicals and plays that were performed at court, such as the comedy staged at Trianon the year before the Queen's Hameau was begun. On 15 July, 1781 a group of Italian actors presented *La Veillée Villageoise,* and judging from the title, the stage setting could have been lifted from a painting acquired by Louis XVI that very year from the Marigny collection at the sale following the Marquis' death: Greuze's well-known 'L'Accordée du Village'.

Les grands were so fascinated by country life that they even staged fêtes in their Paris hôtels with simulated barnyards and real farm animals brought in to complete the picture. One was the Duchesse de Mazarin, whose famous hôtel on the Quai Malaquais was decorated by Bélanger. The large Duchess was noted for her huge, swinging diamond earrings that made her look like a walking chandelier, and for the fact that Murphy's Law seemed inevitably to govern all her parties. The hilarious affair of 1771 was no exception, for the Duchess staged a *grande fête champêtre* in her glorious hôtel, of which Gaston Maugras has left a description:

> When the stage was set and the animals arranged in their proper places, [the Duchess] invited the guests to enter. But as they did so, the animals became terrified; the calf precipitated itself into a large mirror, breaking it into a thousand pieces, then fled to the adjoining salon, followed by an entire flock of sheep who were pursued by a barking dog. The sheep became entangled in the ladies' long robes, as the dog ran from one end of the gallery to the other, barking madly. The Princesse de Lamballe perched upon the chimneypiece, emitting peacock cries, and most of the supper was overturned into the stairwell.[15]

Marie-Antoinette may have been given the notion of adding the Hameau at Trianon by Hubert Robert, as has been suggested, for he certainly collaborated with Mique during its construction. It is a plausible idea, for both its concept and form clearly reflected current painting and literature. Hubert Robert's idea of the garden was that it should be a mobile painting, with one view succeeding another, and the Hameau would become a picturesque motif similar to the mill already seen at Moulin-Joli where Robert worked with Watelet.

The gardener Antoine Richard, who had been solely in charge of planting and maintenance at Trianon since 1782, also played a leading role in the realisation of the gardens. Richard delighted in the presence of the royal children, and he made for Madame Royale a small formal parterre, with her own small flock of lambs and goats. Whereas Mercy Argenteau had been concerned that the Queen was always running off to Paris, by 1779 he complained that she was constantly occupied with her children. When the Hameau was underway in 1781 there were two – Madame Royale, who was three, and the first Dauphin, who was born that year. He was unwell, and the Queen was mourning his death on 2 June, 1789 at the time when the political situation reached a climax in the anguished events of that summer.

Everybody was interested in the new Hameau project, and a group that included the Duc de Polignac and Madame de Chalons went to England to study the manners, climate, gardens, monuments, and celebrities. A perennial favourite was the Duke of Marlborough, and in 1783 a popular spectacle of the Paris theatre was *Le Combat et La Mort de Marlbrough.* France's ancient enemy also lent his name to a burlesque song from Beaumarchais' *Figaro* called 'Malbrouck s'en va-t-en guerre!'. It was revived by the Dauphin's nurse, Madame Poitrine, who sang it to the frail Dauphin who was the constant concern of his parents.

The French visitors to England must have wanted to see the landscape garden at Stowe, as well as the ruins constructed in English gardens by architects like Robert Adam. The Queen had already rejected the idea of *ruinisme* for the Trianon gardens, and although Mique made several sketches for a ruin, no model was given, although some of the buildings in the Hameau were nothing but shams, put there for a picturesque effect.

In 1782 another river had to be excavated in the Queen's garden, widening to form a pond with rushes growing along the banks – the kind of setting required for the feature that Watelet considered indispensable for the irregular garden: a rustic village inhabited by real people. The Queen called her new Hamlet her 'hameau sans prétention'.

A salient feature was a piece of Anglomania that jutted out into the lake, the Tower of Marlborough, which might be regarded as an early example of the troubadour style later popularised by the Empress Josephine. It may have been suggested by the Tower of Gabrielle at Ermenonville (souvenir of a supposed encounter between Gabrielle d'Estrées and Henri IV), which the Queen and court had visited in June 1780. The spiralling staircase of the Marlborough Tower was decorated with simple flowers – geraniums and snapdragons – and the King would take the sickly Dauphin up to the platform, which resembled a lighthouse, for a view of Trianon, the Versailles gardens, and the surrounding countryside.

At the foot of the Tower, and connected to it by an oblique underground passage, was the Queen's Laiterie,[16] designed and built by Richard Mique (1784-6) and destined to become the most famous of all the rustic dairies of the century. The illustration on page 259 shows windows marked with rustications, and the clipped gables seen in the dependencies of early houses along the James River, an English feature in origin. Although of humble appearance, the Laiterie was distinguished by the four white marble

A nineteenth-century view of part of the Queen's Hameau.
The Hameau of the Prince de Condé was certainly the inspiration for Marie-Antoinette's Hameau at Versailles, her last creation at Versailles. The numerous fables that portray the royal famiy playing shepherds and assuming the roles of various rustic characters are exaggerated. As at Chantilly, the rustic village was entirely in accord with the taste of the period, an attempt to escape the luxury and artificiality of court and town. Both the Queen and King wanted their children to become acquainted with the work of a farm, taking a genuine interest in agriculture and husbandry, as the King demonstrated with his flock of merino sheep at Rambouillet. Several families were established at the Hameau, and they carried on real farming operations. Vegetables from the potager, corn ground in the mill, and daily products made in the Laiterie came to the royal table

busts placed on pedestals between the bays – a shepherd, a shepherdess, Diana and a faun.

This was exactly what Watelet advocated – a mingling of Swiss and English features, with a touch of antiquity and Arcadian poetry, as Langner has pointed out. The interior followed the traditional arrangement: walls and floor revetted with marble, a central table, consoles around the walls with four niches furnished with fountains, and refreshing water flowing through a trough. It was more appropriate to its function than Méréville's dairy in the form of an antique temple, or Madame's dairy at Montreuil which also looked like a temple, but with pillars that resembled tree trunks, and a pigeon house on top.

Walking further along the lake, one came to the Farm, a more serious enterprise where the Queen installed twelve poor families in 1785. The Vacherie was erected l July, 1785, and a cowherd, Valy Bussard, from the Touraine arrived a few days later to join his family there. On 11 July Mique asked that water be channelled from Louis XV's old hothouse to the cowshed and the dining room of the Hameau. Real animals inhabited the neat little barns – cows, calves, sheep, goats, and a bull. A note from the

Bagatelle today.
Although the superb original ensemble of pavilion, courtyards, commons, and gardens has been destroyed, the small château remains. Its proportions were spoiled in the 1870s by its English owner, Sir Richard Wallace, and the rushing streams and pools were greatly reduced in number. In the early twentieth century, Forestier and Gravereaux added the famous Roseraie

Opposite: The Comte d'Artois.
The King's youngest brother postures with his rifle and hunting dog, sporting English hunting attire and a hat like a jockey's. Behind him stands a groom in the elaborate dress typically worn by attendants such as Madame Du Barry's page Zamore. Behind his plumed turban may be seen Bagatelle and the woodlands of the Bois de Boulogne. Since he was a major target of the radical press, d'Artois fled France on 16 July, 1789, only two days after the fall of the Bastille, and was followed by many of the nobility who formed the Army of the Emigrés. As Charles X (1824-30), he renewed ties with the ancien régime, *but his repressive measures provoked the Revolution of 1830 and his abdication. In the crisis of 1830 he became the first monarch to use the telegraph*

CHAPTER 21

THE COMTE D'ARTOIS AND BAGATELLE

It is not surprising, from what we have seen of the King's rakehell brother, the Comte d'Artois, that he would have built a pavilion to win a bet. Not a modest *chaumière* or a wooden structure like the Queen's for a one-night party, but a gem of its type designed by perhaps the most accomplished architect in France of the moment, François-Joseph Bélanger.

D'Artois was just the man to endow the Bois de Boulogne with the exquisite pavilion of Bagatelle which still stands on the edge of a pond, for he was preoccupied with pleasure in every form – the theatre, racing, gaming, illicit liaisons, fêtes and, like all his friends, a delectable little house of his own. A leader of the avant-garde at Versailles, d'Artois' name was linked with the Duc de Chartres, who delighted in balloon-ascents and séances with the charlatan Cagliostro. His orgies with cronies at Monceau were common knowledge, and in this garden of *folies,* Chartres gathered around him all those with real or imagined grievances against the Crown. Shockingly, the King's own brother imprudently allowed himself to be drawn into his cousin's diabolical circle.

Unfortunately for Marie-Antoinette, a coterie grew up around her and d'Artois that was 'more snob than royal'.[1] The dramatis personae included Arthur Dillon, Axel de Fersen, the Baron de Besenval, and the Prince de Ligne. Only the Duc de Lauzun (1747-94) came from a conventional noble background.

A key figure of the Queen's circle was the tall, militant Comte de Vaudreuil, an

François-Joseph Bélanger

Like the Duc de Chartres, d'Artois was an Anglophile, naming one of his Paris houses 'Nouvelle Londres'. It was inevitable, then, that he choose as his architect a favourite of the younger aristocracy, François-Joseph Bélanger, who had visited England and knew about the most up-to-date architecture there.

When Bélanger became Designer for the Menus-Plaisirs in 1767, the Prince came into constant contact with him at court. The architect's design in 1770 for Marie-Antoinette's jewel cabinet already exhibited the remarkably advanced Neo-classical style that would appear at Bagatelle seven years later, and it was in that year that Bélanger became an architect to d'Artois' brother, the Comte de Provence. In 1773 d'Artois married Marie-Thérèse de Savoie, and he asked Bélanger to provide plans for his guards' hôtel at Versailles. Four years later, Bélanger bought the post of architect to the young Prince, and in September of that year (1777) he was asked to start the pavilion of Bagatelle.

D'Artois met Bélanger in another context, too, for he was often employed by leading figures in the French theatre, especially the actress Sophia Arnould. Through Bélanger's liaison with Sophie, many commissions came his way from members of the Queen's circle – the Comte de Lauraguais (Sophie's lover before Bélanger) and the Prince de Ligne (her faithful friend). Bélanger's appointment at the Menus-Plaisirs in 1775 – giving him charge of court fêtes and ceremonies – was indirectly due to Sophie as well, for the actress was a friend of Gluck, so generously patronised by the Queen. When the composer gave Sophie the role of Alceste (although it later went to Mercy Argenteau's protégée, Rosalie Levasseur), Bélanger was commissioned to design the décors.

In 1764-7 Bélanger had the opportunity to travel in England, probably under the patronage of Lord Shelburne, Marquis of Lansdowne, who represented the liberal wing of the Whigs. By the 1780s Shelburne's country house at Bowood became a sort of international centre for advanced thinking, and among his foreign acquaintances he had many French friends such as the Abbé Morellet and the beloved Malesherbes, champion of fundamental liberties, Protestant emancipation, and in many ways the French counterpart to Benjamin Franklin. In Paris and at Bowood, Shelburne's set talked of patriotism and liberty, ideas that set the young nobility afire when they fought in the American war.

While Bélanger was drawing up the plans for Bagatelle in 1777, the Scottish architect, Robert Adam, was decorating Bowood and Lansdowne House in London for Lord Shelburne. Shelburne called upon Bélanger, too, and the London town house became a compendium of international Neo-classicism. Among those engaged at one time or another in the gallery, besides Adam and Bélanger, were Joseph Bonomi, Francesco Pannini, George Dance the Younger, Robert Smirke, and a major proponent of the new taste, Charles-Louis Clérisseau.

Bélanger must have been impressed by the creative synthesis of the Adam manner, in which Robert Adam combined passages from Raphael's Vatican loggie, Roman mosaics, Imperial architecture, Diocletian's palace, and antique grotesques to create a highly personal style. Adam's delicate classicism – realised in low-relief stucco for walls and ceilings in pastel colours by Joseph Rose and his assistants – must have appealed to Bélanger, for we find the salon elevations at Bagatelle, by Lhuillier and Roland, treated in the same manner (p.268).

Robert Adam's mentor in Italy and teacher in draughtsmanship had been Charles-

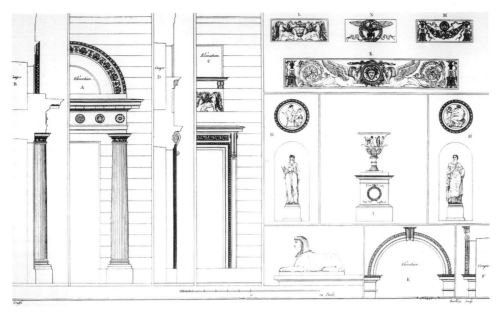

Bagatelle, details.
These include oculi for spandrels, one of the pair of sphinxes at either side of the doorway, panels in low relief (probably for the exterior), classical statuary and vases. No doubt Bélanger's brother-in-law, Démosthène Dugourc, who admired Piranesi and was among the first Frenchmen to employ grotesque decoration, was involved in the designs

Louis Clérisseau (1721-1820), a veritable walking encyclopaedia of antiquity. After twenty years in Italy, Clérisseau returned to Paris in 1768, where he provided a decorative scheme for the influential Hôtel Grimod de la Reynière in 1777, the arabesques executed by Etienne de Lavallée.[5]

Having studied the work of Clérisseau's pupil, Robert Adam, Bélanger now met Clérisseau himself, who brought back to Paris with him another student, the sculptor Nicolas-François Lhuillier (1736-93). Lhuillier had learned the decorative style of Pompeii and Herculaneum under the master, and owned Piranesi's *Diverse maniere di ornare i camini* (1769), a goldmine for Adam and other architects working in the Neo-classical style.

Piranesi's publication became a revelation to Bélanger, who took motifs from it for the décor and furniture of the Duchesse de Mazarin, and for the salons of Mademoiselle Dervieux's hôtel, where he related the house intimately to the garden as he did at Bagatelle. In addition to Piranesi and Adam, Bélanger's personal manner was formed by his contact with Gabriel, for whom he worked in 1768, and the publications of David Leroy, who disclosed the true Greek orders to France.

The Pavilion

The delectable pavilion of Bagatelle was close to perfection when Bélanger completed it, a fascinating variation upon the square type of house so successfully realised in Gabriel's Petit Trianon, as Kaufmann has remarked, and one of the first in the late Louis XVI style. Its dependencies introduced the courtyard before it, a landscape garden was arranged to the right of the courtyard, and behind the house was laid out a French formal garden.

The handsome domestic wing or commons preceded the small château, and the concave façade of the Pages' House was an echo of the Royal Crescent at Bath (1761-5) which had impressed Bélanger. This concave commons behind the pavilion faced the rounded projection on the garden side, an example of the complexity of concavities and convexities playing throughout the composition. A further refinement was the annunciation of themes on the commons' façade (statues in niches, segmental doorways, oculi) that were used elsewhere in the ensemble, a system of 'multiple

Salon panel, Bagatelle.
The eight amazing salon panels of low relief stucco were designed by Bélanger's brother-in-law, Démosthène Dugourc, one of the most outstanding and inventive ornemenistes of his day. They were executed by the sculptor Nicolas-François Lhuillier and Roland, working under Bélanger's direction. A great admirer of Piranesi, Dugourc was among the first to revive the tradition of the fabulous world of Italian grotesques that became a major feature of wall treatments in the Louis XVI period. The panels were reflected in the doors and false windows of the salon that were covered with mirrors; three windows opened on to the garden

Above right: Hubert Robert, 'Mouth of a Cave', 1784.
The only painting in the series of six bearing a signature and date. It features a grotto by the sea adorned with trailing vines, and a group of figures inside, perhaps fishermen. It may recall the caverns Hubert Robert had seen near Naples during his Italian sojourn of 1760. The Comte d'Artois had perhaps first become enamoured of Robert's work when he saw the artist's canvases at Chanteloup, for the disgraced minister the Duc de Choiseul was d'Artois' idol, and the Count was a familiar face at Chanteloup. He must also have been impressed by Hubert Robert's 'Views of the Gardens of Versailles', a royal commission that Robert received in 1775

Opposite: Hubert Robert, 'The Bathing Pool'.
The circular temple evokes the Temple of the Sibyl at Tivoli. A statue of Venus based upon antique models stands within the temple, and the steps are flanked with Jean-Baptiste Pigalle's celebrated 'Venus' and 'Mercury' on pedestals. The lush, feathery greenery with light filtering through the leaves is rendered in the manner of Fragonard, but both Hubert Robert and Fragonard look ultimately to Watteau

announced in the vestibule with four cameo medallions representing Cupid, Venus, Juno and Priapus. The motifs in low relief stucco in the eight salon panels are taken from the Neo-classical repertoire: sphinxes, sheaves, swans, garlands, Psyche's wedding, figures posed on tripods or lyres. A feature seen in Marie-Antoinette's boudoir at Petit Trianon is also found here in the salon – false windows covered with mirrors.

The most lavish and daring use of mirrors, however, was in the boudoir to the right

J.-B. Charpentier (1726-1806), Princesse de Lamballe (1749-1792).
Charpentier, painter-in-ordinary to the Duc de Penthièvre, has painted a sensitive portrait of the Princesse de Lamballe, treating the parasol, the silk and lace of her dress with particular finesse. She sits on a fashionable garden bench, probably in the Rambouillet gardens, with one of the pavilions her father-in-law built for her in the background. Ironically, her resolute enemy was the Duc d'Orléans (formerly Chartres), who was married to the Duc de Penthièvre's daughter. When Lamballe was imprisoned, Orléans is said to have intervened to prevent her release, hoping that his wife would be the only heiress to the immense Penthièvre fortune

CHAPTER 22

THE PRINCESSE DE LAMBALLE AND THE CHAUMIERE AT RAMBOUILLET

In the open fields on the grounds of the château of Rambouillet, where there was once an English garden, stands a modest building with thatched roof on a small island. One would dismiss it as a shed for gardening tools, for there is nothing in the unprepossessing exterior of the Chaumière des Coquillages to suggest for a moment that it had been commissioned by the richest man in France, a grandson of the Sun King and son of the Comte de Toulouse.

The princely patron was the Duc de Penthièvre, a man whose unquestioned probity made him an exceptional member of Louis XV's entourage, and one of the few moral assets at Louis XVI's court. The Comte and Comtesse de Toulouse were Louis XV's great-uncle and aunt, a couple for whom he felt an abiding affection and who were like parents to him. Toulouse enjoyed the honour and right to serve the

Marie-Thérèse-Louise de Savoie-Carignan, Princesse de Lamballe.
The Princesse was blonde like the Queen. One of the courtiers, happening to see Marie-Antoinette with the Princess at her side as they set out for a sleigh ride, commented that they were enveloped in ermine with plumes in their hair, riding in a gilt sleigh with bells attached, pulled by two white horses with velvet harnesses. The Princess was arrested in 1792 and because of her close relationship with the Queen she became the subject of satirical and pornographic lithographs that were totally without foundation

Exterior of the Chaumière des Coquillages.
The exterior of the Chaumière des Coquilles was kept deliberately plain as a contrast to the surprisingly refined interior. This was true of the cottages for the Prince de Condé's Hameau, those of the Queen's Hameau with rush roofs, and of the Duc d'Harcourt's pavilion that looked like a dilapidated peasant's hut

Below left: Salon of the Chaumière des Coquillages.
It was a mark of the Duc de Penthièvre's love for his daughter-in-law that he created for her pleasure a series of delightful pavilions in the park of Rambouillet. The interior of the Chaumière is highly unusual, but was certainly inspired by such French Renaissance grottoes as the one at La Bastide d'Urfé (p.21)

Below right: Dome of the Chaumière des Coquillages.
The ceiling of the luxurious salon is in rotunda form. The ceiling, dome, cornice, fireplace mirror and chimneypiece, drapery swags, pilasters, and medallions of fruit and flowers are all made of shells, marble, clinker and mother-of-pearl

Jean-Honoré Fragonard (1732-1806), 'The Fête at Rambouillet', 1782.
Fragonard's trees are remarkable for their gaiety, verve, and spontaneity and are highlighted, along with
the foliage, by the light of a threatening storm. In 'The Fête at Rambouillet' the shape of the grotto
strongly suggests the pavilions of greenery that P.-A. Paris designed for the Queen's diversions at Marly

Below left and right: Boudoir wall paintings in the Chaumière des Coquillages.
The Princess' small boudoir adjoining the salon is painted in delicate pastels to accord with the intimate
nature of the room. It recalls Le Riche's wall decorations for Marie-Antoinette's Belvédère at Versailles,
with many of the same motifs – flowers, birds, thyrsi, and trophies. The interior of the Chaumière has been
carefully restored, using materials as close to the original ones as possible

with such éclat the pleasures of the landscape garden, as revealed in the exhilarating landscape 'The Fête at Saint-Cloud', which Penthièvre ordered from Fragonard in 1775 for his town house, the Hôtel de Toulouse.

According to tradition, 'The Fête at Rambouillet' was commissioned to record a garden party the Duc de Penthièvre offered to the royal family at Rambouillet in 1782, two years before the property was acquired by Louis XVI. The artist has chosen the moment when the boating party is suddenly surprised by a gust of wind moving across the waters, and the brio of his masterful draughtsmanship heightens the excitement of the approaching storm. The royal barge with silken canopies is moored to the bank, and the lurid light throws into relief the anthropomorphic shape of the trees, picks up the turbulence of the rushing cascades and swirling water, and falls upon the overgrown verdure of the shadowy grotto into which some of the boating party flee.

Among the other distractions of the Rambouillet park that the Duke provided for his son's young widow was the small pavilion that came to be known as the Chaumière des Coquillages. Certainly the *chaumière* concept was no novelty for habitués of the court for, as we have seen, they were ubiquitous in fashionable gardens. They even survived the Revolution, for that disreputable friend of the Empress Josephine, Thérèse Cabarrus (whom the wits called 'government property'), went to live in a *chaumière* surrounded by acacias after she married J.-L. Tallien in December 1794.

The one devised for the Princesse de Lamballe, however, appears to have been a unique example of the type, and its interior reflects the Duc de Penthièvre's fondness for grottoes. The exterior could not have been more modest (p.280), but it differed from most others of its type in a curious way, for there were incorporated into the walls large ox bones to support espaliered vines. This was a traditional structure for peasants' houses in the Prince de Lamballe's native Brittany, and it is possible that the Duke and the Princess brought back the bones for this purpose when they visited Lamballe in 1774.

When the door swings open, there is revealed an astonishingly luxurious salon in rotunda form. Its dome, cornice, fireplace mirror and chimneypiece, drapery swags, pilasters, medallions of fruit and flowers are all made of shells, marble, clinker, and mother-of-pearl worked by remarkably skilled craftsmen (p.280). Most of the shells came from the Normandy beaches, but the coquilles Saint-Jacques that form the frieze, the oyster garlands, the mother-of-pearl of the ceiling are from Dieppe, all worked in the Neo-classical manner.

Although the pavilion survived the Revolution and most of the nineteenth century, during their invasion of France in 1871, the Prussians pried out all of the shells as far up the walls as they could reach. So the interior of the *chaumière* is a careful restoration, patiently carried out with materials as close to the original ones as possible.

The original décor included a suite of chairs by Foliot sculpted with water reeds and four *canapés* covered in green *gros de Tours*, to accord with curtains of the same fabric embellished with green and white pearl fringe. Adjoining the salon is the Princesse de Lamballe's tiny boudoir, its walls and ceiling painted in delicately tinted arabesques (p.281). When the Princess was seated at her dressing table, two mechanical dolls emerged from a closet to present her powder and perfume, reminiscent of those *automates* that had amused Stanislas Leczinski's friends at the Rocher in Luneville.

Georges Le Rouge, Chinese kiosk at Rambouillet.
The garden that the Duc de Penthièvre planned for his daughter-in-law, the Princesse de Lamballe, was among the most imaginative landscape gardens in France, graced by numerous fabriques. Sitting upon a rock formation, the kiosk's whimsical charm is underlined by the ornamental railing

Where did the notion of such an unusual and costly treatment of the salon come from? Among the many properties owned by the Duc de Penthièvre was the château of Sceaux, which contained a cabinet of natural history that had belonged to the Duke's first cousin, Louis-Charles, Comte d'Eu (1712-75), a son of the Duc and Duchesse du Maine. He was a colonel in both the Maine Infantry Regiment and the Swiss Guards, and Governor of the Languedoc. Included in the Count's natural history cabinet were the contents of Louis XIV's old shell collection, which had passed to his grandson (the Comte d'Eu). It may be, therefore, that the shells in the natural history cabinet inspired the grotto-like treatment of the salon's walls.

The Duc de Penthièvre lived frugally in spite of his singular affluence, and was so universally beloved that he was unthreatened by the political situation. But his son-in-law, the Duc de Chartres, perished on the scaffold as Philippe Egalité. The greatest sorrow of the Duke's last days was the terrible death of the Princesse de Lamballe.

Disregarding the dangers of the capital, the Princess left the Château d'Eu on 7 October, 1789 to be near Marie-Antoinette in the Tuileries. Soon afterwards, she was sent to London on a confidential mission, but gave up the safety of England to rejoin the Queen in her extremity, while the Polignacs had rushed to the frontier along with the Comte d'Artois. During the senseless September Massacres in 1792, when half the prisoners in Paris were killed, the Princesse de Lamballe was incarcerated in La Force prison. When she was required to swear an oath of hatred for the King and Queen, she refused. Men with pikes and axes were awaiting her outside, and when the door was opened, she was hacked to pieces in an unusually gruesome manner, her blonde head paraded on a pike under the Queen's window at the Temple prison. It was less than a decade after the party that the Princesse de Lamballe and the Duc de Penthièvre had offered to the royal family at Rambouillet.

The Chaumière des Coquillages did not appeal to everyone. That arbiter of garden structures, the Prince de Ligne, found it insupportable because it reminded him too much of grottoes, a taste which he did not share with the Duc de Penthièvre – or with Hubert Robert, who created so many. 'If you can't be agreeable or sublime, at least be simple,' the Prince advised. 'I sold a house with a grotto . . . of shells, mirrors, paintings . . . sirens, gods, seasons . . . and oh, what a ceiling! May the Lord preserve us from actually creating this sort of thing!'

Façade of the Laiterie de la Reine, Rambouillet.
Thévenin's Laiterie is supposedly based on a design by Hubert Robert. The setting for this austere little building greatly enhanced its beauty, for it was shaded by trees planted close to the walls, and behind it was to have been a landscape garden for which the Dairy was seen as a repoussoir. *The designer of the garden (which was never finished) was Hubert Robert, who laid it out in conformity with the new garden ideal, choosing shrubs for their exotic fragrances. Originally there was a Ménagerie, complete with farm animals, that lent an air of domesticity to the complex*

Opposite: Louis XVI.
The Queen's page, the Comte d'Hézècques, recorded In his memoirs that Louis XVI's bearing was noble and majestic. But the King has been unjustly maligned by many historians, who have uncritically followed Revolutionist propaganda. Although he was indecisive and unable to take a firm stand in moments of crisis, Louis was a devoted husband and father, a devout Christian, and an intelligent, well-educated man who read widely, particularly in history

Ludovicus Decimus Sextus francorum Rex.

CHAPTER 23

THE LAITERIE DE LA REINE AT RAMBOUILLET

The image of Louis XVI perpetrated by historians is as unappealing as it is unfair, and reminds us that Napoleon defined history as an 'agreed-upon fiction'. It is true that this unfortunate monarch was indecisive, unwise at critical moments, and cut a poor figure beside the Queen. But Marie-Antoinette was a young woman whose ingenuous charm had captivated even Louis XV, and it would have required a King with the Sun King's personal magnetism to balance her enormous capacity for social success.

Yet Louis XVI was intelligent, an omnivorous reader (especially of history), a faithful husband, and devoted father. What is more to our purposes, though, is that he was responsible for commissioning a pavilion – the Laiterie de la Reine – which became the single most advanced Neo-classical expression of that particular form.

The King gave significant impetus to the antique style through his exemplary and continuous patronage of the royal factory at Sèvres. Representative of his taste is the most famous service of the period, the Louis XVI Service, with deep blue grounds and mythological scenes in the reserves. It is an example of technical and aesthetic mastery of the highest order, and the King kept the registers in his own hand. For the Council Chamber at Versailles he ordered from Sèvres in 1779 the majestic Belisarius vases now in Boston; in 1783 the monumental vase in the Louvre with deep blue ground, biscuit relief by the sculptor Boizot, and marvellously chased bronzes by Thomire; in 1784 the magnificent Sèvres candelabrum with ormolu by Thomire to celebrate the peace treaty of 1783; in 1787 the large Mars and Minerva vases for the Council Chamber, exploiting the military theme already established for this important state room.

For his private apartments on the first floor of the château, one of the King's last purchases was a pair of vases in the cool antique manner of the 1780s, painted with arabesques and with bronze mounts in the form of goats. To serve as models for the

Sèvres factory, the King desposited there a collection of vases he had purchased from Dominique-Vivant Denon, soon to become a key figure in Napoleon's cultural programme. Their severe Hellenic forms, with subdued, almost monochromatic painting, inspired the Sèvres service in the spare, Etruscan style that became part of the ensemble Louis commissioned for the Laiterie at Rambouillet.

As for Louis XVI's taste in architecture, we have seen that he gave Marie-Antoinette – in the first gesture of his reign – the perfect building of the century, Gabriel's Petit Trianon. As his last gesture, he presented her with the dairy complex of Rambouillet – the veritable culmination of the royal Laiterie tradition and, from every point of view, its most accomplished and complete manifestation.

Louis XVI had long admired the Duc de Penthièvre's château of Rambouillet, with an eye to the vast hunting preserves for the royal chase. But he thought it imprudent to purchase it at a time when the treasury's resources were being strained to meet the demands of the American war. However, after the peace treaty was signed in 1783, Louis asked his cousin to sell it, so on 29 December, 1783 Rambouillet passed from Penthièvre's ownership into the hands of the Crown.

The Queen was curious to see this château which reverberated with memories of François Premier, Henri II and Diane de Poitiers. Of more recent memory were Louis XV's scandalous sojourns with Mademoiselle de Mailly in a pavilion that belonged to the Toulouses, his later excursions with Madame de Pompadour, and finally his visits with Madame Du Barry in the nearby hunting box of Saint Hubert. Louis XV's constant modifications to the hunting lodge at Saint Hubert transformed it into a château. Properly refurbished, it might have been pleased Marie-Antoinette, but Louis XVI felt a certain repugnance at lodging the Queen in an establishment that had been associated with his grandfather's mistresses.

At the end of November 1783, Marie-Antoinette was taken to see the château of Rambouillet, which still retained certain medieval features in spite of modernisations that had been made during the Bien-Aimé's reign. When she stepped from her carriage and caught sight of the two Gothic towers, she spoke for the eighteenth century in general as she exclaimed: 'What would become of me in this Gothic toadpond [crapaudière]?'[1] In spite of his disappointment, the King was not easily dissuaded, and he ordered the Comte d'Angiviller, Director-General of Buildings and Governor of Rambouillet, to have the royal apartments redecorated with an ambiance that might attract the Queen to the new royal domain.

D'Angiviller suggested to the practical King that the property might also serve a useful purpose to the nation. Since the time of Colbert, it had been necessary to import wool – especially from Spain – because of the poor quality of wool obtained from French sheep. So in 1786 Louis decided to establish a model farm with merino sheep at Rambouillet, hoping that the idea of perfumed, beribboned, woolly white lambs might appeal to the Queen – although this was not precisely what the Director-General of Buildings had in mind.

Louis purchased from the King of Spain a troop of merinos, which left Segovia with five Spanish shepherds in June, and spent four months on the road to Rambouillet. The sheep survived, prospered, and lent a pastoral charm to the château, but the Queen – in spite of her delight in the joys of country life – was in no mood to admire the sheep which had arrived in a cloud of dust in October 1786. So the King had to think of something else.

Knowing Marie-Antoinette's fondness for her Dairy at Versailles, Louis decided secretly to build another for her at Rambouillet, and one that would make the Dairy at Trianon pale by comparison. The plans were confided to a protégé of the Comte d'Angiviller, the architect J.-J. Thévenin (active 1780-90), who was equal to the task of designing a structure that was at once impressive, self-contained, and – by virtue of its thick stone walls – capable of retaining the cool temperatures required to conserve perishable dairy products.

For the design, Thévenin took refuge in the security of the French classical tradition, reflecting the increasingly foreboding atmosphere of the late 1780s. He produced a sombre, dignified temple made entirely of white sandstone and marble, without windows and shaded by trees (p.284). The façade is ornamented with two banded columns of the Tuscan order supporting a segmental pediment, which encloses Pierre Julien's white marble medallion of a cow nursing her calf. The exterior walls of the austerely rectangular temple are articulated with horizontal rustications, with voussoirs marking the central doorway. Despite its modest size, the Laiterie achieves an impressive monumentality, and if it were not for Julien's medallion that announces its purpose, the windowless temple might be taken for a particularly refined mausoleum.

The temple stands at the back of a courtyard which originally was decorated with two round basins, and on axis with the carriage approach and gateway with a railing that closes the courtyard. At either side of the entrance are two round brick dependencies with unimposing exteriors. The one at the left was most likely used by the King as a hunting lodge, and it contains an entrance foyer which leads into a circular salon with grisaille wall paintings.

The King guarded the Laiterie as a complete surprise for the Queen, and in June 1787 she was taken to Rambouillet, presumably for a fête. When her party reached the end of the carriage route through the park, it alighted before the open gate, and the Queen was conducted into the round dependency on the left. The Laiterie proper could not be seen, for it had been concealed by a 'hedge' of living greenery that was to disappear at the proper moment. It was probably one of those painted cloths like the one devised for d'Artois' unveiling of his new garden at Bagatelle.

Marie-Antoinette was ceremoniously led into the little round brick building which looked purely utilitarian, but after crossing the foyer, she stepped into a rotunda that might have occurred in the classical world. It appeared to be of cut stone with friezes carved in bas-relief, but it had in fact been painted in *trompe-l'oeil*, and the deep frieze was adorned with four grisailles of dimpled putti busily involved in tasks that appertain to the Four Seasons (overleaf).

They were executed by the accomplished specialist in grisailles, Piat-Joseph Sauvage (1744-1818), who had already painted architectural features in false marble at the Queen's Hameau. The 'reliefs' reflect the spirit of Herculaneum or Pompeii, and their insistent classicism is reinforced by the *trompe-l'oeil* keystones of the windows in the form of rams' heads. They appear so convincingly real, that one must study them for some time to comprehend that Sauvage achieved this remarkable salon entirely with paint.[2] The ram motif reappears in other media throughout the Laiterie as well, and refers to ancient wall paintings as well as to the royal flock of merino sheep.

In perfect accord with the elegant sobriety of the wall decoration was the innovative suite of mahogany furniture designed by Hubert Robert, whose imagination was obviously captured by this challenging commission. For its execution, Hubert Robert chose the superb *ébéniste* Georges Jacob,[3] who – with J.-H. Riesener – was the finest cabinetmaker of the late eighteenth century.

Piat-Joseph Sauvage, the Four Seasons, in the hunting lodge, Rambouillet.
The Four Seasons, a perenially popular theme, are here represented by putti engaged in tasks evoking each of the seasons. They cavort playfully in the countryside, ride goats, brandish classical wreaths, and warm themselves by a fire. Sauvage's allegories in trompe-l'oeil *perfectly imitate marbles, terracottas and bronzes*

Rotunda of the Laiterie de la Reine, Rambouillet.
Under Napoleon the rotunda acquired niches, a marble console running along the wall, the boldly patterned marble floor, and round table at the centre. But the replacements are too heavy-handed and assertive for the chaste white purity of the Dairy as it was originally conceived by Thévenin and Hubert Robert. The ponderous table detracts from the focal point of the entire composition, the snowy-white shepherdess, Amalthea, in the gloomy grotto

Jacob was a great innovator of forms, and his furniture was always in perfect accord with the mood of an interior, like the chairs with stiles and legs wound with vines and flowers in natural colors for the Queen's cheerful trelliswork bedroom at Trianon (p.229). But for the monochromatic, chaste interior of the Rambouillet Laiterie, he abandoned all colour and chose dark, rich mahogany, a material he apparently introduced for furniture making. It was highly favoured because it resembled bronze, recalling the furniture found in the Italian excavations. Mahogany had already been used extensively for English furniture, and the commercial treaty with England of 1786 made it more accessible, aiding and abetting the Anglophobia that captured the French imagination.

Jacob's memorandum of March 1787 states that the Rambouillet chairs are a 'new form of the Etruscan genre' after Hubert Robert's design – palmettes across the top, open lozenges for the backs and seats, which were originally centred with the rams' heads observed in classical wall and vase paintings The legs show the swirled fluting found on ancient sarcophagi, and those of the armchairs take the crossed curule form of Roman senators' seats.

On her visit to Rambouillet that June day of 1787, Marie-Antoinette must have assumed that the elegant salon painted by Sauvage was the reason for her visit. But when she stepped from the doorway of the hunting lodge into the courtyard, the palissade of greenery had been dropped, and before her stood the Laiterie de la Reine. The stern Neo-classicism of the exterior was projected into the rotunda, whose walls were executed with stereometrical perfection. The floor was of white marble, and statues doubtless stood around the wall, which was adorned with four white round marble medallions echoing the form of the room.[4] They represented figures in antique dress engaged in the work of a dairy: milking, making butter, distributing salt and shearing sheep.

The rotunda was lit only by an oculus at the centre of the dome (a direct quotation from the Roman Pantheon), articulated with square coffers centred with crisply sculpted paterae, and rested upon a modillioned entablature. The only touch of colour was the grey-blue ground of the pair of tall doors adorned with gilded crowns of oak leaves (Jupiter's tree) that led into the rectangular salon or grotto room (pp.290 and 291).

The tall doors of the rotunda swung open to reveal an astonishing *tableau vivant*. Instead of the apse one might have expected as a proper termination for the rectangular room, there was a rocky grotto trailing deep-green ivy, within which sat the snowy figure of the nymph Amalthea, holding her goat on a light leash, with streams of water flowing over the stones to fill a dark pool at her feet. The delectable statue of 'Amalthea and Her Goat' by Pierre Julien (1731-1804), was appropriate for a dairy, and although in classical legend Amalthea *is* a goat (as Poussin understood), Pierre Julien took the liberty of transforming her into a nymph for his own purposes. Seated in the Cimmerian gloom of the grotto, Amalthea summed up the theme of the iconological programme.

The grotto room was also lit from above, the barrel-vaulted ceiling decorated with unembellished coffering. Defying classical rules, Thévenin rested the ceiling vault directly upon the walls without an entablature. Cold and austere, far removed from the decorative richness of the Romans, Thévenin's architecture might have been relieved by the introduction of some colour in the way of painting. But this was entirely banished in favour of decoration that was essentially plastic.

The commission for this ambitious sculptural programme was given to Julien, who

had left Paris to recover his health, but was roused to further labour when the challenging commission came to create something for the Queen. The smooth walls of the grotto were interrupted by a high moulding or dado, over which were placed two wide, shallow panels in bas-relief of mythological subjects: 'Mercury Hiding the Sheep of Admetus' and 'Jupiter Reared by the Corybantes'. Again, the sheep referred to the Rambouillet flock, and Jupiter – with his eagle – recalled the statue of Amalthea and the crowns of oak leaves in the door reliefs.

The plaques in low relief were augmented by a large medallion of a 'Mother Nursing Her Child' set over the doorway. This subject enjoyed a great vogue about 1785, for Rousseau had strongly advocated the practice, and Adelaide Labille-Guiard's portrait of Madame Mitoire nursing her child had been exhbited at the 1783 Salon. All of the bas-reliefs related iconographically to the statue of Amalthea, including the four in the rotunda. One can only imagine the chill pagan beauty of the original composition, embellished with perhaps the finest sculptural ensemble of the period by Julien and his atelier, all in place by the spring of 1787.

Springing up along the walls of the grotto room were jets of cold water, alternating with 'Etruscan' vases resting upon bases. The four round tables of Jacob's suite may have been placed in this room as well, probably for serving the products that were a part of the laiterie tradition. The idea was to imitate the ancients, who supposedly took simple repasts consisting of the bounties of Nature – milk, cheese, butter, cream and fruit.

The banal statement has too often been made that the Queen and her ladies were 'playing at being milkmaids', but to see the preoccupation with dairies in these terms was patently absurd, as the Rambouillet Laiterie imagery bears out. It was certainly fashionable among the highest echelons of society to serve one's friends dairy products and fruit in the setting of a laiterie, but when these dairies in the classical manner (that is, the French interpretation of the classical manner) were being built, it was simply another manifestation of the desire to emulate antiquity.

This infatuation with the past reached a pinnacle of the ridiculous in 1788 at the

Opposite and above: Pierre Julien, 'Amalthea and Her Goat' in the Rambouillet grotto room.
In his statue Julien interpreted the Neo-classical ideal with grace and sensitivity (the one seen today in the grotto is a copy). The contents of the Dairy are scattered or destroyed, and none of the sculpture — except the medallion on the façade — is in place

famous dinner party given by the Queen's portraitist, Elisabeth Vigée-Lebrun, just as the finishing touches were being applied to the Rambouillet dairy. The women at Vigée-Lebrun's party were dressed as Athenians, the poet Lebrun came as Anacreon crowned with laurels, enveloped in a purple mantle, Vigée-Lebrun was dressed in a simple white tunic (like the figures in the Rambouillet reliefs), and as the guests entered, a choir sang an air by the Queen's protégé, Gluck. They drank black broth and even sang hymns to Bacchus. It was the same year that Jacques-Louis David painted 'Paris and Helen' — with Georges Jacob's archaeologically correct mahogany furniture — for the Queen's swashbuckling companion, the Comte d'Artois.

The artistic unity of the Laiterie de la Reine was also reflected in the Sèvres service designed by the painter who had worked in the Queen's Bélvèdere, Jean-Jacques Lagrenée, who had been employed since 1785 at Sèvres.[5] The forms of the Sèvres pieces were based on the antique vases purchased in 1786 in the King's name from the collection of Dominique Vivant-Denon, who accompanied Napoleon's extraordinary Egyptian campaign ten years later. The vases were Greek, but architects, artists, and ceramists of this period — Robert Adam and Josiah Wedgwood included — called them 'Etruscan'.

Executed in sepia, black and brick red with touches of yellow or violet but, significantly, with no gold, the approximately fifty-piece Rambouillet service comprised vases, bowls, cups and saucers, shallow vessels embellished with cows and calves, and milk pails in *faux bois* with rams' heads (overleaf). Some of the vases were painted to resemble Greek examples, with shepherds tending merino sheep. Combining a dairy motif with one taken from antiquity were four *bols-sein* — bowls of translucent, delicate, milky-white porcelain modelled upon the Queen's breast, resting upon goats' heads that form a tripodal base, a delicate tribute to the Queen as mother of her people.

Sèvres pail.
This porcelain pail in faux
bois *with rams' heads
adorning the handles was
among the fifty-odd pieces
ordered for the Queen's Dairy
at Rambouillet. It relates to the
theme of merino sheep, cows
and dairy attendants*

Iconography

Johannes Langner explains that the first grottoes were used as
shelters for men, but that the Greeks began to dedicate them to
nymphs, from which comes the term nymphaeum, literally
temple of the nymphs. They were a constant feature of Italian
Renaissance gardens, but their character began to change with
the advent of the 'natural' garden, when grottoes were turned
into *rochers*. During the eighteenth century, when European
travellers sought out the ancient grottoes in Greece, they
discovered that these abodes of the nymphs were always provided
with fresh springs, and sometimes with bas-reliefs and statues of
various subjects, such as nymphs participating in bacchanales.

Even in antiquity, nymphs were associated with shepherdesses. In the second half of
the eighteenth century, this notion of the virtuous nymph/shepherdess/milkmaid
appealed to the collective imagination of a people whose gardens were now furnished
not only with grottoes, but with pristine dairies reminiscent of a primitive Elysium.
The remarkable Rambouillet Laiterie unites the two ideas: the grotto as home of the
nymph and the Arcadian dairy.

Langner attributes the erudite iconography to Hubert Robert. This seems
reasonable in view of the fact that this cultivated artist, a familiar in Madame
Geoffrin's household, moved freely in royal, princely and aristocratic circles.
Moreover, the design is closely related to the dairy that he and Bélanger designed at
Méréville for Jean-Joseph de Laborde (who may have been the first to import merino
sheep). The 'Baths of Apollo' that Hubert Robert had created at Versailles ten years
before (p.166) combines the same elements of grotto, cascades and white marble
sculpture (though from the previous century). But here it forms a garden bosquet,
while the Rambouillet grotto is arranged – unusually – as the termination and focal
point of the main axis *within* the sandstone and marble pavilion.

As originally conceived and carried out, the Queen's Dairy offered a complex
imagery, and an impressive iconographical consistency, carried out by Thévenin,
Hubert Robert, Pierre Julien, Georges Jacob, J.-J. Lagrenée, and their collaborators.
Indeed, one of the intriguing paradoxes of Rambouillet is the mingling of the
eighteenth-century concept of the uncorrupted 'natural' sheepfold of Arcadia with
patently revolutionary concepts in architecture, furniture, and porcelain.

Each artist responded in his own way to the challenge, almost abandoning the
gentle complaisance of the more pliable eighteenth-century manner that still prevailed
in certain quarters. The gracious, smiling classicism of Mique's Bélvèdere, with
sphinxes and low relief decoration, gave way to Thévenin's stark reduction of
architecture in terms of unrelieved elemental geometry. The warm, painted furniture
that Georges Jacob had created for the Queen's apartments at Trianon, now turned to
lozenges and bronze palmettes and the masculine form of an ancient curule. The
porcelain produced at Marie-Antoinette's Paris factory in Rue Thiroux was animated
with ribbons and pink roses. But for the Laiterie, Lagrenée – who had painted
dimpled airborne cupids against a blue sky for the Queen's Bélvèdere – now turned
to sepia and black forms on a strict kylix with a stark geometrical border.

Sadly, the Laiterie de la Reine came too late for Marie-Antoinette to enjoy its
pleasures. For by the time Julien's grotto was completed to his satisfaction in March
1789, riots were already beginning to break out in the capital.

CHAPTER 24

JEAN-JOSEPH DE LABORDE AND MEREVILLE

There were two happy consequences of Louis XVI's purchase of Rambouillet. The first was the magisterial achievement of the Laiterie de la Reine. The second was indirect, but just as impressive in its own way – the most extensive English garden undertaken in France during the eighteenth century, the panoramic Méréville.

The acquisition of Rambouillet set off a labyrinthine train of events. Louis knew the Duc de Penthièvre was grieved to give up a château that had been so closely associated with his family. So in an effort to compensate the Duke for his loss, Louis asked the court banker, Jean-Joseph de Laborde – who was living happily at his château of La Ferté Vidame in 1784 – to sell La Ferté to Penthièvre. As consolation for forfeiting La Ferté, Louis conferred upon Jean-Joseph the title of marquis, whereupon the new Marquis de Laborde acquired another château, Méréville. It was here that he began to create, in 1785, a model English garden on a grand scale.

Laborde is an honoured name in garden history. Jean-Joseph de Laborde was born in Aragon in 1724 and went to Paris when he was thirty-four. He was soon able to replace Paris de Montmartel in 1758 as the last banker to the court, his sudden ascension to this exalted position due, in large measure, to his friendship with the influential Duc de Choiseul. Laborde quickly became one of the richest men in France, and in 1760 he married a daughter of the banker to the court of Vienna, Rosalie Claire de Nettine, sister-in-law of the famous Introducer of Ambassadors and eminent collector, Ange-Laurent de La Live de Jully.

Commensurate with his station, the new Marquis purchased a resplendent Paris

Jean-Joseph, Marquis de Laborde (1724-1794).
The Marquis de Laborde was already sixty when he acquired the château and estate of Méréville. Although he cautioned Bélanger to curb expenses in his projects for the garden pavilions, the admonition went unheeded and Bélanger was dismissed. Finally, however, the Farmer-General/banker spent so lavishly on the grandiose composition at Méréville that it is still regarded as perhaps the most extensive French landscape garden of the eighteenth century

293

Gamble after Constant Bourgeois, the Rostral Column, Méréville, c.1808.
The engraving invokes the poignancy of the monument standing midst weeping willows beside the water and illuminated by moonlight. It is the proper atmosphere for a monument dedicated to the memory of Laborde's young sons who perished at sea. Since a rostral column was traditionally erected to celebrate naval victories, it seems an odd symbol for a marine tragedy

Below left: Neveu after Constant Bourgeois, the Temple of Filial Piety, Méréville.
The temple had to be built twice, for the first one broke through the limestone on which it stood. It was reconstructed upon a promontory so it could be viewed from below

Below right: the Méréville Temple of Filial Piety, now at Jeurre.
Hubert Robert's design was influenced by the Temple of the Sibyl at Tivoli, and also closely resembles Robert's Temple of Philosophy at Ermenonville

Vue prise dans les Jardins de Méréville

hôtel built by the architect Antoine-Mathieu Le Carpentier. Le Carpentier was well known in Paris for designing the pavilion considered to be the veritable Petit Trianon of the capital – the famous Folie Bouexière built by the Farmer-General, Gaillard de la Bouexière, in the Rue de Clichy.

Horace Walpole was invited to dine at the hôtel de Laborde in 1765, and even this sophisticated cosmopolite was impressed, concluding that 'all the houses in London appeared small and miserable' by comparison with the banker's sumptuous establishment. The Englishman was overwhelmed by the luxurious appointments, the bas-reliefs by the sculptor Edmé Bouchardon, the armoires in tortoiseshell and ormolu encrusted with medals in the Boulle tradition, the paintings by Lemoyne hanging in the owner's large study lined with crimson damask bordered with gold, and the canvases by François Desportes that graced the spacious dining room.[1] Walpole remarked upon the fact that fourteen windows of the hôtel looked out upon its immense garden, which he judged to be half as long as The Mall.

Above, left and right: Gamble after Constant Bourgeois, two views of the Grand Cascade, Méréville, c.1808.
The engravings depict the park with cascade as it was during Napoleon's day, when Méréville was frequented by such Empire celebrities as Lucien Bonaparte and René de Châteaubriand. The wild cascade with its frightening rocher was always a favourite spot to visit. As in Hubert Robert's painting (below) the cascade gushes forth from an enormous rock formation. Large rocks are scattered along the shoreline in Robert's painting, but by 1808, the marvellous trees with which Laborde embellished the gardens seem to have taken over

Hubert Robert, the Grotto and Cascade at Méréville, 1786-8. Robert's paintings were intended to capture the essence of a garden, and were not to be taken as a 'photographic' record. As here, fact and fiction are mingled to suit his artistic will, for often his canvases are an artful resumé of salient features – cascades, bridges, rustic pavilions – which he chose to fit his personal concept of a landscape

No one in Laborde's position, however, could afford to be without an important property in the country, so in 1764 he bought from the descendants of Saint-Simon, the huge, still-medieval château of brick and stone, La Ferté Vidame.[2] Laborde was always in a hurry to get things done, but he allowed the architect Le Carpentier four years to carry out its transformation.

It was usual for a man of Laborde's station to set forth pictorially the range of his fiscal enterprises, so he summoned Louis XV's master of seascapes, Joseph Vernet (1714-89), to execute eight large canvases based on the theme 'Four Parts of the Globe on Land and Sea'. Laborde was in such haste to have this decorative series hanging on the walls of La Ferté, that he refused to let them be shown at the Salon of 1769, incurring the wrath of Diderot.

The park of La Ferté was astonishing for its date, for in a period when the Le Nôtre garden was considered hopelessly old-fashioned, Laborde audaciously ordered from his architect a majestic garden that followed the Le Nôtre tradition. There were vast parterres, hidden bosquets, circular reflecting pools ornamented with swans, canals bordered with balustrades, and limitless perspectives created by cutting long tunnels through the forests. It was just the right setting for the magnificent reception that the court banker offered to Marie-Antoinette's brother, the Emperor Joseph II of Austria, when he came to visit Versailles.

Gerard Mabille has noted that the importance of La Ferté's garden lay in its brusque return to classical sources, for Le Carpentier was not simply a late follower of Le Nôtre. The architect's plan for La Ferté represented a conscious nostalgia for the past, reflecting a tendency to look back to a more glorious age that appeared at the end of Louis XV's reign. 'There was more science than dream in the work of Laborde, which was without posterity, but [it contained] a new dimension – a pre-Romantic *sensibilité*.'[3]

It was a real sacrifice for Jean-Joseph to honour the King's request to give up La Ferté on which he had expended so much artistry, energy and money. But on 20 October, 1784 he acquired Méréville from Philippe Antoine de Latour du Pin, and the moment the ground could be turned over the following spring, the inveterate gardener – who was now sixty – began to transform the property over almost the entire decade to come.

Since the Marquis de Laborde was such a prominent figure in Paris and court circles, the banker's latest and most ambitious enterprise caught the attention of the Comte d'Angiviller. The Director of Buildings was interested in Laborde's choice of artists for the garden buildings, and may have applauded his taste when Laborde engaged the accomplished J.-F. Bélanger of the Menus-Plaisirs. As the work progressed, everyone wanted to see it. Joseph Vernet's son reported that the place was enchanting. And Madame Du Barry, then living mostly in her pavilion of Louveciennes, rushed to Etampes to judge the latest additions.

The nine-hundred-acre property of Méréville presented a formidable challenge, for it is situated in the high valley of the Juine, eighteen kilometres from Etampes in the Beauce region, where the Marquis already owned numerous fiefs. On it stood an old château on high ground, overlooking a swampy valley through which flowed the river Juine, and as Bachaumont pointed out, it was first of all necessary to spend millions to gain solidity for this moving, muddy base.

So three or four hundred workers were employed to dig up a mountain, drain and fill in the swampy flatlands, and divert the course of the river, which became a key element in the garden plan. The cursive river made the windmill function, spilled into a lake, disappeared underground, emerged within the grotto of the Dairy – where it gushed from a niche into a basin and flowed across the marble floor, vanished again into a subterranean cavern, only to reappear as a large stream pouring into the lake, and finally fell in a thundering cascade over the rock formation that became a favourite motif for both gardeners and painters. As in the Renaissance gardens of the Villa d'Este and the seventeenth-century masterpiece by Le Nôtre at Vaux-le-Vicomte, water lent animation to the garden, and was valued as much for sound as for sight.

It was in the spring of 1785 that Laborde summoned Bélanger, who described himself as 'an architect by training and a gardener by taste'.[4] The banker was well acquainted with Bélanger's Paris triumphs as a designer of gardens and *folies* such as Bagatelle and a landscape garden for d'Artois at the château of Maisons. In his earliest correspondence with Bélanger, Laborde specified that a temple and a marble column be incorporated into his Arcadia in the Juine valley.

At the same time, Laborde warned the architect that he insisted upon the expenditure being kept under control because of his numerous family, his advanced age, and the huge sums he had already spent at La Ferté. But Bélanger, who was accustomed to profligate clients, lost no time in sending out models of bridges, a windmill, and a fisherman's house as proposals for the required pavilions, along with materials to begin the work. This precipitate haste alarmed Laborde, and there followed a misunderstanding, in which two distinct artistic personalities found themselves in confrontation, for Laborde wanted the garden to represent *his* taste, not his architect's. After all, he had already created some of the most innovative gardens of the second half of the century, and his son, Alexandre de Laborde, was becoming an authority on the subject in his own right, collecting materials for the indispensable book on the art of the garden that would be published in 1808: *Description des nouveaux jardins de la France.*

From Bélanger's point of view, the cost of a temple and a marble column were inconsistent with the owner's injunction of economy, and he impertinently wrote to the Marquis that his intention was 'to put your garden into the country, rather than the country into your garden'.[5] Only a year after he had been hired, Bélanger was dismissed, but not before he had provided a plan for the picturesque park with a large lake, participated in the first planting, placed the alleys and bridges, given two designs for the windmill and the first model for a rostral column.

The variety of bridges that Bélanger conceived to span the curving river were composed on the principles of 'lightness, grace, and surety [practicality]',[6] and before he left Laborde's employ, he had engaged the cabinetmaker Carbillet to execute to his designs the Bridge with Golden Spheres and the Mahogany Bridge. The sculptor L. Auger was employed to carry out another bridge designed by Bélanger, an arch of stones intended to look like a natural rock formation.

It was also Auger who executed Bélanger's drawing for an impressive (and expensive) mahogany pavilion reflecting English taste. This rare material (which had become so highly favoured for furniture in France) could easily be obtained by Laborde, who owned important properties in Santa Domingo, from which island his ships brought all kinds of exotic products, returning with cut stone from France for his building projects on the island.

The remodelling of the château itself was given to J.-B. Barré, a less gifted architect than Bélanger, but one who had worked twenty years for Laborde and complied with his wishes. Barré retained the old pepper-pot towers, for towers had not lost their distinction as a sign of nobility, and he added Neo-classical wings, uniting the disparate parts with a modillion cornice.

Bélanger scornfully described Barré's restoration as 'a so-called Romanesque style', and went on to say that if he had known that this would be the case, he would have changed the style of his windmill to conform to it. A drawing shows Bélanger's fanciful concept of a Gothic windmill, the arms of Laborde over the door set within a

Hubert Robert, view of Méréville, 1791.
The Marquis de Laborde's great château looms in the background, its austere dignity contrasting with the Chinese bridge designed by Bélanger. The Rostral Column is on the left, appropriately set off by weeping willows. The gardener, boating party and group of women and children on the bank contribute to the Claudean tranquillity of the scene

Gothic aedicule.[7] This concept of a Gothic windmill was *à la mode,* for it evoked the nostalgia for the past prescribed for the picturesque garden. Only four years before, Hubert Robert had capitalised upon the presence of a ruined château at the Princesse de Monaco's property at Betz, and conceived a series of Gothic pavilions to set it off.

Apparently the Marquis de Laborde had confided his difficulties with Bélanger to his close friend, the Duc de Choiseul, now in the last months of his life. Since his days as Ambassador in Rome, Choiseul had patronised the painter Hubert Robert, and after the minister's exile, Robert visited him at Chanteloup. As a pre-eminent garden designer for the most distinguished people of the realm, Robert was recommended by Choiseul as the artist best able to meet Laborde's exacting demands.

A refined, tactful man, Robert enjoyed a personal relationship with the King and Queen as Designer for the King's Gardens, Keeper of Paintings, and his work was found in the royal collection. His canvases were eagerly awaited at the Salons and graced foreign courts and the houses of connoisseurs, which included members of France's oldest families. On 29 May, 1786 this 'most amiable of men', as his friend, Madame Vigée-Lebrun described him, arrived at Méréville.

In dramatic contrast to Bélanger's painful tenure, Robert worked in perfect harmony with the Marquis de Laborde, and their relationship matured into a lasting friendship. Robert also found Laborde's architect Barré to be a competent executant of his designs for the English park, so that in July 1786 the painter reported that Méréville was coming along well, and that it must be continued in the 'grandest, simplest, most noble style'.[8]

The column that Laborde had desired in 1785 – for which Bélanger had had his sculptor Lhuillier present a model in pear wood – was intended to celebrate the voyage of two of the Marquis' sons with the expedition of the Comte de la Pérouse. Louis XVI

Left: Gamble after Constant Bourgeois, Monument to Captain Cook, Méréville, c.1808.
Hubert Robert designed Cook's Tomb in August 1786, dedicating it to the English navigator who had perished in 1778. The engraving shows it as it originally stood – upon an island formed by an artificial river which flowed from the large lake. The heavy fluted Doric columns are appropriate to the subject, enframing the sculptor Pajou's superb portrait. Laborde's son, Alexandre, wrote that the collection of foreign trees was intended to evoke the distant lands visited by Cook

Right: The Méréville Monument to Captain Cook, now at Jeurre.
The artistic communion of many years between Hubert Robert and the sculptor Augustin Pajou, accounted for some of the exemplary fabriques for which Méréville became famous. Pajou's sculpture is always distinguished by a technical perfection and grace, and the unusually fine portrait of Cook by one of the finest modellers of the century may be his masterpiece

himself had planned the voyage with the explorer. But both of them were drowned in trying to disembark in long boats which were overturned by the tide.

The household at Méréville went into mourning, and the Marquis decided that the form of the original column honouring his sons had to be modified. At the suggestion of Hubert Robert (1786-9), it became a Rostral Column with a base of turquoise blue marble, the rostrals of bronze, and crowned with a globe of gilt copper (opposite and p.294). For its execution, Robert engaged Le Prince, an artist who was lodged near him at the Louvre.

Hubert Robert's painting dated 1791, with the château at the centre, underlined by the curving bridge and flanked by poplars, and the column rising from the trees beside the lake, looks like a stage setting for the groups disposed along the bank in the foreground. The park was planted with 225 species of trees, and appropriate choices were essential for the presentation of the monuments – weeping willows for the memorial to Laborde's two sons, cypresses for the tombs. Some specimens were later transported to the garden planted at La Vallée-aux-Loups by René de Châteaubriand, who wrote in his *Mémoire d'Outre-Tombe*: 'They will shelter my old age as I have sheltered their youth.'

Méréville was doubly satisfying to Hubert Robert, for as a designer, he could manipulate the gardens as he would a painting, with the architect Barré to carry out his will. Then, he could in turn commit to the canvas a composition that had become *grandeur nature* in Laborde's garden, just as he had done at Versailles with the Baths of Apollo, which he also created and then painted (p.166).

Robert's canvases of Méréville are among his most engaging, and in December 1789 he wrote to Laborde that he was working on the first one, 'which I caress like one of my dearest children'.[9] The word was spread in Paris among patrons of painting that the artist was at work on views of Méréville, and they flocked to his studio to see the latest canvases that immortalised the great garden that was taking shape near Etampes.

Hubert's profound knowledge of materials – rocks, earth, water, and vegetation – is seen in his concept of the huge grotto at Méréville (1786-8). The painting is a transfiguration of nature, for it has been arranged so that the cascades are seen beside the rustic bridge, with a hut surmounting the grotto that was so dear to his artistic sensibilities, and figures silhouetted against the lake (p.295).

At Méréville Robert met Moreau l'Aîné, the older brother of Moreau le Jeune, the artist who recorded the official events of Louis XVI's reign, and whom Robert would already have known in that connection. Their conversations may well be imagined, for Moreau l'Aîné was one of the most enterprising and gifted painters of thatched-roofed cottages and ruined huts, the same leitmotifs that recur in Robert's paintings and in Laborde's gardens.

For the temple that the Marquis de Laborde had insisted upon from the moment he purchased Méréville, it was inevitable that Robert choose his favourite Temple of the Sibyl at Tivoli, a subject that was also found in Choiseul's collection. Robert had studied it during the Italian journey with Fragonard, and the Temple of Philosophy at Ermenonville – where Robert worked several years with its owner, Monsieur de Girardin – closely resembles it. Méréville's Temple of Filial Piety (1787-9) is an exquisite conflation of the Temple of Tivoli and the Temple of Vesta in Rome, with eighteen fluted Corinthian columns meticulously executed, and the entablature of bucrania joined by garlands sculpted with great finesse (p.294).

Both Louis XVI and his banker were fascinated by explorations, and the King was an expert on naval affairs, bringing the French fleet up to the same standard as the the English navy. They assiduously followed the voyages of the English explorer, Captain Cook, but the unfortunate navigator perished 4 February, 1779 in Hawaii during his third voyage.

News of the tragic event did not reach France until 1780, and when it did it provoked the addition of yet another cenotaph to the garden at Méréville. Here Hubert Robert was in his element, for he had already designed a whole Valley of Tombs for the Princesse de Monaco's garden at Betz, with pines and cypresses to augment the melancholy spirit – a *tableau* that Ganay (1932) considered to be the finest of its type in France. For the Monument to Cook ('Monument de Couq' it was called), Robert chose a form that becomes a metaphor for the explorer's character (p.299). The rectangular structure protecting the tomb is supported by heavy, fluted Doric columns of Paestum proportions – masculine, weighty, and grand. Its simplicity is intentional, for the heavy columns provide an appropriate foil for the antique altar within, surmounted by a classical urn, and adorned with Pajou's superb medallion of Cook at the centre which was completed in March 1788.

In spite of the distressing events in Paris during the summer of 1789 and the subsequent imprisonment of the royal family, the Farmer-General Laborde pushed ahead with the gardens, providing work for the inhabitants of the town and taking advantage of Robert's creative genius. Robert had visited Rambouillet with the

Augustin Pajou, Natalie de Laborde.
Natalie, daughter of the Marquis de Laborde, married at sixteen in May 1790. Her husband was Charles, Comte de Noaïlles, but they were soon separated. At Méréville after the Revolution, Natalie conducted a salon for leaders of the new society. Besides this bust, Pajou also executed a standing statue of Natalie de Laborde in the guise of Filial Piety holding a wreath for the Temple at Méréville

Comte d'Angivillers, and he apparently provided the design for Laborde's Laiterie.[10] Like Thévenin's designs for the Queen, the Méréville dairy also assumes a temple front (p.302), but it breaks forward into a belvedere with Ionic columns that were seen from below in its original site. The architect Barré worked at Méréville until January 1791, and was responsible for the Column, the Temple, and the Monument to Cook.

The Marquis de Laborde was Hubert Robert's most faithful patron, and the artist served as 'curator' of Méréville, where Laborde received such illustrious visitors as the Comte and Comtesse d'Angivillers, Madame Du Barry, the Minister of Finance Calonne, the family of the Prince d'Hénin, and the financier Monsieur Boutin, who was credited with being the first to create a large English garden in France.[11] The ancient and illustrious de Noaïlles family were guests, too, and the Marquis de Laborde's daughter, Natalie, married the grandson of the Marechal de Noaïlles, who became the Duc de Mouchy.

The last work at Méréville was being carried out literally in the shadow of the guillotine, and it is astonishing that the banker was still handing out commissions even after the King and Queen were executed in 1793. Laborde seems to have relied on the substantial work that he provided for the poor of the community to save him from the Tribunal, but on 18 April, 1794, he was condemned, and the terrible sentence was carried out the same day. At that time both Bélanger and Hubert Robert were incarcerated in a Paris prison, but they were later freed.

After the Revolution 'had fallen, exhausted, into the arms of Napoleon,' the Marquise de Laborde, her daughter Natalie, and her last son, the writer Alexandre, returned to Méréville, where they entertained the intellectual élite of a new society along with remnants of the decimated *ancien régime* – La Live de Jully, Lucien Bonaparte, Napoleon's painter Baron Gérard, the writer-politician Mathieu-Louis Mollé, Baron Pasquier, and Châteaubriand, with whom Natalie de Laborde's name was romantically – and briefly – linked. Drawings conserved in a private collection portray Natalie de Laborde and her friends in their white, high-waisted Empire gowns perched upon chairs with sabre legs, strumming mandolins.

The château of Méréville passed through a succession of owners, and its marvellous gardens and pavilions were allowed to fall into ruins. But in 1892 four of the most essential *fabriques* – the Rostral Column, the Temple of Filial Piety, the Monument to Cook and the Laiterie façade – were acquired by an enlightened art lover, Henri de Saint-Léon, who had them transported twenty kilometres away, to the park of his château of Jeurre. At Jeurre, the Rostral Column is no longer reflected in a lake, and the flat terrain does not quite do justice to the Laiterie, which was intended to have been viewed from below, rising from a rocky pedestal. A real debt of gratitude is due to the Saint-Léon family which was willing to rescue four crumbling monuments from the once-legendary garden of Méréville, and to care for them so they may be enjoyed in an appropriate setting today.

The Méréville Laiterie façade, now at Jeurre.
Hubert Robert's Laiterie at Méréville was inspired by Palladio. Within was a grotto formed of natural rocks, water from the river flowing from a lion's mouth into a marble basin adorned with the figure of Diana. Although the façade was moved to Jeurre, the grotto still exists at Méréville

Pillement, l'Ile Natalie at Méréville, c.1800.
The small island was named for the Marquis de Laborde's daughter. Although Laborde was guillotined, his wife, daughter and son returned to Méréville after the Revolution, becoming prominent figures in Consular circles

Eleanor von Erdberg, defending the caprices of the eighteenth century, at least insofar as its garden architecture was concerned, wrote:

> . . . the garden buildings of the eighteenth century in their manifold forms reflect the charm of generations who *knew how to play,* and pursued their fancies in spite of the remonstrances of those who thought they knew everything about good taste. The Prince de Ligne was completely happy midst his bizarre and colourful temples, bridges, boats and Chinese figures, and longed for them after the Revolution made him an exile, and ended his style of living.[12]

Elisabeth Vigée-Lebrun described Méréville as a royal habitation, and one can understand why, for at the time it was finished, it was the only French garden that could compare in scope with the majestic, sweeping garden vistas of Blenheim or Stowe.

It is true that Méréville was a wild extravagance, and Olivier Choppin de Janvry calculated that Louis XV's expenses at Trianon over a period of twenty-five years would not amount to one-tenth the sums that Laborde expended for this 'model of an English park'. For Bélanger's biographer, Méréville 'resembled an oasis of Ammon, situated in the midst of the desert'l, where the inhabitants lived happily, separated from the rest of men – one of the most beautiful gardens of France'.[13]

CHAPTER 25

THE FRENCH PAVILIONS IN AMERICA

Towards the end of the second year of Marie-Antoinette's reign – in the early morning of 28 November, 1776 – there appeared off the French coast near Belle Ile a sloop of war flying a flag that had never before been seen. It bore the stars and stripes of the new Republic of Thirteen States, and it carried Mr. Benjamin Franklin who, as one of three commissioners to France, was seeking French help in the colonists' struggle against England. Already welcomed in French scientific circles during his two previous trips, Franklin persuaded the administration to lend material aid, and by 6 February, 1778 he was able to lead the French into a treaty of alliance.

Even before the formal signing, it was known at court. On 21 January, Marie-Antoinette was holding a ball before the Carnival season, with the guests spilling over into the wooden pavilions – *maisons de bois* – that were usually put up for these occasions. It was an unusually brilliant party, with music and laughter under the light of a thousand candles, but there was an air of expectancy. Suddenly silence fell, and the Queen's brother-in-law, Provence, came in from a meeting of the Council and whispered to her the message she expected to hear. It was repeated, the voices grew louder, and the irrepressible Comte d'Artois openly cheered news of the Alliance. By 19 April, a courier reached Versailles with the momentous news that Amiral d'Estaing had sailed from Toulon with twenty ships of the line, and the American campaign was about to begin.

When he had been presented as American plenipotentiary to the King and Queen in the Hall of Mirrors on 20 March, 1778, Franklin's appearance provoked a culture shock. The ritual of receiving foreign ambassadors was observed at Versailles with meticulous protocol – women dressed in splendid ceremonial robes, the glorious gallery filled with grand seigneurs, diplomats, prelates, princes of the blood, dukes, and ministers. But they had never seen an ambassador like this: the seventy-two-year-old Quaker was wearing cotton stockings, a dark wool suit, and – most shocking of all – no wig. He seemed to have stepped from a page by Rousseau, or from a sentimental Greuze painting – the aged father with long white locks come to life.

Lithograph of French Pavilion at West Point in 1782, 1863.
The artist who sketched the West Point pavilion is unknown, although it may have been Major Villefranche, the French officer responsible for its construction. The lithographer was Julius Bien (1826-1909), a German who emigrated to America in 1849. The figures of guests standing under the roof of greenery can just be seen. The insigniae honouring the French and American alliance adorns the exterior

Niderviller faïence, 'Louis XVI and Franklin'.
This biscuit model with fine portraits of Louis XVI and Benjamin Franklin
commemorates the Franco-American Alliance of 1778. It enjoyed a notable success due
to Franklin's popularity in France

The Americans with him were wearing their finest clothes, with the unfortunate effect that they looked like footmen, as Bernard Faÿ uncharitably remarked.

The stunned courtiers thought Franklin must be dressed *en Quaker* or was wearing the costume of an American farmer. In any case, instead of criticism there was admiration. The Queen's coterie was enraptured, and the Paris public made him an idol, for his image appeared on snuff boxes, inkwells, printed cottons, and porcelain. The Comte de Custine, who bought the Niderviller factory in 1793, issued an image of Franklin and the King in biscuit, which became a popular model from 1780 to 1785. The subject was of more than passing interest to Custine, for as a result of the Alliance, the Count joined the French army that went to America, and was present at Yorktown, serving with distinction as Commander of the Saintonge Regiment. In the summer of 1782, Custine presented Martha Washington a set of porcelain from his Niderviller factory in Lorraine. He died on the scaffold in 1793.

When the Alliance was announced, the liberal young nobility were ecstatic, for it was traditionally their metier to go to war for the King, and they were thrilled by the prospects of fighting their ancient foe. Ironically, however, it was at just this time that many prominent Frenchmen were Anglophiles, including Jacques Necker (Minister of Finance), the Orléans family, and the Duc de Lauzun. Furthermore, it was an utterly unprecedented expedition they were about to embark upon, for it meant 'crossing the ocean in spite of English fleets, fighting in a country practically unknown, in conjunction with men of whom even less was known . . . and for a cause which had never before elicited enthusiasm at Versailles, the cause of republican freedom'.[1]

This meeting of the Old and the New Worlds was one of the extraordinary phenomena of the Age of Revolution. For there was temporarily transplanted to American shores some of the flower of the French nobility. Men from the oldest families of France – like the three Saint-Simons, de Bröglie, Chastellux, de Ségur, Noaïlles, de Lauzun – brought closer the glittering court at Versailles, the world of the Paris salons and the academies, and an unaccustomed panoply of warfare that, by tradition, was choreographed like a ballet. At its peak, French civilisation foliated on the banks of the Hudson one bright spring evening in 1782 in the form of a pavilion put up by the French engineers to honour the long-awaited birth of an heir to the throne.

Represented in the expeditionary force were men who stood in the forefront of French scientific, political and humanistic life, such as the philosopher Marquis de Chastellux, whose knowledge of English made him the diplomat of Rochambeau's army. He brought to American shores the allure of the French Academy, and played an active role in planning the Yorktown campaign which terminated in the victory of October 1781.

Many men of the force were officers whose lives were closely enmeshed with the monarchy. When Marie-Antoinette had come to France as Dauphine, she was required by ancient ceremony, to change to French clothes in a wooden pavilion on the island near Kehl. The French noblewoman who met her there was the Comtesse de Noaïlles, Lady of Honour and arbiter of etiquette. The Countess' son, Vicomte Louis de Noaïlles, was among the liberal, idealistic element at court, and was

Elisabeth Vigée-Lebrun, François-Jean, Marquis de Chastellux.
Vigée-Lebrun's portrait of the Marquis de Chastellux, an accomplished writer as well as professional soldier, was painted a few months after his death. Originally Chastellux wore his three decorations (St. Louis, St. Lazarus, and the Cincinnati eagle), but at some later date – no doubt during the French Revolution – they were painted over since they were aristocratic symbols. Chastellux was one of the three major generals, ranking immediately below General Rochambeau, who accompanied the French Expeditionary Force to America

immediately attracted to the idea of the American expedition. De Noailles was among those who were enflamed in America with the desire for 'liberty', and although his family represented an ancient landed dynasty, Louis de Noailles would propose the abolition of nobles' privileges at the National Assembly during the troubled events of August 1789.

The red-haired Marquis de Lafayette was born into the provincial nobility, but his marriage to the Vicomte de Noailles' sister, Adrienne, allied him with this ancient family. Lafayette had already been in America in 1777, where he acquired an aura of glamour in French eyes through his association with Washington. Lafayette's successful campaign in Virginia of 1781 resulted in penning up Cornwallis at Yorktown. He later became head of the National Guard, and a prominent figure in the terrible scenes that ensued at Versailles and in Paris.

Another participant in the American military operations was Lafayette's close friend, Louis-Philippe, Comte de Ségur – a member of the highest nobility, son of the Minister of War, and one of the fast set that gathered around the Queen. He shared her passion for the theatre, was a prolific and eloquent writer, and an habitué of the salons of Mesdames Du Deffand and Geoffrin.

The impulsive Armand-Louis de Gontaut-Biron, Duc de Lauzun – nephew of the Comtesse de Choiseul – was another of the young nobility who was conspicuous at court. Known as the most notorious Don Juan of the kingdom, he embarked with his famous Legion of Lauzun for America in April 1780, and it was he who conveyed Rochambeau's dispatch of 20 October 1781 with the news of Yorktown to the War Minister de Ségur at Versailles.

The Comte de Vaudreuil was apparently unwilling to leave either Yolande de Polignac or the delights of the Queen's theatre for American battlefields. But his family was represented by his young cousin, the Vicomte de Vaudreuil, as well as the count's brother, the Marquis de Vaudreuil, who sailed off with his squadron of thirteen warships and three frigates to play a major role in the critical naval engagement off the coast of Virginia under Admiral de Grasse.

The Swedish nobleman, Comte Axel de Fersen, joined the French forces as an aide to Rochambeau. It was Fersen who later engineered the ill-fated Flight to Varennes, devoting himself wholly to the cause of the royal family in its last days, before he was murdered by a mob on the streets of Stockholm.

The French army of some 60,000 men under the command of the Comte de Rochambeau, embarked from Brest in 1780, landed in Newport in July, and spent the winter of 1780-1 there. A constant refrain of the journal-writers in the French army was their universal fascination with General Washington. When the General went to Newport to confer with Rochambeau, the French were so overwhelmed by the American commander's presence, they offered him the seventeen-gun salute that was usually reserved for a marshal of France. Washington's stoic nobility and his unusually authoritative bearing left such an indelible impression upon the Marquis de Chastellux that he effusively compared Washington to Apollo and Alexander. And when

Rochambeau met with Washington again in Hartford in September 1780, the Frenchman's aides – Axel de Ferson, Mathieu Dumas and the Comte de Damas – begged to go with him in order to study the Virginian once more.

> They could not take their eyes off the commanding figure in the blue coat with buff facings . . . topboots with spurs. He overtopped Rochambeau . . . and in spite of the count's gold embroidered coat, his ribbon and star, the lace at his throat and wrists, [Washington] outshone him, though he had not a single decoration on his breast.[2]

In the spring of 1781 the French met the Continentals on the Hudson, then marched south to Yorktown and the battle that was to determine the outcome of the Revolution. Although it was a distance of 756 miles from Newport to Yorktown, some of the French leaders – the Comtes de Noaïlles and de Custine – walked ahead to encourage their troops. In Philadelphia they were reviewed by Congress, and the President of Congress turned to ask Rochambeau to ask if it would be proper for him to salute the field officers, to which the Count replied that the King of France usually did!

In September the Americans received French naval support, from 'the most powerful fleet that ever appeared on these seas', as Washington put it.[3] Thanks to French supplies, Washington had ammunition in abundance for the first time, and on 9 October the siege of Yorktown began, with more French than Americans participating. When the famous double siege had ended, the impertinent little American flag flew above the redoubt taken by Lafayette and his Americans, the white flag of Rochambeau's Auvergne over the redoubt captured by the French.

At the surrender on 19 October, 1781, Washington ordered that there be no cheering, and General Light-Horse Harry Lee – Washington's outstanding cavalry commander in the southern department and father of Robert Edward Lee – described the scene in which 'universal silence [prevailed] . . . and the utmost decency . . . mingled with commiseration for the unhappy'.

In the spring of 1782 the French army began the long march northward for its embarkation from Boston with Vaudreuil's squadron. In May they were encamped at West Point, the key fort which controlled the navigation of the Hudson River that Benedict Arnold had almost delivered to the English. It was such an important fortress that Rochambeau had gone by boat with General Washington in August 1781 to see it, and the Comte de Clermont-Crèvecoeur described it as being

> in a very formidable position . . . perched on high rocks with very steep sides above a plateau on which 1,200-1,500 men can deploy in line of battle. Six forts . . . defend the approach and protect the troops below . . . one is large enough to provide a very strong *place d'armes* so it is used for the artillery park.[4]

While the army was resting at West Point, they received the joyous news that the Queen of France had at long last given birth to the first Dauphin on 22 October, 1781. It was an event for which the French people had waited for eleven years, and now the succession to the throne was assured.

The birth of a Dauphin, like a royal marriage, always called for the proper civilities, and as we have seen, the City of Paris had offered several days of festivities to the King and Queen in January 1782, and a dinner in the provisional ballroom into which Marie-Antoinette was escorted by comic opera figures in unseemly fashion. Now it was incumbent upon Her Majesty's subjects, who found themselves in a military outpost on the banks of the Hudson River, to plan as distinguished a fête as the Quartermaster's Corps could muster and the resources of the American wilderness could provide.

The strategic fort at West Point, situated beside the Hudson River at a point where

Jonathan Trumbull, 'Surrender of Lord Cornwallis at Yorktown', 1787-c.1828.
Trumbull's painting of the surrender at Yorktown on 19 October, 1781, shows in the centre Major-General
Benjamin Lincoln, with George Washington on a dark horse behind him to the right. The man standing
beside Lincoln is General O'Hara, acting for Lord Cornwallis, who was 'ill'. In the group on the right under
the American flag, General Henry Knox is the first mounted figure just beyond the four standing officers. At
left in the group under the French flag, the Marquis de Chastellux is the sixth mounted figure, with Comte
Axel de Fersen the fifth figure. The Duc de Lauzun, with a feather in his cap, is the first mounted figure.
Rochambeau is astride the dark prancing horse at the end of the French line

it ran through a deep channel formed by lofty mountains, had been an almost impenetrable forest only four years before. But, as the Chevalier de Chastellux remarked, it had been converted by the Americans into a fortification 'bristling with redoubts and batteries'. Now this formidable site would have to be transformed into an appropriate setting for a fête to acclaim the birth of the royal child.

So orders were sent out by the commander, General William Heath, that 'all the Carpenters and Joiners in the Army [were] wanted for a few days at West Point, to assist in erecting and completing an arbour . . . under the direction of Major Villefranche'.[5] He was a French officer who had come to America in 1777, and was serving as an engineer at West Point. These French engineers who entered the American ranks were especially welcome to Washington, for they brought technical skills that were severely wanting in the Continental army, which was largely non-professional. They had been trained by the Ecole des Ponts et Chaussées, mastering advanced architectural principles as well as the art of fortification. Like Lafayette and another French engineer, Pierre l'Enfant, the Chevalier de Villefranche (who became a Lieutenant-Colonel in the Continental army), expended his fortune in the American service.

The ingenious Villefranche, who had been constructing fortifications and drawing the rare, finished maps that were so essential to the French-American forces, now turned his attention to the problem of providing a spacious pavilion to accommodate the dancing and dinner for the important ball. The most appropriate thing for the occasion, he decided, would be a traditional pavilion of verdure, like those leafy *fabriques* that the Menus-Plaisirs put up for the Queen's elaborate court parties (see p.242).

So the corps of engineers set to work. For the next ten days, one thousand men under Villefranche's direction felled trees, cut up tree-trunks, lopped off branches, and wove foliage together to make a roof and walls of greenery. With the cleverest improvisations, using only the materials at hand, they constructed a ballroom 220 feet long and 80 feet wide on the plateau surrounded by military fortifications that rose high above the banks of the Hudson.

The structure was supported by a grand colonnade of 118 pillars made of tree trunks, covered with a roof composed of intricately interwoven boughs, walls formed of the same material, and each end of the room was left open. The interior was adorned with evergreens as only the French can arrange them, festoons of fresh flowers, garlands, emblems in French and American colours symbolising the Alliance, and each pillar was encircled with muskets and bayonets. An anonymous artist made a sketch of the West Point ballroom on the spot (p.303).

Among the Americans at West Point was a Massachusetts doctor serving as surgeon to a Boston regiment, Dr. James Thacher. The practical doctor was amazed by the prodigious amount of labour that the French expended upon a structure intended, as he said, for only a single occasion, and he described the celebration that took place on 31 May, 1782 in his journal:

> [Generals Washington and Knox with their ladies, and the other dignitaries] arrived in their barges . . . and were conducted through the grand colonnade . . . situated on the gently rising ground . . . with a view of all the barracks, encampments, and fortifications of the garrison. The situation was romantic . . . the occasion novel and interesting . . . On the inside every pillar was encirlced with muskets and bayonets, bound round in a fanciful and handsome manner, and the whole interior was decorated with evergreens, festoons of flowers, garlands, emblematical devices, fleur-de-lis, and other ornaments significant of the existing alliance.
>
> This superb structure in symmetry of proportion, neatness of workmanship and elegance of arrangement, has seldom perhaps been surpassed on any temporary occasion; it affected the spectators with admiration and pleasure, and reflects much credit on the taste and ability of Major Villefranche . . .
>
> The whole army was paraded on the contiguous hills on both sides of the river, forming a circle of several miles in open view of the public edifice . . . At the signal designated, by firing three cannons, the regimental officers all left their commands, and repaired to the building to partake of the entertainment . . . prepared by order of the Commander-in-Chief . . . A martial band charmed the senses with music . . . and the cloth being removed [there were] thirteen appropriate toasts [to the Dauphin] . . . each one being announced by the discharge of thirteen cannon and accompanied by music . . .
>
> The Arbor [ballroom] in the evening, was illuminated by a vast number of lights, which . . . exhibited a scene vying in brilliancy with the starry firmament . . . thirteen cannon were again fired as a prelude to a general *feu de joie* . . . throughout the whole line of the army on the surrounding hills . . . the mountains resounded and echoed like tremendous peals of thunder, and the . . . thousands of fire-arms in the darkness . . . could be compared only to the most vivid flashes of lightning from the clouds. [It] was concluded by the . . . fireworks . . . rockets, wheels, fountains, trees, bee-hives, balloons, stars and fleur-de-lis . . .
>
> His Excellency General Washington was unusually cheerful. He attended the ball in the evening, and with dignified and graceful air, having Mrs. Knox for a partner, carried down a dance of twenty couples in the arbor on the green grass.[6]

Washington's partner for the dance, the portly Lucy Knox, was the wife of his energetic and substantial Chief of Artillery, General Henry Knox. Knox had owned a bookshop in Boston before the war broke out, and amused himself by reading the military books. Apparently he knew enough French to be able to decipher a curious volume that appeared in 1757, *Mes Rêveries,* by Louis XV's great general, Maréchal de

Gilbert Stuart, 'General Henry Knox'.
Knox, Washington's Commander of Artillery, is one of the most appealing figures of the American Revolution, and he especially attracted the admiration of the French. Chastellux praised him for his command of the artillery at the siege of Yorktown, for which he was promoted to Major-General. Knox was one of the few American soldiers with even a rudimentary knowledge of French, and Chastellux attributed this to the fact that before the war Knox had spent the time in his Boston bookshop reading military works

Saxe (Carlyle thought it must have been dictated under the influence of opium). In any case, Knox was supposed to have gained his first knowledge of the art of artillery from this book. Fantastic though it may seem, Henry Knox was entrusted with commanding the artillery from the first campaign, and subsequent events proved him to be an exemplary leader.

The ball at West Point was an unqualified success, and word of it soon spread to Philadelphia, where the worthy Chevalier de La Luzerne, French envoy to the United States, was stationed at the time. La Luzerne was just the man to fill such an important post, according to Chastellux, who lodged with him when he was in Philadelphia. Chastellux praised the chevalier as being

> so well fitted for the station he occupies that one cannot imagine that any other but himself could fill it. [He was] noble in his expenditures as befits the Minister of a great monarchy, but as simple in his manners as a republican, he is equally well fitted to represent the King with Congress, or the Congress with the King. He loves the Americans, and his own inclination attaches him to the duties of his mission.[7]

The generous La Luzerne seems to have followed in the footsteps of the Duc de Choiseul (who claimed that he had ruined himself in extravagant entertainments as the King's minister), and he seized the opportunity of the Dauphin's birth to cement American ties with France and to display his 'love for the Americans'. As the King's representative, La Luzerne decided to offer a lavish ball to the political, cultural, and professional leaders of the city and nation at the French Legation, which stood at the corner of Chestnut and Seventh Streets in Philadelphia.

For the dinner and dancing, La Luzerne knew that a large frame pavilion would have to be erected in the grounds of the Legation. Since it had to represent the conspicuous elegance of the French tradition, the Chevalier applied to General Washington for the services of a French engineer engaged in the American army, Pierre-Charles l'Enfant (1754–1825). L'Enfant would be responsible for both the architecture and the landscaping of the adjoining gardens. In fact, he would soon be planning the new city of Washington, and instinctively he would lay it out on the axial principles of a Le Nôtre garden.

By 15 July, the pavilion for La Luzerne's fête was ready to receive the large and distinguished company he had invited to honour the new Dauphin in the City of Brotherly Love. One of Philadelphia's leading citizens, Dr. Benjamin Rush, described the structure in a letter of 16 July, 1782 as 'sixty feet in front and forty feet deep . . . supported by large painted pillars and open all round'.[8] From the time the edifice was started, citizens had crowded around the site, watching the pillars going up, the ceiling being painted with appropriate imagery, and the adjoining gardens being 'cut into walks and divided . . . into artificial groves' – obviously an attempt at a formal French garden. Dr. Rush continued:

For ten days before the entertainment nothing else was talked of. The shops were crowded with customers. Hairdressers were retained; tailors, milliners, and mantua-makers were to be seen covered with sweat and out of breath in every street . . . The morning [of July 15] was ushered in by a corps of hairdressers occupying the place of the city watchmen. Many ladies were obliged to have theirs dressed between four and six o'clock in the morning, so great was the demand.

In the time-honoured French tradition, La Luzerne had intended to provide wine and money for the numerous spectators, but some of the city fathers thought it might cause a riot. When the evening arrived, 'the scene . . . exceeds description . . . numerous lights distributed through the garden, the splendour of the room . . . the size of the company . . . the brilliancy and variety of their dresses . . . the band of music . . . formed a scene that resembled enchantment.'

Benjamin Rush bestowed the highest compliment he could conceive of upon the assembled company – it was, he decided, 'truly republican'. There were 'the president and members of Congress, governors, judges, professionals, former Tories, faculty from the college; an Indian chief in his savage habits and the Comte de Rochambeau in his splendid uniform, talking with each other as if they had been subjects of the same government . . . ' Washington was chatting with John Dickenson (from whom La Luzerne rented the house). The party was international in character as well, for Englishmen, Frenchmen, Scotchmen, Germans, and Irishmen were to be seen 'conversing with each other like children of one father'.

At nine o'clock came the dramatic firework display, followed at midnight by supper. The 'cold collation . . . elegant, handsomely set off' was laid out behind the dancing room 'under three large tents so connected . . . as to make one large canopy', exactly like one of Marie-Antoinette's fêtes at Versailles. The decorum was such that 'the company looked . . . more as if they were *worshipping* than *eating*', and the ode to the Dauphin to be read for the occasion was apparently forgotten altogether.

The French envoy was so delighted with l'Enfant's invention, that he continued to use the dancing pavilion for further entertainments, as he did at the beginning of September when the French troops again paraded before Congress. Among the officers who were in Philadelphia was Jean-François-Louis, Comte de Clermont-Crèvecoeur, whose conscientious help for the American cause foreshadowed the doom of his own family. The entry in Clermont-Crèvecoeur's journal for 3 September noted that:

> The Chevalier de La Luzerne, the French envoy to the United States, had us to dine both days in the pavilion he had had built for the fête he gave to celebrate the birth of the Dauphin. This room was beautifully decorated and the various emblems on its walls very well conceived. Of these I shall cite only two that seemed to me to do honour to the designer. At the east end of the room was a rising sun surmounted by thirteen stars (the arms of America) with an Indian watching the sunrise and apparently dazzled by its rays. Beside the Indian in the same picture was a woman, representing England, emptying a sack of gold into the hands of another Indian, who throws the gold at her feet with obvious contempt. At the opposite end of the room were the arms of France with a sun at its zenith lighting the world . . . The pavilion was 100 feet long; its walls were supported by a colonnade 30 to 40 feet high.[9]

The sun emblem recalled, of course, the reign of Louis XIV, but it was associated with Louis XVI as well, from the very beginning of his reign. At the coronation ceremony in Reims, the sun symbolised the high expectations with which the new monarchy began, and the sun motif had figured prominently in the festival architecture put up by the

Menus-Plaisirs for the coronation fêtes and the *divertissements* that followed.

The fete of 15 July had been such an extraordinary success that newspapers and diarists continued to recount its wonders. 'So distinguished were the guests', said Dr. Rush, that La Luzerne had been compelled to borrow thirty cooks from the French army to prepare a repast that would be 'suited to . . . the dignity of the company'. Dignified it was, for by a fortuitous circumstance, the Comte de Rochambeau and General Washington were, by pre-arrangement, in Philadelphia at the same time.

Rochambeau had served in the major battles of the Seven Years' War, at one time under the legendary Maréchal de Saxe, and would assume another important command upon his return to France. As for Washington, he was venerated by the French visitors, who could not say enough in praise of his unassailable dignity. Chastellux wrote that he gave 'the idea of a perfect whole . . . brave without temerity, laborious without ambition, generous without prodigality, noble without pride, virtuous without severity.'[10] It was a concept of the First President that endured, for James Fenimore Cooper later summed it up in architectural imagery: 'His character was Doric, in all its proportions.'

The results of the French expedition to the New World were fortuitous for the Americans, but disastrous for the French. They tended to idealise the American leaders, and had no idea of what it would cost for so-called 'liberty' to be established on French soil. There was not only the monetary cost, from which France never fully recovered, but 'by patronising a revolt, they prepared a revolution'.[11]

In France, revolution meant bringing a great people into such moral and material ruin that the country fell into the utmost depravity. The Terror 'became a mindless, reasonless machine . . . and fell without discrimination upon all sectors of society[12] . . . The Revolution did not inaugurate, but brought to an end a great age of social transformation.'[13]

Among those who were massacred by a crazed populace, or followed the King, Queen, and Madame Elisabeth to the scaffold, were Madame Du Barry, Chartres (who, as the Duc d'Orléans, had voted for Louis' death), the Princesse de Lamballe, de Lauzun, de Custine, Laborde of Méréville, France's greatest scientiest Lavoisier, and two of the brighest lights of the King's new navy, the Comte de Kersaint and the Comte d'Estaing. After imprisonment, Bélanger and Hubert Robert were freed, but the Queen's architect, Richard Mique, was guillotined, along with the painter of the Queen's gardens and pavilions, Claude-Louis Châtelet. Rochambeau was scheduled for execution, but somehow was overlooked and remained in prison during the Terror. The last title that Louis XVI conferred before his death was upon the Comte de Rochambeau, whom he made a Marshal of France.

Baron de Saint-Simon, youngest of the three Saint-Simons who came to Virginia, was remarkably prescient about the American Revolution. He believed that it 'marked the beginning of a new political era . . . that [it] would set into motion progressive currents in our . . . civilisation, and . . . would before long occasion great changes in the social order then existing in Europe.'[14]

The Comte de Ségur entertained no such premonitions, and spoke for most of the insouciant young nobility when he wrote years later:

> We were all dreaming of Liberty . . . No one thought of a revolution in France. We all wanted to fly to America in the name of philanthropy, and we were destined to bring home the germs of an ardent passion for emancipation and independence . . .
> We marched gaily upon a carpet of flowers which concealed from us the abyss.

NOTES

CHAPTER 2

1. Danis, 4.
2. Verlet, 118. They were engraved by Le Pautre and Chauveau in 1676 with descriptions by Felibien.
3. Saint-Simon, IV, 1008.
4. Alexandre Le Blond, quoted by Berrall, 197.
5. Verlet, 289.
6. Blomfield, 199.
7. Jestaz, 258-86, calls Louis XIV its architect, although the work was supervised by Robert de Cotte and J.-H. Mansart.
8. Marie, 1976, 14.

CHAPTER 3

l. Lebrun prepared a series of drawings for this ceiling, some of which are preserved in the Louvre.
2. On one occasion the King's designer invented for him a headpiece of multiple heads – all resembling the Dauphin – so that no one could tell which was the real face. His costumes were often equipped with cords that could be pulled, allowing the costume he was wearing to fall to the floor, revealing another underneath.
3. The bride and groom were doubly related, for a few years before, Anne-Louise's brother had married Maine's favourite sister, one of the pipe-smoking princesses whose conduct Liselotte so deplored.
4. Lewis, 123.
5. Ibid., 162.
6. Adams, 30.
7. The Grand Condé was Louis II de Bourbon-Condé (1621-86), Fourth Prince of Condé.
8. He chose an axis through the old terrace that had been put up by Montmorency, continuing through the Grand Parterre and across the Canal.

9. Ganay, 1962, 79-80.
10. Loisel, II, 205 ff.
11. Did it inspire the King to build the second pleasure dairy near the Ménagerie at Versailles? This dairy was designed to amuse the twelve-year-old Duchesse de Bourgogne (future mother of Louis XV) who came to court in 1696 and brought sunlight into Louis' painful last years. The little Duchess milked the cows herself, and made cheese that she served to the King.

CHAPTER 4

1. Fontenay was a member of the family of Jean-Baptiste Monnoyer, the greatest flower painter of Louis XIV's day. It is his compositions that we see in the superb Gobelins tapestry series, the 'Maisons Royales'. He was lured to England by the English Ambassador to France, Ralph Montagu, to decorate his London residence, Montagu House, which stood on the site of the British Museum.
2. Clifford, 86.
3. On French maps they are marked 'ah-ah', and were used as early as the end of the seventeenth century. They were ditches with a fence hidden at the bottom, and evolved from defensive military procedures.
4. Keswick, 10.
5. Ibid., 193.
6. Sullivan, 231-2.
7. Keswick, 9.
8. At almost any period, the most conservative architecture in the world is French.

CHAPTER 5

1. The Comte de Toulouse died in 1737, but Louis liked to visit his aunt, the Comtesse de Toulouse and their son, the

Duc de Penthièvre, at Rambouillet. The Countess was like a mother to Louis, and had free access to his Versailles apartments.
2. Le Nôtre, 71.
3. *Madame de Pompadour et la floraison des Arts,* 75.
4. Luynes, IV-X, 225-6.
5. Coursac, 268, states that Mercy was misrepresenting the situation, for the Dauphin even dined with Madame Du Barry and the King at Trianon, and supped thirteen times with the King at Compiègne, where Du Barry would have been present. This does not mean that the the future Louis XVI approved of his grandfather's conduct, which he did not, for he was a devout man. His own father (who had died in 1765) disapproved, too.
6. The hunting pavilion of Marcoussis (1772) has also been attributed to Gabriel.
7. Other hunting pavilions by Gabriel were the Pavillon du Bois de Verrières (1751) between Meudon and Sceaux; the extant two-room Pavillon de Fausses Reposes (1756) between Ville d'Avray and Versailles; and La Muette (1764-75) in the forest of Saint-Germain-en-Laye, being revised when Louis died.

CHAPTER 6

1. The Grand Condé's grandson married a daughter of Louis XIV and Athénaïs de Montespan, Louise-Françoise. Since the Condés sometimes married their close relatives, the peculiarities we noted in the case of our barking friend, Henri-Jules de Bourbon-Condé (father of the Duchesse du Maine), should come as no surprise.

2. Antoine, 131.
3. Schneider, 14.
4. Chantilly is today the centre of equitation in France.
5. Louis XVI, grandson of Louis XV, liked them so much that he had them rendered in Sèvres porcelain.

CHAPTER 8

1. Constans, 60.
2. Verlet, 497.
3. Tadgell, 81.
4. *Louis XV, Un Moment de Perfection de l'Art Français* exhibition catalogue, 7.
5. Verlet, 497.
6. It has been fully documented by Fels, Tadgell, and *Hommage aux Gabriel.*
7. Verlet, 501.
8. Fleming, 110.
9. The building actually had two dining rooms, a larger one followed by a more intimate one. Louis ordered from Loriot a flying table for each one, of the type that he had installed at La Muette and Choisy. The dining room paintings were ordered from Doyen, Pierre, Halle, and Vien, whose canvases were chosen by Madame Du Barry for her own pavilion at Louveciennes (1771).

CHAPTER 9

1. *Madame de Pompadour et la floraison des arts,* 37.
2. Ibid., 68.
3. Levron, 243.
4. *Madame de Pompadour et la floraison des arts,* 99.
5. Blondel, IV, 68.
6. Mitford 1954.

CHAPTER 10

l. Mitford, 1954, 89.
2. Bazin, 226.
3. The Duke still had not paid

Servandoni's widow twelve years after the temple and ice house had been completed.
4. A silk taffeta given a glaze by stretching it over a brazier to make it very brittle, the ultimate in elegance for a boudoir.
5. Gallet, 1972, 114.
6. Sutton, 189.
7. The original château was destroyed in 1800 and later rebuilt.

CHAPTER 11

1. Watson (Snowman 146) was mistaken when he stated that Choiseul's wife was descended from Pierre Crozat, who never married. Her grandfather was Pierre's brother, Antoine Crozat (1655-1738).
2. Port, 3.
3. Soltau, 171.
4. He said that the French should have won at Dettingen. 'What I saw in that battle was one of my principal motives in suggesting to the King in 1763 the military changes I carried out', Soltau, 6.
5. Neither France nor Austria had a general able to oppose him, however, hence the disaster of Rosbach.
6. Quoted by Connolly.
7. 'On l'a remercié' as the French put it – that is, he was thanked, and it was made to sound like a compliment.
8. Maugras, 1924, p.391.
9. Connolly, 5.
10. Watson (Snowman, 156) gave Le Camus de Mézières as Choiseul's architect, but it was Louis-Denis Le Camus. The latter transformed the château of Chanteloup and must have designed many of the pavilions.

CHAPTER 13

1. Richelieu was not the one who procured Jeanne for the King, although he knew her, as Louis himself stated one day to the Duc de Choiseul.
2. Antoine, 925.

3. Castelot, 95.
4. Wilenski, 143. The sophisticated Americans Gouverneur Morris and Thomas Jefferson, both interested in the latest architecture, went out to see the famous pavilion by Ledoux.
5. Those seen in Moreau's version of the inauguration of Louveciennes (p.165) are of plaster, awaiting their execution in marble.
6. Du Barry did, however, buy from Drouais four overdoors for the old house at Louveciénnes that were painted by Fragonard.
7. Eriksen, 123.

CHAPTER 14

1. Faÿ, 288.
2. Behrens, 19.
3. Palmer, I, 282.
4. The architect Gordon Morrill suggests it was also the consequence of economics. The changes in garden design that came about around 1766 were also the result of the high cost of labour and shortage of gardeners.
5. It became so expensive that he let Bélanger go.
6. Conner, 87.
7. Adams, 1979, 104.
8. Erdberg, 141.

CHAPTER 15

1. Hézècques, 14.
2. Wiebenson, 27.
3. It must have been a platonic relationship, for Monsieur was not interested in sex.
4. In 1753 the Marquis d'Argenson wrote that there was no longer anything but friendship between Madame de Pompadour and the King. Pigalle's statue was made in that year, originally ordered for the château of Bellevue. It was in the park of Bagatelle in 1900.
5. Alexandre de Laborde, quoted by Baltrusaitis, 10.
6. It was like a private sanctuary with no visitors admitted. There were over three hundred

paintings by artists from the Low Countries.
7. Weibensen, 73. Watelet also wrote the article on garden buildings (from 1756) for the *Encyclopédie*, becoming recognised as an authority on the subject.
8. Hubert Robert had known Watelet and his companion, Marguerite Lecomte, since they met in Rome in 1763, where he was their guide and dedicated a series of drawings to her. In 1765 Robert sketched the almost dilapidated *moulin* spanning the river, the linen being spread out on the bridge below, and fishermen lounging on a ramp under fulsome trees.
9. Bathilde shared her brother's interest in the occult. Her marriage with a Bourbon-Condé was unusual, for the Orléans and Condés never liked each other. They were separated, and she acquired the Elysée.
10. At one time Pigalle's 'Love and Friendship' (Louvre) was here, perhaps after the Hôtel de Lassay.
11. Père du Halde was in China in 1735, Père Attiret in 1743, Père Bénoit in 1767. The Emperor of China's Yuan Ming Yuan, with artificial mountains, waterfalls, lakes, and four hundred pavilions, was of special interest to them.
12. Quoted by Baltrusaitis, 14.
13. Chalon, 25.
14. The name was taken over by the Comte d'Artois for his own house in 1777-8.
15. *De Bagatelle à Monceau, 1778-1978*, 52.

CHAPTER 16

1. Laudet, 129.
2. Cayeux, 180.
3. Blaikie, 210.
4. Praz, 154.
5. Blaikie, 218.
6. Latour du Pin, 81.
7. Hebert, 167.
8. Dervieux' celebrated Paris hôtel was designed by the Orléans' architect, Brongniart,

and decorated by Artois' architect, Bélanger.
9. Rice, 1972, says he acquired it in 1780, but Schama gives 1776.
10. Gallet, 1972, 73.
11. Schama, 134.
12. Ibid., 135.
13. Ibid.
14. Latour du Pin, 101-2.
15. This child was widely believed to have been that of Madame de Genlis and Chartres. But Madame de Latour du Pin thought she was English, because a friend told her of the child having been purchased and secretly taken to France. Latour du Pin, 103, however, did claim that Félicité de Genlis had an illegitimate daughter by the Duc de Chartres, whom Madame de Genlis hated and gave away.
16. Manceron, 31.
17. Ibid., 33.
18. Quoted by d'Arneville, 91.
19. Blaikie, 210-11.
20. Ibid.
21. Queen Victoria, however, found him 'thoroughly French', the ultimate reproach

CHAPTER 17

1. *De Bagatelle à Monceau, 1778-1978*, 74.
2. Clark, 107.
3. Baltrusaitis, 89.
4. Choppin de Janvry, 1967, 80.
5. Ibid.

CHAPTER 18

1. It is still used today for the same purpose, and the author dined there in the autumn of 1990. Its rotunda was added by the Duc d'Aumale in the nineteenth century to display panelling from a stone hunting pavilion built by the Duc de Penthièvre in the forest of Dreux. Jean Feray states that the pavilion is still there.
2. Bröglie, 309, gives the year as 1774.
3. Manceron, 67.
4. Ibid., 71.
5. Ibid.

Chapter 19

l. Madame Vigée-Lebrun states that the Comtesse de Polignac asked the King to relieve her of her duties, but he refused.
2. Stern, I, 134.
3. Blaikie, 167.
4. Quoted by Verlet, 629.
5. Blaikie, 138.

Chapter 20

1. Goethe was a young student at the time and, as he describes in his *Mémoires,* he took some friends with him to examine the pavilion on the island before it was completed. He was explaining the allegories of the tapestries to his companions and suddenly realized what an unfortunate choice they were for the forthcoming royal wedding – Jason and Medea.
2. Moulin, 33.
3. Alain Gruber states that it impossible to say if it were 1781 or 1782.
4 Gruber, 114.
5. Ibid., 147.
6. Mercklein created the ingenious mechanical devices of the table made by Riesener, delivered to the Queen's bedchamber when Madame Royale was born in 1778.
7. The Redoute Chinoise was such a success that the Duc d'Aumont and Moreau gave parties there on 6 and 15 September, 1781.
8. Cobban, 106.
9. Nolhac, 1927, 134.
10. Ibid., 138.
11. Moulin, 32.
12. Her *Mémoires* are highly embroidered, and Verlet called her a hypocrite. Yet, when she has no reason to be anything but objective, certain details that she reports are useful.
13. Cobban, 117.
14. Quoted by Claude Arnaud in Alcouffe et al., 19.
15. Maugras, 1893, 356.
16. It was really in two parts, for on the other side of the path was the Laiterie de Preparation,

where the work of making butter, cream, and cheese was done.
17. Quoted by Verlet, 638.
18. *Marie-Antoinette: archduchesse, dauphine, et reine,* No.742.
19. Latour du Pin, 98. Granted she was speaking of the year 1789, but even earlier in the reign, Louis was not notably in touch with events of the day.

Chapter 21

1. Claude Arnaud, in Alcouffe et al., 18.
2. Saint-Amand, 176.
3. Hauser, 34.
4. The Marquise de Latour du Pin was a high-ranking but atypical member of this society, for like Madame Elisabeth (the King's young sister who was so beloved by Marie-Antoinette) she was a model of Christian probity.
5. Etienne de Lavallée, called Lavallée-Poussin (1722-1802), was a student at the French Academy in Rome, where he met Piranesi and Clerisseau. When he returned to Paris in 1777, he decorated several houses in the new manner, including the Grimod de la Reynière residence and Madame Du Barry's Louveciennes. Mary L. Myers has published a sheet of his arabesques in *French Architectural and Ornament Drawings of the Eighteenth Century.*
6. Kaufmann, 172.
7. Stern, 1, 70.
8. Ibid., 205.
9. The work of Robert Adam, too, was 'denatured' in the nineteenth century, when several of his finer rooms – like the gallery at Harewood – were 'improved' by the architect Sir Charles Barry.
10. *De Bagatelle à Monceau,* 19.

Chapter 23

1. Le Nôtre, 20.
2. Possibly intended for the other round pavilion was a

panorama of Rome painted by Le Masson in fifteen sections, ordered by d'Angiviller in the King's name. It seems to have been an ancestor of those panoramas printed as wallpaper under the Empire, and a descendant of Carmontelle's scenes of gardens and pavilions painted on rolls of paper.
3. The suite of furniture by Georges Jacob included four armchairs, ten straight chairs, six stools, a rather large round table (*gueridon*), and four small round tables. Guth, 74, believed that the Jacob suite was placed in the rotunda of the round pavilion. Langner thought the large round table, surrounded with chairs, occupied the rotunda of the principal pavilion, with the smaller round tables in the rectangular room. It is interesting to speculate upon how the furniture by Jacob for David's atelier may have influenced this commission.
4. Langner places these in the rotunda, where the niches are now. Guth, 80, believes they were principally in the grotto room.
5. Lagrenée's designs for the Rambouillet porcelain are in the Sèvres archives.

Chapter 24

l. Laborde was not a true collector, as Ferdinand Boyer has shown, for the furniture and paintings of his hôtel stayed there even after it was bought by Grimod de la Reynière just before the Revolution.
2. This was not his only château. His son, Alexandre de Laborde, author of *Description des nouveaux jardins de la France,* stated that his father built a landscape garden at Saint-Leu after 1774, a property later acquired by the financier Beaujon, who built the famous Paris folly. Laborde also engaged an English architect in 1773 to build a garden for his

château of Taverny. He owned the château de Laborde near Beaune, as well as the great château of Châtelet in Lorraine, which he acquired from the heirs of La Live de Jully in 1786.
3. Lassus, 1975, 35.
4. Ibid., 33.
5. Ibid., 35.
6. Lassus, 1976, 275.
7. This was discarded, but another design for the windmill, also by Bélanger, was ultimately realised. The drawing was supposedly in the Wrightsman Collection, but has not been located.
8. Lassus, 1976, 280.
9. Ibid., 283.
10. Gallet, 1975, II, 53, credits Bélanger with the Laiterie at Méréville, but Lassus, 1976, 285, quotes a letter from Hubert Robert to Laborde stating that he designed it in the manner that his patron desired.
11. Cayeux, 137.
12. Erdberg, 142.
13. Stern, I, 166.

Chapter 25

1. Speech by Ambassador Jusserand at Harvard University, 1912.
2. Whitlock, I, 215.
3. Rice, 1963, II, 371.
4. Rice, 1972, I, 41.
5. Quoted by Boynton, 158.
6. Thacher's Military Journal; *New Jersey Gazette,* 12 June, 1782.
7. Rice, 1963, I, 179.
8. This and all subsequent quotations from Dr. Rush are taken from Butterfield, 278-83.
9. Quoted by Rice, 1972, I, 77.
10. Rice, 1963, 113.
11. Chalon, 157.
12. Cobban, 233. He noted that of those executed after trial, 85% belonged to the Third Estate, some 6.5% to the clergy, and 8.5% to the nobility.
13. Ibid., 260.
14. Quoted by Bonsal, 207.

BIBLIOGRAPHY

Adams, William H., *Atget's Gardens*, New York, 1979.

Alcouffe, Daniel et al., *La Folie d'Artois*, Paris, 1988.

Anonymous, *Les Folies du Marquis de Brunoy, ses mille et une extravagances*, Paris, 1804, 2 vols.

Anseaume, L., *Théâtre de M. Anseaume*, Paris, 1766, 3 vols.

Antoine, Michel, *Louis XV*, Paris, 1989.

Arneville, Marie-Blanche d', *Parcs et Jardins sous le Premier Empire*, Paris, 1981.

Ashton, Leigh (trans.), *Lettres et Mémoires du Prince de Ligne*, London, 1927.

Babelon, Jean-Pierre (ed.), *Le Château en France*, Paris, c.1986.

Baltrusaitis, Jurgis, preface in *Jardins en France 1760-1820*, exhibition catalogue, Paris 1977.

Baulez, Christian, 'Deux Sièges de Foliot et de Sené pour Versailles', *Revue du Louvre*, 1-1991, pp. 76-81.

Baulez, Christian, 'Buffault et Le Service de Madame Du Barry', *Revue du Louvre*, 3-1993, pp. 58-60.

Bazin, Germain, *The Baroque: principles, styles, models, themes*, Greenwich, Connecticut, c.1968.

Behrens, C.B.A., *The Ancien Régime*, London, 1967.

Berger, Robert W., *In the Garden of the Sun King*, Washington D.C., 1985.

Berrall, Julia S., *The Garden*, New York, 1966.

Blaikie, Thomas, *The Diary of a Scotch Gardener at the French Court at the End of the Eighteenth Century*, London, 1931.

Blomfield, Reginald, *History of French Architecture from the death of Mazarin till the death of Louis XV*, London, 1921.

Blondel, J.-F., *Cours d'Architecture*, Paris, 1773, vol. IV.

Bonsal, Stephen, *When the French Were Here*, Garden City, New York, 1945.

Boynton, Edward C., *History of West Point and its Military Importance during the American Revolution and the Origin and Progress of the U.S. Military Academy*, New York, 1863.

Bröglie, Raoul de, 'Le Hameau et la Laiterie de Chantilly', *Gazette des Beaux-Arts*, October-December, 1950, p.309.

Butterfield, Lyman (ed.), *Letters of Benjamin Rush, Vol.1: 1761-1762*, Princeton, 1951.

Cailleux, Jean, *Hubert Robert et Louis Moreau*, Galerie Cailleux, Paris, 1957.

Campan, Jeanne-Louise-Henriette, *The Private Life of Marie-Antoinette*, New York, 1887.

Carrogis, Louis, called Carmontelle, *Le Jardin de Monceau*, Paris, 1779.

Castelot, André, *Madame Du Barry*, Paris, c.1989.

Cayeux, Jean, *Hubert Robert*, Paris.

Chalon, Jean, *Chère Marie-Antoinette*, Paris, 1988.

Chandernagor, Françoise, *L'Allée du Roi*, Paris, 1981.

Choppin de Janvry, Olivier, 'Avant que disparaisse a jamais le Désert de Retz', *L'Oeil*, September 1967, p.31.

Choppin de Janvry, Olivier, 'Méréville', *L'Oeil*, December 1969.

Choppin de Janvry, Olivier, 'Cassan', *Revue Française*, 1975.

Choppin de Janvry, Olivier, 'Les jardins promenades au seizième siècle', *Revue des Monuments Historiques de la France*, 1976, no. 5, p.7.

Clark, Kenneth, *Landscape into Art*, London, 1979.

Clifford, Derek, *A History of Garden Design*, New York, 1963.

Cobban, Alfred, *A History of Modern France*, New York, 1965.

Conner, Patrick, *Oriental Architecture in the West*, London, 1979.

Connolly, Cyril, and Zerbe, Jerome, *Les Pavillons*, New York, 1962.

Constans, Claire, *Versailles, Château de la France et orgueil des rois*, Paris, 1989.

Coursac, P., Girault de, *L'education d'un Roi*, Paris, 1972.

Curl, James S., *English Architecture*, London, 1977.

Danis, Robert, *La Première Maison Royale de Trianon (1660-1687)*, Paris, 1928.

De Bagatelle à Monceau, 1778-1978, exhibition catalogue, Paris, 1978.

Desjardins, Gustave, *Le Petit Trianon*, Versailles, 1885.

Ducros, Louis, *French Society in the Eighteenth Century*, New York, 1927.

Dufort, Jean-Nicolas, Comte de Cheverny, *Mémoires de Comte Dufort de Cheverny* (ed. Robert Crevecoeur), Paris, 1909, 2 vols.

Dumont-Wilden, L., *La Vie de Charles-Joseph de Ligne*, Paris, 1927.

Dunlop, Ian, *Versailles*, London and New York, 1970.

Erdberg, Eleanor von, *Chinese Influence on European Garden Structures*, Cambridge, Massachusetts, 1936.

Eriksen, Svend, *Early Neo-classicism in France*, London, 1974.

Faÿ, Bernard, *Louis XVI*, Chicago, 1968.

Fels, Comte de, *Agne-Jacques Gabriel*, Paris, 1924.

Fleming, John (with Hugh Honour and Nikolaus Pevsner), *The Penguin Dictionary of Architecture*, Harmondsworth, England, 1972.

Forbes, Alan, and Cadman, Paul F., *France and New England*, Boston, Massachusetts, n.d., vol.1.

Furcy-Raynaud, M., *Inventaire des Sculptures executées au XVIII siècle pour la Direction des Bâtiments du Roi*, Paris, 1927.

Gallet, Michel, *Paris Domestic Architecture of the Eighteenth Century*, London, 1972.

Gallet, Michel, *Palladio, sa vie, son oeuvre*, Paris, 1975.

Gallet, Michel, *Les Monuments Historiques de la France*, 1975.

Gallet, Michel, *Charles de Wailly 1730-1798*, Paris, 1979.

Ganay, Ernest de, 'Le gout du Moyen Age et des ruines aux jardins du dix-huitième siècle', *Gazette des Beaux-Arts*, October 1932, pp.183-97.

Ganay, Ernest de, 'Fabriques aux jardins du dix-huitième siècle', *Revue de l'Art Ancien et Moderne*, LXIV, July 1933, p.49.

Ganay, Ernest de, *Les Jardins de France*, Paris, 1949.

Ganay, Ernest de, 'Fabriques aux jardins du dix-huitième siècle, *Gazette des Beaux-Arts*, May-June 1955, p.287.

Ganay, Ernest de, *Châteaux Royaume de France*, Paris, 1956.

Ganay, Ernest de, *André Le Nostre*, Paris, 1962.

Girardin, Fernand, Marquis de, *Maisons de plaisance française, parc et jardins, l'Ile de France*, Paris, 1920.

Goncourt, Jules et Edmond de, *Portraits intimes du dix-huitième siècle*, Paris, 1807.

Gontaut, Armond Louis de, Duc de Lauzun, *Mémoires de Duc de Lauzun et du Comte de Tilly*, Paris, 1862.

Gontaut, Armond Louis de, Duc de Lauzun, *Un Duc et pair au service de la Revolution, le Duc de Lauzun, 1791-1792: correspondence intime*, Paris, 1906.

Gromort, G., *Le Hameau de Trianon*, Paris, 1928.

Gruber, Alain-Charles, *Les grandes fêtes et leurs décors à l'époque de Louis XVI*, Paris, 1972.

Gurrieri, Grancesco, and Chatfield, Judith, *Boboli Gardens*, Florence, 1972.

Guth, Paul, 'La Laiterie de Rambouillet' *Connaissance des Arts*, May 1958, pp.74-81.

Hauser, Arnold, *The Social History of Art*, New York, 1958, vol. 3.

Hazlehurst, Franklin H., *Jacques Boyceau and the French Formal Garden*, Athens, Georgia, 1966.

Hebert, Monique, 'Les demeures du Duc d'Orléans et de Madame de Montesson à la Chausée d'Antin, *Gazette des Beaux-Arts*, July 1964, p.161.

Hézècques, Comte d', *Souvenir d'un page a la cour de Louis XVI*, Paris, 1873.

Hommage aux Gabriel, exhibition catalogue, Paris, 1982.

Jestaz, B., 'Louis XIV, architecte', *Gazette des Beaux-Arts*, November 1969, p.259.

Jones, Barbara, *Follies and Grottoes*, Glasgow, 1953.

Kaufmann, Emil, *Architecture in the Age of Reason*, New York, 1968.

Keswick, Maggie, *The Chinese Garden, History, Art and Architecture*, Hong Kong, 1980.

Kochno, B., *Le Ballet en France du quinzième siècle a nos jours*, Paris, 1954.

Lablaude, Pierre-André, *Jardins de Versailles*, Paris, 1995.

Laborde, Alexandre de, *Description des nouveaux jardins de la France*, Paris, 1808.

La Gorce, Jerome de, *Berain: dissinateur du roi soleil*, Paris, 1986.

Lamb, Carl, *Die Villa d'Este in Tivoli*, Munich, 1966.

Lange, L., 'La grotte de Thetis a Versailles', *Art de France*, Paris, 1961.

Langner, Johannes, 'Architecture pastorale sous Louis XVI', *Art de France*, Paris, 1961, p.171.

Lassus, Simone de, 'Les fabriques de Méréville et de Jeurre', *Information Histoire de l'Art*, XX/I, 1975, pp.32-6.

Lassus, Simone de, 'Quelques détails inedits sur Méréville', *B.S.H.A.F.*, 1976, pp.273-87.

Latour du Pin, Henrietta-Lucy Dillon, Marquise de, *Memoirs of Madame de Latour du Pin* (ed. Félice Harcourt), New York, 1971.

Laudet, Fernand, *L'Hôtel de Toulouse*, Paris, n.d.

Leclerc, Tristan, *Hubert Robert et Les Paysagistes Français du dix-huitième siècle*, Paris, 1913.

Lehmann, Karl, 'The Dome of Heaven', *Modern Perspectives in Western Art History* (ed. W. E. Kleinbauer), New York, 1971.

Le Nôtre, G., *Le Château de Rambouillet*, Paris, 1930.

Levron, Jacques, *La Vie Quotidienne à la Cour de Versailles aux XVII et XVIII siècles*, Paris, 1965.

Lewis, W.H., *The Sunset of the Splendid City*, New York, 1954.

Loisel, Gustave, *Histoire des ménageries de l'antiquité à nos jours*, 3 vols., Paris, 1912.

Louis XV, Un Moment de Perfection de l'Art Français, exhibition catalogue, Paris, 1974.

Luynes, Charles-Philippe d'Albert, Duc de, *Mémoires du Duc de Luynes sur la cour de Louis XV, 1735-1758*, Paris, 1860-5, 17 vols.

Macon, Gustave, *Chantilly et le Musée Condé*, Paris, 1925.

Madame Du Barry: de Versailles à Louveciennes, Marly-le-Roi/Louveciennes, exhibition catalogue, 1992.

Madame de Pompadour et la floraison des arts, exhibition catalogue, Montreal, 1988.

Manceron, Claude, *Le bon plaisir 1782-1785*, Paris, 1976.

Marie, Alfred, *Jardins français crées a la Renaissance*, Paris, 1955.

Marie, Alfred, *Marly*, 1947.

Marie, Alfred, *La Naissance de Versailles*, Paris, 1968.

Marie, Alfred, *Mansart à Versailles*, Paris, 1972, 2 vols.

Marie, Alfred, *Versailles au Temps de Louis XIV*, Paris, 1976.

Marie, Alfred, *Versailles au Temps de Louis XV*, Paris, 1984.

Marie-Antoinette: archduchess, dauphine et reine, exhibition catalogue, Versailles, 1955.

Masson, Georgina, *Italian Villas and Palaces*, New York, 1959.

Mauclair, Camille, *Versailles*, Paris, 1926.

Maugras, Gaston, *Le Duc de Lauzun et la cour intime de Louis XV*, Paris, 1893.

Maugras, Gaston, *Le Duc de Lauzun et la cour de Marie-Antoinette*, Paris, 1902.

Maugras, Gaston, *La disgrace du Duc et de la Duchesse de Choiseul*, Paris, 1903.

Maugras, Gaston, *Le Duc et la Duchesse de Choiseul*, Paris, 1924.

Miller, Naomi, *French Renaissance Fountains*, New York, 1977.

Mitford, Nancy, *Madame de Pompadour*, New York, 1954.

Mitford, Nancy, *The Sun King*, New York, 1966.

Montclos, J.M. Perouse de, *Etienne-Louis Boullée*, Paris, 1969.

Mosser, Monique, 'M. de Marigny et les jardins; Projets Inedits des Fabriques pour Ménars', *Société de l'Histoire de l'Art Français*, 1972.

Mosser, Monique, and Georges Teyssot, *The Architecture of Western Gardens*, Cambridge, Massachusetts, 1991.

Moulin, Jean-Marie, *Le Chateau de Compiègne*, Paris, 1987.

Neave, Christine Corty, *Marly-le-Roi*, Paris, 1968.

Nolhac, Pierre de, *Versailles, Residence de Louis XIV*, Paris, 1925.

Nolhac, Pierre de, *Versailles au dix-huitième siècle*, Paris, 1926.

Nolhac, Pierre de, *Trianon*, Paris, 1927.

Nolhac, Pierre de, *Le Trianon de Marie-Antoinette*, Paris, 1927.

Nolhac, Pierre de, *Marie-Antoinette, Dauphine*, Paris, 1929.

Nolhac, Pierre de, *Marie-Antoinette*, Paris, 1929.

Palmer, R.R., *Age of the Democratic Revolution*, Princeton, 1959, 2 vols.

Port, C., *Le train de vie de la Maison du Duc de Choiseul, 1763-1766*, Paris, 192(?).

Praz, Mario, *Mnemosyne*, London, 1974.

Reiset, Gustave, Comte de, *Modes et usages au temps de Marie-Antoinette*, Paris, 1885, 2 vols.

Rice, Howard C., Jr. (ed.), *Travels in North America in the Years 1780, 1781 and 1782 by the Marquis de Chastellux*, Chapel Hill, North Carolina, 1963, 2 vols.

Rice, Howard C., Jr., and Anne S.K. Brown (eds.), *The American Campaigns of Rochambeau's Army, 1780, 1781, 1782, 1783*, Princeton University Press, New Jersey, and Brown University Press, Providence, Rhode Island, 1972.

Rice, Howard C., Jr., *Thomas Jefferson's Paris*, 1976.

Rey, Léon, *Le Petit Trianon et Le Hameau de Marie-Antoinette*, Paris, 1936.

Saint-Amand, Arthur Léon Imbert de, *Les Beaux Jours de Marie-Antoinette*, Paris, 1879.

Saint-André, Claude, *Madame Du Barry*, Paris, 1915.

Saint-Simon, Louis de Rouvray, Duc de, *Mémoires complètes de Louis de Rouvray, Duc de Saint-Simon*, Paris, 1965, 20 vols.

Schama, Simon, *Citizens*, New York, 1989.

Schlumberger, E., 'Grand Trianon', *Connaissance des Arts*, August 1966, p.33.

Schneider, Pierre, *World of Antoine Watteau, 1684-1721*, New York, 1967.

Scott, Barbara, 'King Stanislas of Poland at Lunéville', *Apollo*, February 1968, p.100.

Scott, Barbara, 'Pavillon de Musique de Madame', *Apollo*, May 1972, p.390.

Scott, Barbara, 'Madame Du Barry, A Royal Favourite with Taste', *Apollo*, January 1973.

Scott, Barbara, 'The Duc de Choiseul', *Apollo*, January 1973, p.42.

Scott, Barbara, 'Pierre Crozat', *Apollo*, January 1973, p.11.

Scott, Barbara, 'Le Comte d'Angiviller', *Apollo*, January 1973, p.78.

Siren, Oswald, 'Le Désert de Retz', *Architectural Review*, CVI, 1949, p.327.

Snowman, A. Kenneth, *Eighteenth Century Gold Boxes of Europe*, London, 1966.

Soltau, Roger H., *The Duke de Choiseul*, London, 1909.

Souchal, François, *French Sculptors of the 17th and 18th Centuries*, London, 1977.

Stern, Jean, *A l'ombre de Sophie Arnould*, Paris, 1930, 2 vols.

Stryienski, Casimir, *La Galerie du Regent, Philippe d'Orléans*, Paris, 1913.

Sullivan, Michael, *The Arts of China*, Berkeley, California, c.1984.

Sutton, Denys, 'The Final Flowering of the Medicis', *Apollo*, September 1974, p.189.

Tagdell, Christopher, *Ange-Jacques Gabriel*, London, c.1978.

Thacher's Military Journal, *New Jersey Gazette*, 12 June, 1782.

Thiery, Luc-Vincent, *Guide des Amateurs et des Etrangers voyageurs dans le maisons royales*, Paris, 1788.

Tilly, Alexandre, Comte de, *Mémoires du Comte de Tilly* (trans. Françoise Delisle), New York, 1932.

Treasure, G.R.R., *Seventeenth Century France*, London, 1966.

Verlet, Pierre, *Versailles*, 1985.

Vigée-Lebrun, Elisabeth-Louise, *The Memories of Madame Elizabeth-Louise Vigée Lebrun* (trans. Gerard Shelley), New York, n.d.

Vinson, Robert-Jean, 'Bagatelle', *Connaissance des Arts*, January 1977, p.79.

Walpole, Horace, *Essay on Modern Gardening*, 1770.

Watson, Francis J.B., 'The Choiseul Boxes' in Snowman.

Whitlock, Brand, *Lafayette*, New York, 1929, 2 vols.

Wiebenson, Dora, *The Picturesque Garden in France*, Princeton, New Jersey, 1978.

Wilenski, R.H., *French Painting*, New York, 1973.

Wolf, John B., *Louis XIV*, New York, 1968.

Index

Page numbers in italics indicate illustrations